Foundations of Assessment in Early Childhood Special Education

Effie P. Kritikos
Northeastern Illinois University

Phyllis L. LeDosquet
Northeastern Illinois University

Mark E. Melton
Northeastern Illinois University

Boston   Columbus   Indianapolis   New York   San Francisco   Upper Saddle River
Amsterdam   Cape Town   Dubai   London   Madrid   Milan   Munich   Paris   Montreal   Toronto
Delhi   Mexico City   São Paulo   Sydney   Hong Kong   Seoul   Singapore   Taipei   Tokyo

Vice President and Editorial Director: Jeffery W. Johnston
Executive Editor and Publisher: Stephen D. Dragin
Editorial Assistant: Jamie Bushell
Marketing Manager: Weslie Sellinger
Senior Managing Editor: Pamela D. Bennett
Production Manager: Fran Russello
Art Director: Jayne Conte
Cover Designer: Suzanne Behnke
Cover Art: Boy painting © Jacek Chabraszewski/Fotolia
Full Service Production and Composition: Mohinder Singh/Aptara®, Inc.
Printer/Binder: Courier Companies, Inc.
Text Font: Times

Credits and acknowledgments borrowed from other sources and reproduced, with permission, in this textbook appear on appropriate page within text.

Every effort has been made to provide accurate and current Internet information in this book. However, the Internet and information posted on it are constantly changing, so it is inevitable that some of the Internet addresses listed in this textbook will change.

Library of Congress Cataloging-in-Publication Data

Kritikos, Effie P.
  Foundations of assessment in early childhood special education / Effie Kritikos, Phyllis LeDosquet, Mark E. Melton.
    p. cm.
  ISBN-13: 978-0-13-606423-7
  ISBN-10: 0-13-606423-X
  1. Children with disabilities-Education (Early childhood)   2. Early childhood special education.   I. LeDosquet, Phyllis
II. Melton, Mark   III. Title.

LC4019.3.K75 2012
371.9'0472—dc22

2011009984

www.pearsonhighered.com

ISBN 10:   0-13-606423-X
ISBN 13: 978-0-13-606423-7

PREFACE

Implementing effective assessment practices in early childhood special education settings can be a complex process, especially for young children with exceptionalities. The process has been referred to as a fact-finding mission that requires a broad array of approaches to capture fully the performance of children. To aid service providers in this fact-finding effort, *Foundations of Assessment in Early Childhood Special Education* is anchored in a holistic perspective that details formal and informal assessment processes with recognition of natural settings as contexts, cultural variations that inform assessment practices, the collaboration needed to ensure quality assessment, and the legal mandates that underpin assessment procedures. Educators and related personnel play a critical role in this important component of early childhood education, and this text is designed to be a reference for this topic. Grounded in research-based practices, the goal of the authors in preparing this text is to do the following:

- Provide a readable, easy-to-use text that is accessible to a variety of disciplines.
- Make available up-to-date information on assessment tools and practices.
- Highlight the importance of collaboration and its role in assessment.
- Emphasize the central place that families have in the assessment process.
- Understand the role of diversity in assessment decisions.
- Illustrate how children's development affects assessment.
- Acknowledge the connections among assessment, intervention, and program planning.

Included in each chapter are field-based case studies that capture typical scenarios for early childhood special education settings. Breakpoint Practices (each chapter has two or more of these sets of exercises) will aid the reader in applying new knowledge. Each chapter concludes with websites and activities that may be used for self-assessment and to promote further research and exploration of key concepts.

The primary purpose of assessment for young children with exceptionalities, beyond determining eligibility for services, is to aid teachers, parents, and other key stakeholders in making instructional decisions and in devising support strategies that will enhance children's developmental outcomes. The exponential changes in growth and development for children in the early childhood years increases the complexity for accurately assessing their development and requires a continuum of assessment options and considerations to be effective. *Foundations of Assessment in Early Childhood Special Education* offers a wide range of theoretical perspectives, best practices, the delineation of assessment tools, and application activities to assist the reader in attaining this goal.

NEW! COURSESMART ETEXTBOOK AVAILABLE

CourseSmart is an exciting new choice for students looking to save money. As an alternative to purchasing the printed textbook, students can purchase an electronic version of the same content. With a CourseSmart eTextbook, students can search the text, make notes online, print out reading assignments that incorporate lecture notes, and bookmark important passages for later review. For more information, or to purchase access to the CourseSmart eTextbook, visit www.coursesmart.com.

ACKNOWLEDGMENTS

We would like to thank our reviewers for their valuable suggestions and input: Brent Askvig, Minot State University Center of Excellence; Mike Cass, McNeese State University; Marlaine Chase, University of St. Francis; Barbara Feicht, Utah State University; Dr. Colleen Klein-Ezell, Southeastern Louisiana University; Mary Ann Marchel, University of Minnesota–Duluth; Jane Squires, University of Oregon; Vicki Stayton, Western Kentucky University; Candra Thornton, University of North Carolina–Wilmington; Cathy Thorsen, University of Wisconsin–Eau Claire; and Yaoying Xu, Virginia Commonwealth University.

I would like to express my deepest appreciation to the many students and colleagues at Northeastern Illinois University who provided valuable input in the development of this book. I would also like to thank my family, including Harry; Anton; Lia; my parents, Aglaia and Tom; and my sister, Vicky, for their immeasurable encouragement.

Effie P. Kritikos

I would like to express my greatest appreciation to the hundreds of families of infants, toddlers, and young children, all of whom welcomed me into their homes and into their lives at a time when their worlds were consumed by a roller coaster of emotions as they looked for answers, support, and knowledge about their children and the future. I would also like to thank my parents, Lovella and Francis Laqua, who taught me the importance of compassion, especially for those who had unique learning needs, and to my children, Michelle and Melissa, who supported me unconditionally through my years of service to young children and their families.

I would especially like to dedicate this book to my lovely granddaughter, Eleanor Rose MacPhail, who was born on October 26, 2007, with Trisomy 12p. Eleanor; her parents, Melissa and Will MacPhail; and all of the families with whom I have worked have taught me—and continue to teach me—invaluable lessons about life, love, learning, and the authenticity of family when a child has exceptional needs.

Ella, you were on my mind and in my heart through every hour as I researched, reflected and wrote about assessment of not only you, but all young children with exceptional learning needs.

Phyllis L. LeDosquet

I dedicate this book to the many children and families whom I have been fortunate to know over the course of my career and whose influence continues to inform my practice and sustain my passion for the important work of early childhood special education. I am also grateful for the love and support of my parents, Merle and Martha Melton, and that of my family and friends, whose invaluable contributions to my professional and personal life are beyond measure. Finally, I wish to acknowledge Mrs. Mary Lou Clutts, an early "pioneering mother" who worked tirelessly on behalf of children with special needs before special education was their right. She saw my potential for this work as a young boy and nurtured me in my journey to become a special education teacher. Her loving guidance remains an important imprint for which I am enormously grateful.

Mark E. Melton

BRIEF CONTENTS

CONTENTS

PART One

FOUNDATIONS OF ASSESSMENT IN EARLY CHILDHOOD SPECIAL EDUCATION

PART OUTLINE

Introduction to Children with Special Needs

CHAPTER 1

INTRODUCTION

All parents dream of giving birth to healthy, typically developing children. In most cases, this is exactly what happens. However, early intervention programs and services are provided to more than 200,000 eligible infants and toddlers and their families, while about 6.5 million children and youth receive special education and related services to meet their individual needs (Archived: History of the IDEA, n.d.).

The causes of disability are numerous. Some children are identified at birth or within the first few months of life; others show complex characteristics that perplex parents, teachers, and medical professionals, with no clearly defined link to a specific diagnosis. In addition, within the parameters of a single diagnosis are a multitude of factors that influence the ways in which a disability may manifest itself, resulting in unique individuality among children with the same disability. The common ground is that each child is first, a young child, and second, has exceptional learning needs (ELN).

HISTORY OF EARLY CHILDHOOD SPECIAL EDUCATION

Friedrich Wilhelm Froebel, a German scholar who coined the term *kindergarten*, "a garden for children," established the first formal early education program in 1837. However, the earliest account of education for young children with exceptional learning needs was Maria Montessori's work in the early 1900s. She used a scientific, strategic approach to teaching young children deemed incapable of learning. Her work continues to influence guiding principles in special education programs today.

It was not until President Lyndon Johnson declared his "unconditional war on poverty" that government funded programs for young children who were at risk for educational failure. President Johnson believed that the poor socioeconomic environments in which many children lived were underlying causes for developmental delays and future academic problems. He pledged to allocate funding for compensatory programs starting in early childhood, believing that these purposeful efforts would provide the intellectual growth and development needed to ensure future educational success (Zigler & Valentine, 1979). The outcome was the establishment of Head Start, which initially served 500,000 4- and 5-year-olds in 2,500 communities

(Gargiulo & Kilgo, 2005). Eventually, Head Start included programs such as Project Follow Through, which ensured that educational success continued once children entered elementary schools, and Home Start, which brought the quality learning environments into the homes of low-income families. Head Start programs continue to provide high-quality early experiences for children who are at risk, and they require that 30% of their enrollment be children who have diagnosed exceptionalities.

In the 1960s, more special education programs were urgently needed because of the rubella epidemic, which resulted in more than 20,000 babies born with deafblindness. Recognizing the critical need for trained teachers and more programs, the federal government appropriated considerable funding for assessment, programming, and teacher training in special education (Fewell, 2000). One initiative in particular, the Elementary and Secondary Education Act (ESEA), established several special education programs and laid the groundwork for subsequent amendments that ensured future allocations of financial support for children who were at risk or diagnosed with exceptionalities (Hooper & Umansky, 2009).

In 1968, the Handicapped Children's Early Education Assistance Act was passed; it established guidelines for early childhood special education. In 1975, landmark legislation, the Individuals with Disabilities Act (IDEA), established rights for all children with exceptionalities. Over the next several years, numerous amendments and reauthorizations followed, continually improving the quality of education for young children.

Caldwell (1973) labeled three distinct historical periods in special education over an 80-year span: "Forget and Hide Period" (1900–1950), "Screen and Segregate Period" (1950–1960), and "Identify and Help Period" (1960–1980). During the "Forget and Hide Period," society viewed children with ELN as an embarrassment to their families, and these children were kept out of the public eye. The second period, "Screen and Segregate" assessed, labeled, and then isolated children in institutional settings because it was believed that children with ELN were not capable of living in the mainstream of society. The "Identify and Help Period" recognized the importance of providing support as early as possible and advocated for early screening and intervention.

Shonkoff and Meisels (2000) named the present era "Educate and Include." They state that the goal at the present time is

> to contain the consequences of disabling conditions, prevent the occurrence of more severe disorders, empower the families of children with special needs, and increase the opportunities for all children to reach their full potential by integrating them as fully as possible into regular classrooms and society at large. (p. 10)

HISTORY OF ASSESSMENT

Through the years, several early childhood special education programs were established and mandated; however, leaders in the field were concerned that many assessment tools were not sensitive to the unique needs of young children. Assessments authored in the 1940s and 1950s were used to make diagnostic decisions, and many felt that outcomes were inaccurate, resulting in mislabeling, misdiagnosis, and inappropriate placement of young children (Fewell, 2000). Bronfenbrenner (1977) stated that "much of contemporary developmental psychology is the science of the strange behavior of children in strange situations with strange adults for the briefest possible period of time" (p. 513). The scrutiny and critique of existing assessment tools led to the development of several new assessments, which were intentionally designed to meet the unique developmental, cultural, and linguistic needs of children who were at risk for developmental delay (Hanson &

Bruder, 2001). Assessments such as the Peabody Developmental Motor Scales (Folio & DuBose, 1974) and Developmental Activities Screening Inventory (Dubose & Langley, 1977) became cutting-edge assessments, with assessment through play in natural settings and mindful of curricula designed to meet the unique needs of young children with ELN (Fewell, 2000).

Neisworth and Bagnato (2004) stated that the assessment of young children has continued to benefit the evaluator specifically, and concern continues about the lack of sensitivity to cultural and social bias and the misrepresentation of children's potential. Fortunately, leaders in the field continue to research existing evaluation procedures, looking for ways to improve the accuracy and appropriateness of assessment of young children with exceptional learning needs.

OVERVIEW OF THIS TEXT

Part I: Foundations of Assessment in Early Childhood Special Education

In Part I, you will learn about the legal issues that shape special education in our country today. The evolution of guidelines has influenced the assessment process with young children, especially as we moved from the categorical approach to the noncategorical approach (developmental delay and children at risk) in identification of young children with ELN. Recent decades have witnessed an exponential increase in programs and services for young children with disabilities (Hodapp & Ly, 2005). These changes reflect an increasing national priority for providing comprehensive special education services for all children, regardless of disability status (Martin, Martin, & Terman, 1996).

Part I also discusses the involvement of families in the assessment process and family considerations, topics that increase awareness of biased unfair assessment with young children. Family assessment and how it is an integral part of the holistic approach to assessment will be discussed. You will also learn about the models that you would utilize in assessing families, the need and the means for engaging in self-reflection, and strategies that address families' needs from a culturally diverse perspective.

Finally, Part I will discuss collaboration models and the influence each approach may have on the assessment process.

Part II: Assessment Approaches and Considerations

Part II explains the interpretation of standardized or norm-referenced test results. Although standardized testing is rarely used with young children, norm-referenced testing may be part of the comprehensive assessment of the child. Norm-referenced standardized testing is used to determine difficulties, which could give information regarding delay but could also give information needed for a diagnosis, thus making a child eligible for services, especially as the school-age child moves from noncategorical to categorical identification of learning needs.

Part II will discuss numerous alternative assessment models used when assessing young children with ELN. It will also discuss the critical issue of assessment in natural settings as well as the spectrum of assessment methods considered best practice in the field of early childhood special education.

Finally, Part II will discuss early childhood settings, focusing on the context in which children learn, grow, and thrive through the development of skills associated with cognition, language, and socialization. The goal of early childhood education is to support children in the development of their abilities for understanding the world around them, gaining mastery of their environments, and assuming the dispositions necessary for participation in future academic settings.

Part III: Developmental Domains

Knowledge of typical development is needed to understand a child's specific learning needs. Part III will address typical growth and development in each developmental domain as well as relevant issues that influence assessment outcomes, especially with young children.

This unit also addresses sensory skills, with the premise that in the first six years of life, learning is a result of processing information through sensory channels and that the coordination of this information helps to bring meaning to the world. Sensory issues must be addressed in a unique way when assessing a child who has or is suspected of having exceptional needs.

Part III will provide an understanding of the basic components of language development in young children and methods of assessment in the areas of receptive and expressive language. These two areas are the major components of language that are the focus of the communication assessment process.

Cognitive and social-emotional skills are two distinct but highly interrelated domains that are critical to children's success in school. Although there has been a tendency to focus on these domains separately as predictors of school success, research indicates that the combination of these skill sets is critical to ensuring school success (Leerkes, Paradise, O'Brien, Calkins, & Lange, 2008). Part III will discuss these components of early childhood development and their role in healthy growth and development. Emphasis will be on the role of assessment in determining appropriate interventions for meeting the needs of children with special needs.

The development of movement is a complex, comprehensive process. When children struggle with acquisition of gross and fine motor skills, it affects learning overall. A keen knowledge of motor development and the needs of children with motor involvement influences curriculum design in the early intervention setting.

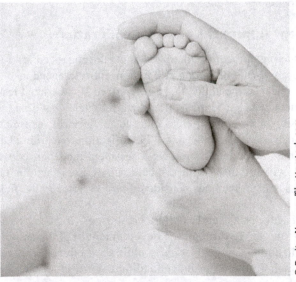

© Dmitry Naumow/Shutterstock.com

Part III will discuss the development of appropriate self-help behavior as a critical issue in the assessment and programming of young children with special needs. When young children have difficulties with self-help skills, they struggle acquiring the skills needed to meet their personal needs, show social responsibility, and respond appropriately in a variety of situations (Dunlap & Powell, 2009).

USING THE TEXT

Each chapter in the text is organized using a set of learning objectives, a case study about a young child with exceptionalities, and what we call breakpoint practices, which offer application exercises, including reflection and discussion of key issues regarding assessment. In addition, Chapters 2 to 12 includes key terms for understanding early childhood special education assessment and provides you with a vocabulary that will build your expertise in the use of terminology common to the field.

Best practices, including those regarding assessment, are commonly informed by the work of leaders in our field who provide guidance around standards of practice to help practitioners in the assumption of effective, evidence-based intervention services. The National Association for the Education of Young Children (NAEYC) and the Council for Exceptional Children/Division for Early Childhood (CEC/DEC) provide two key sets of standards. These standards are available on the CEC and NAEYC websites. The standards anchor the content in this text.

Finally, each chapter concludes with suggested activities and websites that may be useful in facilitating your learning. We encourage you to use these resources as a means of furthering your learning and applying the relevant principles presented in this text.

Conclusion

Personnel in early childhood special education environments are given the task of providing appropriate services that effectively support children and their families. Knowledge in our field, particularly in the area of assessment, has grown exponentially through research that guides our practices. This text is designed to enhance your learning so that you are prepared to meet the exciting challenges associated with the evaluation of children with exceptionalities.

The causes and manifestations of exceptional development are numerous and often difficult to define. Therefore, adequate preparation of professionals for assuming this important role and responsibility in service provision is essential. Again, we begin with the notion that each child is, first, a child. We hope that, by starting from this important premise, this text will contribute to your knowledge and promote your own growth and development in understanding the fundamental elements of assessment for young children with exceptional learning needs while recognizing their unique contributions to our world.

References

Archived: History of the IDEA. (n.d.). U.S. Department of Education. Retrieved April 18, 2010, from http://www.ed.gov/policy/speced/leg/idea/history30.html

Bronfenbrenner, U. (1977). Toward an experimental ecology of human development. *American Psychologist, 32*, 513–530.

Caldwell, B. M. (1973). The importance of beginning early. In M. B. Karnes (Ed.), *Not all little wagons are red: The exceptional child's early years*. Arlington, VA: Council for Exceptional Children.

Cattell, R. (1940). *Infant intelligence scale*. New York: Psychological Corporation.

Danaher, J., Shackelford, J., & Harbin, G. (2004). Revisiting a comparison of eligibility policies for infant/toddler programs and preschool special education programs. *Topics in Early Childhood Special Education, 24*(2), 59–67.

DuBose, R. F., & Langley, M. B. (1977). *Developmental activities screening inventory*. Hingham, MA: Teaching Resources Corporation.

Dunlap, G., & Powell, D. (2009). Promoting social behavior of young children in group settings: A summary of research roadmap to effective intervention practices #3. Tampa: University of South Florida, Technical Assistance Center on Social Emotional Intervention for Young Children.

Fewell, R. R. (2000, Spring). Assessment of young children with special needs: Foundations for tomorrow. *Topics in Early Childhood Special Education, 20*(1), 38–42.

Fewell, R. R., & Langley, M. B. (1984). *Developmental activities screening inventory* (2nd ed.). Austin, TX: PRO-ED.

Folio, R., & Dubose, R. F. (1974). *Peabody developmental motor scales—Revised experimental edition*. Nashville, Tenn: George Peabody College for Teachers.

Folio, R., & Fewell, R. F. (2000). *Peabody Developmental Motor Scales* (2nd ed.). Austin, TX: PRO-ED.

Gargiulo, R., & Kilgo, J. (2005). *Young children with special needs*. Clifton Park, NY: Thomson Delmar Learning.

Gesell, A. L., & Amatruda, C. S. (1947). *Developmental diagnosis* (2nd ed.). New York: Paul B. Hoeber.

Hanson, M. J., & Bruder, M. B. (2001, January). Early intervention: Promises to keep. *Infants and Young Children, 13*(3), 47–58.

Hodapp, R. M., & Ly, T. M. (2005). Parenting children with developmental disabilities. In T. Luster & L. Okagaki (Eds.), *Parenting: An ecological perspective* (2nd ed., pp. 177–201). Mahwah, NJ: Erlbaum.

Hooper, S. R., & Umansky, W. (2009). *Young children with special needs* (5th ed.). Upper Saddle River, NJ: Merrill/Pearson Education.

Howard, V. F., Williams, B., & Lepper, C. E. (2010). *Very young children with special needs: A foundation for educators, families, and service providers* (4th ed.). Upper Saddle River, NJ: Merrill/Pearson Education.

Leerkes, E. M., Paradise, M., O'Brien, M., Calkins, S. D., & Lange, G. (2008). Emotion and cognition processes in preschool children. *Merrill-Palmer Quarterly, 54*, 102–124.

Lerner, J. W., Lowenthal, B., & Egan, R. (2003). *Preschool children with special needs: Children at risk, children with disabilities* (2nd ed.). Boston: Allyn & Bacon.

Martin, E. W., Martin, R., & Terman, D. L. (Spring 1996). The legislative and litigation history of special education. *The Future of Children, 6*(1), 25–39.

Neisworth, J. T., & Bagnato, S. J. (2004). The mismeasure of young children: The authentic assessment alternative. *Infants and Young Children, 17*(3), 198–212.

Shackelford, J. (2002). *Informed clinical opinion* (NEC-TAC Notes No. 10). Chapel Hill: University of North Carolina, FPG Child Development Institute, National Early Childhood Technical Assistance Center. Retrieved November 14, 2009, from http://www.nectac.org/pubs/pdfs/nnotes10.pdf

Shackelford, J. (2006). *State and jurisdictional eligibility definitions for infants and toddlers with disabilities under IDEA* (NECTAC Notes No. 21). Chapel Hill: University of North Carolina, FPG Child Development Institute, National Early Childhood Technical Assistance Center. Retrieved November 14, 2009, from http://www.nectac.org/~pdfs/pubs/nnotes21.pdf

Shonkoff, J. P., & Meisels, S. J. (2000). *Handbook of early childhood intervention*. New York: Cambridge University Press.

Stutsman, R. (1948). *Merrill-Palmer scale of mental tests*. Wood Dale, IL: Stoelting.

U.S. Department of Education. (2007). *Thirty years of progress in educating children with disabilities through IDEA*. Retrieved January 10, 2010, from http://www.ed.gov/policy/speced/leg/idea/history30.html

Zigler, R., & Valentine, J. (Eds.). (1979). *Project Head Start: A legacy of the war on poverty*. New York: Free Press.

Legal Issues

CHAPTER 2

CHAPTER OBJECTIVES

By the end of this chapter, you will be able to respond to the questions posed based on your understanding of special education law as it relates to assessment, especially in relation to the case of Huan. This chapter introduces you to historical perspectives regarding early childhood special education services and the progression of legislative efforts to increase and enhance early childhood special education services, including assessment. Specific components of federal legislation that direct services for young children with disabilities and their families, including trends for assessment and intervention in the field, are also discussed. You will be able to discuss key components of the federal law regarding the rights, procedures, and safeguards afforded children and families who participate in early childhood special education settings. This chapter addresses Council for Exceptional Children (CEC) Standards 1 (foundations) and 8 (assessment).

Assessing Huan

Huan is a 28-month-old toddler who was recently screened by the local early intervention agency because of his pediatrician's concerns about delays in the areas of speech, language, and socialization. In particular, Huan appears to lack a sense of curiosity and motivation, which can be indicators of developmental delay. Huan's mother and father heeded the advice of their pediatrician to seek further evaluation, but they are not certain that they agree with the notion that their son has developmental delays.

Huan's family moved to the United States when he was 18 months old. His parents believe that his delays may be a response to his change in environment and the use of Chinese as the primary language in their home. As recent immigrants, they are also unfamiliar with the U.S. educational system, especially support services for children with exceptional needs. Huan's parents were very apprehensive at the evaluation meeting that determined his eligibility for services for Part C services. Although they have functional skills in speaking English, they were confused by terminology used by the multidisciplinary team and are unclear about their ongoing role in developing services and where those services may lead. At the time of the evaluation, Huan's parents felt that it was inappropriate to offer "too much feedback" because they saw this as disrespectful to the professional team. Because the family largely deferred to the professionals and their decisions during the meeting, conclusions regarding Huan's eligibility were based largely on formal assessments only.

Now that a determination of eligibility has been made and an individualized family service plan (IFSP) has been written to outline early intervention (Part C) services, Huan's parents are reluctant to engage in these services. They feel that Huan can make gains in his own environments and around those who are familiar with him. The multidisciplinary team strongly believes that Huan is at risk for developmental delays and that intervention is necessary to support better outcomes.

Huan is the member of a close-knit family whose members have many supportive friends and relatives in their community. His parents often rely on their community because they are both employed full-time and are of limited financial means. While they want to do what is best for their son, they are concerned about having the time and resources to do so. They remain reluctant to use early intervention services as a means for supporting their son.

What information do you think is most relevant for this multidisciplinary team to collect in order to best serve Huan and his family? What does the law say about the family's role in collaborating with teams to design services? What are the family's rights for accepting or denying services?

As an educator, you will work collaboratively with other professionals (e.g., speech-language pathologists, occupational therapists) in ongoing assessment activities to answer these questions. In addition, you will work closely with family members of the children you serve, as is dictated by law and best practice, to determine appropriate methods and outcomes. This chapter concentrates on key components of special education law as it relates to assessment, the assessment context, and specific factors associated with early childhood special education settings.

HISTORY OF LEGISLATION

Recent decades have witnessed an exponential increase in programs and services for young children with disabilities (Hodapp & Ly, 2005). These changes reflect an increasing national priority for providing comprehensive special education services for all children, regardless of disability status, that began with the Great Society programs of the 1960s. Prior to the 1960s, children with disabilities were largely ignored by the public school system, either by lack of access or through inappropriate service models (Martin, Martin, & Terman, 1996).

Beginning with the landmark Supreme Court decision, *Brown v. Board of Education* (1954), the United States began focusing on the inequalities of racial segregation, poverty, and the disenfranchisement of its citizens. As a result, the nation also began focusing on the needs of young children who were at risk and their families. The consequence of this national movement has been the inclusion of many children in educational programs for whom access was previously denied (Antoinette, 2003).

According to the United States Department of Education (2003), roughly 8.9% of children between the ages of 6 and 21 are receiving special education services. Preschool programs for children age 3 to 5 comprise 5.25% of children served, and early intervention services for children at birth to age 3 have witnessed a 31% increase in enrollment from 1998 to 2001. This evident trend demonstrates the critical role that special education plays in the public education arena today.

Education of All Handicapped Children Act (Public Law 94-142)

Prior to the enactment of federal legislation, the picture for children with disabilities was vastly different. For example, the National Council on Disability (2000) reports that, in 1970, the United States educated only one in five students with disabilities, excluded more than 1 million students from public schools, and provided inappropriate services to an additional 3.5 million students. In addition, their findings suggest that approximately 200,000 school-age children with mental retardation or emotional disabilities were institutionalized. Compounding this problem was the likelihood of exclusion based on demographics, such as low-income status, belonging to an ethnic or racial minority, or living in a rural community.

While many legislative efforts were significant for the national movement toward full equality in educational programs (see Figure 2.1), the **Education of All Handicapped Children Act** (also known as **Public Law 94-142**) was a monumental achievement that set the nation's course in ensuring equal access to U.S. public school programs. Passed in 1975, the legislation marked the first time in the nation's history that students with disabilities were guaranteed civil rights, and states were directed to educate all of their citizens. The stated purposes of the act were as follows:

a) To ensure that all children with disabilities have available to them a free appropriate public education that emphasizes special education and related services designed to meet their unique needs and prepare them for employment and independent living;
b) To ensure that the rights of children with disabilities and their parents are protected;
c) To assist states, localities, educational service agencies, and federal agencies to provide for the education of all children with disabilities; and
d) To assess and ensure the effectiveness of efforts to educate children with disabilities.

Effective implementation of the law hinges on six main principles: (a) zero reject, (b) nondiscriminatory assessment, (c) procedural due process, (d) parental participation, (e) least restrictive environment, and (f) an individualized education plan (IEP) (Murdick, Gartin, & Crabtree, 2002).

Zero reject is the foundation of the act and defines a **free appropriate public education** **(FAPE)**, which guarantees that children with disabilities, regardless of severity or type, can participate equally in public education services at public expense.

Nondiscriminatory assessment mandates that children with special learning needs are evaluated for a diagnosis and education plan to meet their individual needs. The requirements for an appropriate assessment include the following:

- Evaluation in all areas of suspected disability
- A team of evaluators knowledgeable and trained in the use of the tests and other evaluation materials
- Use of a variety of proven evaluation materials and procedures, including information gathered from a variety of sources, which do not discriminate on a racial or cultural basis or subject children to unnecessary testing
- Use of the information to determine eligibility for special education, related services, and planning an individualized plan for meeting the child's needs

Procedural due process guarantees and safeguards the rights of students with disabilities to receive an appropriate, publicly funded education. Based upon this principle, parents and

Legislation	Goals and Outcomes for Early Childhood Special Education
1965 Project Head Start	Federal program that established early education program for young children who were economically disadvantaged.
1968 Handicapped Children's Early Education Act	Provided federal funds for establishing experimental and model educational programs for young children.
1975 P.L. 94-142 Education for All Handicapped Children Act (EHCA)	Considered to be landmark legislation that established rights to public education for children with disabilities, including a free and appropriate public education and the mandate for special education services for children ages 5–21.
1986 P.L. 99-457	The ECHA amendments of 1986 that expanded Part B services to children ages 3–5 and established Part H as a grant program to encourage states to provide special education services to children from birth to age 3.
1990 P.L. 101-476	The ECHA amendments of 1990, renamed The Individuals with Disabilities Education Act (IDEA), expanded the entitlement for public education in all states to ages 3 to 21 with funding for infant and toddler early intervention programs.
1991 P.L. 102-119	The IDEA amendments of 1991 strengthened Part H services for infants and toddlers with disabilities and their families, and included the creation of the Federal Interagency Coordinating Council and states' discretion in implementing IFSPs and related family-centered service models.
1997 P.L. 105-17 Reauthorization of IDEA	The reauthorization of IDEA in 1997 strengthened the requirements for the provision of early intervention services in "natural environments" by requiring that the IFSP contain a statement regarding placement in these settings.
2001 P.L. 107-110 The No Child Left Behind Act	The reauthorization of the Elementary and Secondary Education Act of 1965 in 2001 to improve the performance of public school students by increasing standards of accountability for states and local school districts, requiring "highly-qualified teachers," and allowing for parental choice in placement decisions when schools do not meet federal standards.
2004 P.L. 108-446 Individuals with Disabilities Improvement Education Act (IDEIA)	The IDEA amendments of 2004 were named the Individuals with Disabilities Education Improvement Act (IDIE) and served to align IDEA with NCLB, including requirements for "highly-qualified teachers," the participation of students with disabilities in local and state testing, performance goals and indicators linked to the goals of NCLB, and an option for states to extend Part C services from age 3 until the child is eligible for kindergarten.

FIGURE 2.1 Legislative History of Early Childhood Special Education.

teachers play an equal role in decision-making processes and both parties are ensured the right of due process to resolve disagreements.

Parental participation is closely tied to procedural due process and allows the parent or guardian of the student to be equally involved as members of the multidisciplinary team that develops educational goals and services. Specific parental rights include (a) providing written permission for assessment; (b) participating in the development of the IEP; (c) participation in eligibility determination and annual review meetings; and (d) advocating for their child, including giving or withholding consent for services.

The **least restrictive environment (LRE)** is premised on the notion that all children should first be considered for placement in the general classroom with their nondisabled peers so that:

a) to the maximum extent appropriate, children with disabilities, including children in public or private institutions or other care facilities, are educated with children who are not disabled, and

b) special classes, separate schooling or other removal of children with disabilities from the regular educational environment occurs only when the nature or severity of the disability is such that education in regular classes, with the use of supplementary aids and services cannot be achieved satisfactorily.

The law refers to this consideration as the "continuum of alternative placements" in which the multidisciplinary team, after considering modifications, adaptations, and support, deems the general education classroom inappropriate to meet the individual needs of the student.

An **individualized education plan (IEP)** is required for all students who receive special education services. Using current evaluation information, the IEP team develops a written document that clearly identifies an individualized plan of instruction and support for each child with disabilities. Components of the IEP include the following:

- Present level of performance
  - Academic achievement
  - Functional performance (including social and behavioral)
  - The means by which the student's disability affects her or his involvement and progress in the general education curriculum
- Measurable annual goals
  - A statement of measurable annual goals, including both academic and functional goals
  - Means for the student to be involved and progress in the general education curriculum and to meet other educational needs associated with the disability
- Report of student's progress
  - The IEP must include a description of how the student's progress will be measured and the periodic timeframes when student progress toward annual goals will be reported (i.e., quarterly reports or student report cards)

BREAKPOINT PRACTICE

1. What are factors to be considered in nondiscriminatory assessment? What factors might be most relevant to Huan and his family?
2. What is the role of the parent in the IEP process? How is the parental role being carried out by Huan's family?
3. Discuss the least restrictive environment (LRE) and how this "might look" across different types of exceptionalities and service settings. What might the LRE be for Huan, given his age and developmental needs?
4. Define the six principles that are the foundation of special education law.

INDIVIDUALS WITH DISABILITIES EDUCATION ACT (IDEA)

The public law has been reauthorized on several occasions to expand the rights of public education to all citizens and to strengthen its approach to special education services. Amendments in 1986 (P.L. 99-457) were significant for their guarantee of services for preschool-age children (ages 3 through 5) and the provision of funding for the planning and implementation of early intervention services for children from birth to age 3, and their families. Renamed the **Individuals with Disabilities Education Act (IDEA)** in 1990 (P.L. 101-476), the act was further amended in 1991 (P.L. 102-119, renamed the Program for Infants and Toddlers) to reauthorize early intervention services.

A significant departure from the original act was the inclusion of the **individualized family service plan (IFSP)** for children and families participating in the infants and toddlers program. The act specifies that the IFSP must include (a) information about the child's status, (b) family information, (c) outcomes, (d) early intervention services, (e) other services, (f) dates, (g) duration of services, (h) service coordinator, and (i) transition from Part H (now Part C) services.

The 1997 reauthorization (P.L. 105-17) further delineated the critical role that the law plays in the lives of children with disabilities and their families. Specifically, the amendments require that students' with disabilities:

* Participate and make progress in the general education curriculum.
* Have an equal opportunity for participation in nonacademic and extracurricular activities.
* Participate in education with their nondisabled peers to the maximum extent appropriate (i.e., in the least restrictive environment).
* Be removed from the general education environment (i.e., self-contained classes or separate schooling) only if placement in the general education setting with supplementary aides and services is insufficient.
* Be included in districtwide assessments with appropriate accommodations and modifications or participate in alternate assessment programs.
* Have an IEP team that consists of the parent, at least one regular education teacher, one special education teacher, an administrator or his or her designee, and the child, if appropriate.

IDEA includes 14 categories for determining eligibility for special education services (see http://www.nichcy.org/disabilities/categories/pages/default.aspx), including **developmental delay**, a nonmandatory category that may be utilized at states' discretion.

Structure of the IDEA

IDEA was most recently revised in 2004, named the Individuals with Disabilities Education Improvement Act (IDEIA), and is now structured in four parts: subparts A, B, C, and D (see Figure 2.2). The combination of these parts define the law, determine its funding, establish procedural safeguards for students with disabilities and their families, and establish a national agenda for research and dissemination to improve outcomes for children with disabilities. For purposes of early childhood special education, we will focus on Parts B and C.

Part B Services

Part B of IDEIA, also called the Assistance for Education of All Children with Disabilities, delineates the rights, roles, and responsibilities for the provision of special education services for children age 3 through 21 through public education agencies. In addition to the six principles of

Structure of IDEA	
Part A	General provisions, including the purposes of the act and definitions.
Part B	Provisions relating to the education of school-age and preschool children relating to evaluations, eligibility determinations, IEPs, and educational placements.
Part C	Provisions for the Program of Infants and Toddlers with Disabilities relating to multidisciplinary evaluations, eligibility, family participation, and placement (including the use of "natural environments").
Part D	Contains requirements for various national activities designed to improve the education of children with disabilities.

FIGURE 2.2   Structure of IDEA

Source: Information from Congressional Digest, 2005.

the act previously discussed, Part B also includes specific language relevant to early childhood special education settings, including (a) *child find* (plans and procedures for identifying children from birth to age 6 with disabilities who are not served), (b) use of developmental delay as a category, (c) extended school year services, and (d) transition services.

A significant component of the law is the mechanism for identifying all children with disabilities who may be eligible for special education services. The law requires states to have policies and procedures in effect that ensure that all children residing in a state, including children with disabilities who are homeless or wards of the state, and children with disabilities attending private schools, who require special education and related services are identified and evaluated. In addition, the law allows for another category of eligibility to address children for whom problems may be apparent but not definitively so. The law defines this category as **developmental delay** and allows states to adopt definitions for children age 3 to 9 or a subset of that category. This provision is especially helpful for children from vulnerable populations (i.e., homeless, highly mobile) who present unique challenges in assessment and placement.

States that choose to include developmental delay in its definition of eligibility must define the term precisely and ensure that it is consistent with definitions set forth in IDEA. States can also determine the age range of children who qualify for this category from birth to age 9, or a subset of that age range (e.g., 3 through 5). States may not require local education agencies (LEAs) to adopt or use the term *developmental delay* and LEAs are prohibited from use of this category if it is not included in state regulations. Use of the category must conform to a state's definition of the term and the age ranges that the state has adopted (National Dissemination Center for Children with Disabilities, 2009).

Part B also allows for **extended school year services** "as necessary to provide FAPE." When deemed appropriate by the IEP team, these services are provided to children in addition to services rendered during the school year. Restriction of extended school year services based on types or severity of disability is unlawful.

Last, Part B services provide for effective **transition** of children from Part C to Part B services in order that children will experience a smooth and effective transition from one program of services to another. To fulfill this mandate, states must have in effect policies and procedures to ensure successful transition occurs through the identification of lead agencies that will coordinate with LEA efforts on behalf of young children transitioning from one program to another. This mandate places significant responsibility on early intervention personnel to ensure that the IFSP targets transition goals and effectively coordinates with LEAs to guide implementation of those goals.

Part C Services

Part C of IDEA, *also called* Infants and Toddlers with Disabilities, delineates the rights, roles, and responsibilities for the provision of special education and family support services for children from birth to age 3. The goal of Part C is preventive because it is hoped that early intervention will ameliorate developmental disabilities, thus allowing children to progress to the regular education curriculum. According to the most recent data from the U.S. Department of Education, however, the majority of children enrolled in Part C services (approximately 62.6%) continue in special education through a transition to Part B services (2003). See Figure 2.3 for a comparison of Part B and Part C services.

Part C programs are often referred to as **early intervention services** and, as noted in Figure 2.3, they contain several provisions that are unlike those for children enrolled in Part B services. Part C is largely defined by its unique purposes, namely, (a) identification of interagency coordinating councils, (b) different eligibility criteria, (c) use of individualized family service plans (IFSPs), and (d) natural environments as intervention settings.

In sum, Congress established the early intervention program in 1986 in recognition of "an urgent and substantial need" to:

- enhance the development of infants and toddlers with disabilities;
- reduce educational costs by minimizing the need for special education through early intervention;
- minimize the likelihood of institutionalization, and maximize independent living; and
- enhance the capacity of families to meet their child's needs. (National Early Intervention Longitudinal Study, 2007)

A key change to the reauthorization of IDEA (2004) is the flexibility for states to allow parents the decision for continuing Part C services for children from age 3 to their eligibility for kindergarten. This provision in the law applies to children who have previously received Part C services and who are eligible for Part B services. The continuation of Part C services must include an educational component that promotes school readiness and incorporates preliteracy (language and numeracy skills) until children enter or are eligible under state law to enter kindergarten.

BREAKPOINT PRACTICE

1. Define and describe key differences between Part B and Part C services, including the individualized education plan (IEP) and the individualized family service plan (IFSP).
2. Describe reasons the law requires a transition plan for young children moving from one service setting to another.
3. What factors must you consider in using the label *developmental delay* to categorize a student for special education services? How might this inform your assessment of Huan?

KEY PROVISIONS OF PART C SERVICES

Interagency Coordinating Councils (ICCs)

The Program for Infants and Toddlers with Disabilities (Part C of IDEA) operates as a federal grant program to assist states in implementing a comprehensive statewide system of early intervention

	Part C (Birth to Age 3)	Part B (Ages 3–21)
Focus	Family as primary change agent in promoting children's development.	Child-centered focus related to individual educational needs.
Eligibility	Children who are experiencing a developmental delay (as determined by individual state criteria) or have a diagnosed condition that is highly likely to result in a developmental delay.	Special education services must be provided for children who fit into one or more of the following categories: *Autism* *Deafblindness* *Deafness* *Developmental delay (ages 3–9)* *Emotional disturbance* *Hearing impairment* *Intellectual disability* *Multiple disabilities* *Orthopedic impairment* *Other health impairments* *Specific learning disability* *Speech or language impairment* *Traumatic brain injury* *Visual impairment*
Individualized plans	Individualized family service plan (IFSP)	Individualized education plan (IEP)
Services	Early intervention services are designed for the child and family to meet the needs of the child and to promote the family's abilities to meet the needs of the child. A service coordinator, a role typically assumed by the person whose expertise is most relevant to the child's needs, is assigned to guide the family and facilitate communication and services among agencies and assist parents in obtaining necessary supports.	Special education and related services are designed to meet the educational needs of the child and, to the maximum extent possible, ensure that the child participates in the general education curriculum.
Service settings	To the maximum extent possible, services are provided in natural environments, including home and community locations where children without disabilities would typically participate, and emphasizing rhythms and routines of daily life as a context for development and learning.	Services are provided with consideration for the least restrictive environment (LRE), including maximum exposure to educational settings with nondisabled peers.
Family involvement	Families participate in all team decisions regarding the individualized plan for their children's services. Families may receive additional services to improve their abilities for meeting the needs of their children with disabilities.	Families participate in all team decisions regarding the individualized education plan for their children's services.

FIGURE 2.3   Comparison of Part C and Part B Services.

services for infants and toddlers with disabilities and their families. Receipt of federal monies is contingent on states' plans for ensuring that services are available to every eligible child and family and organized through an identified lead agency that is chosen by legislative authority in each state. Unlike Part B services, which are primarily housed within the public school sector, Part C services represent a coordinated group of services that may be housed in public school systems, health departments, mental health agencies, or other service settings deemed appropriate by the state for administrating the program. Consistent across all states is the mandate for an interagency coordinating council (ICC), which includes parents of young children with disabilities, to advise and support the lead agency. Currently, all states and eligible territories are participating in the Part C program.

Assessment and Eligibility

Unlike Part B services, states have some discretion in setting eligibility requirements for children enrolled in Part C services. While minimum components are established by federal law, discrepancies exist across states in determining eligibility for services (see www.nectac.org/~pdfs/pubs/nnotes21.pdf for information on state eligibility definitions). Among the more notable differences is states' discretion for serving children deemed at risk. IDEA defines **established conditions of risk** as developmental challenges that, left unattended, may result in developmental delays. These risk factors include biological, medical (i.e., chromosomal abnormalities, genetic or congenital disorders, sensory impairments, exposure to toxins, severe attachment disorders), or environmental conditions (i.e., parental substance abuse, family social disorganization, poverty, homelessness, parental developmental disability, child abuse or neglect). Effective assessment relies largely on informed clinical opinion, or the combination of knowledge and skills among multidisciplinary team members, including parents, used to better understand children and their development within a "socially valid context," or otherwise defined as children's abilities and needs within their own natural environments (Shackelford, 2002, p. 3).

Like Part B services, evaluation is provided to families of infants and toddlers at no cost to the parents. The evaluation process includes a **multidisciplinary approach** (see Chapter 4) in which a team of early intervention personnel use evidenced-based tools to evaluate children for developmental delays and provide recommendations based in their area of clinical expertise. Assessment occurs in the following developmental domains: (a) cognition, (b) physical (fine and gross motor), (c) social-emotional, (d) speech and language, and (e) hearing and vision (see Chapters 5–8).

Natural Environments

A significant feature of Part C is the mandate that, to the maximum extent possible, early intervention services are to be provided in **natural environments** that are typical for the child (e.g., home and community settings) and in which children without disabilities would typically participate. The law does allow for exceptions to the mandate if members of the multidisciplinary team, including the child's parents, determine that outcomes can be achieved successfully in an alternative setting, such as a center-based program.

Individualized Family Service Plan (IFSP)

The IFSP is the vehicle through which effective early intervention is implemented in accordance with Part C of IDEA. The IFSP is developed after eligibility is determined by the IFSP team members, including the parents and others involved in the evaluation and assessment of the identified child, developing the written plan. The IFSP is based on a multidisciplinary evaluation of the child's development and the concerns, priorities, and needs of the family related to the child's development.

The IFSP must include a statement of the child's functional ability across five developmental areas: physical (including vision and hearing), cognitive, communication, social/emotional, and adaptive functioning. The document must state the major outcomes to be achieved by the infant or toddler and the family with specific strategies, including criteria, procedures, and time-lines, to demarcate milestones for achievement. In light of the rapid developmental changes that occur in the early years, IFSPs are reviewed at least semiannually, or more frequently as determined by the multidisciplinary team and the family.

A significant difference between the IFSP and the IEP is the global nature of support to families with infants and toddlers with disabilities. Within that paradigm, the IFSP may also include other services needed by the child and family, such as assistance with housing, food, clothing, education, or medical care, with assistance provided in accessing these services.

A major component of Part C services is the identification of a service coordinator who will be responsible for implementing the IFSP and coordinating services among agencies, personnel, and the family. In some states, this function can be carried out by the family; in others, this role is assumed by professional team members. The service coordinator serves as the axis for the team in determining and ensuring effective intervention. The law defines this critical role as including the following:

- Coordinating the performance of evaluations and assessments;
- Facilitating and participating in the development, review, and evaluation of IFSPs;
- Assisting families in identifying available service providers;
- Coordinating and monitoring the delivery of available services;
- Informing families of the availability of advocacy services;
- Coordinating with medical and health providers; and
- Facilitating the development of a transition plan to preschool services, if appropriate. (Bruder, 2005).

Last, the IFSP must include a plan for transition to support infants and toddlers with disabilities and their families in moving from Part C to Part B services. The multidisciplinary team, including the parents, begins preparing for a transition around the age of 30 to 32 months, but no less than three months prior to the child's third birthday. A transition planning meeting is held to discuss next steps, particularly as they relate to a child's preparation for entrance into the Part B service system.

© Monkey Business Images/ Shutterstock.com

BREAKPOINT PRACTICE

1. Compare and contrast the differences between Part B and Part C services related specifically to contexts and settings for service delivery.
2. Early intervention services are defined as "family centered." How does this distinction affect the ways that professionals collaborate with families? How might a family-centered approach support Huan's family members in their search for support?
3. What leeway do professionals have in deciding to use natural environments in Part C services? How might natural environments meet the needs of Huan and his family?
4. What is the role of the service coordinator? Why is this role deemed necessary for infants, toddlers, and their families?

NO CHILD LEFT BEHIND (NCLB) AND IDEIA

Significant to assessment and intervention for children with disabilities is understanding the mandated congruence of No Child Left Behind (NCLB), which is legislation designed to set high standards and measurable goals for improving children's educational outcomes, with the IDEIA of 2004. It is clear that Congress is demonstrating its commitment to improving educational outcomes for all students, especially those with disabilities (Elliot, 2003). Handler (2006, p. 6) suggests that the law creates "multiple layers of accountability, programming, and assessment for educators serving students with disabilities." For personnel working within early childhood settings, accountability to outcomes, which has been a historical focus, is now embedded into legal mandates for ensuring that all children achieve at outcomes expected for their age group and abilities.

Of particular importance in the legislation is the requirement that children with disabilities participate in assessments with their nondisabled peers. This fundamental shift holds all parties more accountable to the educational process and requires greater effort on the part of educators to ensure that evidence-based strategies are employed, with appropriate assessment for measurement of development that will actuate developmental potentialities.

For effective implementation of this goal, educators must seek effective collaborations that cross the lines of general and special education services, including parties outside the school system who may be of assistance in supporting children and families. While this may prove difficult at times, it is suggested that collaboration can lead to shared knowledge among regular and special education teachers in a manner that "makes transparent" those special education processes and practices that all teachers can assume and use to support all students (Garriott, Miller, & Snyder, 2003; Handler, 2006).

EARLY CHILDHOOD SPECIAL EDUCATION ASSESSMENT AND LEGAL TRENDS

The public law solidifies the historical foci of early childhood special education services, namely, that families are central to the process; children, regardless of disability status, need to participate in the educational system with their age-appropriate, nondisabled peers in order to achieve optimal developmental outcomes; and effective assessment is the linchpin of effective intervention. In addition, the law sets high standards for both teacher and student performance in an effort to ensure that all children reach their educational potential in a timely fashion. These goals should be familiar to early childhood special education personnel. Contextualizing young children with disabilities within family, school, and community settings is at the core of early childhood special education services.

In particular, **family-centered** service delivery is a primary focus of many early childhood programs in both regular and special education settings. Dunst (2002) has described this philosophical approach as a set of beliefs and practices that mobilizes supports and resources to undergird families in heading their children toward optimal outcomes. Despite a proliferation of research to support this intervention philosophy, accomplishing this goal has been described as elusive (Bruder, 2000). Yet the law has integrated the family in a very central role, both in the context of Part C services and in partnership and decision-making responsibilities throughout Part B services. Clearly, the trend toward family-centeredness in early childhood special education services can be viewed as both a best practice approach and a legal requirement.

Similarly, a definite trend is moving the fields toward the **inclusion** of children with disabilities in the mainstream of educational and community settings. While parents report mixed feelings about inclusion, they are more prone to push for inclusive settings to allow participation with their children's nondisabled peers to promote social competencies (Brown, 2001). The use of inclusion practices are gaining wider support as a paradigm for service delivery and mirror the ecological systems approaches (Bronfenbrenner, 1979) that are the foundation of early childhood special education services (Guralnick, 2005). This is most apparent in the use of **natural environments** for infants and toddlers that promote positive, trusting parent-professional partnerships in the implementation of services within home and community-based settings (Soodak & Erwin, 2000). As inclusion becomes a more routine practice, special educators will be responsible for assessment consistent with these goals and for revamping curricula to meet both the social-emotional and academic needs of young learners (Cross, Traub, Hutter-Pishgahi, & Shelton, 2004).

The reconceptualization of early childhood special education services toward increased family-centeredness and inclusion of children in "typical environments" directly affects the role of assessment, including the use of functional behavioral assessments (FBAs) (see Chapter 7) and response to intervention (RTI) (see Chapter 14) approaches and culturally sensitive measures that supplement traditional evaluation tools for evaluation and placement (Blair, Umbreit, Dunlap, & Jung, 2007).

In alignment with NCLB, IDEIA of 2004 makes central the role of assessment in determining placement, evaluating performance, and guiding ongoing decisions regarding educational interventions for children with disabilities. Most significant are requirements for ensuring that students with disabilities participate in state- or districtwide assessments, including the use of modifications and alternate assessments, and the evaluation of the implementation of IEP in determining disciplinary action as a result of children's behavior.

The assessment of young children with exceptionalities poses unique challenges to professionals and families. While the law sets forth clear parameters for assessment and intervention, the nature of children's development and latitude within the law make empirical judgments limited, at best. Much of the assessment process entails the collection of disparate pieces of information, gathered through formal, informal, anecdotal, observational, and other means, to draw the best conclusions about a child's developmental picture and how a child's identified needs can best be met by families and other significant people in their environments. To put it simply, the process can be daunting.

Children's development in the early years is dynamic by nature. Developmental changes may occur rapidly, as do the support needs of children's families. The support needs of children and families will vary with the characteristics of their development, skills, culture, values, beliefs, preferences, and interests. It requires great skill, and informed clinical judgment, to integrate these variables into schemes that make assessment accurate and effective.

Advances in our understanding and assessment of young children with exceptionalities continue to guide the field in new directions and is reflected in law. For example, the adoption of developmental delay as a category for consideration, the continuation of Part C services through toddlerhood, or the focus on natural environments are necessary supports for effective practice. However, they add a new set of dimensions to the numerous factors that professionals must consider in order to be effective in their work. For early childhood special education professionals, effectiveness in moving through this maze is largely anchored in an awareness of the laws that guide intervention and the intent of the law for the adoption and use of best practices.

Clearly, the field faces significant challenges in assuming assessment procedures that respond more adequately to the multifaceted nature of the law. Successful adherence to the law requires that personnel involved in early childhood special education services are fully aware of legal mandates, evidence-based practices for effective intervention, and the dynamic shifts that are pushing the field toward new paradigms in service delivery. A progressive history of legislation regarding young children with disabilities has resulted in definitive directives for the future of the field. Effective implementation relies on practitioners successfully integrating these directives in their day-to-day practices.

BREAKPOINT PRACTICE

1. IDEIA of 2004 mandates that students with disabilities participate in state- and districtwide testing. How might this affect the need for collaboration between regular classroom teachers and early childhood special education teachers in assessment processes?
2. Inclusion is a growing trend in considering the LRE for students with disabilities. How might this trend affect approaches to assessment?
3. The field of early childhood special education promotes family-centered practices. Yet Bruder (2000) describes our efforts toward this goal as elusive. What factors do you believe may impede the field's full embrace of this philosophical approach?
4. What do you consider as the pros and cons of aligning IDEA with the goals of NCLB within early childhood special education settings?
5. How do you see legal mandates as being a potential help or hindrance to your clinical practice?

Revisiting Huan

Huan's family came to the early intervention program on the recommendation of their pediatrician to determine the nature of observed developmental delays. Huan's family is reluctant to participate in early intervention services and seem unclear about the parameters of the program and their intended outcomes. At the beginning of this chapter, you were asked to consider the information you might want to gain from the assessment, the role of the family in collaboration, and the rights of the family in determining services. After reading this chapter, you should have been able to draw some preliminary conclusions about Huan's case. Among those conclusions might be the following:

- A review of assessment practices to ensure a family-centered approach
- Issues of culture and their relationship to nondiscriminatory assessment
- More accurate identification and definition of the concerns, priorities, and resources of the family
- The financial needs of the family and how this affects their view of services
- The close-knit community in which this family lives and their role in providing natural environments as promoters of development

Families often come to early childhood special education services with various resource needs, levels of ability, and levels of commitment to their children and family. The role of the early childhood special education professional is to listen to the family members' stories and, based on their input, use the mechanisms associated with the law to organize an effective response.

Clearly, Part C services were designed for a family, like Huan's. The law is family-centered in its approach, setting a collaborative alliance with families and making parents the "drivers of services." The goals of the IFSP, which include global assessment, strategies, services, and timelines for intervention, are clearly poised to guide your intervention.

Last, Huan enters the service delivery system at 28 months of age. Did his age trigger your thinking? Huan is fast approaching the age where children exit Part C services. Therefore, you want to think about Huan's transition at the very start of your intervention or, with his family, begin thinking about the extension of Part C services if that option is available in their setting. Within two months, the law requires a beginning of the transition process. Knowing from the beginning that your relationship with the family will be short term would obviously affect the development of your relationship with the family. Consequently, the practitioner may want to use personnel from Part B service systems to begin working with the family from the start, should this be the direction of Huan's future placement. Thinking about these factors at the beginning will set in motion the provisions of the law that work to integrate Parts B and C services so that families experience a seamless transition between these distinct service paradigms.

When we left Huan's family, they were still undecided about their participation in early intervention services. This is not an unusual phenomenon. The question is, Is their resistance something that can be solved within the contexts of the law and best practice to engage them in services for their son? Doing so requires knowledge of the law and the law's intents for family-centered supports within effective assessment paradigms. These foundations are necessary to achieve the aims of federal legislation for support of children with exceptional needs and must be employed judiciously to achieve quality outcomes.

Activities

1. Think of ways in which your community could enhance its outreach to families eligible for early intervention services through child find initiatives.
2. Discuss the pros and cons of formal versus informal assessment approaches for the evaluation and identification of children with exceptional needs.
3. Describe ways in which cultural diversity may affect assessment and how you might improve your practices to account for this variable in evaluation, eligibility, and intervention approaches.
4. Devise a protocol or checklist for embedding the evaluation of developmental skills within natural environments.

5. Observe an IEP or IFSP meeting so you can more clearly identify the application of the six principles that comprise special education law.

Websites

Council for Exceptional Children
http://www.cec.sped.org

Council of Chief State School Officers
http://www.ccsso.org/

National Association for the Education of Young Children
http://www.naeyc.org

National Association of Directors of Special Education
http://www.nasdse.org/

National Association of School Psychologists
http://www.nasponline.org/about_nasp/pospaper_eca.aspx

National Dissemenation Center for Children with Disabilities (NICHCY)
http://www.nichcy.org/Pages/Home.aspx

National Early Childhood Technical Assistance Center
http://www.nectac.org/

United States Department of Education
http://www.ed.gov

Wrightslaw
http://www.wrightslaw.com/

References

Antoinette, M. L. (2003). Examining how the inclusion of disabled students into the general classroom may affect non-disabled classmates. *Fordham Urban Law Journal, 30*(6), 203–209

Blair, K., Umbreit, J., Dunlap, G., & Jung, G. (2007). Promoting inclusion and peer participation through assessment-based intervention. *Topics in Early Childhood Special Education, 27*(3), 134–147.

Bronfenbrenner, U. (1979). *The ecology of human development: Experiments by nature and design.* Cambridge, MA: Harvard University Press.

Brown, K. T. (2001). *The effectiveness of early childhood inclusion: Parent's perspectives.* (Report No. PS-029-342). Baltimore, MD: Loyola College. (ERIC Document Reproduction Service No. ED451898)

Brown v. Board of Education, Topeka, Kansas, 347 U.S. 483 (1954).

Bruder, M. B. (2000). Family-centered early intervention: Clarifying our values for the new millennium. *Topics in Early Childhood Special Education, 20*(2), 105–115.

Bruder, M. B. (2005). Service coordination and integration in a developmental systems approach to early intervention. In M. J. Guralnick (Ed.), *The developmental systems approach to early intervention* (pp. 29–58). Baltimore: Brookes.

Cross, A. F., Traub, E. K., Hutter-Pishgahi, L., & Shelton, G. (2004). Elements for successful inclusion for children with significant disabilities. *Topics in Early Childhood Special Education, 24*(3), 169–183.

Dunst, C. J., (2002). Family-centered practices: Birth through high school. *Journal of Special Education, 36*(3), 139–147.

Education of All Handicapped Children Act, P.L. 94-142, 20 U.S.C. § 1400 et seq. (1975).

Education of All Handicapped Children Act Amendments, P.L. 99-457, 20 U.S.C. § 1400 et seq. (1986).

Elliot, J. L. (2003). IDEA 2003: Reauthorization or retrofit? *School Administrator, 60*(3), 28–30.

Garriott, P. P., Miller, M., & Snyder, L. (2003). Preservice teachers' beliefs about inclusive education: What should teacher educators know? *Action in Teacher Education, 25*(1), 48–54.

Guralnick, M. J. (2005). An overview of the developmental systems model for early intervention. In M. J. Guralnick (Ed.), *The developmental systems approach to early intervention* (pp. 3–28). Baltimore: Brookes.

Handler, B. (2006). Two acts, one goal: Meeting the shared vision of No Child Left Behind and Individuals with Disabilities Education Improvement Act of 2004. *Clearing House: A Journal of Educational Strategies, Issues and Ideas, 80*(1), 5–8.

Hodapp, R. M., & Ly, T. M. (2005). Parenting children with developmental disabilities. In T. Luster & L. Okagaki (Eds.), *Parenting: An ecological perspective* (2nd ed., pp. 177–201). Mahwah, NJ: Erlbaum.

Individuals with Disabilities Education Act Amendments, P.L. 105-17, 20 U.S.C. § 1400 et seq. (1997).

Individuals with Disabilities Education Act Amendments, P.L. 102-119, 20 U.S.C. § 1400 et seq. (1991).

Individuals with Disabilities Education Act Amendments, P.L. 101-476, 20 U.S.C. § 1400 et seq. (1990).

Individuals with Disabilities Education Improvement Act of 2004, P. L. 108-446, 20 U.S.C. § 1400 et seq.

Martin, E., Martin, R., & Terman, D. (1996). The legislative and litigation history of special education. *The Future of Children, 6*(1), 25–39.

Murdick, N., Gartin, B., & Crabtree, T. (2002). *Special education law.* Upper Saddle River, NJ: Merrill/Pearson Education.

National Council on Disability. (2000, January 25). *Back to school on civil rights.* Washington, DC: National Council on Disability. Retrieved November 7, 2007, from http://www.ncd.gov/newsroom/publications/2000/backtoschool1.htm

National Dissemination Center for Children with Disabilities (NICHCY). (2009, April). Categories of disability under IDEA. Washington, DC: Author.

National Early Intervention Longitudinal Study (NEILS). (2007). *Early intervention for infants and toddlers with disabilities and their families: Participants, services, and outcomes.* Menlo Park, CA: Author.

No Child Left Behind Act, 2001, 20 U.S.C. § 6301 et seq. (2001).

Shackelford, J. (2002). *Informed clinical opinion* (NEC-TAC Notes No. 10). Chapel Hill: University of North Carolina, FPG Child Development Institute, National Early Childhood Technical Assistance Center.

Shackelford, J. (2006). *State and jurisdictional eligibility definitions for infants and toddlers with disabilities under IDEA* (NECTAC Notes No. 21). Chapel Hill: University of North Carolina, FPG Child Development Institute, National Early Childhood Technical Assistance Center.

Soodak, L. C., & Erwin, E. J. (2000). Valued member or tolerated participant: Parents' experiences in inclusive early childhood settings. *Journal of the Association for Persons with Severe Handicaps, 25,* 29–44.

U.S. Department of Education, Office of Special Education and Rehabilitative Services, Office of Special Education Programs. (2003). *25th Annual (2003) Report to Congress on the Implementation of the Individuals with Disabilities Education Act.* Retrieved June 30, 2008, from http://www2.ed.gov/about/reports/annual/osep/2003/25th-vol-1-front.pdf

Family Diversity and Assessment

CHAPTER 3

CHAPTER OBJECTIVES

Based on the case study that follows, you will be able to discuss the questions that follow and learn to describe frameworks that you may use in assessing families from diverse cultures, understand the need and the means for engaging in self-reflection, and articulate strategies that address families' needs from culturally diverse perspectives.

This chapter addresses Council for Exception Children (CEC) Standards 2 (Development and Characteristics of Learners), 9 (Professional and Ethical Practice), and 10 (Collaboration) and National Association for the Education of Young Children (NAEYC) Standard 2 (Building Family and Community Relationships).

Assessing Sarah

Emily and Tariq were referred to the local early intervention program by their pediatrician because their 2-year-old daughter, Sarah, is not developing expressive language; is withdrawn from others, including her parents; and increasingly demonstrates patterns of behavior that do not align with age-appropriate play skills of discovery and mastery. Emily was 18 years of age and 3 months pregnant when she married her husband Tariq, who was 19 at the time of their marriage. Because the couple came from different religious and cultural backgrounds, their marriage was contentious for both sides of their families, with whom they have strained relationships.

Emily and Tariq currently live in a studio apartment that is "cramped" with their child. Tariq works at a low-wage job, and Emily is staying home with her child because of her concern for Sarah's development and the cost of childcare. They would like to have more children, socialize more with others, and rent a larger apartment, but the costs of living in a major metropolitan area, coupled with Sarah's needs, leave them financially strapped and isolated.

Both Emily and Tariq describe their extended families as "pushy and opinionated," offering unsolicited advice that is more aligned with their own beliefs, values, and personal agendas than those of Emily and Tariq. While Emily grew up in the United States, her husband immigrated to this country as a 13-year-old, learning a new language and customs.

At the initial meeting, the parents appear cautious in their request for help, although it is clear that Tariq speaks more authoritatively for his family. It is apparent that, while they need, and are seeking support, they do not want to be "told what to do. Rather, they want to become competent parents who are autonomous of professional advice. Tariq appears especially sensitive to this issue. For example, when the early interventionist makes suggestions, he often responds that they have "tried that already" or "have already been working on these issues," even though that does not appear to be the case.

As a member of the transdisciplinary team that supports Sarah and her parents, you are working with your colleagues to better understand this family's orientation to parenting, the beliefs and values that underlie their decision making, and the models and strategies you should use in forming effective alliances and goals that meet the family's identified concerns, priorities, and resources. Here are some questions that should guide your thinking: (a) What types of information do you think the team needs to gather to support this family effectively? (b) What may be the "lens" that the team can use in assessing and understanding this family? (c) How can this information be applied in support of this family and to produce growth for Sarah's, her parents', and the team's development?

DIVERSITY IN THE UNITED STATES TODAY

The face of the United States is rapidly changing. Recent U.S. Census data (U.S. Census Bureau, 2008) suggests that groups currently labeled as minorities will collectively become the majority of the U.S. population by 2042. These demographic shifts pose unique challenges for family-centered service delivery in early childhood education settings. By law and best practice, early childhood special education practitioners are obligated to engage families effectively in collaborative, trusting alliances to mutually address the developmental needs of young children with disabilities. Given the complexities of family life, this can be a challenging task. This task can be more challenging when families possess cultural views and behaviors that may be different from our own.

For the early childhood educator, the role of the family cannot be underestimated. With increasing diversity being a hallmark of the field, enhancing the profession's competencies for working successfully with families from diverse backgrounds and experiences is paramount. However, a recent survey of new teachers by the National Comprehensive Center for Teacher Quality and Public Agenda (2008) found that, while 76% reported receiving training in the area of support to diverse families, only 39% reported that their training "helped a lot," ranking diversity training as the least effective of their subjects studied. Finding comfort in working with families from different cultural perspectives is an essential ingredient in realizing effective family-centered intervention. The field of early childhood special education has long recognized the central role of the family members as the primary teachers of their children and the context in which optimal developmental can occur (Bailey et al., 1998; Bruder, 2000; McBride & Brotherson, 1997). This chapter addresses that need by focusing on elements of diversity to guide professionals in more accurately assessing and engaging with all families in successful, collaborative partnerships.

The goal of effective early childhood programs is to understand fully the needs of families in their roles as parents and to use tools and strategies that will enhance collaboration and parenting practices unique to the needs of parents' children and that will work within the context of the family's rhythms, rituals, and routines. While this goal is at the heart of best practices in service delivery, it is complicated by the diversity of cultural ideals representing many values, beliefs, and goals with regard to childrearing and perspectives on children with disabilities.

© DNF Style/Shutterstock.com

FAMILY SYSTEMS THEORY

Regardless of status, all families have an identifiable structure. In concert with ecological principles (Bronfenbrenner, 1979), family systems theory (Bowen, 1978; Minuchin, 1974) defines the following set of parameters that are relevant for effectively assessing family structure, the ways in which families interact, and the manner in which families perform the tasks of daily living: boundaries, roles, rules, hierarchy, and equilibrium. Regardless of cultural identity, this set of parameters punctuates family life. These parameters are used to organize and evaluate the family's functioning across all contexts.

Boundaries

Boundaries relate to the limits that families put on togetherness and separateness and define who is "let in" and who is "kept out" (Barker, 1992). Some families are open to new people and new ideas and are able to make decisions on their own. These families tend to be more independent, valuing autonomy over belonging. In other families, the boundaries tend to more closed and restrictive. These families emphasize togetherness, belonging, and emotional connectedness (Christian, 2006).

Depending on the relationship (e.g., family, friends, professionals), families enact their boundary definitions to meet their unique needs and definitions of family and their interactions with the outside world. While professional relationships tend to be bounded by roles and tasks, interactions with families in early childhood special education settings tend to move through a continuum of relationship dimensions, such as information sharing, strategy development, and emotional support (Lord-Nelson, Summers, & Turnbull, 2004). As educators navigate these dimensions, they note the ways in which families are willing to use relationships of support. For example, some families may be willing to engage around ideas of intervention, but demur from discussing personal information or joining in friendly conversation. Other families may rely heavily on the educator and wish to join in friendship and support that may appear outside the typical bounds of the professional relationship. In each case, families are demonstrating their interaction style with the outer world and indicating the posture the educator should assume in approaching them.

Roles

Roles have been defined as the prescribed and repetitive behaviors that inform the reciprocal activities of family members (Barker, 1992; Steinhauer, Santa-Barbara, & Skinner, 1984). In most families, these roles are not assigned in a formal manner, but rather they are the understood way that family members perform their tasks. These roles prescribe the behavioral actions that family members take and are observed by others. For example, a mother may assume the day-to-day responsibility for the education of her child and be a frequent visitor at the school, while the father's involvement may occur only when major decisions are to be made about educational planning or outcomes. Family members enact their prescribed functions to ensure that the family works effectively according to the constructs of the family's goals, values, and beliefs. The behaviors that family members assume illustrate the functions of their task performance and the role that is ascribed to each member.

Rules

Rules, in concert with role performance, helps families maintain a sense of stability. Family rules are best described as "understanding or agreements in families that organize the family members' interactions" (Hecker, Mims, & Boughner, 2003, p. 53). These rules may be spoken or unspoken. Or as family therapist Virginia Satir said, "[R]ules exist for all other contributing factors that make it possible for people to live together in the same house and grow or not grow" (Satir, 1996, p. 168).

Examples of spoken rules may be a child's curfew or required attendance at family meals. Examples of unspoken rules may be the fact the children "just know" to never argue with their father or that a disabled sibling's needs "just come first." Rules are often embedded in a cultural context (Hecker et al., 2003) and therefore may contribute to the discontinuity that parents feel when implied; lived-by rules are dissimilar to the settings where their children receive services.

Hierarchy

As Christian (2006) suggests, **hierarchy** helps answer the question, Who's the boss? Hierarchy is a characteristic related to decision making, control, and power in the family. For example, in the "traditional" family, the father might assume the roles of decision maker and the leader of the family. In other families, this role may fall to the mother. In families with ineffective hierarchical structures, this role may disproportionately fall to an older sibling. In most families, parents typically share responsibilities and assume the hierarchical stance based on the situation or the task at hand.

As you can see, hierarchies are a shifting dynamic. Power and control may shift based on the individual talents of a family member or change when a new member enters the picture, such as a new stepparent. A family's hierarchy is certainly affected by the referents of microcultures, such as religion, age, gender, and ethnic identity, which will be discussed later in this chapter. At times, the messages about who is the boss may be clear and at other times it is not. For example, an early interventionist reported that she had worked weekly with a mother regarding her child's development. She naturally assumed that, at the individualized family service plan (IFSP) meeting, she would continue her dialogue with the mother regarding the family's concerns, priorities, and resources. Upon attending the meeting, however, she quickly realized that the child's father and an elder uncle would be the spokespersons for the family and the ultimate decision makers about issues previously shared between the interventionist and the mother.

The diversity of families presenting in early childhood settings makes the need for the understanding of hierarchy in families a must for educators. With rapidly evolving family structures, these characteristics are shifting with new and emerging configurations of which educators must be aware.

Equilibrium

All families engage in patterns that are recursive in nature or in patterns that tend to repeat themselves (Hecker et al., 2003). **Equilibrium** can best be understood as the family's attempts at achieving balance, or a steady state, especially during times of crisis, stress, transition, and change. This is a particularly relevant characteristic for consideration because many families we see have recently learned the news about the child's difficulties with development and are working to organize this information into their family life. Consistency in families can be difficult to maintain (Christian, 2006), but it is particularly difficult when stressors, such as a child's disability, are an imposition on the family structure and result in disequilibrium. However, the inherent nature of the family structure is its ability to seek equilibrium, or homeostasis, as a means to adjust to new realities and to incorporate new dynamics and interactional patterns that better meets the needs of the family in new or challenging situations. A central goal of any family unit or structure is the ability to move effectively from disequilibrium to equilibrium with the greatest degree of comfort and holding intact the family's basic sense of identity.

While an understanding of family systems theory can guide observation and assessment, it is suggested that the theory alone is not a therapeutic practice, only a lens through which to organize our thinking about families (Simon, 1995). To be successful in our interventions, we must hold the belief that families are uniquely equipped to alter their patterns of behavior in order to accommodate necessary changes that will support effective family functioning. The analysis of these patterns is difficult at best, but such analysis can be further complicated by cultural referents for which we may be unfamiliar.

BREAKPOINT PRACTICE

1. Given your knowledge of Sarah's family, how do you view the hierarchy in this family? What is apparent? What may be missing that you would like to know?
2. How are boundaries potentially affected by Emily and Tariq's relationship with their families? How might this be reflected in meetings with professionals?
3. What specific steps might you suggest for Sarah's family to work toward a greater sense of equilibrium? What would equilibrium for Sarah's family look like to you?

CULTURE DEFINED

Although all families operate within certain frameworks, such as the use of boundaries, roles, and rules, the enactment of family life within these parameters is largely characterized by cultural experience. Defining cultures is no easy task; each of us has his or her unique conceptions of the term. **Culture** may best be defined as the ways in which one perceives, believes, evaluates, and behaves (Goodenough, 1987). You may also refer to culture as one's life map or the blueprint by which decisions are made and the actions of others are evaluated. The term *culture* can be subdivided into subcategories, into macro- and microcultures. According to Banks (2001), "the United States consists of a common overarching culture, or macroculture, and microcultures that consist of unique institutions, values, and cultural elements that are non-universalized and are shared primarily by members of specific cultural groups" (p. 11). In the United States, typical **macroculture** values individualism, assertiveness, utilizing new or modern methods to solve problems, or the importance of seeking wealth. Conversely, the United States is composed of an almost infinite number of **microcultures** that punctuate U.S. life and contribute to its immense diversity. Among these microcultures are race, ethnicity, gender, age, geography, religion, income, and language (Turnbull, Turnbull, Erwin, & Soodak, 2006).

To begin, it is appropriate to discuss a basic similarity that all families bring to the educational setting. Although expressed in differing ways, all cultures have patterns of attachment and bonding with their children that serve to guide their relationships over the life span. Similarly, most parents report a desire for achieving this outcome, along with a wish to see their children exceed their own accomplishments. Too often, in discussions of diversity, there is a singular focus on the differences that characterize family life rather than the similarities that tend to intertwine with our own views and perspectives. If we begin from the premise that most families want what is best for their children, we are in a better position to listen and learn about the unique ways in which all families strive for success. To listen well, however, we must first know what to listen for. The goal of understanding diverse family perspectives is to promote alliances with educators that are effective; enduring; honor the family; and recognize how the interactions of differing values, perceptions, and beliefs may affect the relationship with the school team.

Race and Ethnicity

Race and ethnicity play a critical role in the way families have experienced the world and the perceptions they bring to the working alliance with education professionals. Parenting practices in different racial and ethnic groups may be situated from various perspectives. For example, Park and Bauer (2002) studied parenting practices and their relationship to academic achievement along four dimensions: supervision, strictness, support, and involvement. Similarly, research has utilized Baumrind's (1966, 1967) early notions of parenting styles (authoritative, authoritarian, and permissive) and how these may be evidenced in certain parenting practices that are uniquely employed from different cultural perspectives. Rodrilquez, Donovick, and Crowley (2009) build on these notions and suggest that parenting styles package complex information regarding sets of attitudes and behaviors along dimensions of warmth, autonomy granting, supportive demandingness, nonsupportive demandingness, and their relationship to child outcomes.

While there is clear evidence that racial and ethnic groups engage in a range of parenting practices unique to their culture and experience, it is also clear that much research remains to be done to understand fully the impact of these styles and the cautionary stance one must take in making assumptions about parenting behavior or inaccurately generalizing outcomes based on these styles. As is suggested, the complex nature and interactions of cultural referents and parenting provide a lens for understanding the unique focus of particular parenting styles, but these topics remain an active area of research for which evolving knowledge bases continue to emerge.

Gender

Gender also influences the manner in which families enact their roles, including the tasks of parenting and the ways in which communication takes place with helping professionals. In most cultures, the role of the mother is dominant in childrearing, especially in the early years (Rotundo, 1985). However, that dynamic is changing with the increase of women in the workforce and the rise in the number of stay-at-home dads who are assuming primary caretaking duties of children in the home (Palkovitz, 2002). In certain cultures, women may assume the primary responsibilities for childrearing, but fathers are the communicators with the world outside the family and may take the lead for facilitating services with educators. For example, in many Arab American households, fathers play a dominant role in decision making for the family, and offers of assistance to the family may need to begin with the father (Hildebrand et al., 2008). In other cultures, however, family leadership may emanate from the eldest female in the household. A newer dimension in our evolving understanding of parenting is the role of parents who are gay and lesbian and the effects of this shared role in same-gender relationships.

Religion

Religion as well as beliefs and customs are critical factors in families' views and perspectives, especially as they relate to their children with disabilities. For example, Zhang and Bennett (2001) suggest that perspectives on disability are uniquely intertwined with religious beliefs and that cultures vary in their interpretations of disability: from "special gifts" from God, leading to beliefs about protection and nurture, to punishments from God, leading to rejection and alienation.

Religious life plays a large role for many families regarding the rituals that they observe. For example, most religious groups perform rituals that demarcate the developmental milestones of children as they progress toward adulthood (e.g., bar or bat mitzvah, first communion, naming of the baby, and circumcision). Depending on the ritual, these milestones may be skewed or missed for children with special needs, which is something that families experience as a sense of loss.

The importance of religious and spiritual values may be most apparent in the manner that families use these referent points to explain a child's disability with terms such as *punishment*, *gifts*, or *learning opportunities for growth and meaning making*. It is important to keep in mind that, within most religions and belief systems, more than one explanation of disability exists. The understanding of beliefs and religious practices is used most often in the educational setting to comprehend more fully the context in which parents accommodate their child with special needs and incorporate this experience into their value systems.

Age

The age at which people start parenting children has a tremendous impact on their experience, abilities, and viewpoints. For teenage mothers, there is evidence that lack of experience, education, and skills and an incomplete role identity that is generally assumed following adolescence affects their capacities for parenting (Hurlbut & McDonald, 1997). Because of problems in families such as illness, death, incarceration, or unfit parenting, many grandparents find themselves assuming the role of parents for their grandchildren. This growing phenomenon is captured by

U.S. Census data (U.S. Census Bureau, 2000), which reflects a dramatic increase in grandparents serving as parents and the fact that, since 1993, the American Association for Retired Persons (AARP) has devoted considerable resources through its Grandparents Information Center to support older Americans who are raising children. Educators must not assume that parents of differing ages bring the same sets of skills, resources, or energies to the tasks of parenting. Generational differences can be noted in the roles that parents play in childrearing practices, as well as their capabilities for doing so.

Geography

Geography is an often overlooked but critical variable in understanding family perspectives. In the broadest sense, geography can be defined as native or non-native to the United States. On a regional scale, however, many differences exist within U.S. culture that are based on geography and affect service delivery for children with disabilities. First, despite the increasing homogenization of the United States, people from different parts of the country tend to display unique characteristics of their region, such as Southern hospitality or Midwest pragmatism. While there is a wide variation in the demonstration of these characteristics, they do affect the way relationships are approached and conducted. Second, a tremendous difference often exists between families living in rural versus urban settings. People living in urban settings likely have more access to resources and services for their children, regardless of disability. However, there are also stressors associated with what Turnbull et al. (2006, p. 19) describe as "complicated, energy draining urban environments." In addition, there is evidence that urban and rural parents approach parenting differently. For example, there might be an urban emphasis on social development (e.g., making new acquaintances) and a rural emphasis on homogenous grouping and more time spent with parents (Coleman, Ganong, Clark, & Madsen, 1989). Consequently, urban families tend to use friendship networks more often for the exchange of social support, including money, whereas this role tends to be performed by family members in rural areas (Hofferth & Iceland, 1998).

Income

Income and the disparity of resources are critical determinants of parents' choices in childrearing. The most recent census data reports that 39% of the nation's children live in low-income families, a disproportionate number of these children coming from African American, Latino, and Native American families (Douglas-Hall, Koball, & Chau, 2006). When families face economic hardships, they tend to be less effective at parenting because of a multitude of stressors related to poverty and psychological distress (Magnuson & Duncan, 2002; McLoyd, Jayaratne, Ceballo, & Borquez, 1994), including less warmth, harsher discipline, and less stimulating home environments (McLoyd, 1998; Duncan & Brooks-Gunn, 1997). Despite these findings, there is evidence that not all low-income families meet this profile (Turnbull et al., 2006) or that higher levels of income necessarily correlate to good parenting practices. However, the dynamic of income level and access to resources tends to be a key indicator regarding families' opportunities and success in parenting endeavors.

Language

Language tends to be an immediately noticeable characteristic of differences between cultures, especially when families do not speak English. The nonverbal components of communication, such as use of eye contact, gestures, posture, and facial expressions, may also be used differently

Age of parent.
Marital/relationship status.
Community acceptance/affiliation.
Access to health and mental health resources.
Employment status.
Socioeconomic status.
Adequate housing.
Access to adequate food and nutrition.
Strategies for coping.
Extended family or relationship networks.
Parenting and interaction styles.
History of life experience and events.

FIGURE 3.1   Examples of Variables That May Affect Parenting.

than the communication styles of the mainstream culture. This can pose a dilemma for families who enter the special education world, where jargon and acronyms are commonplace (e.g., the LRE [least restrictive environment], or the IEP [individualized education plan]) and the use of meetings are an understood phenomenon. Because language is the primary mode of communication between families and professionals, the inability to communicate effectively can seriously impair the establishment of effective working alliances and is defined as a major barrier to receiving special education services (Shaprio, Monzó, Rueda, Gomez, & Blancher, 2004; Turnbull et al., 2006). As language diversity increases in U.S. schools, educators will need to respond to this trend with strategies that address communication barriers that may inhibit trusting alliances between families and service personnel. (See Figure 3.1.)

Contextualizing Culture

In reviewing these elements of culture, it is critical to understand that many families from racial and ethnic minorities have often experienced discrimination and prejudices that affect their views of others, including helping professionals. For example, African American families have often been described as "dysfunctional and in disarray" (Massaquoi, 1993), with myths about the roles of mothers and fathers frequently perpetrated (Bennett, 1988). Latino families are often portrayed in the media as a dysfunctional underclass (Méndez-Méndez & Alverio, 2003), despite evidence that the "Three R's" of relationships, respect, and responsibility are at the core of their cultural identity (Hildebrand, Phenice, Gray, & Hines, 2008). However, the evidence shows that social class generally plays a much larger role in determining family functioning, suggesting, for example, that a comparison of African American, Latino, and European American families within the same social class will likely reveal very similar childrearing practices (Lareau, 2003).

Based on media representations (or misrepresentations), assumptions about race and ethnicity regarding family life, parenting styles, and educational goals for children are often misperceived, misunderstood, or misguided. As families seek to enter the educational system, especially during the assessment phases, they confront real, or perceived, barriers to their effective participation based on assumptions that may not accurately reflect who they are. The approach that racial and ethnic differences uniquely inform parenting and family is different from assuming that unique characteristics are necessarily a detriment to effective family functioning or incongruent with the goals of the U.S. educational system.

BREAKPOINT PRACTICE

1. From what you know about the Sarah's family, what microcultural values would you identify as being relevant to understanding her family's situation?
2. Using the characteristics of cultural diversity (e.g., income, age, geography, etc.), what specific information might you want to gain to better assess the family's current level of need as it applies to your intervention?
3. How do you think Sarah's parents would describe their concerns, priorities, and resources for their child and family life?

FAMILY-CENTERED SERVICE DELIVERY

Dunst (2002) suggests that **family-centered** approaches are characterized by beliefs and practices that treat families with dignity and respect; are individualized, flexible, and responsive; and allow parents to make informed decisions about childrearing that are optimal for child, parent, and family outcomes. Dunst and Trivette (1996) state that family-centered practices are comprised of both **relational practices** (e.g., active listening, empathy, nonjudgmental stance, professional beliefs about families) and **participatory practices** (e.g., providing flexible, individualized services in a responsive fashion and actively involving families in decision making) that undergird effective approaches to fully including the family. Realizing effective outcomes depends on an accurate assessment of family needs and appropriate intervention, especially as they relate to issues about diverse cultural reference points regarding parenting and childhood development.

Family-centered services are based on **ecological principles** that consider the contexts and transactions between children and their environments and their impacts on development. Based on an ecological perspective (Bronfenbrenner, 1979), family-centered services do not assess and intervene on behalf of a child as a singular unit of focus, but rather as a member of a complex system of transactions among a variety of contexts, primarily the family. Bronfenbrenner defined four layers of context that encase the child: **microsystems** and **mesosystems** (e.g., immediate relationships and environments in which children frequently participate, such as the school or playground, and parents and consistent caregivers), **exosystems** (e.g., extended relationships with other family members, neighbors, religious groups, or places of employment), and **macrosystems** (e.g., broader cultural ideas, values, policies, and customs that inform societal mores and practices). To be succinct, and for purposes of the early educational setting, these systems could be viewed as family, community, and society (see Figure 3.2).

A primary benefit of Bronfenbrenner's theory was the inclusion of early childhood services designed to both assess and intervene on behalf of the child with recognition of the environments in which she or he grows and develops. Simply stated, to understand the child is to know the family. This basic assumption supposes the critical role of the family and the educator's need for understanding children and families as defined by the layers of their participation in society, based on family systems theory and cultural variations that inform and affect families' experiences and opportunities based on these definitions.

A primary purpose of effective assessment is the support of the family in promoting children's developmental outcomes. Establishing relationships that encompass empathy, reciprocity, and support increases the likelihood that families will share their histories, their feelings, and

FIGURE 3.2 Family Systems Model.

their strengths (Seligman & Darling, 1989). When families feel safe and accepted, they are more likely to engage with early childhood professionals in a manner that builds trust and mutually defined agendas for ongoing intervention and assessment.

Brinker (1992) suggests that educators often assume that family-centered intervention is based on a "dominant prototype of families as autonomous, self enhancing centers of decision making" (p. 313). However, in a complex, multicultural society, this prototype may conflict with the cultural practices and desires of some families (Gilkerson & Stott, 1997). Therefore, it is necessary for educators to evaluate their own assumptions about cultural referents and their approaches for effectively aligning with families.

As you can see, there are many dimensions and dynamics that punctuate family life. The complexity of understanding families makes effective assessment difficult, at best. However, early childhood providers are best suited to provide effective services to families when they are culturally competent in their approaches and when their approaches involve increasing awareness of various cultural variables relevant to family support and asking the right questions about clinical practices. With the vast diversity of cultures represented in many of today's schools, however, one could not possibly be an expert on all cultures, which means that professionals should be involved in an ongoing learning process of these fluid and changing dynamics.

BREAKPOINT PRACTICE

1. In assessing Sarah's family, what would you want to know about the family members' contexts (micro-, exo-, and macrosystems)? Why would this information be relevant to your assessment of their needs and to those of Sarah?
2. Do you view Sarah's family as an autonomous, self-enhancing family unit, or do you view them as in need of greater support and guidance?
3. Given your knowledge of Sarah's family, what specific relational and participatory strategies do you think would be necessary to engage and support them effectively?

KNOWLEDGE FOR DEVELOPING CULTURAL COMPETENCIES

Kalyanpur and Harry (1999) suggest that assuming a "posture of cultural reciprocity" can help you develop a habit of **reflective practices**, or systematic approaches to self-evaluation of clinical and professional practices, that will lead to effective parent–professional collaboration without requiring a great deal of culturally specific information. Lynch and Hanson (1996) suggest three essential components of **cross-cultural competence** leading to this outcome: (a) self-examination and values clarification, (b) culture-specific knowledge, and (c) the ability to apply this knowledge at both interpersonal and systems levels. Storti (1999) defines the following building blocks upon which cultures uniquely engage:

- Concept of self
- Personal versus societal responsibility
- Concept of time
- Locus of control
- Styles of communication

Explanations of particular behaviors may be based on these building blocks and can guide our examination and understanding of cultural competencies.

One's cultural reference dictates his or her perspective regarding the building blocks identified by Storti. For example, in some cultures the **concept of self** is defined by individualism or an emphasis on self-reliance, while in others, collectivism or an emphasis on one's belonging to a group predominates. Similarly, one's view of personal versus social responsibility runs along a continuum of universalist cultures, which tend to rely on rules rather than relationships in decision making, to particularistic cultures, which tend to rely on "thinking from the heart" and friendship arrangements in decision making.

The U.S. culture is typically defined by an individualistic rather than a collectivist approach. This macrocultural dimension informs many areas of our lives. The old adage of "pulling one's self up by the bootstraps" typifies this perspective. When groups are more collectivist in their thinking, they are prone to associate and make decisions with a greater awareness of how their actions work for both themselves *and* their group. This dynamic could be briefly described as individualistic (solving) to considering what is good for everyone (collectivist). See Figure 3.3.

The **concept of time** is another way that cultures define themselves. Certain cultures treat time as a premium and encourage its efficient use (monochronic). This is typical of the U.S. culture.

Individualistic	Collectivist
Direct conversational styles (low context).	Indirect conversation styles (high context).
Less use of nonverbal communication.	More use of nonverbal communication.
Decision making based on facts and evidence.	Decision making based on intuition and experience.
Tendency toward persuasion to find solutions.	Tendency toward harmony to find solutions.
Short-term relationships of a strategic nature.	Long-term relationships that are enduring.
Higher reliance on written communication.	Lower reliance on written communication.
Flexible and open in utilizing relationships.	Greater distinction between in-group and out-group.
Schedules are more important than relationships.	Relationships are more important than schedules.

FIGURE 3.3   Examples of Individualistic versus Collectivist Approaches.

Phrases such as "procrastination is the thief of time" or "time is money" capture this U.S. trait. Other cultures quantify time in the moment (polychronic); members of these cultures care less about schedules and deadlines and more about the quality of the task or interaction at hand.

The orientation to time is also relevant to the broader goals of child development, such as the age range defining infancy or the expected ages for independence and autonomy from the parent. For example, some parents push for early independence in the early childhood years, which demonstrates the child's competencies to the parents; other parents view the same period as a time for protection and nurture, with less emphasis given to childhood autonomy (Owens, 2008). Understanding the time orientation of families is critical to working collaboratively with them so that goal setting is measured by standards that are relevant to the family and incorporates their unique perspectives.

Families are also defined by their beliefs about **locus of control**, or whether outcomes of their actions are contingent on what they do (internal control) or on events outside their personal control (external control) (Zimbardo, 1985). See Figure 3.4. A family's beliefs about its locus of control are a significant factor in the family members' confidence and capacities for responding to environments external to the family, such as educational settings. When parents feel they have the capacities to meet the needs of their children, they are more effective in their parenting, and outcomes are apparent in their children's course of development (Silsby, 2003). Parents tend to disavow their capacities if they believe a lack of education, language, social, or adequate parenting abilities will hinder their ability to join with professionals in solving problems and designing strategies. This may explain, in part, those families who appear passive, or resigned to their fate, and those who are active and eagerly take charge. Too often, these parents might be described, respectively, as lazy or pushy. More likely, the difference lies in a family's perception of control.

Styles of communication used by families are likely the most noticeable difference associated with interactions between people of different cultures. Broadly speaking, the differences

External Locus of Control	Internal Locus of Control
The belief that behavior and outcomes are guided by fate, luck, or other external circumstances.	The belief that personal efforts and specific steps in decision making guide behavior and outcomes.

FIGURE 3.4   External versus Internal Locus of Control.

can be summarized by styles that are low context (direct) or high context (indirect) (Owens, 2008). For example, groups in high-context cultures more often rely on less verbally explicit communication; less formal, written communication; internalization rather than communication of their understandings verbally; stronger boundaries about insiders and outsiders; and personal, face-to-face encounters. Conversely, groups from low-context cultures generally rely on rules and codified norms for bounding relationships, make more interpersonal connections that are of shorter duration, are more task-focused and use a division of responsibilities for goal completion, and depend on schedules and deadlines. U.S. society is typically defined as a low-context culture, although each of us partakes in settings that are both high- (e.g., our families) and low-context (e.g., formal meetings) throughout our day.

Clearly, family behaviors are not as dichotomous as presented in the previous examples. Rather, culturally defined behaviors tend to fall on a continuum between the polarities presented. Imagine how you might feel, however, if you were task-oriented and desirous of getting to work on behalf of your child, only to be met with the parameters of a high-context culture? Or imagine the frustration of families who want to take time to build a relationship with professionals, only to be met with strict timeframes and professional boundaries associated with a low-context culture? The extent to which we feel comfortable in our way of being is often defined by our comfort with the context in which we are interacting.

To assess family participation effectively requires an understanding of parental goals and behaviors and parents' underlying meanings in order to align clinical practices with family strengths and thus meet their needs. It also requires self-awareness about our own worldviews and how these may affect our relationships with the families we serve. The manner in which we communicate, or the ways we approach others and our expectations of that interaction, are highly personal. Adapting interaction styles to increase comfort and understanding of families can be used more effectively when knowledge of cultural differences and personal reflection are inherent in approaching work with families (Lynch & Hanson, 1996). Although cultural clashes between service providers and families are bound to occur because of differences in beliefs, values, behaviors, and language, knowing our own worldviews is an essential first step in moving toward culturally responsive service delivery (Lynch & Hanson, 2004). While it is impossible to know and fully understand the complex dynamics of all cultures, recognizing our own perspectives, biases, and values allows us to pinpoint differences more quickly and with less discomfort; it also allows us to move more judiciously in responding appropriately to families from a collaborative framework that respects the family and moves intervention initiatives forward.

BREAKPOINT PRACTICE

1. Using Storti's model, consider your own referent points in these domains and consider how these referent points might potentially conflict with those of Sarah's family.
2. Would you describe yourself as individualistic or collectivist? High or low context? Do you have an internal or an external locus of control? What might you need to address in your own style or preferences to be able to engage and assess families effectively?
3. What might Tariq's style of communication in the initial meeting suggest about him and your approach to ensuring a more comfortable alliance with him?

SKILLS FOR DEVELOPING CULTURAL COMPETENCY

Kalyanpur and Harry (1999) posit a posture of cultural reciprocity, or steps for engaging explicitly with families to bring "an openness of mind, the ability to be reflective in practice, and the ability to listen to the other perspective" (p. 118):

Step 1: Identify the cultural values that are embedded in the professional interpretation of a student's (family's) difficulties or in the recommendation of service.

Step 2: Find out whether the family being served recognizes and values these assumptions and, if not, how their views differ from that of the professional.

Step 3: Acknowledge and give explicit respect to any cultural differences identified, and fully explain the cultural basis of the professional assumptions.

Step 4: Through discussion and collaboration, determine the most effective way of adapting professional interpretations or recommendations to the value system of this family.

See Figure 3.5 for some sample questions to consider when working with culturally diverse families.

Taylor and Whittaker (2009) offer a "case decision-making scaffold" that operationalizes a process for effective case analysis. This model allows for both the identification of problems and the promotion of family strengths as remedies that are mutually beneficial to families and professionals.

- Recognize the problem
  - Are there trigger events that cause you to recognize the problem?
  - What facts do we know about the family's context (e.g., micro-, meso-, exo-, and macrosystems)?
- Reframe the problem
  - What underlying assumptions, values, or beliefs do we hold about each of the problems?
  - What values or beliefs regarding the problems do we hold in common with the family?
- Search for alternatives
  - What can we learn about the problem from others with greater experience and expertise?
  - What alternatives might address the problem?

Who are the key members of this family system?

Who speaks (makes decisions) for this family?

Is this family group-oriented (collectivist) or individual-focused (individualistic)?

Is this family system open or closed to outsiders (boundaries)?

What is this family's view or perspectives about disability?

How is this family situated in its community?

What are the family's apparent rhythms, routines, and rituals?

What are the family's parameters and expectations regarding discipline?

How does this family use helping relationships?

What values and beliefs guide the family's expectations and decision making?

FIGURE 3.5 Sample Questions to Consider When Working with Culturally Diverse Families.

- Develop and implement a plan of action
  - How do we prioritize the goals?
  - What resources and supports are necessary to support the family?
- Evaluate progress
  - What is the satisfaction of both families and professionals?
  - What new problems have developed?
  - What revisions to the plan need to be made?

One would be justified in asking how educators can acquire all of the proficiencies necessary to meet the needs of culturally diverse families. Simply put, there are no short-cuts. In fact, Christian (2006) suggests that the way we usually find out about unspoken family rules of behavior is by first breaking the rule and then experiencing the consequences. In other words, we often learn from our mistakes. However, deliberate steps can be taken toward gaining greater cultural competency. Increasing knowledge and awareness is a first step.

While formal measures, which are discussed later in this text, may be used to assess families, frameworks and approaches for observing and understanding families can offer insight into the workings of the family that may not be captured through formal means. This information about the family is most beneficial in both child and family assessment.

Evidence suggests that family-centered practices that facilitate parental involvement leads to enhanced developmental outcomes for children (Dunst, 2002). However, there is also evidence to suggest that services offered to families often do not match their perceptions of need (Wade, Mildon, & Matthews, 2006). As Wade, Mildon, and Matthews suggest, families' and educators' needs and goals should be similar. When families enter the assessment phase for their children, they are facing their own assessment, too. As early childhood services are predicated on ecological and systems theory approaches, the context of the child's development, the family, becomes a highly relevant focus of attention.

Families need support not only in the interpretation and application of assessment measures for their children; they also need overt recognition of their referents for family life and the ways in which services can be provided to complement their approaches. To use the family as an optimal context for development, practitioners must be aware of the unique ways in which their clients "express family" and use this expression in support of parenting.

See Figure 3.6 for a list of practices for working with culturally diverse families.

Use approaches that honor and respect family and cultural diversity in all interactions.

Seek to find family assets and strengths for collaboration toward mutual goal setting.

Facilitate assessment using the family's interests, ideas, and frames of reference.

Employ individualized and flexible approaches consistent with the family's identity.

Suspend judgment when approaching issues for which you are unfamiliar or uncomfortable.

Communicate clearly how the family can be involved in intervention services.

Use family-friendly language to describe and engage families in assessment practices.

FIGURE 3.6 Practices for Working with Culturally Diverse Families.

BREAKPOINT PRACTICE

1. What specific strategies can you undertake to achieve the goals set forth by Kalyanpur and Hanson?
2. How would you describe your own boundaries in terms of working with families? How does this help or hinder you?
3. Using the case decision-making scaffold as defined by Taylor and Whittaker, define one issue for each of the following questions that you may begin to assess about the needs of Sarah's family:
   a. What is your recognition the problem?
   b. How might your reframe the problem?
   c. What are possible alternatives for action?
   d. What might be your action plan?
   e. How would you evaluate your plan?

STEPS FOR SELF-REFLECTION

Culture is a part of all of us. We express it in our daily interactions through our values, perspectives, and decisions. To separate from our cultural views is a demanding task that requires the consistent use of reflective practices that challenge our worldviews and open our minds to new alternatives.

Ecological and systems perspectives hold that families are adaptable and self-correcting units that, with appropriate supports, can thrive despite the stressors they endure. As Salvadore Minuchin states: "When families come to me for help, I assume they have problems not because there is something inherently wrong with them, but because they've gotten stuck—stuck with a structure whose time has passed, and stuck with a story that doesn't work" (Minuchin & Nichols, 1993, p. 43).

Educators can gain the necessary knowledge, attitudes, and skills to engage families from diverse cultures in meaningful, productive, and more effective working alliances. To do so, service providers must recognize their own lack of acceptance of unfamiliar customs and work toward strategies that promote comfortable alliances with families. Here are some suggestions:

- Gain firsthand knowledge from members of other cultural communities about their experiences.
- Recognize stereotypical reactions that are more aligned with perceptions about a "group" rather than the family sitting in front of you.
- Encourage open, reflective environments in which practitioners are comfortable in addressing one another's lack of acceptance or misperceptions about families.
- Realize the strengths of diversity and use those strengths to build strategies that are tailored to the family's concerns and priorities.

The failure to accept and use the family's diversity can result in detrimental outcomes for both families and educators because of incongruence in perceptions and understandings around goal setting and attainment within the context of the family. It is clear that educators must take deliberate steps for developing the knowledge, attitudes, and skills required to support all families, regardless of their cultural affiliation.

BREAKPOINT PRACTICE

1. After reading this chapter, what stereotypes of your own may hinder your work with families? How might these stereotypes affect your assessment of a child or family?
2. List the ways that you can gain more firsthand experience with people of different cultures in order to enhance your skills and competencies for working with families from diverse backgrounds.
3. What steps can you take to promote open, reflective environments in which families can participate?
4. What strengths of diversity do you think Sarah's family might bring that can be used for meeting their concerns, priorities, and resources?

Revisiting Sarah

Sarah's family members are unique; like many of the families who come to us for services, however, they are similar because they are new to parenting and the challenges of a child with special needs, are in need of additional resources, and have distinct characteristics in which they express their ideas of family. As you are now probably aware from reading this chapter, a few points are worth noting:

- The age of the parents
- The strained relationship with their extended family
- Potential value conflicts between cultural views of parenting
- Economic struggles
- Geography
- Ambivalence about receiving help

In combination, these factors should suggest avenues for thinking, planning, and intervention that the practitioner may use to support Sarah's family. Based on the content of this chapter, you should be able to contextualize these issues within frameworks, strategies, and general ways of thinking that more accurately inform your positive perceptions of the family and lead you to strategies that

are commensurate with their perceived needs. Among these strategies are the following:

- Accurately assessing and understanding the context of the family
- Selecting and using relational and participatory strategies to meet their needs
- Recognizing the complexity of their situation and the holistic approach that may be needed to support them and Sarah's developmental outcomes
- Understanding the family's actions based on their locus of control
- Reframing your perception of the problem to accommodate the worldview of Sarah's parents
- Increasing your awareness of family boundaries, values, and beliefs and how these may be affected by both culture and life experience

The goal of assessing any family, including Sarah's, is to discover their strengths; find pathways for smooth, comfortable working alliances; and optimize the family's functioning in support of the child, in this case, Sarah. The story of the Sarah's family is imbued with many aspects of diversity that may have triggered your thinking and making assumptions of your own. For example, what are the value differences between the families, and why? Why are the extended family members so "pushy"? Does the name Tariq suggest something about the father's origins, religion, or values? How about the names Emily and Sarah? Did any of these questions come to mind for you? It is likely that these or similar questions arose. That is the point. When we meet families, we tend to begin a journey of observation and assessment that begins with questions that help us fill in the blanks regarding family members and their roles and values. When we begin this journey from the assumption of family competence, we are more likely to join with families in a way that promotes awareness of their own abilities while increasing our self-awareness. When we are able to avoid stereotypes and join with families as they are, we are more likely to adopt stances and strategies that are more universal in their application while empowering families and ourselves in the assessment process (Kalyanpur & Hanson, 1999).

Activities

1. List the resources in your area that may be of help to Sarah's family.
2. Devise inservice training that could help your agency engage in thinking about cultural diversity and means for bettering alliances with all families.
3. Identify your reflective practices, and those of your agency, with an emphasis on promoting more opportunities for this to occur.
4. Start brown bag lunch meetings with a small group of concerned professionals in which the issues in the previous questions may be addressed.
5. Find opportunities in your community to participate in culturally diverse activities and thus increase your comfort and awareness of others' rhythms, routines, and rituals for family life.

Websites

Diversity Council
http://www.diversitycouncil.org

Estefania's Website
*http://ows.edb.utexas.edu/site/estefanias-website/
linguistic-and-cultural-diversity*

Family Village
http://www.familyvillage.wisc.edu/

Institute for Cultural Partnerships
http://www.culturalpartnerships.org/

National Dissemination Center for Children with Disabilities
http://www.nichcy.org/Pages/Home.aspx

National Early Childhood Technical Assistance Center
http://www.nectac.org/default.asp

World Institute on Disability
http://www.wid.org/

References

Bailey, D. B., McWilliam, R. A., Darkes, L. A., Hebbler, K., Simeonsson, R., Spiker, D., & Wagner, M. (1998). Family outcomes in early intervention: A framework for program evaluation and efficacy research. *Exceptional Children, 64*, 313–327.

Banks, J. A. (2001). Multicultural education: Characteristics and goals. In J. A. Banks & C. A. McGee-Banks (Eds.), *Multicultural education: Issues and perspectives* (4th ed., pp. 3–30). New York: John Wiley & Sons.

Barker, P. (1992). *Basic family therapy* (3rd ed.). London: Blackwell.

Baumrind, D. (1966). Effects of authoritative parental control on child behavior. *Child Development, 37*(4), 887–907.

Baumrind, D. (1967). Child care practices anteceding three patterns of preschool behavior. *Genetic Psychology Monographs, 74*(1), 43–88.

Bennett, A. T. (1988). Gateways to powerlessness: Incorporating Hispanic deaf children and families into formal schooling. *Disability, Handicap & Society, 3*, 119–151.

Bowen, M. (1978). Family therapy is clinical practice. New York: Jason Aronson.

Brinker, R. (1992). Family involvement in early intervention: Accepting the unchangeable, changing the changeable, and knowing the difference. *Topics in Early Childhood Special Education, 12*, 307–332.

Bronfenbrenner, U. (1979). *The ecology of human development*. Cambridge, MA: Harvard University Press.

Bruder, M. B. (2000). Family centered early intervention: Clarifying our values for the new millennium. *Topics in Early Childhood Special Education, 20*(2), 105–115.

Christian, L. G. (2006). Understanding families: Applying family systems theory to early childhood practice. *Young Children, 61*(1), 12–20.

Coleman, M., Ganong, L. H., Clark, J. M., & Madsen, R. (1989). Parenting perceptions in rural and urban families: Is there a difference? *Journal of Marriage and Family, 51*, 329–335.

Douglas-Hall, A., Koball, H., & Chau, M. (2006). *Basic facts about low-income children, birth to age 18*. New York: National Center for Children in Poverty, Columbia University Mailman School of Public Health.

Duncan, G. J., & Brooks-Gunn, J. (Eds.). (1997). *Consequences of growing up poor*. New York: Russell Sage Foundation.

Dunst, C. J. (2002). Family-centered practices: Birth through high school. *Journal of Special Education, 36*(3), 139–147.

Dunst, C. J., & Trivette, C. M. (1996). Empowerment, effective help-giving practices and family-centered care. *Pediatric Nursing, 22*, 334–337, 343.

Gilkerson, L., & Scott, F. (1997). Listening to the voice of families: Learning through caregiving consensus groups. *Zero to Three, 18*, 9–16.

Goodenough, W. (1987). *Multicultural education in a pluralistic society*. Columbus, OH: MacMillan.

Hecker, L. L., Mims, G. A., & Boughner, S. R. (2003). General systems theory, cybernetics and family therapy. In L. L. Hecker & J. L. Wetchler (Eds.), *An introduction to marriage and family therapy* (pp. 39–61). New York: Haworth Clinical Practice Press.

Hildebrand, V., Phenice, L. A., Gray, M. M., & Hines, R. P. (2008). Knowing and serving diverse families (3rd ed.). Upper Saddle River, NJ: Merrill/Pearson Education.

Hofferth, S. L., & Iceland, J. (1998). Social capital in rural and urban communities. *Rural Sociology, 63*, 574–598.

Hurlbut, N., & McDonald, A. (1997) Adolescent mothers' self-esteem and role identity and their relationship to parenting skills knowledge. *Adolescence, 32*, 639–655.

Kalyanpur, M., & Harry, B. (1999). *Culture in special education: Building reciprocal family–professional relationships*. Baltimore: Brookes.

Lareau, A. (2003). *Unequal childhoods: Race, class, and family life*. Berkeley: University of California Press.

Lord-Nelson, L. G. L., Summers, J. A., & Turnbull, A. P. (2004). Boundaries in family–professional relationships: Implications for special education. *Remedial and Special Education, 25*, 153–165.

Lynch, E. W., & Hanson, M. J. (2004). *Developing cross-cultural competence: A guide for working with young children and their families*. Baltimore: Brookes.

Lynch, R. W., & Hanson, M. J. (1996). Ensuring cultural competence in assessment. In M. McLean, D. B. Bailey, & M. Wolery (Eds.), *Assessing infants and preschoolers with special needs* (2nd ed., pp. 69–94). Upper Saddle River, NJ: Merrill/Pearson Education.

Magnuson, K. A., & Duncan, G. J. (2002). Parents in poverty. In M. Bornstein (Ed.), *Handbook of parenting. Vol. 4, Social conditions and applied parenting* (2nd ed., pp. 95–121). Mahwah, NJ: Lawrence Erlbaum.

Massaquoi, J. (1993, August). The Black family nobody knows. *Ebony*, pp. 28–31.

McBride, S., & Brotherson, M. J. (1997). Guiding practitioners toward valuing and implementing family-centered practices. In P. J. Winton, J. A. McCollum, & C. Cattlett (Eds.), *Reforming personnel preparation in early intervention* (pp. 253–276). Baltimore: Brookes.

McLoyd, V. C. (1998). Socioeconomic disadvantage and child development. *American Psychologist, 53*, 185–204.

McLoyd, V. C., Jayaratne, T. E., Ceballo, R., & Borquez, J. (1994). Unemployment and work interruption among African American single mothers: Effects on parenting and adolescent socioemotional functioning. *Child Development, 65*, 562–589.

Minuchin, S. (1974). *Families & family therapy*. Cambridge, MA: Harvard University Press.

Minuchin, S., & Nichols, M. P. (1993). *Family healing*. New York: Free Press.

National Comprehensive Center for Teacher Quality. (2008). Lessons learned: New teachers talk about their jobs, challenges, and long-range plans. *Teaching in Changing Times, 3*. Retrieved on June 20, 2008, from http://www.tqsource.org/publications/LessonsLearned3.pdf

Owens, R. E. (2008). *Language development: An introduction* (7th ed.). Upper Saddle River, NJ: Pearson Education.

Palkovitz, R. (2002). *Involved fathering and men's adult development: Provisional balances.* Mahwah, NJ: Erlbaum.

Park, H., & Bauer, S. (2002). Parenting practices, ethnicity, socioeconomic status and academic achievement in adolescents. *School Psychology International, 23,* 386–397.

Rodriguez, M. M., Donovick, M. R., &. Crowley, S. (2009). Parenting styles in a cultural context: Observations of "protective parenting" in first-generation Latinos. *Family Process, 48*(2), 195–210.

Rotundo, E. A. (1985). American fatherhood: A historical perspective. *American Behavioral Scientist, 29*(1), 7–25.

Satir, V. (1996). The rules you live by. In K. Galvin & P. Cooper (Eds.), *Making connections: Readings in relational communication,* Los Angeles: Roxbury Publishing.

Seligman, M., & Darling, R. B. (1989). *Ordinary families, special children: A systems approach to childhood disability.* New York: Guilford.

Shaprio, J., Monzó, L. D., Rueda, R., Gomez, J. A., Blancher, J. (2004). Alienated advocacy: Perspectives of Latina mothers of young adults with developmental disabilities on service systems. *Mental Retardation, 42*(1), 37–54.

Silsby, C. (2003). Parental predictors of behavioral outcomes for children with developmental disabilities. Doctoral dissertation, Boston College, Chestnut Hill, MA. *Dissertation Abstracts International, DAI-A 57/08,* 3385.

Simon, G. M. (1995). A revisionist rendering of structural family therapy. *Journal of Marital and Family Therapy, 21*(1), 17–26.

Steinhauer, P. D., Santa-Barbara, J., & Skinner, H. (1984). The process model of family functioning. *Canadian Journal of Psychiatry, 29,* 77–88.

Storti, C. (1999). *Figuring foreigners out: A practical guide.* Yarmouth, ME: Intercultural Press.

Taylor, L., & Whittaker, C. (2009). *Bridging multiple worlds: Case studies of diverse educational communities* (2nd ed.). Boston: Allyn & Bacon.

Turnbull, A. P., Turnbull, H. R., Erwin, E., & Soodak, L. (2006). *Families, professionals, and exceptionality: Positive outcomes through partnership and trust* (5th ed.). Upper Saddle River, NJ: Merrill/Pearson Education.

U.S. Census Bureau. (2000). Grandparents living with grandchildren: 2000. Census brief. Retrieved June 25, 2008, from http://www.census.gov/prod/2003pubs/c2kbr-31.pdf

U.S. Census Bureau. (2008, August 14). An older and more diverse nation by midcentury. Press release. Suitland, MD.

Wade, C. M., Mildon, R. L., & Matthews, J. M. (2006). Service delivery to parents with an intellectual disability: Family-centred or professionally centred? *Journal of Applied Research in Intellectual Disabilities, 20*(2), 87–98.

Zhang, C., & Bennett, T. (2001). Multicultural views of disability: Implications for early intervention professionals. *Transdisciplinary Journal, 11*(2), 143–154.

Zimbardo, P. G. (1985). *Psychology and life.* Glenview, IL: Scott Forsman.

Collaboration

CHAPTER OBJECTIVES

After reading this chapter, you will be able to define *collaboration* and identify the three main collaboration models used for assessment in early childhood special education. You will be able to give examples of each team approach, and discuss the strengths and weaknesses of each with regard to the assessment process and the assessment summary meeting, including best practices for

collaborative assessment in early childhood special education.

This chapter addresses Council for Exceptional Children/Division for Early Childhood (CEC-DEC) Standard 10 (collaboration) and National Association for the Education of Young Children (NAEYC) Standard 3 (Observing, Documenting, and Assessing to Support Young Children and Families).

Assessing Michelle

Janet, the early childhood interventionist, was deep in thought after her final assessment of 5-year-old Michelle. Michelle, a petite child with dark eyes and long curly brown hair, was referred for assessment just before midyear break because of academic concerns and observations of atypical social behaviors. Her teacher voiced concerns about Michelle's communication skills, especially when it came to understanding directions or answering questions appropriately. She also had difficulty carrying on a conversation with an adult or with her peers, and usually preferred to play alone in the block area.

As Janet walked to the door, she heard someone call her name. It was the speech pathologist who had completed her assessment of Michelle

earlier that week and she wanted to discuss her thoughts with Janet.

The speech pathologist reported that Michelle's skills are mostly within age range but she has difficulty with pragmatic skills, especially when playing with the other children.

Janet had also talked with the occupational therapist, who had completed his assessment, and she shared the information that he had provided about Michelle's eye-hand coordination with the speech pathologist. Janet and the occupational therapist had both agreed that they had also observed Michelle's difficulty with eye-hand coordination tasks and wondered if the vision consultant had completed her evaluation.

"E-mail me," stated Janet. "That is the best way to contact me. I haven't talked with the school psychologist yet. However, I am having coffee with Michelle's mother tomorrow to get her input before the meeting. I have to run because I have another assessment in 20 minutes. I will see you at the meeting!"

At the assessment meeting, Janet welcomed Michelle's parents and offered them a cup of coffee. They appeared to be nervous, and Janet, aware of this, engaged in casual conversation with them. As they waited for the meeting to begin, some team members carried on private conversation regarding another student's assessment results, and the principal was on her cell phone planning another meeting. The classroom teacher rushed in and announced her apologies for being late due to an unplanned conference with a parent.

"Okay, everyone, let's get started," announced the principal. "I want to thank Mr. and Mrs. Lassey for attending this meeting today to hear the test results. I am not sure if we have time to cover everything in an hour, but we should be able to talk about LRE." The principal then organized the meeting by assigning tasks such as taking notes and monitoring the time.

What collaboration approach is evident in this scenario? How comfortable are the parents in this team meeting? What best practices are evident? What are the strengths and weaknesses of the collaborative setting?

COLLABORATION

For several years, special education has considered collaborative teaming as best practice in early childhood special education (Reed-Victor, 2004); leaders in the field have recognized the need to address the young child as a whole, with development in each domain being interdependent (Golin & Ducanis, 1981). The overlapping complexity of developmental issues with young children required professionals to work as a unit instead of independently (Fewell, 1983). Therefore, the effective **team** approach developed in response to the need to organize and generate educational outcomes based on multidimensional assessment process, which included numerous professionals and family members. Dettmer, Thurston, and Knackendoffel (2008) define **collaboration** as an interactive process used in most general and special education settings. It includes support and related services personnel, the child's family, and sometimes the child or student, all working together and sharing the knowledge and expertise needed to devise the optimal education program for the child.

By using the collaborative model during assessment planning, the assessment process, and reporting of assessment results, the team is forced to look at children all-inclusively, which results in optimal educational planning for children whose needs are not met adequately when professionals act alone (Dettmer, Thurston, & Knackendoffel, 2008). In a quality collaborative environment, team members realize their skill limitations and learn and expand their own perspectives and knowledge by accepting and responding to the unique expertise that each member brings to the collaboration (Beckman & Bristol, 1991). If this construct holds precedence in team process, the ideal outcome will be a rich connection between assessments and interventions, resulting in "goodness of fit" (Reed-Victor, 2004, p. 77) for our young children with exceptional learning needs.

In Michelle's case, cognitive, social/emotional, and language development were enmeshed in her play skills. Her disinterest in play with children and materials in her world created a barrier to learning through avenues that were most natural for children. This situation was further complicated by her lack of interest in exploring and playing with materials that enhanced fine motor growth. It is evident how intertwined her overall fine motor skill development is with her skills in other developmental domains and how crucial the cadre of expertise would be in carrying out valid assessment of her strengths and needs.

BREAKPOINT PRACTICE

1. Discuss the value of collaboration in early childhood special education and how it affects the assessment process.
2. How would you describe the quality of collaboration among the members of Michelle's team?
3. Discuss wherein the early childhood assessment process you see collaboration as most valuable. Where would it be least valuable?

Team Process

The concept of working together as a team is an idealistic vision because collaboration is not a process that happens naturally. We bring a gamut of professional and personal baggage to the collaborative process, including personal and professional **paradigms**, conflicts and stressors, a variety of personalities and working styles, personality conflicts, unique communication styles, and areas of interest and expertise. The erroneous belief is that, during the assessment process and the assessment summary meeting, everyone will get along, like each other, and agree on all issues. The actuality is that "[c]ollaborators do not compromise and cooperate so much as they confer and contribute" (Dettmer, Thurston, & Dyck, 2005, p. 7). Not everyone may agree, but everyone agrees to work together.

> The occupational therapist (OT) and physical therapist (PT) arrived at Mari's home with the intention of updating her developmental profiles and assessments, which were needed for the upcoming review. Mari's mom had just finished reading about collaboration and smiled as she reported this to the therapists. "Here we are . . . collaborating!" smiled the OT. As the visit progressed, the OT reminded Mari's mother that, as early interventionists, the OT and the PT prefer that she interact with Mari, and they will instruct and guide, but the outcomes will most authentic when Mari is interacting with someone with whom she has developed a bond, especially her parent. Although it was quite evident that the two professionals worked well together, the OT was a little hesitant regarding the PT's directives and stated, "If you don't mind, I really like to try and facilitate a skill first and then observe the same activity with someone who is familiar." They agreed to disagree and it worked.

In Michelle's case, the team members completed their individual assessments. During this process, it wasn't necessary for them to compromise or cooperate with each other unless they were administering assessments simultaneously. We aren't given an accurate glimpse of the working relationships fostered in this team effort. We do know, however, that they shared information regarding their individual assessment results in anticipation of constructing an accurate and complete picture of Mari's strengths and needs.

The Individuals with Disabilities Education Improvement Act (IDEIA) (2004) has specifically included language that mandates parental involvement in the assessment process, including educational outcomes resulting from assessment findings. Legislation also requires program members to work collaboratively with parents and families as they move through the assessment process. An optimal collaborative environment fosters active involvement from parents. Therefore, team members should strive to make this a safe community for all group members, especially the parents. Collaboration with the family during the assessment process increases the likelihood that the assessment results and program plan will be accepted and carried out by families in home environments (Hooper & Umansky, 2009).

The members of Michelle's assessment summary team may be aware of the role her parents play as crucial and equal team members. However, many team members did not convey this message to her parents. The cliché "Actions speak louder than words" was evident in Michelle's situation, except for Janet, the early interventionist, who welcomed the parents as part of the group. Whether this was an intentional effort on her part is unknown. She had already attempted to establish a rapport with Michelle's mother based on the contacts she previously had with her. Also, she may have the personality and social etiquette skills that invite people into the setting and create an immediate comfort level. She may not be aware of how this can be part of a deliberate strategy that sets the tone for a productive collaborative setting.

Some parents may have specific reasons for wanting a team approach used during the assessment process and assessment summative meeting. These families may not be able to afford services from any other sources and, as a result, this becomes a high-stakes procedure (Brink, 2002; Meisels, 1989). It is crucial that an accurate picture of the child be obtained through the assessment and at the summary meeting (Brink, 2002) because this may be the only opportunity to secure the services and program that is most appropriate for the child.

Michelle's assessment meeting was an example of one possible scenario of what can transpire when administration and other professionals attempt to create a high-quality, productive collaborative milieu. However, as the schedules of special educators and other school personnel become overloaded due to a high-number caseload and deadline crunches, intentional collaborative practice may lose priority because these specialists may feel pressured to meet minimum requirements and move on to the next assignment. To avoid ineffective assessment procedures, group members should be trained to facilitate best team practice with ongoing review and reflection regarding their role in the collaborative process.

COLLABORATION MODELS

Three models, or approaches, are identified when defining collaborative assessment in early childhood special education. Each approach, the **multidisciplinary approach**, **interdisciplinary approach**, and **transdisciplinary approach**, is designed to produce the most effective outcomes, depending on various child and family needs and circumstances.

Multidisciplinary Approach

The conventional model used in educational assessment and program planning is multidisciplinary assessment. It emerged from what has been referred to as the medical model and has been compared to the parallel play observed in young children: "side by side, but separate" (Peterson, 1987, p. 484). The overall premise of this model is that those trained in that specific field are the only ones who hold the expertise to assess the needs of the child accurately. For example, an occupational therapist has been trained to observe unique fine motor skills and development and would be the only professional that could accurately assess fine motor skill development. As a result, assessments are conducted independently from each other, and the expert who administered the assessment would be responsible for reporting the outcomes to the family and other team members.

The term *multidisciplinary* is used in IDEIA (2004) when referring to assessment as an "a timely, comprehensive, multidisciplinary evaluation of the functioning of each infant or toddler with a disability . . ." (IDEIA, §635.3, 2004). This statement can be misconstrued as referring to the assessment process. Instead, *multidisciplinary*, in this circumstance, refers to the importance of using a variety of assessments such as standardized assessments, performance-based assessments and professional judgment, as well as assessment across the spectrum of developmental domains. It does not require that the team process or assessment process be a multidisciplinary approach.

The steps in the multidisciplinary approach begin with the skeleton team meeting to discuss the referral to the special education program, consisting of only those who are required by law to attend: parent(s), administrator, classroom teacher, and the special educator/case manager. The outcomes of this meeting dictate who will be contacted and asked to complete assessments. Each professional who will be conducting an evaluation then contacts the family or school and arranges a time to complete the assessment. Minimal consideration is given for other assessment outcomes, little or no communication occurs across disciplines; it is considered a time-efficient approach (Gargiulo & Kilgo, 2005).

For the infant or toddler who is not attending a center-based program, the parents may be asked to bring the child to a clinic or the office of the person administering the assessment. Parents may or may not be present during the actual evaluation; in some situations, parents may be encouraged to leave and return in an hour because the professional may think that the infant or toddler may perform better without the distraction of the parent in the room. An early interventionist shared the following about experiences recalled from the 1980s:

> Our program was a center-based program for infants and toddlers, and we completed our assessments in what we referred to as the playroom. Parents usually waited and watched the assessment process from an observation room with a two-way mirror. Sometimes the parent chose to run errands, and agreed to return in an hour to hear the results of the assessment. If it could be arranged, the others involved in the assessment process would wait and observe from the observation room or sit quietly on the sidelines in the playroom, awaiting their turns to complete their assessments. Many of the team members came from other agencies, and it seemed like a highly coordinated way to gather the necessary expertise and to complete the assessments in a time-efficient manner. As I look back at what we saw as best practice, it appeared that we had little regard for what the parents may be feeling as we scrutinized the abilities of their beloved little one. I know that we were always pleasant to families and worked to make them feel comfortable. But it was also quite evident that we were the experts and they were the parents.

When the assessment results are shared in the multidisciplinary model, those who completed assessments attend the meeting with a written assessment report and their specific plan for intervention. The team members do not confer with one another in advance nor do they have prior knowledge of the outcomes of the other assessments. If this was the model used in Michelle's case, the early interventionist would not have taken time to talk with the speech pathologist in the hallway as she was on her way to another appointment. They would not have discussed their own concerns, and they would not have known or shared the concerns of other team members. It may be a convenient, quick, and efficient way for professionals to complete numerous assessments under strict time constraints, but it leaves much room for disjointed programming and miscommunication on the part of the team members who are striving to set up the best program possible for the young child.

Although this assessment approach was most common before the mid-1980s, it continues to be used in some school districts because it takes little effort to implement. Working within the federally guided timelines, each evaluator is responsible for completing a particular portion of the assessment by the set date. Unfortunately, the meetings may result in surprises that can affect the overall program planning to follow.

The multidisciplinary approach is not considered family friendly (Gargiulo & Kilgo, 2005). Families learn about assessment results in a meeting where most of the professionals have had no contact with one another before the meeting. Here, parents are regarded as listeners instead of as active participants in the reporting of the specific results and in program planning. It is contrary to best practice regarding the inclusion of families in the assessment process as described in IDEIA (2004).

Interdisciplinary Approach

The interdisciplinary approach transpired from concerns that the multidisciplinary approach was not meeting the needs of the educators or families, especially when it was time to use the assessment results to plan the appropriate interventions. Misunderstandings regarding the accuracy of developmental profiles and contradicting outcomes based on individual observations were common, and they caused tensions and disagreements during assessment summary meetings. The interdisciplinary approach alleviated these disconnects and appeared to be an expedient method that accommodated the busy schedules of professionals and respected the expertise of various disciplines. When this model is implemented, professionals conduct their assessments independently yet confer with each other prior to the assessment summary meeting. For infants and toddlers, assessments are typically conducted in the home environment. It is common for two or three professionals to visit a family at the same time; however, each completes his or her specific assessment, commenting on and confirming each other's observations as they do so.

If the child is attending a school-based program, the evaluator arranges for the assessment to take place in the classroom or in another setting in the school environment. This approach is not considered best practice when the child is removed from the natural setting and expected to perform tasks that are taken out of context or in the presence of an adult with whom the child is not familiar.

Michelle's team functioned as an interdisciplinary team. The early interventionist and others had conducted their independent evaluations yet consulted with each other, confirming their assessment outcomes and observations. They did not formally meet before the meeting to discuss results, but they communicated informally through conversation and e-mail and were aware of each other's findings prior to the meeting. This approach is common in many school settings; although many professionals are not consciously aware of the style that is being implemented, it works well for them, especially if it is a group of professionals who have worked together for an extended period of time.

A teacher recently described the electronic assessment summary template used in her school district. As assessment results were inserted, they were readily available for all team members to view. This gave them the opportunity to consult with each other if there were questions about any assessment outcomes prior to the assessment summary meeting.

Transdisciplinary Approach

The transdisciplinary approach is considered the preferred collaboration model in early childhood special education. What separates this approach from the others are two unique features: Team members share roles, and team members cross discipline boundaries by appointing a primary therapist (Gargiulo & Kilgo, 2005). Bruder (1994) stated that the purpose of the transdisciplinary model is "to pool and integrate the expertise of team members so that more efficient and comprehensive assessment and intervention services may be provided" (p. 61). This assessment typically happens in a play setting or within the natural environment and is conducive to family involvement in the assessment process (Brink, 2002). It is also sometimes described as arena assessment, referring to the arrangement of several professionals gathered in one area and observing the child, who interacts with an assigned designee (Guillory & Woll, 1994). When members of the transdisciplinary team come together to share assessment results, all members, including the parents, are familiar with the outcomes. There is open reciprocal dialogue at this meeting, and all members, including the parents, partake in an interactive discussion about the assessment results and the implications for program planning (Bruder, 1994).

The intent of this process is to decrease compartmentalization and fragmentation (Gargiulo & Kilgo, 2005) and to increase continuity of service delivery that is more utilitarian for parents and professionals. Ultimately, all team members strive toward a common goal and learn from one another as they share their discipline expertise (Bruder, 1994).

The transdisciplinary approach is commonly used to evaluate infants and toddlers in their home environments because it is convenient and less invasive for families. Realistically, it may take several weeks for professionals to schedule appointments around the busy schedules of families with children with exceptional needs due to issues such as illness, transportation, and doctor appointments (Meyers & McBride, 1996). A single appointment would alleviate these scheduling issues and accommodate time constraints experienced by families. However, the downside to this approach is finding a convenient time for all professionals to meet simultaneously with the family and the child, which again requires concerted collaboration of all team members.

For transdisciplinary assessment to work, the whole team must buy into the concept and be able to relinquish professional boundaries. It requires each team member to believe in collaboration as best practice for building teams that work together from beginning to end. It requires time and effort; some, especially in our busy work worlds, view it as a tedious process, defined by the needs of the situation rather than by discipline-specific characteristics. However, the strengths far outweigh the weaknesses because the child is the one who, in the end, benefits from the time and effort invested by all.

BREAKPOINT PRACTICE

1. In small groups, compare and contrast the collaboration approaches using your own words and according to your understanding of each.
2. Which approach(es) have you experienced in a work or other setting?
3. Which approach would you feel most comfortable facilitating? Why?
4. Think about each approach and how it is structured for assessment and the assessment summary meeting. Do you see a mix-and-match among approaches based on the age of the child and the educational setting? If you do, discuss your reasons for this.

BEST COLLABORATION PRACTICE

Assessment in early childhood special education is a comprehensive process, beginning with a planning session where the team makes decisions regarding which assessments will be administered and concluding with a summary meeting where the assessment outcomes are shared and used to plan appropriate developmental or educational intervention. IDEIA (2004) requires that the core team include a school administrator or administrative representative, parent(s) or parent representative, a general education teacher (if the child is participating in a general education setting), and a special education teacher. Those who become part of the assessment team may vary based on their areas of expertise as well as considerations for the unique needs of children and their families. Best collaborative practice is not accidental. It encompasses the comprehensive approach and is integrated intentionally into all components of the assessment process (Friend & Bursuck, 2006). Successful team process takes time and ultimately ensures high-quality child assessment and programming. Therefore, there must be a conscious effort on the part of all team members to make the process as productive as possible. Michelle's team was comprised of integral key players. However, one could speculate about the purpose of including all the professionals who took part in the assessment process and whether this influenced the parents' comfort level during the meeting.

An effective team appoints a facilitator who sets the parameters by clearly articulating the meeting's purpose and assigns the roles and responsibilities of team members. The facilitator designates a recorder whose responsibilities include documentation of the meeting outcomes. A timekeeper is appointed to monitor on-task discussions. Most professionals and parents are juggling busy schedules and have planned a block of time for the particular meeting; therefore, staying on task allows for succinct reporting of assessment outcomes.

All team members become collaborative participants when they take responsibility for respecting the input of others, even if they have opposing views. Being respectful of the input of others means being mindful of effective listening; asking for clarification when needed; serving as an equal participant; and using overall evidence-based, collaborative practice (Friend & Cook, 2010). This also includes being cognizant of characteristics that may jeopardize team effectiveness (Gutkin & Nemeth, 1997), such as a majority-rule mentality, even while continuing to show serious concern for the accuracy of a specific decision.

BREAKPOINT PRACTICE

1. Consider this statement from the first paragraph of this chapter section: "Best collaborative practice is not accidental." Discuss your feelings about this statement and support your views with personal experience.
2. How common or realistic is the structured team setting in your educational setting or according to your experiences in education?
3. Discuss the concept of effective team practice and how it relates to each collaborative approach.
4. In a structured team setting, which role are you most comfortable implementing? Do you see yourself capable of taking responsibility for each role at various times?
5. Identify and list collaborative practices that took place in Michelle's assessment summary meeting.

© Art3d/Shutterstock.com

Fostering Collaborative Assessment Relationships

The most effective collaborative relationships are characterized by three major factors: mutual trust, respect, and effective communication (Turnbull, Turnbull, Erwin, & Soodak, 2005).

Mutual trust occurs when team members acknowledge the character, ability, and truthfulness of the other members (Turnbull et al., 2005). For group participants to share their information and ideas with one another, they must feel that others will listen to what they have to say. Team members need to view parents as important members of the assessment team and believe that they have a wealth of knowledge about their child, the family, the home, and community environments (Hooper & Umansky, 2009). Mutual trust also results from professionals trusting what parents say and believing that they are being truthful as they report their child's abilities, temperaments, responses, likes, and dislikes (LeDosquet, 2010).

Respect is essential for interpersonal reciprocity of a collaborative team. It includes respect for and sensitivity to the cultural diversity of families as well as other team members. To respect differences, each team member must understand what shapes her or his biases (LeDosquet, 2010). Team members should ask themselves the following questions:

- Do I have a bias toward the age, experience, and/or expertise of other team members?
- Do I respect unique problem-solving approaches, including differing philosophies, viewpoints, and interaction styles of team members?
- Do I have a bias toward particular characteristics associated with family life, for example, level of education, involvement of fathers in the educational process, socioeconomic status, geographical background, diverse parent roles (gay-lesbian parents, live-in partners, single parents), and/or diverse parenting styles?
- Do I respect the level of involvement in the assessment process chosen by the parent(s)?

When reflecting on these questions, we must consider personal paradigms, which shape the ways in which we perceive the world, based on past experiences (Amatea, 2009). Every team member walks into the meeting room or the assessment process with paradigms or mental images of the outcomes. They are shaped by past experiences as well as embedded belief systems that lead to the activation of categorical thinking. They affect the way in which others perceive our messages and the way in which we perceive theirs. When we gain perspective toward another's view of her or his social world, the phenomenon is called a paradigm shift. Amatea (2009) calls this the Aha! Experience (p. 23). The Aha! Experience may take place when the professional completes an assessment in the child's home environment, giving insight regarding routines, communication styles, attitudes, temperaments, as well as other family styles that may affect the learning and development of the child.

BREAKPOINT PRACTICE

1. Reflect on your experiences regarding trust with parents, teachers, or other educational personnel. Discuss positive and negative experiences.
2. Discuss ways in which you can show respect, other than what has been addressed in this chapter.
3. Think about your personal paradigms and how they may shape the ways in which you respond to others. Can you recall a meeting or assessment in which your outcomes were influenced by your personal beliefs or paradigms?

Effective Communication

Communication is defined as a means of exchanging information, including individual ideas, needs, and desires. It consists of encoding, transmitting, and decoding the intended message (Owens, 2008) and is comprised of three main elements: the message, the sender, and the receiver (Dettmer et al., 2005). Communicative competence refers to the degree to which a speaker is successful in communicating a message and it is measured by the clarity of the message (Owens, 2008).

The communicative pathway is complicated by numerous factors, including belief systems, professional relationships, and personal and professional paradigms. It is also affected by factors such as environmental conditions, which can include room arrangement, room temperature, member proxemics, and the time of day. Turnbull, Turnbull, Erwin, and Soodak (2005) suggest that effective communication with other team members includes the following attributes: friendliness, ability to listen, clarity, and honesty.

Friendliness, in this case, is not a personal endeavor but a characteristic used to create a welcoming atmosphere for the family that is both comfortable and invites participation. One might assume that in Michelle's meeting, the friendly environment was compromised by behaviors that appear disengaged with the task at hand.

Effective listening fosters understanding. Rogers (1961) believed that miscommunication happens when the receiver has a tendency to pass judgment, evaluate the intent, or choose to approve or disapprove of the message. He stated that true communication occurs when the receiver listens with understanding, is aware of the other person's point of view, and has a sense of how the person is reacting to how the message was conveyed. Effective listening is possible only when the listener stops talking and shows interest through congruent body language, including eye contact, nods of affirmation, and reflecting back on the speaker's words to affirm that he or she heard the information as it was meant.

Clarity is achieved when the original intent of a message is conveyed. Team members had observed that Michelle was not interacting with her peers. The message is unclear when the observer reports that Michelle does not like to play with other children. However, the message is clear when it is reported that during playtime, Michelle plays alone in the block area.

The use of professional jargon in a meeting where others may not be familiar with the terms commonly used in education also prohibits clarity in communication with other team members, especially parents. **Professional jargon** refers to the use of terms and acronyms that are used regularly within a professional discipline. For example, special educators regularly use acronyms such as IEP (individualized education plan), IFSP (individualized family service plan), LRE (least restrictive environment), IQ (intelligence quotient), LD (learning disability), MR (mental retardation), with little consideration for parents and other team members understanding of these terms.

Miscommunication and confusion may have been avoided in Michelle's case if the team had been aware of the profession terms that were casually used during the summary meeting. Each acronym could easily have been replaced with the actual terms, such as individualized education plan instead of IEP, or the administrator could have clarified the acronym LRE by referring to it as least restrictive environment.

Professional jargon is frequently used when assessment results are reported. Telling a parent that the standard score on the Battelle is 74 may have little or no meaning for a parent. Converting to percentages may also cause confusion to someone who is unfamiliar with standardized assessment. Educators must further clarify this information so that parents can process how this may affect the outcomes of the meeting and possible program plan.

> As a special educator, I sat in on numerous assessment meetings where results were shared. I especially appreciated working with a team member who always shared her information verbally but accompanied the words with diagrams that she drew as she talked. If she was referring to a percentile score, she would draw a line and label one endpoint 0 and the other 100. She would then draw a line in the middle, which she labeled 50. As she did this, she explained its meaning in terms of percentile scores. Then, with a marker or pencil of a different color, she would place the child's percentile, describing what that meant in terms of the number line. If she needed to talk about standard deviation, she used the line concept again. Parents always seemed to respond well to this and felt empowered to ask questions based on the knowledge they had just received.

While team members should exercise caution in the use of professional jargon, it is equally important to gauge discussions to avoid oversimplification. It is in the moderation of our content and interaction styles that we best achieve common ground and parity in problem solving.

Honesty is reflected in the reporting of the results and outcomes. Parents deserve the truth. One might conclude that there is a fine line between sounding too harsh and sugarcoating the diagnosis. Some families are disappointed when there is no diagnosis, especially when they are looking for reasons why their child is experiencing development delay or academic failure. Yet some are relieved that their child does not qualify for early intervention. The professional's responsibility is not to predict the parent's reaction but to report the facts as they are presented and to allow the parents the right to respond in their own way.

Clarity and honesty are also reflected in paralinguistic cues, which account for over 90% of the relayed message (Mehrabian, 1971). When our body language does not match our words, mixed signals are given. This can be avoided by developing a keen sense of awareness about how our messages are conveyed and interpreted by others.

BREAKPOINT PRACTICE

1. Talk about your own communication style. How do you think you are perceived in a group setting?
2. Discuss the four characteristics of effective communication. Describe situations where these characteristics are either present or absent. How does their presence or absence affect the communication of the group?
3. Discuss your own personal paradigms that may affect your ability to work with others.
4. Think about your profession or how you think you would be in the role of an early interventionist. How easy would it be to allow someone trained in a field other than education (occupational therapist, physical therapist, etc.) to assess a child for cognitive or social emotional development? How comfortable would you be assessing fine motor or gross motor development?
5. What professional jargon is commonly used in the area of early intervention? Discuss situations where you have felt confused or excluded due to the overuse of professional jargon.

Revisiting Michelle

Michelle was referred for assessment because of concerns about her delays in social skills, speech and language, and fine motor skills. Assessments were administered by the appropriate personnel, and an assessment summary meeting was planned. As we revisit the collaborative approaches and strategies used throughout Michelle's assessment process, it is apparent that the team administered assessment using the interdisciplinary model.

During the summary meeting, team members needed to be mindful of the atmosphere that was fostered by their involvement or lack of involvement at the outset of the meeting. They needed to be aware of the parents' comfort level. They also needed to remind themselves of best team practice and the positive outcomes of effective collaboration and communication throughout the assessment process as well as during the assessment summary meeting with the parents. A friendly environment was compromised by the distractions of team members and the administrators. Also, professional jargon was used, without concern for the parents' understanding of this terminology. Awareness about these dynamics of collaboration and effective communication would ensure positive and productive outcomes for Michelle and her family.

Activities

1. Interview the parents of a young child with exceptional learning needs regarding their experiences with collaboration during the assessment process. Share their experiences with others in your class.
2. Role-play an assessment summary meeting based on the collaborative approaches. Discuss the outcome of each role play and how team members perceived the experience.
3. Brainstorm lists of professional jargon used in various professions. Some examples are the educational, medical, and psychology professions. Discuss how parent participation is affected by overuse of professional jargon and practitioners' lack of sensitivity concerning this issue.
4. Share your collaboration experiences and the strengths and weaknesses that affected the outcome of each situation.

Websites

Center for Effective Collaboration and Practice
http://cecp.air.org/

Collaboration and Consultation
http://www.circleofinclusion.org/english/pim/four/coll.html

Collaboration between General and Special Education
Teachers
*http://www.teachervision.fen.com/teaching-methods/
resource/2941.html*

Collaborative Teaching—Special Education in
Collaborative Classrooms
*http://learningdisabilities.about.com/od/
publicschoolprograms/p/collaboration.htm*

How to Develop Collaboration Skills
*http://www.ehow.com/how_2060519_develop-collabora-
tion-skills.html*

Seven Personal Skills for Effective Collaboration
*http://www.anecdote.com.au/archives/2008/09/seven_
personal.html*

What Is Teacher Collaboration, and How Does it Relate to
Other Current School Practices?
http://www.slc.sevier.org/tcollab.htm

References

Amatea, E. S., (2009). *Building culturally responsive family school relationships.* Upper Saddle River, NJ: Pearson Education.

Beckman, P. J., & Bristol, M. (1991). Issues in developing the IFSP: A framework for establishing family outcomes. *Topics in Early Childhood Special Education, 11*(3), 19–31.

Brink. M. B. (2002, Summer). Involving parents in early childhood assessment: Perspectives from an early interventionist instructor. *Early Childhood Education Journal, 29*(4), 251–257.

Bruder, M. B. (1994). Working with members of other disciplines: Collaboration for success. In M. Wolery & J. S. Wilbers (Eds.), *Including children with special needs in early childhood programs* (pp. 45–70). Washington, DC: National Association for the Education of Young Children.

Dettmer, P., Thurston, L. P., & Dyck, N. J. (2005). *Consultation, collaboration, and teamwork for students with special needs* (5th ed). Upper Saddle River, NJ: Pearson Education.

Dettmer, P., Thurston, L. P., & Knackendoffel, A. (2008). *Consultation, collaboration and teamwork for students with special needs* (6th ed.). Upper Saddle River, NJ: Pearson Education.

Fewell, R. R. (1983). The team approach to infant education. In S. G. Garwood & R. R. Fewell (Eds.), *Educating handicapped infants: Issues in development intervention.* Rockville MD: Aspen.

Friend, M., & Bursuck, W. D. (2006). *Including students with special needs: A practical guide for classroom teachers* (4th ed.). Boston: Allyn & Bacon.

Friend, M., & Cook, L. (2010). *Interactions: Collaboration skills for school professionals* (5th ed.). Upper Saddle River, NJ: Merrill/Pearson Education.

Gargiulo, R., & Kilgo, J. (2005). *Young children with special needs* (2nd ed.). Clifton Park, NY: Delmar Cengage Learning.

Golin, A. K., & Ducanis, A. J. (1981). *The interdisciplinary team.* Rockville, MD: Aspen.

Guillory, A. W., & Woll, J. (1994, November). How professionals can work with families to assess children's disabilities. *Education Digest, 0013127X*(60), 3.

Gutkin, T., & Nemeth, C. (1997). Selected factors impacting decision making in pre-referral intervention and other school-based teams: Exploring the intersection between school and social psychology. *Journal of School Psychology, 35*(2), 195–216.

Hooper, S. R., & Umansky, W. (2009). *Young children with special needs* (5th ed.). Upper Saddle River, NJ: Merrill/Pearson Education.

Individuals with Disabilities Education Improvement Act of 2004. 20 U.S.C. § 1400 et seq.

LeDosquet, P. (2010). Early childhood. In E. P. Kritikos (Ed.), *Special education assessment: Issues and strategies affecting today's classrooms.* Upper Saddle River, NJ: Merrill/Pearson Education.

Mehrabian, A. (1971). *Silent messages.* Belmont, CA: Wadsworth.

Meisels, S. J. (1989). *Developmental screening in early childhood: A guide* (3rd ed.), Washington, DC: National Association for the Education of Young Children.

Meyers, C. L., & McBride, S. L. (1996, Spring). Transdisciplinary, play-based assessment in early childhood special education: An examination of social validity. *Topics in Early Childhood Special Education, 16*(1), 102–126.

Owens, R. E., (2008). *Language development: An introduction* (7th ed.). Boston: Pearson.

Peterson, N. (1987). *Early intervention for handicapped and at risk children: An introduction to early childhood special education.* Denver, CO: Love.

Reed-Victor, E. (2004, January). Individual differences and early school adjustment: Teacher appraisals of young children with special needs. *Early Childhood Development and Care, 174*(1), 59–79.

Rogers, C. (1961). *On becoming a person: A therapist's view of psychotherapy.* London: Constable.

Turnbull, A. P., Turnbull, R., Erwin, E. J., & Soodak, L. C. (2005). *Families, professionals and exceptionality: Positive outcomes through partnership and trust* (5th ed.). Upper Saddle River, NJ: Merrill/Pearson Education.

Technical Aspects of Assessment

CHAPTER OBJECTIVES

By the end of this chapter, you will be able to answer the questions included in Judy's case study, which is included in Chapter 5. You will also be able to explain how publishers design standardized, norm-referenced testing. You will be able to name, explain, and interpret reliability and validity types based on coefficients. You will also be able to use this information to choose appropriate tests for students. In addition, you will be able to discuss test administration, including basals and ceilings. You will know scales of measurement, measures of central tendency (mean, median, mode), dispersion (range, deviation from the mean, variance, and standard deviation), and relative position (z-scores and percentile rank). You will also be able to interpret standard scores.

This chapter addresses Council for Exceptional Children (CEC) Content Standard 8, which concentrates on assessment. Reliability, validity, interpretation, and norm-referenced testing are discussed in this standard (see http://www.cec.sped.org/ps/perf_bases_stds/standards.html).

Assessing Judy

Judy is a 35-month-old toddler in your preschool classroom. She has frequent tantrums where she bangs her head against the door for over a minute at a time unless physically stopped. She does not regularly interact with the other children. When she does play with peers, it is usually parallel play activities. She sometimes participates in group art and music activities. According to the test results you have received, Judy has a moderate delay in language and social skills. Judy's mother reports that Judy appeared to be developing at a normal rate in the areas of language and social skills in her earlier stages of development. At about 24 months, however, there appeared to be a regression of these skills. Judy did not speak the words she had once used. Judy's mother added that these skills were continuing to deteriorate.

Judy's mother asks you if you think it is more than a speech and language delay. She says that she is upset and feels a high level of stress regarding Judy's overall development. What do you tell her? What information do you share with her? What contact information do you give her? What does this information mean in relation to the testing information you received? How does this information tie into your classroom objectives?

NORM-REFERENCED, STANDARDIZED TESTING

The required testing in individual states mandated in No Child Left Behind (NCLB) (2001) was implemented by 2006, and an intensified focus on testing has emerged in the literature (Olson, 2006). Children who are very young in age are often not placed in disability groups but are reported in terms of how much of a delay exists (Cook, Klein, Tessier, & Daley, 2004). Norm-referenced, standardized testing is used to determine difficulties that could give information regarding delay but could also give information needed for a diagnosis, thus making a student eligible for services.

Norm-referenced tests are tests where a student can be compared to other students of the same age or grade level. This comparison of a child's scores to a sample group's scores is at the core of norm-referenced testing (McLean, Wolery, & Bailey, 2004). **Standardized tests** are tests that use the same materials, testing procedures, scoring procedures, and interpretation of test results (McLean, Wolery, & Bailey, 2004).

Standardized tests not only have standardized procedures, but also include a test manual with detailed information regarding construction of the test (McAfee & Leong, 2007). Standardized measures attempt to ensure that no matter who gives and scores the test, similar results would be achieved by the student. Technical aspects represent the structural features in these norm-referenced, standardized measures. The concepts of test reliability and validity allow educators to understand if a test is technically sound. It is important to have a valid and reliable instrument because the data collected from the test will be used for instruction of the student (Fewell, 2000; McConnell, 2000).

If a test is not valid, an invalid label and inappropriate services could be recommended for the child. Standardized testing is used for eligibility. Testing of intelligence in the early years is a controversial topic in the area of validity and is discussed heavily in the literature (Bagnato, 2005; Freeman & Miller, 2001; Maisto & German, 1986; Neisworth & Bagnato, 1992; Neisworth & Bagnato, 2004; Skiba, Knesting, & Bush, 2002; Tusing & Ford, 2004). Testing of infants is not predictive. One example of these concerns is that theories connected to testing are sometimes taken from data related to adults and then applied to the early childhood setting (Meisels & Fenichel, 1996).

Application to the Classroom

Teachers are involved with norm-referenced, standardized testing at multiple levels, and they can influence which test, or tests, are chosen for their district, school, or program. Information related to development of the test (e.g., norm sample), reliability, and validity guides professionals in choosing appropriate tools. Cronbach (1990) reported that cost, time needed for testing, and testing and scoring ease were other items for consideration when choosing tests for younger children. Multiple formal tools (Appl, 2000), in addition to informal measures (Guilory & Woll, 1994; Trivette & Dunst, 1990; Whitehead & Deiner, 1990), give a robust picture of the child and his or her family, which is the child's context (Carpenter, 1997; Dunst, 2000, 2002). For example, observations, family interviews, teacher interviews, samples, play-based assessments, and dynamic assessments are essential early childhood assessment components.

Teachers may also need to administer, score, and interpret standardized measures (McAfee & Leong, 2007). A thorough understanding of testing, including coursework, purpose of a particular test, reading of the test manual, and practice with administration and scoring of tests will generally be required. Statistical measures allow the assessor to apply scores on the normal curve in order to achieve these results. Teachers match raw scores to derived scores based on age levels in test manuals. The derived scores allow teachers to see how students performed in comparison to their peers. In other words, statistics enable and empower the assessor to understand test performance.

Important technical aspects include reliability, validity, normative sample, test administration (basals and ceilings), scales of measurement, measures of central tendency (mean, median, mode), dispersion (range, deviation from the mean, variance, standard deviation), and relative position (z-scores, percentile rank). The teacher must often communicate assessment results to co-workers, family members, and other professionals. Co-workers and professionals can include administrators, teachers, psychologists, speech-language pathologists, occupational therapists, physical therapists, and childcare providers (Mindes, 2007).

Textbooks, research articles, publishers, professional organizations, and review websites offer valuable information regarding the technical aspects of tests. The Mental Measurements Yearbook (Spies & Plake, 2005), Pearson's website (http://www.pearsonassessments.com), and content area websites (i.e., Council for Exceptional Children, Learning Disabilities Association, American Speech-Language Hearing Association, and American Educational Research Association) can be very helpful in learning more about this pertinent information.

RELIABILITY

Reliability refers to the consistency of test scores (Cook, Klein, Tessier, & Daley, 2004). It is also a prerequisite of validity (Kritikos, 2010). For a test to be valid, it must be reliable.

Correlation coefficients.   Correlation coefficients are often used in interpreting reliability. Coefficients measure the relationship between two or more sets of scores (Wortham, 2008) and are indicated by the letter r or Greek ρ. Coefficients measure observed and predicted values. Coefficients are always between $+1$ and -1. In standardized tests, reliability and validity for tests ranges from 0 to 1. A cutoff of .9 is generally used for assessment guiding diagnostic decisions (Nitko & Brookhart, 2006). It is important to note that many instruments do not meet this standard. It is also important to note that relationship does not refer to causality.

Direction.   Coefficients can be positive or negative, or they can have no direction. Two or more scores going in the same direction (i.e., both positive and both negative) indicates a positive relationship. A plus sign or no sign is used before the number. For example, a positive direction can be indicated with a $+.81$ or $.81$. An example is intelligence and academic achievement (Atkinson, Atkinson, Smith, & Bem, 1992). A negative direction includes a set of scores that increase as another set of scores decrease. A minus sign precedes the number when the relationship is negative. For example, a $-.77$ indicates a negative relationship. The number of absences and test scores is an example of this relationship. When two sets of scores are not connected, there is no relationship or a zero relationship. Hair thickness and test score results is an example of scores not related at all. In a scatter plot, scores are randomly scattered all over the plot with no pattern (Everitt, 2002).

Strength.   Strength is another important aspect of coefficients. As the number gets closer to $+1$ or -1, the coefficient is stronger (Steel & Torrie, 1960). Also, direction does not affect the strength of a coefficient. So $-.5$ and $+.5$ have equal strength. Furthermore, .9 is stronger than .85. It is also significant to note that rarely does a perfect relationship of 1 or -1 occur. Typically, a cutoff of .9 is used as a measure of adequate strength. For example, if a test has a strength of .75 in the area of test-retest reliability, it would not be adequate. If a test has a .92 reliability, it would have adequate strength.

BREAKPOINT PRACTICE

1. State the direction of the following coefficients:
   a. .51
   b. +.62
   c. −.77
   d. .00
2. State whether the strength of the following coefficients is adequate in making educational decisions:
   a. .83
   b. .22
   c. .95
   d. .89

Reliability Types

Common reliability types used include test-retest reliability, alternate forms of reliability, inter-rater reliability, internal consistency, and measurement error. The first step is for the assessor to examine which reliability types were conducted. In general, the more types of reliability reported by the test makers, the more information the educator has regarding the strength of the test. It is important to look at composite and individual subtests. Composite scores typically have higher reliability coefficients than do individual subtests. In addition, it is important to look at scores by age and grade level. At times, variability may occur. Matching the child's information helps the educator decide whether the test is a good choice. For example, if a cutoff score is .9 and a score falls below that level, one may choose to use a different test (Kritikos, 2010). See Table 5.1 for more information about types of reliability.

TEST-RETEST. In **test-retest reliability**, a group of students is administered the same test at two different times. The scores are then compared to yield an *r*. The coefficient indicates consistency

TABLE 5.1 Types of Reliability

Reliability Type	Number of Groups	Number of Forms	Number of Testing Sessions
Test-retest	1	1	2
Alternate forms	1	2	1 or 2
Inter-rater	1, 2 raters	1	N/A
Internal consistency	1	1	N/A
Measurement error	1	1	N/A

over time. An acceptable score is usually .9 or higher when making educational decisions. Two to four weeks is an acceptable timeframe between testing times. A lesser time period inflates r because of the learning experience from the first testing. Waiting more than four weeks lowers r due to developmental changes (Cohen & Spenciner, 2010).

ALTERNATE FORMS RELIABILITY.   **Alternate forms reliability** means consistency of item samples in different forms of the same test. Alternate forms reliability is otherwise known as equivalent or parallel forms reliability. This type of reliability is used when more than one form of a test exists (i.e., form A and form B). The two forms have different items, which are matched for difficulty. The students are given both forms, sometimes during the same testing period. The more time between the administration of the instruments, the more the chance of a change in scores (Salvia & Ysseldyke, 2007). A score of .9 or higher is generally accepted as appropriate when making educational decisions.

INTER-RATER RELIABILITY.   Inter-rater, inter-scorer, or inter-observer reliability refers to consistency of rater scores. **Inter-rater reliability** includes two or more raters who score the same test independently. Differences in ratings negatively affect reliability coefficients. More structure and less subjectivity in tests increase coefficients. A cutoff score of .9 is generally used in this type of reliability (Cohen & Spenciner, 2010).

INTERNAL CONSISTENCY.   **Internal consistency** focuses on stability or consistency over items within a test. That is, items are compared to other items within the same test. Therefore, one administration of the test is used. In some cases, half the test items are compared to the other half (split-half method). In other cases, an average correlation of all possible split halves occurs (Kuder-Richardson formulas) (Salvia & Ysseldyke, 2007).

STANDARD ERROR OF MEASUREMENT.   Standard error of measurement (SEM) involves true and observed scores. **Standard error of measurement (SEM)** is the difference between the true score and the observed score. When a child or caregiver completes a test, an observed score is revealed. An observed score includes measurement error, yielding a range of possible scores. So, a true score is never pinpointed. If more error exists within a test, a larger range is established. Therefore, the test is less reliable. This measure tells us how confident we can be regarding the score. Educators add and subtract standard error of measurement to or from an observed score to find a true score range (Taylor, 2009). For example, a score of 85 and an SEM of 5 yields a range of 80 to 90.

Factors that negatively affect reliability include test length, item difficulty, test error, examinee error (e.g., thirst), or an error within the environment (e.g., low temperature level) (Linn & Gronlund, 2000). Additional issues that can increase error when testing young children include a short attention span, language maturity, motor maturity, psychosocial factors, and the fact that young children tire more easily than do older individuals (Puckett & Black, 2008).

BREAKPOINT PRACTICE

1. Think of an everyday example and apply the concepts of test-retest, alternate forms, internal consistency, and inter-rater reliability.
2. Which form of reliability would be the most difficult to establish in an educational test for infants and toddlers? Why?

VALIDITY

Validity is at the heart of choosing and using instruments because the data collected from the test will be used for instruction of the student and is the most important technical aspect of testing (Popham, 2000). **Validity** tells the educator about the quality of the test. Common validity types are content, construct, and criterion-related (concurrent and predictive) validity. As with reliability, the more types of validity that are reported by the test makers, the stronger the test (Kritikos, 2010). See Table 5.2 for more information about types of validity.

Validity Types

CONTENT VALIDITY. Content validity determines how well the content area is manifested within the test. **Content validity** is the measurement of an area of study or domain. It is the most important type of validity. Appropriate test items represent the area tested. Too broad or too narrow a testing field has negative results in the area of content validity because the domain would not be well represented (American Educational Research Association, Psychological Association, & National Council on Measurement in Education, 1999). Format interfering with the content area also has a negative effect on content validity. For example, investigating receptive language and asking the student to supply a written answer could negatively affect the area of content validity.

CONSTRUCT VALIDITY. **Construct validity** is the measurement of how well a psychological theory is covered. Construct validity measures how well a test measures a theory or construct. Examples include intelligence, language, and motor skills. Test makers define a construct and show evidence linking their test to a theory. Construct validity is the most difficult to establish. Borich and Tombari (2004) reported procedures to improve construct validity. These procedures included delineating the construct domain, identifying multiple indicators related to domains, focusing on assessment tasks relevant to selected construct, and choosing appropriate directions connected to processes.

CRITERION-RELATED VALIDITY. **Criterion-related validity** is a comparison of an instrument's scores to another measure. **Concurrent validity** is a type of criterion-related validity often used. Test makers usually compare their test to another widely used and respected test. When this occurs, tests should be administered at around the same time (i.e., not more than two weeks apart) (Overton, 2006). A cutoff of .85 to .9 is commonly used for this type of validity. Predictive validity measures how well a test forecasts another behavior or event. The Reasoning Test of the Scholastic Aptitude Test (SAT) and tests of the American College Testing (ACT) predict future performance in college or readiness for college.

Factors that can negatively influence validity include low reliability, examinee factors, test factors, assessor factors, and weak norms. Tests that are not appropriate because of diversity

TABLE 5.2 Types of Validity

Validity Type	Definition
Content	Content area manifested with the test
Construct	Test measures scientific theory
Criterion-related	Test scores related to another measure
a. Concurrent	Comparison of two tests
b. Predictive	Test forecasts a behavior

considerations should be examined. Examples include sampling, test content, translation issues, and cultural misunderstanding on the part of the examiner. Social context guides learning (Das, 1995; Smagorinsky, 1995; Vygotsky, 1978). It is the responsibility of the educator to follow protocol that takes these aspects into consideration. If these aspects are not appropriately understood, these norm-referenced, standardized tests are not valid instruments. Therefore, one cannot use those instruments' standard scores and measures.

BREAKPOINT PRACTICE

1. When choosing a test for an evaluation, which validity type is most important to you?
2. Which validity type is the most difficult to establish? Why?
3. How are reliability and validity related?

CURRICULUM-BASED MEASUREMENT AND VALIDITY AND RELIABILITY

Curriculum-based measurement is an important area of assessment, especially as connected to instruction (Fuchs & Fuchs, 1999; Fuchs & Fuchs, 2002; Hosp & Hosp, 2003). Curriculum-based measurement is an assessment tool used for measuring students' academic growth over time. The measurement is repeated, and additional strategies are determined and used to support students and to ascertain if additional diagnostic testing is needed (Howell & Nolet, 1999). A number of research articles have addressed the technical adequacy of curriculum-based measurement tools (Deno, 1985; Fuchs, Fuchs, Karns, Hamlett, Dutka, & Katzaroff, 2000; Ardoin, 2006; VanDerHeyden, Broussard, & Cooley, 2006). Coefficients were used to support the concepts of reliability and validity.

For example, VanDerHeyden, Witt, Naquin, and Noell (2001) reported on the reliability and validity of readiness probes with kindergarten students. Alternate forms reliability; inter-rater reliability; internal consistency; and concurrent, predictive, and social validity types were investigated with math, reading, and writing probes assessed in a group setting. Results revealed acceptable technical adequacy results. Shin, Deno, and Espin (2000) reported acceptable alternate-form reliability in maze tasks for reading. Some researchers have found that curriculum-based measures in mathematics have lower reliability measures than so those in reading (Foegen, Jiban, & Deno, 2007).

Martson, Pickart, Reschly, Heistad, Muyskens, and Tindal (2007) discussed acceptable reliability and validity in literacy measures. Espin, Busch, Shin, and Kruschwitz (2001) reported moderate alternate-form reliability for vocabulary-matching curriculum-based measurements as an indicator in social studies performance. On the other hand, researchers have found a need for further study in technical adequacy of curriculum-based measurement in written expression (McMaster & Espin, 2007).

CURRICULUM-BASED ASSESSMENT

Curriculum-based assessment is used to assess students' performance on the curriculum utilized (Gickling & Havertape, 1981). Burns, Tucker, Frame, Foley, and Hauser (2000) investigated test-retest, alternate-form, internal consistency, and inter-rater reliability in curriculum-based assessment in reading curriculum-based assessments. The researchers found reliability results well within acceptable levels.

Thurman and McGrath (2008) focused on the importance of contextual validity when assessing young children. The researchers discussed the authentic quality of assessment that takes place in the natural environment. Macy, Bricker, and Squires (2005) supported the use of curriculum based assessments with authentic environments related to toddlers. They also noted that a realistic context connects the assessment to the instructional loop. That is, assessment feeds instruction, which in turn feeds assessment in a continuous fashion.

Curriculum-referenced or curriculum-based assessment (Neisworth & Bagnato, 1986) is widely used in the context of early childhood and refers to meeting a determined objective (Bailey, Jens, & Johnson, 1983; McLean, Wolery, & Bailey, 2004). In this case, the child is not compared to other children, but instead is compared to his or her improvement in regard to his or her skills. Useful in the assessment-to-instruction link is the association of the assessment criterion with an individualized education program (IEP) criterion (Overton, 2006). Technical information about these types of tests can be located in test manuals, research studies, and websites provided by publishers. Some widely used examples of curriculum-based assessments include: Assessment, Evaluation, and Programming System for Infants and Children (Bricker & Pett-Frontczak, 1996), Brigance Diagnostic Inventory of Early Development—Revised (Brigance, 1991), Carolina Curriculum for Preschoolers with Special Needs (Johnson-Martin, Jens, Hacker, & Attermeier, 1990), and Hawaii Early Learning Profile—Birth to 3 (Parks, 1994). Reliability and validity sections of these tests are not reported in the same way as they are in norm-referenced tests. See Chapter 10 for more information regarding curriculum-based measurement.

BREAKPOINT PRACTICE

1. What are some areas in which reliability and validity testing have been addressed in curriculum-based measurement?
2. Which content areas have favorable reliability and validity data?

Norms and Testing

Educators use standard scores to make comparisons in the determination of student performance levels based on normed data. The process of connecting numerical values to test performance allows the assessor to interpret test performance (Linn & Miller, 2005) and is of great importance to standardized testing in early childhood (Urbina, 2004). An example is whether the student is performing at age or grade level. The normal curve with standard deviations is used to examine various content areas (i.e., adaptive skills). Norms along the normal curve allow evaluators to compare test performance. See Figure 5.1.

Different cutoff levels are used for different content areas when dealing with standard deviation. For example, in the cognitive domain, two standard deviations below the mean or above the mean (i.e., gifted) can be used as a cutoff score, whereas in the language domain, one standard deviation below the mean is a common cutoff score. See Figure 5.2 for more information regarding standard scores and standard deviations.

Normative sample.   Means for various age and grade levels of the normative sample are established for comparative purposes. According to Sattler (2002), at least 100 individuals for each grade or age level must be included in the normative sample for statistical purposes. A norm sample should have at least 1,000 individuals (Mindes, 2007). In addition, the norm group data should be no more than 15 years old (Salvia & Ysseldyke, 2007).

When test makers develop tests, the normative samples or norm groups for those tests are essential. Assessors can then make inferences from samples based on population data (Salvia & Ysseldyke, 2007). In the beginning, an initial sample is used in the developmental version of a test. After any difficulties are resolved from the initial testing version, a larger norm group consisting of thousands of participants is used. It is important that the sample be stratified and representative. Regions, income levels, gender, parental education, and urban-rural settings are areas

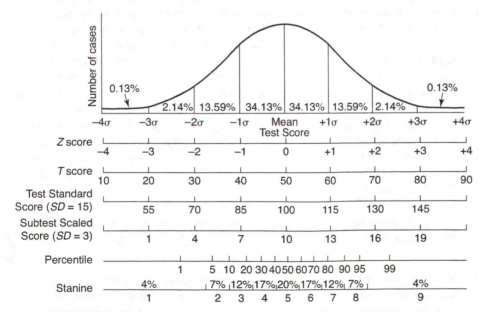

FIGURE 5.1   Normal Curve with Standard Deviations and Percentage of Individuals at Each Segment of the Normal Curve.

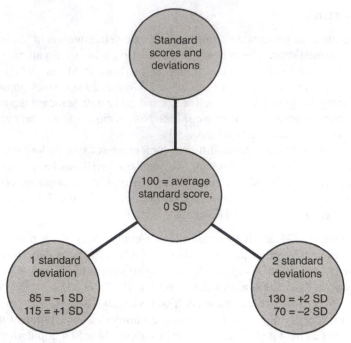

FIGURE 5.2   Standard Scores and Standard Deviations.

that help the assessor determine representativeness. When representativeness is questionable, validity concerns arise (Fotheringham, 1955).

One example would be an individual who is culturally and/or linguistically different from the mainstream. Lack of representativeness in the sample poses sample bias (American Educational Research Association, Psychological Association, & National Council on Measurement in Education, 1999; Borich & Tombari, 2004; National Association for the Education of Young Children & National Association of Early Childhood Specialists in State Departments of Education, 2003). As in the aforementioned examples, validity and equity issues arise. The issue of representativeness in addition to other factors (i.e., examiner bias) (Biggar, 2005; Kritikos, 2003; Rhodes, Ochoa, & Ortiz, 2005; Wesson, 2001) leads some researchers to question standardized assessment practices and equity issues regarding individuals who are culturally and/or linguistically diverse (Jensen, 1998; Reschly, 1981). The term *measurement invariance* refers to a possible nonequivalent performance among different groups (Byrne, Shavelson, & Muthen, 1989). One example is behavior measurement for both boys and girls (Willoughby, Kupersmidt, & Bryant, 2001).

BREAKPOINT PRACTICE

1. Why does lack of representativeness in a norm group pose a problem?
2. Why could it be challenging to achieve true representativeness of a sample?
3. What percentage of the curve falls under +1 or −1 standard deviations?

Chronological age.   To use age levels, it is important to determine chronological age. One could determine chronological age by subtracting the child's age from the testing date. Start with days, months, and then years when subtracting. The child's age is generally given in years and months. Thirty days are borrowed for each month, regardless of which month is used. For example, if a child is born on 03/14/2006 and the date of the evaluation is 06/04/2008, the following computations would be determined:

Year	Month	Day
2008	06	04
−2006	03	14
2008	06 − 01 = 05	04 + 30 = 34
−2006	03	14
2	02	20

In this case, 1 month was borrowed, which translated in 30 days to add to the days column. Twelve months would be borrowed from 1 year if months were needed in the subtraction process. It is important to note that, because years and months are often looked at in this case, the outcome would be 2–3 (2 years, 3 months). The child's age is 3 months because 20 days rounds up the month. If the days number less than 15, then the result would have been 2–2. So, 15 is the cutoff in terms of rounding off the number of months. Grade and age level scores are deemphasized in assessment reports because they could be misleading.

BASALS AND CEILINGS.   Once the chronological age has been determined, the evaluator checks with the test manual to see which item number to begin testing the examinee. Some tests start with the first items, but others have a certain number or section item to begin. A **basal** is where a test "begins" and a **ceiling** is where it "ends." Basals and ceilings are used to shorten the span of the number of items on a test to an appropriate span of items. Checking the basal and ceiling rules assists the assessor in determining if he or she could continue administering the test. Basals and ceilings are very important. If the basal and ceiling rules are not followed, the test results are not considered valid. Errors on basals and ceilings are one of the most common errors (Peterson, Steger, Slate, Jones, & Coulter, 2006). It is assumed that any item number below the basal is correct and any item above the ceiling item is incorrect. Test makers have different rules regarding basals and ceilings.

One example is if the basal and ceiling are both part of three consecutive items. In this case, if the child gets all three items first administered correct, the assessor could move on to the next items. When the student gets three consecutive items incorrect (the ceiling), the evaluator stops administering the test. If the student gets one of the three items incorrect when first taking this test, the evaluator follows the rules specified in the test manual for this scenario. One possible solution given by tests is to go backward by item number until the student gets three correct and then continue from the point in the test where one started. Sometimes students do not establish a basal at all. In that circumstance, one could not use the score compared to the norm group due to validity issues. In other circumstances, numbers could yield two basals. That is, if the basal is three correct consecutive items, items 12–14 could be correct and items 20–22 could be correct. This is especially common when subtests are given in their entirety (Mayes, 1997). The lowest basal would then be used.

BREAKPOINT PRACTICE

1. What would you do if you miscalculated a basal or a ceiling of a test?
2. What does it mean when a basal cannot be established?
3. What does it mean when a ceiling cannot be established?

SCALES OF MEASUREMENT.   It is important to discuss four scales of measurement before discussing the evaluation of test scores. Those four scales include the nominal, ordinal, interval, and ratio scales. The **nominal scale**, the weakest scale, is used to identify or name items. For example, numbers on players' shirts in hockey are used as names rather than ranking or counting. The **ordinal scale** serves as a ranking measure. An example is height. In the third level of measurement, the **interval scale**, items have equal points. One could add and subtract points. So a score of 45 is 5 more than 40. However, scores in this scale are not multiplied or divided. Also, no absolute zero exists in this type of scale. In the **ratio scale**, all qualities of the lesser scales and an absolute zero are available. If one looks at time, naming, ranking, adding, subtracting, multiplying, dividing, and an absolute zero (i.e., 0 seconds) are inherent in the scale.

Standardized scores.   Standardized scores are based on inferential statistics, which allows educators to interpret data. Inferential statistics allows individuals to draw conclusions from data collected from a random sample (Upton & Cook, 2008). One first obtains a raw score of the student from each test. The raw score is generally the amount of correct items based on where the tester started, basal and ceiling. Weights are sometimes connected with certain items (McAfee & Leong, 2007). The assessor can determine derived scores from norm tables located in test manuals. Examples of derived scores include standard scores, percentile ranks, stanines, z-scores, grade equivalents, age equivalents, normal-curve equivalents, and other standardized scores (i.e., W-scores).

CENTRAL TENDENCY.   Central tendency is related to how data cluster about the mean. The mean, median, and mode are three **measures of central tendency**. The **mean** is also known as the average. In this case, the scores are added and then divided by the number of scores. So $10 + 9 + 8 + 5 + 3 = 35/5 = 7$. The mean in this distribution is 7. The **median** is the middlemost score. Half of the scores fall above the median and half of the scores fall below the median. In the distribution we just gave, it is 8. When the distribution has an odd number of items, it is the middle score. When there is an even number of items, average the two middle scores. If the distribution had been $10 + 9 + 8 + 6 + 5 + 3$, then the median would be $8 + 6/2$, or 7. The **mode** is the most frequently occurring score. In our initial distributions, no score occurs twice, so there is no mode. However, if the distribution had been 10, 9, 8, 8, 5, and 3, then 8 would be the mode. A distribution can have more than one mode. If it has two modes, it is a bimodal distribution. If more than two modes exist, then it is multimodal (Best & Kahn, 2005).

BREAKPOINT PRACTICE

Calculate the mean, median, and mode of the following distribution:

Student	Score
James	98
Lucy	92
Shirley	83
Frank	77
Hillary	74
Randy	74

MEASURES OF DISPERSION.   **Measures of dispersion** seem to be the opposite of central tendency. Dispersion shows how data or scores are spread about the mean. Range, deviation from the mean $(x - \bar{x})$, variance (s^2 and σ^2), and standard deviation (s and σ) are four common measures of dispersion. S is used for the sample and Greek σ is used for the population. The **range** involves the distance or difference between the highest and lowest scores (Best & Kahn, 2005). In the example from the last chapter subsection, the range is $10 - 3 = 7$. The **deviation from the mean** shows how far each score of the distribution is from its mean. Each score is subtracted from the mean of the distribution. In the example from the last subsection, the deviations from the mean would be calculated as follows:

Score	Deviations from the mean
10	$10 - 7 = \quad 3$
9	$9 - 7 = \quad 2$
8	$8 - 7 = \quad 1$
5	$5 - 7 = -2$
3	$3 - 7 = -4$

This example has five scores and five deviations from the mean. When adding all of the deviations from the mean, zero is the result. When rounding takes place, however, the result is not zero.

Variance and standard deviation.   Variance and standard deviation also indicate how scores are spread about the mean. **Standard deviation** is the square root of variance. These concepts are critical to using the normal curve in translating what is within normal limits. For example, one standard deviation below the mean is a common cutoff for achievement skills. Therefore, standard deviations are often used as cutoffs for recommending services to children. In theory, if a sample reflects the population and the tool is technically sound, using the normal curve distribution is a sound and fascinating practice.

Variance calculations serve as precursors to finding standard deviation. Standard deviation is the square root of variance and variance is the square of standard deviation (Overton, 2008). If variance is 16, standard deviation is 4. If standard deviation is 2, variance is 4. Variance is calculated by summing all of the squared deviations from the mean of the distribution and then dividing that number by the number of scores (variance $= \Sigma(x - \bar{x})2/N$).

Continuing with our example, we would make a column to square the deviations from the mean and then add that column. We would then divide that result by the number of scores (5), as follows:

Score	Deviations from the mean	Deviations from the mean squared
10	$10 - 7 = 3$	$3 \times 3 = 9$
9	$9 - 7 = 2$	$2 \times 2 = 4$
8	$8 - 7 = 1$	$1 \times 1 = 1$
5	$5 - 7 = -1$	$-1 \times -1 = 1$
3	$3 - 7 = -4$	$-4 \times -4 = 16$

$$31/5 = 6.2 = \text{variance}$$

The standard deviation would then be the square root of 6.2, or 2.5.

BREAKPOINT PRACTICE

Calculate the range, deviation from the mean, variance, and standard deviation of the distribution from the previous Breakpoint Practice. The scores are repeated here for your convenience.

Score
98
92
83
77
74
74

Measures of relative position.   How scores relate to other scores in the same distribution is what measures of relative position do. **Z-scores** and **percentile ranks** are common relative position scores. Relative position scores help educators to determine how a student does compared to others within his or her distribution (Ary, Jacobs, Sorensen, & Rezavieh, 2009). Sometimes, scores are deceiving because of several factors. If we look at a score of 40, we do not have an indication of how that student performed. For example, we might not know how many points a test is worth. It could be worth 50, 100, or more points. Not having this information would leave us clueless of how a student has done. Also, difficulty level is another factor. If a test is very easy, most students could have received a perfect score. On the other hand, if a test is very difficult, very few perfect scores could have been achieved. A relative position score takes away the effects of those variables.

A z-score indicates how many standard deviations a score is away from the mean (Ary, Jacobs, Sorensen, & Rezavieh, 2009). An average score is anything between positive and negative 1. A positive score of positive 1 or larger shows that the child did significantly better than the mean. A negative score of negative 1 or lower shows that the child did significantly below the mean. The z-score formula is as follows: $x - \bar{x}/SD$.

Continuing with our example, the score of 8 would have a z-score of $8 - 7/SD$.

Percentile rank is another type of relative position score (Cohen & Spenciner, 2010). A score of 81 tells us that the child did the same or better than 81% of the children who took the test. A percentile rank is always between 1 and 99. The formula for percentile rank is as follows: $100 - (100\,\text{rank} - 50)/N$.

Measures of central tendency, dispersion, and relative position allow us to take children's raw scores, convert them into derived scores, and compare children to other children of the same age or grade level. This concept is extremely powerful because we can take a child's test scores and determine whether educational services are needed for the success of the student. This would require the use of several formal assessments as well as informal assessments.

Data gathered from technical measures give teachers a wealth of information regarding students. Not only does test information provide identification of student needs, it also reveals strengths of students. Formal subtest information provides detail in each domain area. The student may have difficulty using semantic language in expressing age-appropriate utterances. However, receptive and expressive vocabulary may be strengths to be used in achieving those goals.

In addition, informal information gathered from conducting tests can support student learning. Student response mode, body posturing, and assistive technology information can help the teacher plan appropriate classroom instruction. Repetition of administered items, idiosyncratic responses, and other information during testing can assist the evaluators in appropriate referrals for students.

Testing information can serve as a baseline or progress check over time, in terms of student progress. Valuable information can be used for purposes of the individualized family service plan (IFSP), individualized education program (IEP), and classroom planning activities. Also, reevaluation is useful in assessing progress over time.

BREAKPOINT PRACTICE

Calculate the z-score and percentile rank of the scores 92 and 83 in the distribution from the previous Breakpoint Practice. The scores are repeated here for your convenience.

Score

98

92

83

77

74

74

Revisiting Judy

The first step in looking at Judy's case would be to reread the evaluation report. Examining the testing date would provide critical information. You would then ask Judy's mother whether she agreed with the testing results at the time of the report, and if she found a change of skills since that time and for how long. You would also ask for examples, and you would supply examples from your classroom.

If Judy's mother agreed with the results at the time of the report and saw a deterioration of skills since that point, a referral to a physician and a team for a reevaluation based on new information would be warranted. You would continue to provide support for the skills noted in the report and for needs found via ongoing classroom assessment and discussed with Judy's mother. If Judy's mother would like parent support group or social work services, you could offer referrals through your agency.

Activities

1. A new student enters your kindergarten class. You have concerns regarding the accuracy of the findings of his report in the area of phonetic awareness. He seems to be at a much higher level than the report indicates. What do you do?
2. A student in your first-grade class seems to be at a much lower level in the area of writing than his report indicates. What do you do?
3. A student is falling below 1 standard deviation from the mean in multiple areas of assessment (i.e., achievement, language, and motor skills). What could this suggest? What other information would you need to determine the student's needs?
4. You look at a test manual and see coefficients for reliability ranging from .8 to .95. What does this information mean? What other information would you need to determine whether to use this test?

Websites

AERA Position Statement on High-Stakes Testing in Pre-K–12 Education
http://www.aera.net/?id=378

Council for Exceptional Children: A Well-Prepared Special Education Teacher
http://www.cec.sped.org/content/navigationmenu/ professionaldevelopment/professionalstandards/ well-prepared-final.pdf

Research Institute on Progress Monitoring: Report #2
http://www.progressmonitoring.net/pdf/techrep2.pdf

State Educational Technology Directors Association
http://www.setda.org/web/guest/petireliability

Wright's Law
http://www.wrightslaw.com/advoc/articles/ tests_measurements.html

References

Ardoin, S. (2006). The response in response to intervention: Evaluating the utility of assessing maintenance of intervention effects. *Psychology in the Schools, 43*(6), 713–725.

American Educational Research Association, Psychological Association, & National Council on Measurement in Education. (1999). *Standards for Educational and Psychological Testing*. Washington, DC: American Educational Research Association.

Appl, D. J. (2000). Clarifying the preschool assessment process: Traditional practices and alternative approaches. *Early Childhood Education Journal, 27*(4), 219–225.

Ary, D., Jacobs, L. C., Sorensen, C., & Razavieh, A. (2009). Introduction to research in education (8th ed.). Belmont, CA: Thomson Wadsworth.

Atkinson, R. L., Atkinson, R. C., Smith, E. E., & Bem, D. J. (1992). *Introduction to psychology* (11th ed.). Forth Worth, TX: Harcourt Brace Javonovich.

Bagnato, S. J. (2005). The authentic alternative for assessment in early intervention: An emerging evidence-based practice. *Journal of Early Intervention, 28*(1), 17–22.

Bailey, D. B., Jens, K. G., & Johnson, N. (1983). Curricula for handicapped infants. In S. G. Garwood & R. R.

Fewell (Eds.), *Educating handicapped infants* (pp. 387–415). Rockville, MD: Aspen.

Best, J. W., & Kahn, J. V. (2005). *Research in education* (10th ed.). Upper Saddle River, NJ: Pearson Education.

Biggar, H. (2005). NAEYC recommendations on screening and assessment of young English-language learners. *Young Children, 60*(6), 44–47.

Borich, G. D., & Tombari, M. L. (2004). *Educational assessment for the elementary and middle school classroom* (2nd ed.). Upper Saddle River, NJ: Pearson Education.

Bricker, D., & Pett-Frontczak, K. (1996). *Assessment, evaluation, and programming system for infants and children.* Baltimore, MD: Paul Brookes.

Brigance, A. (1991). *Brigance diagnostic inventory of early development—revised.* North Billerica, MA: Curriculum Associates.

Burns, M., Tucker, J. A., Frame, J., Foley, S., & Hauser, A. (2000). Interscorer, alternate-form, internal consistency, and test-retest reliability of Gickling's model of curriculum-based assessment for reading. *Journal of Psychoeducational Assessment, 18*(4), 353–360.

Byrne, B. M., Shavelson, R. J., & Muthen, B. (1989). Testing for the equivalence of factor covariance and mean structures: The issue of partial measurement invariance. *Psychological Bulletin, 105*, 456–466.

Carpenter, B. (1997). Early intervention and identification: Finding the family. *Children & Society, 11*, 173–182.

Cohen, L., & Spenciner, L. (2010). *Assessment of children and youth with special needs* (4th ed.). Upper Saddle River, NJ: Merrill/Pearson Education.

Cook, R. E., Klein, M. D., & Tessier, A., with Daley, S. E. (2004). Adapting early childhood curricula for children in inclusive settings (6th ed.). Upper Saddle River, NJ: Merrill/Pearson Education.

Cronbach, L. J. (1990). *Essentials of psychological testing* (5th ed.). New York: Harper & Row.

Das, J. P. (1995). Some thoughts on two aspects of Vygotsky's work. *Educational Psychologist, 30*, 93–97.

Deno, S. L. (1985). Curriculum-based measurement: The emerging alternative. *Exceptional Children, 52*, 219–232.

Dunst, C. J. (2000). Revisiting "rethinking early intervention." *Topics in Early Childhood Special Education, 20*(2), 95–104.

Dunst, C. J. (2002). Family-centered practices: Birth through high school, *Journal of Special Education, 36*(3), 139–147.

Espin, C., Busch, T., Shin, J., & Kruschwitz, R. (2001). Curriculum-based measurement in the content areas: Validity of vocabulary-matching as an indicator of performance in social studies. *Learning Disabilities Research & Practice, 16*(3), 142–151.

Everitt, B. S. (2002). *Cambridge Dictionary of Statistics* (2nd ed.). Cambridge, England: Cambridge University Press.

Fewell, R. R. (2000). Assessment of young children with special needs: Foundation for Tomorrow. *Topics in Early Childhood Special Education, 20*(1), 38–42.

Foegen, A., Jiban, C., & Deno, S. (2007). Progress monitoring measures in mathematics: A review of the literature. *Journal of Special education, 41*(2), 121–139.

Fotheringham, W. C. (1955). Drawing highly representative samples from large populations. *Educational Research Bulletin, 34*(4), 95–97.

Freeman, L., & Miller, A. (2001). Norm-referenced, criterion-referenced, and dynamic assessment: What exactly is the point? *Educational Psychology in Practice, 17*(1), 3–16.

Fuchs, L. S., & Fuchs, D. (1999). Monitoring student progress toward the development of reading competence: A review of three forms of classroom-based assessment. *School Psychology Review, 28*, 659–671.

Fuchs, L. S., & Fuchs, D. (2002). Curriculum-based measurement: Describing competence, enhancing outcomes, evaluating treatment effects, and identifying treatment nonresponders. *Peabody Journal of Education, 77*, 64–84.

Fuchs, L. S., Fuchs, D., Karns, K., Hamlett, C. L., Dutka, S., & Katzaroff, M. (2000). The importance of providing background information on the structure and scoring of performance assessments. *Applied Measurement in Education, 13*, 83–121.

Gickling, E. E., & Havertape, S. (1981). *Curriculum-based assessment.* Minneapolis, MN: School Psychology Inservice Training Network.

Guillory, A. W., & Woll, J. (1994). How professionals can work with families to assess children's disabilities. *Education Digest, 60*(3), 58–60.

Hosp, M. K., & Hosp, J. (2003). Curriculum-based measurement for reading, math and spelling: How to do it and why. *Preventing School Failure, 48*(1), 10–17.

Howell, K. W., & Nolet, V. (1999). *Curriculum-based evaluation: Teaching and decision making* (3rd ed.). Belmont, CA: Wadsworth.

Jensen, A. (1998). *The "g" factor: The science of mental ability.* Westport, CT: Praeger.

Johnson-Martin, N., Jens, K., Hacker, B., & Attermeier, S. (1990). *Carolina curriculum for preschoolers with special needs.* Baltimore, MD: Paul Brookes.

Kritikos, E. P. (2003). Speech-language pathologists' beliefs about language services for bilingual/bicultural individuals. *American Journal of Speech-Language Pathology: A Journal of Clinical Practice, 12*, 73–91.

Kritikos, E. P. (2010). *Special education assessment: Issues and strategies affecting today's classrooms.* Upper Saddle River, NJ: Merrill/Pearson Education.

Linn, R. L., & Gronlund, N. E. (2000). *Measurement and assessment in teaching* (8th ed.). Upper Saddle River, NJ: Merrill/Pearson Education.

Linn, R. L., & Miller, D. M. (2005). *Measurement and assessment in teaching* (9th ed.). Upper Saddle River, NJ: Merrill/Pearson Education.

Macy, M. G., Bricker, D. D., & Squires, J. K. (2005). Validity and reliability of a curriculum-based assessment approach to determine eligibility for Part C services. *Journal of Early Intervention, 28*(1), 1–16.

Maisto, A. A., & German, M. L. (1986). Reliability, predictive validity, and interrelationships of early assessment indices used with developmentally delayed infants and children. *Journal of Clinical Psychology, 15*(4), 327–332.

Martson, D., Pichart, M., Reschly, A., Heistad, D., Muyskens, P., & Tinda, G. (2007). Early literacy measures for improving student reading achievement: Translating research into practice. *Exceptionality, 15*(2), 97–117.

Mayes, S. D. (1997). Potential scoring problems using the Bayley Scales of Infant Development II—Mental Scale. *Journal of Early Intervention, 21, 36*(1), 36–44.

McAfee, O., & Leong, D. J. (2007). *Assessing and guiding young children's development and learning* (4th ed.). Upper Saddle River, NJ: Pearson Education.

McConnell, S. R. (2000). Assessment in early intervention and early childhood special education: Building on the past to project into our future. *Topics in Early Childhood Special Education, 20*(1), 43–48.

McLean, M., Wolery, M., & Bailey, D. B. (2004). *Assessing infants and preschoolers with special needs* (3rd ed.). Upper Saddle River, NJ: Merrill/Pearson Education.

McMaster, K., & Espin, C. (2007). Technical features of curriculum-based measurement in writing: A literature review. *Journal of Special Education, 41*(2), 68–84.

Meisels, S. J., & Fenichel, E. (Eds.). (1996). *New visions for the development assessment of infants and young children.* Washington, DC: Zero to Three National Center for Infants, Toddlers, and Families.

Mindes, G. (2007). *Assessing young children* (3rd ed.). Upper Saddle River, NJ: Pearson Education.

National Association for the Education of Young Children & National Association of Early Childhood Specialists in State Departments of Education. (2003). *Early childhood curriculum, assessment, and program evaluation: Building an effective, accountable system in programs for children birth through age 8.* Washington, DC: Author. Available online at http:www.naeyc.org.

Neisworth, J. T., & Bagnato, S. J. (1986). Curriculum-based developmental assessment: Congruence of testing and teaching. *School Psychology Review, 15,* 180–199.

Neisworth, J. T., & Bagnato, S. J. (1992). The case against intelligence testing in early intervention. *Topics in Early Childhood Special Education, 12*(1), 1–20.

Neisworth, J. T., & Bagnato, S. J. (2004). The mismeasure of young children: The authentic assessment alternative. *Infants and Young Children, 17,* 198–212.

Nitko, A. J., & Brookhart, S. (2006). *Educational assessment of students* (5th ed.). Upper Saddle River, NJ: Merrill/Pearson Education.

Olson, L. (2006). Department raps states on testing. *Education Week, 25*(42), 1, 36–37. No Child Left Behind Act. (2001). Public Law 107–15.

Overton, T. (2006). *Assessing learners with special needs* (5th ed.). Upper Saddle River, NJ: Merrill/Pearson Education.

Overton, T. (2008). Assessing learners with special needs: An applied approach (6th ed.). Upper Saddle River, NJ: Merrill/Pearson Education.

Parks, S. (1994). *Hawaii early learning profile (birth to 3).* Palo Alto, CA: Vort Corp.

Peterson, D., Steger, H., Slate, J., Jones, C., & Coulter, C. (2006). Examiner scores on the WRAT—R. *Psychology in the Schools, 28*(3), 205–208.

Popham, W. J. (2000). *Test! Testing! What every parent should know about school tests.* Boston: Allyn & Bacon.

Puckett, M. B., & Black, J. K. (2008). *Meaningful assessments of the young child: Celebrating development and learning* (3rd ed.). Upper Saddle River, NJ: Merrill/Pearson Education.

Reschly, D. J. (1981). Psychological testing in educational classification and placement. *American Psychologist, 36*(10), 1094–1102.

Rhodes, R. L., Ochoa, S. H., & Ortiz, S. O. (2005). *Assessing culturally and linguistically diverse students: A practical guide.* New York: Guilford.

Salvia, J., & Ysseldyke, J. (2007). *Assessment* (10th ed.). Boston: Houghton Mifflin.

Sattler, J. M. (2002). Assessment of children: Behavioral and clinical applications (4th ed.). San Diego, CA: Jerome M. Sattler, Publisher, Inc.

Shin, J., Deno, S., & Espin, C. (2000). Technical adequacy of the maze task for curriculum-based measurement of reading growth. *Journal of Special Education, 34*(3), 164–172.

Skiba, R. J., Knesting, K. & Bush, L. D. (2002). Culturally competent assessment: More than nonbiased tests. *Journal of Child and Family Studies, 11*(1), 61–78.

Smagorinsky, P. (1995). The social construction of data: Methodological problems of investigating learning the zone of proximal development. *Review of Educational Research, 65*, 191–212.

Spies, R. A., & Plake, S. (Eds.) (2005). *The sixteenth mental measurements yearbook.* Lincoln, NE: Buros Institute of Mental Measurement.

Steel, R. G. D., & Torrie, J. H. (1960). *Principles and procedures of statistics,* New York: McGraw-Hill.

Taylor, R. L. (2009). *Assessment of exceptional students: Educational and psychological procedures* (8th ed.). Upper Saddle River, NJ: Merrill/Pearson Education.

Thurman, S. K., & McGrath, M. C. (2008). Environmentally based assessment practices: Viable alternatives to standardized assessment for assessing emergent literacy skills in young children. *Reading & Writing Quarterly, 24*(1), 7–24.

Trivette, C. M., & Dunst, C. J. (1990). Assessing family strengths and family functioning style. *Topics in Early Childhood Special Education, 10*(1), 16–35.

Tusing, M. E., & Ford, L. (2004). Examining preschool cognitive abilities using a CHC framework. *International Journal of Testing, 4*(2), 91–114.

Upton, G., & Cook, I. (2008). *Oxford Dictionary of Statistics.* Oxford, UK: Oxford University Press.

Urbina, S. (2004). *Essentials of psychological testing.* New York: Wiley.

VanDerHeyden, A. M., Broussard, C., & Cooley, A. (2006). Further development of measures of early math performance for preschoolers. *Journal of School Psychology, 44*(6), 533–553.

VanDerHeyden, A. M., Witt, J. C., Naquin, G., & Noell, G. (2001). The reliability and validity of curriculum-based measurement readiness probes for kindergarten students. *School Psychology Review, 30*(3), 363–382.

Vygotsky, L. S. (1978). *Mind in society.* Cambridge, MA: Harvard University Press.

Wesson, K. A. (2001). The "Volvo effect": Questioning standardized tests. *Young Children, 56*(2), 16–18.

Whitehead, L. C., & Deiner, P. L. (1990). Family assessment: Parent and professional evaluation. *Topics in Early Childhood Special Education, 10*(1), 63–77.

Willoughby, M., Kupersmidt, J., & Bryant, D. (2001). Overt and covert dimensions of antisocial behavior in early childhood. *Journal of Abnormal Child Psychology, 29*(3), 177–187.

Wortham, S. C. (2008). *Assessment in early childhood education* (5th ed.). Upper Saddle River, NJ: Merrill/Pearson Education.

Assessment Models

CHAPTER OBJECTIVES

By the end of the chapter, you will have a clearer understanding of alternative assessment approaches and will be able to articulate informed responses to the questions following Anna's case. The chapter will discuss curriculum-based assessment as an alternative to conventional assessment in early childhood and will introduce you to a variety of models commonly used to administer assessment in early childhood special education settings. Finally, you will be able to make knowledgeable decisions about assessment models

that best fit the unique needs of a child with exceptional learning needs.

This chapter content addresses Council for Exceptional Children/Division for Early Childhood (CEC/DEC) Standard 2 (Development and Characteristics of Learners), CEC/DEC Standard 8 (Assessment), and National Association for the Education of Young Children (NAEYC) Standard 3 (Observing, Documenting, and Assessing to Support Young Children and Families).

Assessing Anna

Anna is a 2-month-old infant who was referred for early intervention services by the local children's hospital. She was born at 30 weeks of gestation (normal gestation is 40 to 42 weeks) weighing 3 pounds, 4 ounces. At that time, she was transported to the neonatal intensive care unit (NICU) and within 48 hours, the nurse noticed a rhythmic movement of her left limbs. She was placed on medication for possible seizure activity that was later confirmed by an electroencephalogram (EEG). Anna was also diagnosed as having retinopathy of prematurity stage 5 (a cause of

visual impairment or blindness in premature infants). This resolved within the first few weeks of her hospitalization. She showed signs of apnea and continues to be monitored with an apnea monitor. Presently, she startles frequently to environmental sounds, causing irritability. She is bottle-fed and is experiencing colic on a regular basis.

Anna is the first child and first grandchild for the maternal and paternal grandparents. Her parents, Mindy and Wyatt are well educated: Mindy has a master's degree in special education and Wyatt has a teaching degree in middle school social studies.

> After 25 days, Anna was discharged from the NICU and within the first week at home, the family was contacted by the area early intervention program. An appointment was set up and Anna's family received a visit from an early interventionist who explained the program to them. At this meeting, a second meeting was scheduled for completion of the initial developmental assessment. A team comprised of an early interventionist, nurse, occupational therapist, and physical therapist would visit the family. You are the early interventionist who will be providing support to Anna and her family. You know very little about the family except for what has been included in the hospital reports.

Based on this case study, what other information would you like to know about the family in order to conduct the initial assessment? Where would the initial assessment take place? Are there unique assessment considerations that would allow you to understand the needs of Anna and her family? What assessment model would best fit the needs of this family?

ALTERNATIVE ASSESSMENT MODELS

Alternative assessment approaches have been explored for decades in early childhood special education. When the Individuals with Disabilities Act (IDEA) mandated programs and supports for young children, the field of assessment was dominated by standardized measurements used primarily for diagnosis and evaluation of older students with exceptionalities. Traditional measurements focused on performance rather than process and gathered normative information from typically developing children, without consideration for the unique growth and development of children with exceptional learning needs. There were also concerns that some programs used standardized screening tools to qualify young children for early intervention services (McLean, Wolery, & Bailey, 2004). Many questioned whether one could accurately quantify the intellect of infants and toddlers, especially because infant intelligence is measured through **sensorimotor development**, while older children and adult intelligence is measured primarily through language skills. Researchers also asserted that developmental characteristics are not consistent from infancy through adulthood and therefore cannot be measured using the same assessment tools (Neisworth & Bagnato, 1992).

Early childhood educators were frustrated with erroneous outcomes for many reasons. However, most were concerned that the assessments resulted in wrongful placement, inaccurate program planning, and unreliable monitoring of ongoing developmental growth (Neisworth & Bagnato, 2004). Thus, **curriculum-based assessment** tools were designed as authentic and functional alternatives to standardized assessment (Deno, 2003; Macy & Bricker, 2006; Macy & Hoyt-Gonzalas, 2007). These measurements identified a child's strengths and needs according to skills embedded in the program curriculum and served several purposes, including program planning and a feasible way to monitor child progress (Hooper & Umansky, 2004). Over the past several years, several curriculum-based assessments have been developed. Measurements commonly used in early childhood special education are Brigance Inventory of Early Development II, Carolina Curriculum for Infants and Toddlers with Special Needs and Carolina Curriculum for Preschoolers with Special Needs, Transdisciplinary Play-Based Assessment, and Hawaii Early Learning Profile (HELP).

Brigance Inventory of Early Development II (Brigance IED II, 2004) is an example of a curriculum-based assessment initially developed in 1978. The initial purpose of administering this assessment was to assist in creating program plans for children. It assesses the overall development of children from birth through age 7. It includes comprehensive assessments and screening tools and has a standardized component that is frequently administered to determine eligibility when a child transitions from an early intervention program or is about to enter a school-based program.

Carolina Curriculum for Infants and Toddlers with Special Needs and Carolina Curriculum for Preschoolers with Special Needs, Third Edition (2004), has become a popular curriculum-based assessment specifically designed to measure the growth and progress of young children with exceptionalities. Both assessments categorize skills in the five developmental domains: gross motor, fine motor, language, cognition, and social-emotional. A child's needs are measured primarily through observation and are linked to curriculum activities with ongoing evaluation of acquisition and skill mastery.

Transdisciplinary Play-Based Assessment, Second Edition (2008), was developed in 1990 by Toni Linder. It assesses cognitive, language, social-emotional, and sensorimotor skills through observation in a highly structured play environment that is organized into five phases:

- *Phase 1:* The child initiates all of the play activities.
- *Phase 2:* The assessor initiates some but not all of the play activities.
- *Phase 3:* The child interacts with a peer.
- *Phase 4:* The child interacts with her or his parents.
- *Phase 5:* The session concludes with a snack given to the child and the peer.

Hawaii Early Learning Profile (HELP) is a curriculum-based assessment that measures ongoing development from birth to 36 months of age. It categorizes skills into six developmental domains, including cognitive, language, gross motor, fine motor, social-emotional, and self-help skills. It is designed to be a play-based assessment, with the environment being prearranged by the evaluator. The assessment package includes an activity guide to be used by the educator, activities for the home environment, and wall charts for parents and teachers to log ongoing and emerging progress in each developmental domain. The assessment has been updated several times since its first edition; the most recent update occurred in 2007.

A multiplicity of alternative approaches emerged to accommodate both curriculum-based assessments and informal and observational assessment tools. These models include the following:

- Performance-based
- Authentic
- Judgment-based
- Portfolio
- Play-based
- Dynamic

Each model was founded in best practice, intending to ensure the most reliable picture of the young child. However, many educational programs have combined various models and use an individualized approach based on the needs of the family and the child.

BREAKPOINT PRACTICE

1. When thinking about Anna, discuss the advantages and disadvantages of traditional testing versus curriculum-based testing.
2. Which assessment tool would give the most comprehensive and accurate information about Anna?
3. What challenges do you see in providing assessment in the home environment?
4. When administering assessment through alternative methods, can you think of any threats to assessment validity?

Performance-Based Assessment

Performance-based assessment looks at the child's performance in a variety of situations and can encompass other assessment models such as portfolio assessment (Lerner, Lowenthal, & Egan, 2003). An example is giving the child the opportunity to drink from a cup during snack time, after free play, in the morning, and at the end of the day, and using a variety of cups of different shapes and sizes. Through observation, information is gathered on the child's ability to perform this task in each situation and then decisions are made about whether the skill is mastered.

Performance-based assessment is easy to implement because the evaluator has control over the settings and the activities. Typically, the setting is designed to simulate a real-life experience. However, a natural setting is optional and is not required in order to observe a specific skill.

Authentic Assessment

Authentic assessment became a common assessment model when the concept of **natural environment** emerged as a key issue in service delivery to infants and toddlers with exceptional learning needs. It differs from the performance-based model because assessment takes place in natural settings through real-life situations (Cohen & Spenciner, 2007).

Authentic assessment is easily implemented in home-based programs with infants and toddlers. For example, while observing a 6-month-old infant who is lying on a blanket on the floor with toys within reach, the evaluator(s) can observe skills in all five developmental domains. Gross motor development is to observe as the infant naturally explores the environment. Fine motor skills are assessed by watching the baby reach for and play with toys, and language skills are assessed through observation of spontaneous vocalizations as well as interactions with a familiar person.

Authentic assessment is also easily implemented in the preschool setting through observation of a child's movements and interactions throughout the day. The daycare or early childhood

© michaeljung/Shutterstock.com

classroom is also conducive to ongoing assessment over a period of time and lends itself to observations of a specific skill in a variety of settings at various times during the day.

Judgment-Based Assessment

Bagnato and Neisworth (1990) introduced **judgment-based assessment (JBA)** to early childhood special education and designed the System to Plan Early Childhood Services (SPECS), which includes professional opinions when making critical decisions about educational placement. JBA is considered a **transdisciplinary approach** that meets the Individuals with Disabilities Education Improvement Act (IDEIA) 2004 criteria for using informed clinical opinion as part of comprehensive assessment of young children (Individuals with Disabilities Education Improvement Act [IDEIA], 2004). Professional opinion encompasses the expertise of all members of the assessment team, including parents and caregivers. The expected outcome is that significant information that otherwise could be overlooked by a formal assessment is shared with the team and valued in the decision-making process (Fleischer & Belgredan, 1990).

Judgment-based assessment also considers information gathered from checklists, questionnaires, anecdotal records, and interviews or conversations with family members and professionals who have observed the child in a variety of settings (McLean, Wolery, & Bailey, 2004). The model allows for consideration of several different variables such as temperament, behavior, and environmental characteristics (Fleischer & Belgredan, 1990). Many times, parents and caregivers complete these assessments, providing valuable information about a child's behavior across several environments and time periods, for example, information about sleep habits or play with siblings, and information about food preferences, eating habits, favorite play toys, and favorite activities.

The JBA model works well when collecting data about the abilities of children with significant exceptional needs, especially when it is difficult to obtain accurate assessment information through formal and informal assessments. In these situations, JBA typically provides the supplemental information needed to fill in the gaps due to limited responses of these children (Lerner, Lowenthal, & Egan, 2003).

A commonly used developmental screening tool that is administered using the judgment-based model is the Ages and Stages Questionnaire (Bricker et al., 1999). It is frequently distributed to parents and teachers in Head Start programs and child find programs and by pediatricians.

Portfolio Assessment

Children with exceptional learning needs have notoriously been portrayed according to their needs rather than their abilities. Ever since educators have been writing individualized goals and objectives, they have concentrated on what the child needs to learn rather than strengths in skills or skill development. Campbell, Milbourne, and Silverman (2001) conducted a study involving 65 caregivers who were instructed on how to complete a portfolio for a child with exceptional learning needs who was attending their daycare programs. The outcomes showed that the portfolio process overwhelming emphasized the child's strengths and abilities rather than weaknesses and created a more positive communication and rapport between those running the program and the family.

Portfolio assessment is a comprehensive process that is usually completed by the classroom teacher over a period of several months or the school year. It is a collection of information that documents the skills, abilities, and performance in all developmental areas. It can be used to record developmental change or improvement over the school year. It can be a time-consuming process; however, the benefits are well worth the time and effort needed to successfully employ this assessment model (Gelfer & Perkins, 1998).

The portfolio can serve as a positive communication tool between educators and parents because it provides concrete documentation of the improvements made over a period of time and is easy to understand (Cohen & Spencer, 2007). Sometimes educators use the portfolio as a "book" about the child that includes pictures (possibly a school portrait on the cover), hand prints, and growth charts throughout the year. When the portfolio concentrates on what the child can do instead of what the child can't do, it creates a positive, relaxed communication between the family and the school.

Gelfer and Perkins (1998) suggest that the portfolio include important documents such as individualized education program (IEP) information; test results, including checklists and curriculum-based assessments; program goals and objectives; work samples; teacher observations; progress notes and data collection; parent meeting summaries; and documentation of communications with parents. Additional portfolio artifacts can include writing and drawing samples, cutting and coloring samples, art projects, photos of projects, play preferences, activities within the school day, videos, and audiotapes.

The portfolio can be organized in a variety of ways, including three-ring binders, file boxes, and electronic files. Electronic portfolios can be complicated mostly because it requires the educator to be technologically savvy, with expertise on web-page design and uploading pictures and scanning artifacts. It would also require that family members have access to technology and that they have the technology literacy needed for locating and viewing the portfolio. The key to maintaining a portfolio is to be organized and comprehensive in what is collected. Ensure that it is a comprehensive profile of the child's abilities and needs. Here is an example of the organization of one portfolio:

Background information

    Demographic information

    General health and medical information

    Permission slips

    IEP or other program plan

Learning characteristics

    Description of play skills

    Play environment preferences and dislikes

    Activity preference and dislikes

    Learning style preferences and dislikes

    Supporting evidence as appropriate (protocols, checklists)

Developmental strengths and needs

    Observations, assessment in developmental areas

    Completed protocols and checklists

    Bullet points of developmental abilities

    Behavior logs

    Anecdotal records

Recommendations

    Activities for families to incorporate in the home

    Adaptations and modifications

BREAKPOINT PRACTICE

1. Which assessment models complement each other in the assessment process?
2. How would you conduct authentic assessment for a 3-year-old child who is blind and living in a foster home?
3. Discuss situations where performance-based assessment would be more appropriate than authentic assessment.
4. What would be some pros and cons of implementing portfolio assessment?

Play-Based Assessment

Play-based assessment was first considered a best practice in the assessment of young children in the early 1990s when Toni Linder (1993) developed the Transdisciplinary Play-Based Assessment. The play-based model is developmental, transdisciplinary, holistic, and dynamic. It makes sense that children's abilities are most authentic when doing what they do best, and that is play. Play-based assessment takes place in any environment where there are developmentally appropriate play materials readily available to the child. It is an informal process that facilitates natural behavior and thus shows more typical developmental skills (Lerner et al., 2003).

Myers and McBride (1996) conducted a study on the developmental assessment of 40 children under the age of 3. They divided the children into two groups, with one group being assessed using the multidisciplinary, standardized assessment and the other assessed using a transdisciplinary play-based assessment. The outcomes showed that the play-based approach yielded an array of positive outcomes, including the fact that it was more time efficient. In a multidisciplinary assessment process, it may take weeks or even months for professionals to schedule appointments around typical family issues such as illnesses, family activities, and transportation availability. In play-based assessment, the professionals and family meet on the same day at the same time, which alleviates the need to work around many busy schedules.

Play-based assessment facilitates quality assessment of skills in all developmental domains. The play setting is typically arranged to fit the needs of the assessment. For example, if the purpose of the assessment is to evaluate social-emotional behavior, the setting may include play items such as dolls to represent family members. If the primary purpose of the assessment is to observe motor skills, then climbing toys, slides, tricycles, and steps may be in the play area (Linder, 1993; Dykeman, 2006).

Play-based assessment is arranged so that only the child, parent(s), and facilitator are in the immediate play area, with the facilitator sitting a comfortable distance from the parent–child interaction. The other team members, who are gathering information, position themselves on the perimeter of the area and observe targeted skills in their area of expertise (Linder, 1993; Meyers & McBride, 1996). For a 3-year-old girl who has global developmental delay, her team may consist of an early childhood teacher, special educator, occupational therapist, physical therapist, and a speech-language pathologist. The assessment may take place in her early childhood classroom in the kitchen area. Her mother would be interacting with her in this area, with her early childhood teacher serving as the assessment facilitator. Each team member would be positioned around the perimeter of the play area, allowing natural interaction between the parent and child, yet close enough to observe the child's developmental abilities. Periodically, a team member, such as the occupational therapist, may request that the parent or coach introduce an activity that may require the use of a specific skill, such as finger dexterity. The teacher would facilitate this by placing materials in the play area that elicit this skill, such as play dough for making cookies. Following the assessment, the team convenes to discuss results and share observations.

Dynamic Assessment

The **dynamic assessment** model is based on Vygotsky's theory of the **zone of proximal development** and the premise that there is an ongoing relationship between learning and development. Lidz (1991) stated that "dynamic assessment is typically contrasted with static assessment. This reflects the fact that dynamic assessment focuses on learning process, in contrast to the traditional assessment focus on already learned products" (pp. 3–4). Dynamic assessment is an approach to learning that is so logical that most educators believe that they are already implementing it (Lidz, 1991). Those who support this model as best practice in assessment of young children agree that it is a reliable indicator of potential instead of performance (McLean, Wolery, & Bailey, 2004). With dynamic assessment, learning is supported by **scaffolding**, or the provision of supports that allow learning to take place (Vygotsky, 1978). The two most common dynamic assessment designs are test-teach-retest and successive cueing. Both techniques contribute to the successful measurement of child learning across all developmental domains (Campione, Brown, Ferrara, & Bryant, 1984).

The test-teach-retest approach begins with the evaluator's assessment of a child's skill acquisition. If mastery is not observed, the evaluator then provides remediation and the supports necessary for successful completion of the task. The skill is tested again. If the task still could not be completed independently, more supports and/or remediation is provided to assist the child in reaching task mastery (Lidz, 1991; Campione et al., 1984). The steps are repeated until the child is able to complete the task alone. For example, the educator may want to assess Erin's cutting skills. As Erin works on a project in the art center, the teacher observes her ability to successfully cut a piece of paper into two pieces (initial test of this skill). If the teacher observes that Erin is unable to hold the scissors in order for the blades to open and close for cutting, the remediation may include hand-over-hand assistance in placing her fingers in the openings and helping her open and close the scissors without actually cutting the paper. If she is then successful at operating the scissors, the scissors and paper are again given to her (retest). If she is successful, the skill is considered mastered. If she is not, the teacher provides more assistance and may modify the materials, perhaps using loop scissors and a thicker piece of paper. This process repeats until Erin is able to independently use a pair of scissors to cut a piece of paper into two pieces.

With successive cueing, there is no test-and-retest format. Instead, as the child engages in an activity, supports are offered as needed in order to attain successful task completion (Lidz, 1991; Campione et al., 1984). In Erin's case, instead of testing and retesting her skill level, the evaluator may observe her unsuccessful attempts to cut with a pair of scissors and provide levels of support until she can cut successfully. Prompting or cueing may be as involved as providing hand-over-hand support or as simple as having her cut with loop scissors.

Revisiting Anna

The first step in looking at the assessment process for Anna and her family is to reread the medical information, noting any information that would affect the assessment process or assessment results. In this situation it would be easy to assume that the family needs are minimal. However, this should not be assumed based on the education and possible knowledge base of the family. It is best to visit with Anna's parents and find out specific information regarding Anna's personality, temperament, likes, and dislikes and most comfortable environments and times of the day when she is most alert. Because of her age and medical conditions, assessment in the home environment may best fit the family needs. However, this must be discussed and decided in collaboration with the family. Also, a play-based model would be optimal for gathering accurate information about her developmental strengths and needs. Because of Anna's age, she may not be awake or alert during part of or possibly the entire planned assessment visit. Therefore, judgment-based assessment would be beneficial in providing valuable information about her skills and abilities that may not be observed during the assessment period. A number of curriculum-based assessments can give thorough information about Anna's strengths and needs. Also, it may be helpful to consider the unique characteristics of a child who is born prematurely.

Activities

1. When thinking about Anna and the assessment models, which particular assessments do you think best fit her needs? Which would be least appropriate?
2. When looking at the unique characteristics of Anna's family, what information would you assume and/or attempt to elicit in the family interview?
3. Assessment of a young infant may be difficult for what reasons?
4. Assume that you will conduct a play-based arena assessment. Draw a diagram of how the room would look; include which professionals would be part of the assessment process.

Websites

Authentic Assessment
http://uclid.org:8080/uclid/pdfs/
  Practice_Guide_Authentic_Assessment.pdf

Dynamic Assessment
http://www.dynamicassessment.com/index.html

Early Childhood Education and Assessment
http://www.hoagiesgifted.org/eric/faq/ec-asses.html

Evaluation Methodology
http://www.nectac.org/topics/quality/evalmeth.asp

Hawaii Early Learning Profile
http://www.vort.com/training/help4-3.html

Performance-based Assessment
http://www.projectappleseed.org/assesment.html

The Power of Play-Based Assessment
http://speech-language-pathology-audiology.advanceweb.
  com/Article/The-Power-of-Play-Based-Assessment-2.
  aspx

References

Bagnato, S. J., & Neisworth J. T. (1990). System to plan early childhood services (specs). Manual for a team assessment/intervention system. Circle Pines, MN: American Guidance Service.

Bricker, D., Squires J., Potter L., Nickel R., Twombly, E., & Farrell J. (1999). *Ages and stages questionnaires.* Baltimore, MD: Brookes.

Campbell, P. H., Milbourne, S. A., & Silverman, C. (2001). Strengths-based child portfolios: A professional development activity to alter perspectives of children with special needs. *Topics in Early Childhood Special Education, 21*(3), 152–162.

Campione, J. C., Brown, A. L., Ferrara, R. A., & Bryant, N. R. (1984). The zone of proximal development; Implications for individual differences and learning. In B. Rogoff & J. V. Wertsch (Eds.), *Children's learning in the zone of proximal development. New directions for child development.* San Francisco: Jossey-Bass.

Cohen, L. G., & Spenciner, L. J. (2007). *Assessment of children and youth with special needs* (3rd ed.). Upper Saddle River, NJ: Pearson Education.

Deno, S. L. (2003). Developments in curriculum-based measurement. *Journal of Special Education, 37*(3), 184–192.

Dunst, C. J. (2000). Re-visiting "rethinking early intervention." *Topics in Early Childhood Special Education, 20*(2), 95–104.

Dykeman, B. F. (2006). Alternative strategies in assessing special education needs. *Education, 127*(2), 265–273.

Fleischer, K. H., & Belgredan, J. H. (1990). An overview of judgment-based assessment. *Topics in Early Childhood Special Education, 10*(3), 13–24.

Gelfer, J. I., & Perkins, P. G. (1998). Portfolios: Focus on young children. *Teaching Exceptional Children, 31*(2), 44–51.

Hooper, S. R., & Umansky W. (2004). *Young children with special needs* (4th ed.). Upper Saddle River, NJ: Merrill/Pearson Education.

Individuals with Disabilities Education Improvement Act (IDEIA). (2004). Retrieved on February 6, 2008, from http://IDEIA.ed.gov/explore/home

Lerner, J. W., Lowenthal, B., & Egan, R. W. (2003). *Preschool children with special needs: Children at risk and children with disabilities* (2nd ed.). Boston, MA: Allyn & Bacon.

Lidz, C. S. (1991). *Practitioner's guide to dynamic assessment.* New York: Guilford Press.

Linder, T. (1993). *Transdisciplinary play-based assessment: A functional approach to working with young children* (rev. ed.). Baltimore, MD: Paul H. Brookes.

Macy, M., & Bricker, D. (2006). Practical applications for using a curriculum-based assessment to create embedded learning opportunities for young children. *Young Exceptional Children, 9*(4), 12–21.

Macy, M., & Hoyt-Gonzalas, K. (2007). A linked system approach to early childhood special education eligibility assessment. *Teaching Exceptional Children, 39*(3), 40–44.

McLean, M., Wolery, M., & Bailey, D. B. (2004). *Assessing infants and preschoolers with special needs* (3rd ed.). Upper Saddle River, NJ: Merrill/Pearson Education.

Meyers, C. L., & McBride, S. L. (1996). Transdisciplinary, play-based assessment in early childhood special education: An examination of social validity. *Topics in Early Childhood Special Education, 16*(1), 102–126.

Neisworth, J. T., & Bagnato, S. (1992). The case against intelligence testing in early intervention. *Topics in Early Childhood Special Education, 12*(1), 1–20.

Neisworth, J. T., & Bagnato, S. J. (2004). The mismeasure of young children: The authentic assessment alternative. *Infants and Young Children, 17*, 198–212.

Vygotsky, L. S. (1978). *Mind in society: The development of higher psychological processes.* Cambridge, MA: Harvard University Press.

Environmental Analysis

CHAPTER 7

CHAPTER OBJECTIVES

This chapter is designed to provide you with a foundation for understanding the role of the environment in supporting student learning and the means to implement an environmental analysis. You will be able to identify formal and informal assessments, the reasons you might choose both types, and the ways in which the curricula can be tied to assessment outcomes. Finally, you will be able to articulate special considerations unique to children with special needs, and their families, that should be a factor in your decision making regarding environmental assessment.

This chapter addresses Council for Exceptional Children/Division for Early Childhood (CEC/DEC) Standard 5 (Learning Environments and Social Interaction) and National Association for the Education of Young Children (NAEYC) Standard 1 (Promoting Child Development and Learning).

Assessing Carlos

Carlos is a 4-year-old who came to preschool with many behaviors that caused concern for his parents. Carlos's parents described him as very rambunctious, failing to recognize limits, and using very risky behavior that they feared would hurt him. At school, Carlos even has difficulty maneuvering his environment and tends to be "at odds" with his teachers and peers. He insists on his own agenda. When excited, Carlos can be found "walking around on his toes," making loud sounds, running into other children "without noticing," and becoming very upset when others are playing with "his toys" or routines and schedules change.

The members of the teaching staff are aware of his parents' concerns, but they are increasingly frustrated both with Carlos's behavior, which they feel is taking away from other children, and his parents' frequent questions about their success with him. The teachers are attempting to manage Carlos's behavior by using time out; behavioral rewards; and, when required, physical restraint to keep Carlos from running away. The preschool staff members are focused on doing group activities at tables, and they are particularly frustrated that Carlos does not want to sit down, focus on their activities, or interact with other children around these activities. Carlos complains that people are "mean to him" at school.

Carlos's parents both work full-time and have two other children. They are active, involved parents, but, as recent immigrants, they are still learning the U.S. school system. They rely on the preschool for assessment of their son's needs and to provide a comfortable learning environment to meet his needs. They are starting to feel that this is not happening. They would like Carlos to have more fun at preschool. They are particularly upset that he has to sit at a table and work on things that are difficult for him. Carlos's parents have asked the staff members to modify the curriculum and accommodate the environment, but the staff members are unclear about how to do so.

What assessments, formal or informal, might you use to assess Carlos's performance in the preschool setting? How might observations help with understanding his needs and the program response? What useful information can observations and assessments provide for curriculum planning?

By the conclusion of this chapter, you will be able to answer the questions posed in the case study about Carlos. In addition, you will be able to identify assessments that might be appropriate to address Carlos's, and his family's, needs. You will be able to describe checklists and rating scales, and provide examples, that support your work with Carlos.

EARLY CHILDHOOD ENVIRONMENTS

Early childhood environments provide the contexts in which children learn, grow, and thrive through the development of skills associated with cognition, language, and socialization. The goal of early childhood education is to support children in the development of their abilities for understanding the world around them, gaining mastery of their environments, and assuming the dispositions necessary for participation in future academic settings. Through hands-on experiences, a foundation is formed by which children use their practical knowledge to master abstract thinking and to engage in purposeful pursuits that increase academic abilities.

Through play and social interactions, children increase competencies in managing themselves and others while learning important concepts that organize their thinking and assist them in mentally mapping their actions within the parameters of the learning environment. Quality environments are known to support development in the critical domains of the early childhood curriculum (Gomby et al., 1995; Bowman, Donovan, & Burns, 2001), so it is vital that early childhood educators consider the environment along with curricular approaches that support children across a variety of developmental trajectories. This work on the part of early childhood educators must include both typically developing preschoolers and their peers with special needs.

Early childhood programs must be designed carefully to enhance and optimize learning opportunities for children. Children need to "see, hear, touch, and connect with their surroundings" (Blaustein, 2005, p. 4). Consideration of the educational setting for ensuring these opportunities is at the heart of environmental assessment.

It has long been known that children must construct their own meaning in order to learn new knowledge, integrate that knowledge into meaningful schemas, and assume the roles of both follower and leader as they engage in socially mediated learning and plans of action (Piaget,

1955; Vygotsky, 1978). Maria Montessori, the Italian physician who developed the Montesorri approach, suggests that early childhood curricula include sensorimotor experiences on which children can build skills of observation and exploration, and develop higher learning skills through self-directed action. These learning experiences support the development of the whole child across the critical domains that bind experience with enhanced cognition and socialization.

Environment has been defined as the "circumstances, objects, or other conditions by which one is surrounded" (www.merriam-webster.com). Optimal development for children is contingent on the experiences they have in early learning environments. A basic assumption is that high-quality environments are growth-producing and must be carefully constructed in order to realize outcomes consistent with the development of skills and dispositions necessary for life in school and beyond. This intent must be clearly articulated in the organization of space; materials; and the interplay among children, adults, and peers as a means to that end. Given what is known about the importance of quality environments, early childhood professionals must create environments that engage children, including children with special needs, in learning activities that promote their development across all domains.

Environmental Analysis

An **environmental analysis** can be defined as the systematic examination of environments for elements that promote the development of young children with special needs. Many questions may come to mind in thinking about an environmental analysis. For example, does the environment reflect what you intend? What does the environment look like from the child's perspective? The family's perspective? Do curriculum, materials, and teaching approaches adequately support development?

Using an ecological framework designed by Apter and Conoley (1984), Sheridan and Gutkin (2000, p. 489) set forth four basic assumptions in addressing the needs of all children within the context of their development:

1. Each student is an inseparable part of a small social system;
2. Disturbance is not viewed as a disease located within the body of the student but, rather, as discordance (a lack of balance) in the system;
3. Discordance may be defined as a disparity between an individual's abilities and the demands or expectations of the environment—"failure to match" between child and system; and
4. The goal of any intervention is to make the system work.

For intervention to be successful with young children, especially those with exceptional developmental needs, it is important to understand these ecological assumptions that suggest that a child, situated within a context or place, can thrive or fall behind based on the necessary tools provided by the environment.

Early childhood special education personnel should pay close attention to the environments they create because environment is clearly a critical factor and indicator of child performance. Whether one is evaluating seating arrangements, material selection, or the use of relationship-based approaches, the ultimate goal is the provision of environments that are conducive to learning and that promote development across all domains (Dunst et al., 2001).

Numerous initiatives have been undertaken by state departments of education and national organizations to address the roles and goals of early childhood settings since the

National Association for the Education of Young Children (NAEYC) issued their position statement (Bredekamp, 1987) regarding **developmentally appropriate practices**, or evidence-based (or research-based) practices used as guiding principles for intervention, such as the Regional Educational Laboratories' Early Childhood Collaboration Network (1995) report highlighting eight indicators appropriate for the evaluation of environments for young children:

1. Children receive age and developmentally appropriate care and education.
2. Learning experiences allow children to work, learn, and grow at their own rate and developmental level.
3. The environment is flexible and includes age, developmentally, and culturally appropriate activities that support active learning.
4. Children are engaged in learning through play; exploration; and child-initiated, hands-on activities that are supported by adult guidance and encouragement.
5. Children's progress is assessed through developmentally appropriate methods.
6. Care and education assessment practices relate directly to the needs of individual children, including their special needs, and are reviewed as the children grow.
7. Policies and practices promote continuity of care and education as children progress through various early childhood settings and services.
8. Adult learning opportunities support cross-agency implementation of services that reflect understanding of child and family development. (p. 88)

Various guidelines exist to drive evidence-based practices and decision making in creating and sustaining appropriate environments. **Evidence-based practices** are principles based on empirical research that promote quality outcomes for children. The National Association for the Education of Young Children's (2009) position statement on developmentally appropriate, evidence-based practices provides five broad domains for consideration:

1. Creating a caring community of learners;
2. Teaching to enhance development and learning;
3. Planning curriculum to meet important goals;
4. Assessing children's development and learning; and
5. Establishing reciprocal relationships with families

The Division of Early Childhood (DEC) of the Council of Exceptional Children (CEC) includes 240 practices within seven strands (Sandall, Hemmeter, Smith, & McLean, 2005):

1. Assessment;
2. Child-focused interventions;
3. Family-based practices;
4. Interdisciplinary models;
5. Technology applications;
6. Personnel preparation; and
7. Policies, procedures, and system change.

It is important for educators of young children to consult best-practice models for intervention, which are available through various agencies and organizations, to employ more successfully recommended practices and to create environmental contexts that support children, families, and the ongoing evaluation, including self-assessment, reflection, and program improvement.

© poplasen/Fotolia

BREAKPOINT PRACTICE

1. Do you believe the environment for Carlos is flexible and meets his developmental level? Why or why not?
2. Do you believe the classroom offers Carlos developmentally appropriate instruction? If not, what would you suggest as a way to evaluate his needs in this regard?
3. How might the teachers work with Carlos, and other students, to create a more caring community?

ENVIRONMENTAL RATING SCALES

Researchers at the Frank Porter Graham Child Development Institute (University of North Carolina) have given considerable focus to the development of scales that evaluate early childhood environments. **Environmental rating scales** are defined as research-based instruments that have been designed to evaluate early childhood environments and settings. Among the measures they have devised is the Early Childhood Environment Rating Scale—Revised (ECERS–R) (Harms, Clifford, & Cryer, 1998), the Infant Toddler Environment Rating Scale—Revised (ITERS–R) (Harms, Cryer, & Clifford, 2003), and the Family Child Care Environment Rating Scale—Revised (FCCERS–R) (Harms, Cryer, & Clifford, 2007).

The ECERS–R is designed to evaluate the quality of programs for children from ages 2.5 to 5. The inventory is completed through observation of a classroom setting for a minimum of 2 hours, with additional time allotted as needed, and is based on a 7-point Likert scale. The inventory provides for interviews following the observation and "notes for clarification" that may bring greater definition to items that are difficult to capture through the observation process. The ECERS–R is comprised of 43 items organized into seven subscales: (a) space and furnishings, (b) personal-care routines, (c) language-reasoning, (d) activities, (e) interactions, (f) program structures, and (e) parents and staff.

The ECERS–R is a reliable, valid instrument that is easy to score. It provides summary scores across items in each subscale with rating sheets that are described as "simple to use." The inventory can be used for self-assessment and for program evaluation and improvement. Because the ECERS–R encompasses basic elements of most early childhood settings, it can be used in a number of venues, including community and childcare programs.

The ITERS–R (Harms, Cryer, & Clifford, 2003) is modeled after the ECERS, but it is slightly different in its focus on early development, replacing "language-reasoning" with "talking and listening" as a subscale. The instrument is designed to evaluate the quality of programs and interventions for children from birth to age 2.5. Similar to the ECERS–R, the infant-toddler scale relies on direct observation and is followed up with interviews to determine rankings across items and subscales. Like the ECER–R, evaluation of each item is based on a 7-point Likert scale, with administration lasting approximately 3 hours.

Because many children spend a significant amount of time in childcare settings, the FCCERS–R (Harms, Cryer, & Clifford, 2007), comprised of 37 items organized into seven subscales, serves as an effective evaluation tool for family childcare settings. The seven subscales are very similar to the constructs for the ITEFS–R and ECERS–R, as are the scoring procedures. Based on the initial instrument designed in 1989, the revisions include, among others, updated indicators regarding the use of technology as a tool with children and a greater focus on the cultural sensitivity needed to meet the diversity reflected in many preschool settings today. See Figure 7.1 for a comparison of subscales and items for this series of assessment tools.

Paradigms in early childhood special education are changing, including legal and best-practice policies regarding the use of **natural environments** to support young children's learning and development (Dunst, Bruder, Trivette, & Hamby, 2005). Part C of the Individuals with Disabilities Education Act (IDEA, 1997) denotes that "to the maximum extent appropriate to the needs of the child, early intervention services must be provided in natural environments, including the home and community settings in which children without disabilities participate." This emphasis calls for evaluation of environments beyond the traditional settings of preschool, childcare, and related environments.

The Home Observation and Measurement of the Environment (HOME) (Caldwell & Bradley, 1984) was designed to "measure the quality and quantity of stimulation and support available to a child in the home environment. The focus is on the child in the environment and the child as a recipient of inputs from objects, events, and transactions occurring in connection with the family surroundings" (Totsika & Sylva, 2004, p. 25).

The HOME scales are actually comprised of four different instruments for children from birth to adolescence. The Infant-Toddler HOME Inventory (IT-HOME) (ages 0–3) is comprised of 43 items in six subscales: (a) parental responsivity, (b) acceptance of the child, (c) organization of the environment, (d) learning materials, (e) parental involvement, and (f) variety in experience. The IT-HOME examines the interactions between parents and children, including the manner in which the child is disciplined. Additional items evaluate how the child's time is organized, how space is utilized, and the use of daily routines. As is evidenced in these categories, a significant factor in the evaluation involves the effective and physical responses toward the child by the parent(s). Example items include the manner in which the mother vocalizes to the child and the availability of the father in daily care routines. Items to measure the quality of materials (e.g., toys, games) that support development and appropriate equipment for the very young child (e.g., car seat, high chair) are also included.

The Early Childhood HOME (EC-HOME) is designed for use with children between 3 and 6 years of age. The tool contains 55 items grouped into eight subscales: (a) learning materials,

Subscales	Items for ITERS–R	Items for ECERS–R	Items for FCCERS–R
Space and furnishings	1. Indoor space 2. Furniture for routine care and play 3. Provision for relaxation and comfort 4. Room arrangement 5. Display for children	1. Indoor space 2. Furniture for routine care, play, and learning 3. Furnishings for relaxation and comfort 4. Room arrangement for play 5. Space for privacy 6. Child-related display 7. Space for gross motor play 8. Gross motor equipment	1. Indoor space used for childcare 2. Furniture for routine care, play, and learning 3. Provision for relaxation and comfort 4. Arrangement of indoor space for childcare 5. Display for children 6. Space for privacy
Personal Care Routines	6. Greeting/departing 7. Meals/snacks 8. Nap 9. Diapering/toileting 10. Health practices 11. Safety practices	9. Greeting/departing 10. Meals/snacks 11. Nap/rest 12. Toileting/diapering 13. Health practices 14. Safety practices	7. Greeting/departing 8. Nap/rest 9. Meals/snacks 10. Diapering/toileting 11. Health practices 12. Safety practices
Listening and Talking (ITERS–R; FCCERS–R) **Language-Reasoning (ECERS–R)**	12. Helping children understand language 13. Helping children use language 14. Using books	15. Books and pictures 16. Encouraging children to communicate 17. Using language to develop reasoning skills 18. Informal use of language	13. Helping children understand language 14. Helping children use language 15. Using books
Activities	15. Fine motor 16. Active physical play 17. Art 18. Music and movement 19. Blocks 20. Dramatic play 21. Sand and water play 22. Nature/science 23. Use of TV, video, and/or computer 24. Promoting acceptance of diversity	19. Fine motor 20. Art 21. Music/movement 22. Blocks 23. Sand/water 24. Dramatic play 25. Nature/science 26. Math/number 27. Use of TV, video, and/or computers 28. Promoting acceptance of diversity	16. Fine motor 17. Art 18. Music and movement 19. Blocks 20. Dramatic play 21. Math/number 22. Nature/science 23. Sand and water play 24. Promoting acceptance of diversity 25. Use of TV, video, and/or computer 26. Active physical play

FIGURE 7.1   Subscales and Items for ITERS–R, ECERS–R, and FCCERS–R. (*continued*)

Subscales	Items for ITERS–R	Items for ECERS–R	Items for FCCERS–R
Interaction	25. Supervision of play and learning 26. Peer interaction 27. Staff–child interaction 28. Discipline	29. Supervision of gross motor activities 30. General supervision of children (other than gross motor) 31. Discipline 32. Staff–child interactions 33. Interactions among children	27. Supervision of play and learning 28. Provider–child interaction 29. Discipline 30. Interactions among children
Program Structure	29. Schedule 30. Free play 31. Group play activities 32. Provisions for children with disabilities	34. Schedule 35. Free play 36. Group time 37. Provisions for children with disabilities	31. Schedule 32. Free play 33. Group time 34. Provisions for children with disabilities
Parents and Staff (ITERS–R; ECERS–R) **Parent and Provider (FCCERS–R)**	33. Provisions for parents 34. Provisions for personal needs of staff 35. Provisions for professional needs of staff 36. Staff interaction and cooperation 37. Staff continuity 38. Supervision and evaluation of staff 39. Opportunities for professional growth	38. Provisions for parents 39. Provisions for personal needs of staff 40. Provisions for professional needs of staff 41. Staff interaction and cooperation 42. Supervision and evaluation of staff 43. Opportunities for professional growth	35. Provisions for parents 36. Balancing personal and caregiving responsibilities 37. Opportunities for professional growth 38. Provisions for professional needs

FIGURE 7.1 (*continued*)

(b) language stimulation, (c) physical environment, (d) parental responsivity, (e) learning stimulation, (f) modeling of social maturity, (g) variety in experience, and (h) acceptance of the child. The EC-HOME continues to evaluate critical interactions between parents and their children with a move toward higher-level skills, including activities directed toward intellectual development, verbal interactions that promote language development, and the use of boundaries in the caregiver–child relationship. Great emphasis is placed on the relationships between parents and children, as is evidenced in the final subcategory (acceptance), which addresses parents' use of appropriate discipline strategies for enhancing the relationship and promoting prosocial behavior.

Both the IT-HOME and the ET-HOME are structured in the form of yes or no questions, and administration takes approximately 1 hour for each. Both tools employ a semistructured interview (conversational style) format to elicit information from parents. Both tools have acceptable validity and reliability rates for use with diverse populations of families with young children (Bradley, Corwyn, McAdoo, & Garcia Coll, 2001; Totsika & Sylva, 2004).

While the evaluation of a "good environment" is appropriate for all children, it is important to consider that some children have difficulty thriving, even in "good environments." This is particularly true for children with exceptionalities, whose needs may fall outside environments that typify quality approaches.

BREAKPOINT PRACTICE

1. How might the ECERS–R be used to help staff members in organizing the environment to meet Carlos's needs?
2. Which of the subscales in the ECERS–R do you think is most important to understanding needed accommodations or modifications to the environment?
3. How might the ET-HOME be utilized with Carlos's family? What do you hope to learn from his family members using this assessment?

FUNCTIONAL BEHAVIORAL ASSESSMENT

For children whose behavioral challenges present obstacles to effective developmental outcomes, the use of a functional behavioral assessment (FBA) is indicated. **Functional behavioral assessment (FBA)** can be defined as a problem-solving process, including environmental analysis, for determining causes and functions of behavior. The FBA process, along with the development of **positive behavioral supports (PBS)** plans, or strategies designed to prevent and replace problem behaviors, can assist intervention teams in the analysis of a child's environment and the construction of positive supports to promote appropriate behaviors that are conducive to learning and development.

Use of an FBA approach is a systematic attempt to understand challenging behavior and to determine the antecedents (what happened before the behavior) and consequences (what happened after the behavior). Simply put, the FBA is an approach to understand more fully the how's and why's of behavior beyond broad interpretations or simple definitions of "bad behavior." Environmental factors are a critical component of this assessment. This problem-solving method presumes that when behaviors recur, it must serve a purpose for the child. Implementing an FBA helps identify patterns of behavior and the circumstances, including the environment, that better describe the "function" of a behavior: why the child engages in this behavior, when the child is more likely to demonstrate this behavior, and situations and environments in which this behavior is most likely to occur. The functional behavioral assessment is a process that collects global and specific information related to the child and carefully examines the environments and contexts in which the behaviors occur.

The components of a functional behavioral analysis include (a) identification of the behavior, (b) a concrete definition of the behavior (e.g., in observable, behavioral terms), (c) identification of the context in which the behavior occurs, and (d) the generation of hypotheses (brainstorming) regarding the context for the occurrence of behaviors and the consequences that continue the behavioral sequence. Assessment techniques may include indirect assessment (e.g., interviews, a review of child records), direct assessment (e.g., observations, use of standardized instruments, checklists), and (c) analysis of the data to determine patterns of behavior.

An FBA can assist in determining the appropriateness of a child's present placement; services that may be necessary to support growth, development, and learning; and how these changes may support the child in using more "acceptable" behavior. A key goal is identifying positive interventions that will help in reducing undesirable behavior and the appropriate behaviors that may be substituted to support the child in greater autonomy while using prosocial actions. Some questions that educators and interventionists might consider are the following:

- What activity is the child engaging in when the behavior occurs?
- What do you see as the purpose of the child in using this behavior?
- Who is present when the behavior occurs?
- What was the preceding activity?
- Do you observe signs or subtle cues that indicate a child's increase in frustration?
- What environmental factors are present that appear to initiate or sustain the behavior?
- What are relevant social factors, including the child's family experience, that may contribute to this behavioral pattern?

The intent of challenging behavior has been described along three dimensions: (a) behavior that gains attention and elicits desired activities and objects; (b) behavior that allows a child to avoid or escape demands or other undesired events/activities, and (c) behavior that occurs because of its sensory consequences, such as brining pleasure, relieving pain, or attempts at finding self-regulation. For young children, it is important to consider that self-regulation is a maturational process on which preschool and early learning programs focus. As such, special care should be taken in consideration of behaviors that may appear inappropriate but serve to identify next steps in support, rather than punitive measures to "correct" the behavior. Often, corrective measures serve to make behaviors more rigid because children may be unable to understand corrective measures as a response to their specific behavioral sequence (cause and effect) or be able to integrate the corrective measures into a prosocial action plan.

Barnes, O'Flynn, and Saile (2009, pp. 127–128) offer a series of important considerations that should be incorporated into plans for implementing a positive behavioral support plan for children on the autism spectrum. These considerations are appropriate for all learners in early childhood settings.

- Effective intervention occurs within relationships.
  - It takes time and effort build a positive, productive relationship.
  - Familiarity and trust allow children to respond to redirection and limit setting by adults.
- All children benefit from predictable structure and rehearsal.
  - The environment and schedules need to be organized so that children develop successful routines of prosocial performance.
  - Supports, such as cueing, modeling, and visual schedules and activity choices, support transitions necessary for successful participation.
- Supports need to account for a child's learning styles, sensory needs, and interests.
  - Providing strategies that are commensurate with a child's learning styles and interests increases motivation for participation in learning activities.
  - Respecting a child's reluctance to participate, as a response to anxiety, is necessary to help children face sensory challenges and increase risk taking.
- Learning appropriate ways for managing stress.
  - Knowing that particular environments or activities are difficult for a child suggests strategies that may reduce anxiety and promote self-regulation.
  - The identification of feelings in self and others, through role play, games, and children's books, allows children to assume alternative viewpoints about their behaviors and those of others and to build better self-perception about their own.

A systematic response to challenging behaviors requires manipulating the environment to see how children's behavior might change. The framework above provides insights into ways that the environment may be evaluated and altered to assess child performance more effectively.

While the function of the FBA is largely designed to manage challenging, disruptive behaviors, the philosophy and principles of the approach are particularly well suited to supporting children in preschool settings. For example, many children with developmental disabilities fail to communicate their needs effectively, leading to behavioral reactions that appear defiant and disrespectful. Using an environmental scan to determine the context of behavioral schemes and then manipulating that environment to observe behavioral changes form a central basis for the effective use of the FBA/PBS approach in supporting young children with special needs. The use of environmental rating scales, both formal (e.g., ECERS–R, ITERS–R) and informal (e.g., checklists, use of recommended practices), contributes to the understanding of children within their contexts of development.

BREAKPOINT PRACTICE

1. Why would you choose to use an FBA for Carlos? What would you hope to learn? What would be useful to know so that you can make appropriate environmental changes?
2. How might Carlos's family's status as new immigrants affect their views of behavior, discipline, or preschool approaches?
3. How would the use of the FBA help you in discussing potential environmental changes with Carlos's family?

SUPPORTING ASSESSMENT TOOLS

It is clear that early childhood development occurs within the contexts of the environment, relationships, and the unique characteristics of children. For children with special needs, the supports required may not be as evident without the use of measures to investigate various types of environmental characteristics relevant to the child's functioning in a given situation or setting. Snow and Hemel (2008) suggest a number of inventories that are appropriate for this purpose. For a complete list and a more comprehensive review of these measures, see http://www.acf.hhs.gov/programs/opre/hs/national_academy/reports/early_child_assess/early_child_assess.pdf.

The Assessment Profile for Early Childhood Programs (APECP; Abbot-Shinn & Sibley, 1992) is an observational checklist for the global assessment of the preschool classroom environment. It includes the following scales: (a) learning environment (the provision of and accessibility to materials and space for and accessibility of materials and space conducive to child independence); (b) scheduling (a balance and variety of activities; (c) curriculum (degree to which alternative techniques are employed, the degree to which children are encouraged to be active learners, and the role of the teacher in facilitating learning); (d) interacting (positive interactions, responsiveness, and management of children), and (e) individualizing (support for individualized learning experiences through assessment, communication with families, and children with special needs). The ACEP includes 75 items that are scored using a yes or no format. Typical observations are 15 to 20 minutes in length and occur over a 3-hour period (one observation per hour).

The Early Childhood Classroom Observation Measure (ECCOM; Stipek & Byler, 2004) focuses on classroom quality from the perspective of teacher sensitivity and classroom management.

Thirty-two descriptors are housed within three subscales: (a) management (teachers provide choices across contexts; routines are clear but flexible; children are given developmentally appropriate responsibilities; and discipline is brief and nondisruptive, and promotes a child's problem solving), (b) social climate (teachers display warm, responsive, attentive, and respectful interactions with children; there is flexibility in tasks and activities that are individually adapted to a child's needs and consider skills and interests; communication is taught through naturally occurring events and social conflicts), and (c) learning climate and instruction (individualized, clearly articulated standards; coherent instruction that focuses on understanding and participation; a broad array of literary experiences; and mathematical activities that emphasize process and problem solving). Item ratings are made at the conclusion of observations, and each item is rated from 1 (practices are rarely observed) to 5 (practices predominate). The instrument includes a classroom resources guide.

The Caregiver Interaction Scale (CIS; Arnett, 1989) is primarily focused on teacher–child interactions. The instrument contains 26 items in four subscales: (1) sensitivity (e.g., shows enthusiasm about child efforts), (2) harshness (e.g. appears unnecessarily harsh when disciplining children), (3) detachment (e.g., gives considerable time to activities not involving children), and (4) permissiveness (e.g., expectations for children to exercise self-control beyond their developmental abilities). Items are scored using a 4-point Likert scale from 1 (not at all) to 4 (very much). The measure solely focuses on teacher–child interactions; another measure should be used if other aspects of the environment are to be assessed.

The Supports for English Language Learners Classroom Assessment (SELLCA; National Institute for Early Education Research, 2005) is comprised of eight items with scores ranging from 1 (minimal evidence) to 5 (strong evidence). This tool assesses the degree to which teachers incorporate the cultural backgrounds of children, encourage the participation of families, and support English language acquisition with the encouragement of children in the use of their native language. In addition to observations, an interview with the teacher is required to complete the scale.

In addition to these scales, many local, state, and national agencies and organizations provide checklists for their recommended practices that may be used in performing an environmental scan. For example, the state of Iowa has user-friendly checklists that evaluate early childhood environments for alignment of services with state-level standards and the recommended practices of NAEYC (http://www.iowa.gov/educate/; http://www.iowa.gov/educate/index.php?option=com_content&task=view&id=681&Itemid=805#Guiding%20Practices). A review of state departments of education websites, among other related websites, provides numerous examples of measures that evaluate the physical, educational, and social-emotional aspects of learning environments. It is important to seek out these types of resources because they aid in the assessment of environments, the inclusion of evidence-based practices, and effective program evaluation.

BREAKPOINT PRACTICE

1. Why might you be interested in assessing teacher–child interactions as a means of supporting Carlos's development?
2. What might the assessment of materials and activities tell you about active, self-guided learning in Carlos's classroom?
3. What do you want to learn from the SELLCA that might support Carlos and his family?

ENVIRONMENTAL ANALYSIS AND CURRICULUM

A key component of an environmental analysis is making application of the assessment to children's learning. Tying assessment results to actual change is made easier with curricula that incorporate essential elements of environmental designs for learning and development.

High/Scope's (2003) Preschool Program Quality Assessment (PQA) relies on research and evidence-based practices to assess the environmental aspects of the preschool setting, including relationships between children and staff members; involvement of families; and creative, supportive work environments for staff members. The PQA is comprised of 63 items clustered in seven key areas related to program quality: learning environment (9 items), daily routine (12 items), adult–child interactions (13 items), curriculum planning and assessment (5 items), parent involvement and family services (10 items), staff qualifications and staff development (7 items), and program management (7 items). Raters observe the program, interview appropriate program personnel, and record supporting evidence for each item being evaluated. Quality ratings are circled from 1 (low) to 5 (high).

The PQA is one of many instruments and curricula developed over 40 years ago by David Weikart and his team at the Perry Preschool Program in Ypsilanti, Michigan. The purpose of their initiative was to support the success of children from disadvantaged backgrounds in school and society. High/Scope's comprehensive approach of program assessment, coupled with an array of instruments and curricula to support learning (http://www.highscope.org/), provides a continuum of evaluation methods to support the goals of the environment analysis across a wide range of settings. A longitudinal study found that children who participated in the High/Scope approach were better suited to meet the demands of society and had higher educational and employment levels than children in the control group (Schweinhart & Weikart, 1997). In addition, the High/Scope curriculum offers a way to align the curriculum with federal and state special education standards and Head Start programs. A quick guide to evaluating the implementation of the curriculum and an explanation of concepts is available at http://www.state.nj.us/education/ece/curriculum/tools/highscope.pdf.

The Creative Curriculum for Preschool (Dodge, Colker, & Heroman, 2002) provides a comprehensive approach to the assessment of environments, which is stated to be the foundation for the use of the curriculum. The Creative Curriculum for Preschool Implementation Checklist allows for assessment in the following categories: (a) physical environment, (b) structure, (c) teacher–child interactions, (d) assessment, and (e) family involvement. Each section includes descriptions of what to observe in the classroom. Areas of consideration regarding the arrangement of the physical environment include steps for evaluating and creating "interest areas" for children and the effectiveness of the physical environment in meeting the goals of the curriculum. Using a series of message statements (see Figure 7.2), the teacher can examine the qualitative aspects of the environment in addition to the physical properties and arrangements.

"This is a good place to be."
"You belong here."
"This is a place you can trust."
"There are places where you can be by yourself when you want to."
"You can do many things on your own here."
"This is a safe place to explore and try out your ideas."

FIGURE 7.2 Message Indicators for Considering the Intent of the Environmental Design.

High/Scope and Creative Curriculum are examples of curricula providing direct resources that align environmental assessment with practical strategies for implementation. For example, schedules and routines are a significant component in both curricula, with clear direction about how these might be arranged to optimize outcomes in a learning environment. Both inventories have been thoroughly researched; validity and reliability standards available on their websites (www.highscope.org, www.teachingstrategies.com). The Creative Curriculum for Preschool also offers a way to align the curriculum with federal and state special education standards and Head Start programs.

Special Needs and the Learning Environment

Children with special needs are entering preschool programs at greater rates than was previously the case. In addition, greater focus has been given to the role of the No Child Left Behind Act and the expansion of the law's provisions at the early childhood education level. While there is disagreement about this expansion (Commission on the No Child Left Behind Act, 2006), clearly, there is an emphasis on the examination of programs for quality initiatives that enhance developmental outcomes for all children, including those with special needs.

The Individuals with Disabilities Education Improvement Act (IDEIA, 2004) stipulates the responsibility of educators for working in teams, which include families, to better address the needs of children whose learning, behavioral, and communication styles may differ from the norm. Attention has been paid to the unique supports that are inherent in the joint curricula of early childhood education and early childhood special education programs that better serve the needs of young children with exceptionalities (Odom & Wolery, 2003). The variables that make a program beneficial for children's individual learning experiences are a necessary consideration, particularly for students with developmental disabilities. Important considerations for environmental assessment that are unique to serving children with special needs are included as perspectives in the use of instruments for environmental evaluation.

Health and Safety

Many children with special needs enter the preschool arena with a variety of health and physical needs that must be addressed in the environmental evaluation and design. For children with physical disabilities, appropriate handling is a concern for both the safety of the child and the staff members who may be physically handling the child for movement and positioning related to instruction. For children with regulatory challenges, unpredictable behavior may be a threat to those supporting the child or to the child's peers. Consideration should be given to these unique factors as an adjunct to other tools and inventories related to environmental analysis and design. An example of a comprehensive inventory for evaluation of health and safety in preschool programs is the CCHP Health and Safety Checklist—Revised (California Childcare Health Program, 2005), an 82-item checklist covering issues related to emergency procedures, proper labeling and storage of medication, and requirements for food preparation and sanitation. A copy of this instrument is available at: http://www.ucsfchildcarehealth.org/pdfs/Checklists/UCSF_Checklist_rev2.0802.pdf.

Families as Partners

It is well established in the law that families take a central role in the education of children with special needs. The individual family service plan (IFSP), which is developed for children from infancy to age 3, places the families' concerns, priorities, and resources at the center of the planning and implementation of services. The individualized education plan (IEP) incorporates parents as team members whose status is equal to that of other members. Families are viewed as the context in which relationships begin and are nurtured, and they provide the primary teaching responsibilities within natural settings.

Natural Environments

Whether "education" occurs in or outside the classroom, the premise of natural settings is the inclusion of everyday learning opportunities that lead to natural learning outcomes (Dunst et al., 2001). In programs for children from birth to age 3, the emphasis has shifted exclusively to natural environments, including the home, daycare, and related community settings. The goal of preparing children through common routines and interactions is intended to provide meaningful learning opportunities that will be internalized and sustained in a sequential manner that supports future learning and participation.

Relationships

It is generally agreed that the importance of nurturing relationships is an essential feature and is evidenced to be a critical factor in children's development (Shonkoff & Phillips, 2000). The relationships that young children have with their caregivers are known to have a major impact on children's development across all domains. When these relationships are "warm nurturing, and individualized," they are growth-producing in their impact and are "characterized by a high level of 'goodness of fit'" (p. 341).

Inclusion

The inclusion of children with special needs in general education and preschool environments has become a subject gaining widespread attention in the use of best practices for early childhood special education (Bredekamp & Copple, 1997; Odom, 2000; Vakil, Welton, O'Connor, & Kline, 2009; Winton, McCollum, & Catlett, 2008). **Inclusion** means that children with disabilities receive individualized instruction and related supports within general education and preschool settings alongside their same-age peers. According to the DEC/NAEYC joint position statement on inclusion, a defining characteristic of inclusion programs is the active engagement and participation of children with and without disabilities (DEC/NAEYC, 2009). A full report regarding their joint position statement is available at the NAEYC website: www.naeyc.org.

Assessment of environments for young children with special needs requires an analysis of those factors that promote inclusion (see Figure 7.3). Checklists for ensuring appropriate practices should be used in environmental analysis for promoting philosophies and strategies associated with inclusion practices. Examples of checklists for the evaluation of inclusive practices can be found at www.nectac.org and www.circleofinclusion.org.

Encourage interactions among all children, including those with exceptionalities.
Answer children's questions about exceptionalities.
Assist in communication for children with exceptionalities.
Teach children how to interact and include children with exceptionalities.
Seek to illuminate similarities among all children, including those with exceptionalities.

FIGURE 7.3   Factors for Promoting Inclusive Environments.

Grouping

Decisions about grouping children for instructional and social purposes present unique challenges and opportunities for teachers of young children with special needs. **Grouping**, in this context, refers to the arrangement of children to optimize instruction and social development. DEC/CEC professional standards for early childhood special education practitioners support the importance of designing learning environments so that active participation in group activities is highlighted. Preschool is noted for its focus on social skills necessary for successful participation in learning environment, so it is important to consider the types of cooperative learning groups that may be designed to aid students with special needs in this critical endeavor (Johnson, Ironsmith, Snow, & Poteat, 2000).

Scaffolding and Mediation

The effective use of relationships may best be evidenced in the role of scaffolding and the use of socially mediated approaches for supporting children's development (Vygotsky, 1978). **Socially mediated learning** approaches, including **scaffolding**, can be defined as temporary support and guidance from more competent adults or peers that structures tasks, materials, and personal support to guide the learning process until a child has gained mastery of a new skill (Hall, 2002). Adults are significant in their roles as guides, models, and encouragers of children's growth through greater mastery.

Embedded Instruction

Embedded learning opportunities are appropriate for all young children, but especially for children with exceptionalities. **Embedded instruction** has been defined as giving opportunities for children to practice individual goals and objectives within naturally occurring activities or events "in a manner that expands, modifies or adapts the activity/event while remaining meaningful and interesting to children" (Bricker, Pretti-Frontcak, & McComas, 1998, p. 13). Goals for children's development are identified and situated within everyday activities, routines, and transitions to promote their skill acquisition and the generalization of newly acquired skills. For example, a child who is working on using social greetings may have this goal embedded into a morning circle activity or a classroom's arrival rituals to provide the appropriate context for learning and use of this skill.

The goal of embedded instruction is the incorporation of systematic learning trials within naturally occurring events to enhance children's learning opportunities. Embedded instruction maximizes a child's motivation for learning by considering that child's interests and preferences for opportunities to practice and learn identified skill targets within contexts that are important to the child. Embedded instruction promotes mastery and maintenance of skills that are more effectively generalized across multiple settings.

Positive Behavioral Supports

The use of positive behavioral supports (PBS) is an effective approach for supporting all children, but especially those with unique educational needs. A major objective of PBS is the incorporation of strategies that prevent, rather than react to, the manifestation of challenging behaviors in children. The primary goal of PBS is to accurately define, explicitly teach, and consistently note positive behaviors through purposeful intervention strategies that can be tailored to the multiple levels of a child's experiences.

According to Fox et al. (2003), factors associated with the development of PBS include positive relationships with children, families, and colleagues; classroom prevention practices; social and emotional teaching strategies; and intensive individualized interventions. These factors are built on a foundation of effective systems policies and personnel who can sustain these approaches across time and settings.

While early childhood education programs incorporate universal goals that are appropriate for children with special needs and their families, considerations for special education learners should be incorporated in the context for early childhood environments and dictate commensurate practices that are achieved through these outlined goals.

BREAKPOINT PRACTICE

1. What do you believe the preschool should do to make sure that schedules and routines are created and followed effectively? How might this help Carlos?
2. What factors do you think might be most important for your analysis of the health and safety of the environment?
3. How might an observation in natural settings help you understand Carlos and his family better? How might this help your relationship with his family?
4. What considerations might you give to grouping Carlos with other students? What configurations might you use and why?
5. What do you want to know about building relationships with Carlos? What do you believe are key factors to understand from your analysis that may be affecting Carlos's behavior and development?

Reassessing Carlos

Carlos's parents brought him to the local early intervention program regarding behaviors about which they were concerned. Carlos was described by his parents as being very rambunctious, failing to recognize limits, and using very risky behavior that they feared would hurt him. Teachers have observed that Carlos tends to have difficulty managing his environment and relationships with both teachers and peers. The teaching team's frustrations include difficulty in grouping Carlos with other children, his running away from staff members, and his general lack of availability to the learning environment.

At the beginning of this chapter, you were asked to consider what types of assessments you would choose to assess Carlos's performance in the preschool setting and the information you would want to gain from those assessments. By now, you have probably drawn some preliminary conclusions about Carlos's case. Among those conclusions the following might be important:

- The need for a systematic environmental analysis to determine causes and functions of behavior.
- The inclusion of both formal and informal measures to capture a more complete picture of Carlos's environments and their effects on his learning and socialization.
- The importance of observational assessments for organizing and capturing a better snapshot of environments for young children, including Carlos.

- The use of multiple assessments across environments and settings (e.g., home, school, childcare) allows for a cross-analysis of findings to determine themes and functions of behavior.
- The evaluation of grouping arrangements and their impact on Carlos's learning and socialization needs.
- The role of the family in behavioral schemes, their perceptions of their son's behavior, and the need for the intervention program to include them.
- The need to tie curricular approaches to those findings gained from environmental analysis.

High-quality early childhood programs provide a rich environment for which children gain a variety of critical skills in the areas of cognition, language, and socialization, among others. The evidence suggests that children learn best in environments that are developmentally appropriate for their age and stage. The use of consistent routines, social interactions, and developmentally appropriate play and exploration contributes to meaningful learning that allows for children's competencies to increase exponentially. This is especially important for children with exceptional learning needs. They require targeted attention to the critical elements of learning and maturation that will support them now and in the future. The goal of environmental assessment and design is to comprehend factors that may not be readily apparent and thus ensure that children's success is realized.

Activities

1. Design an inservice training for your colleagues to discuss the important elements of environmental assessment and how these may be used to support development.
2. Create a database of assessment tools that teachers might find easy to access for use in their classrooms.
3. Organize curriculum groups to discuss the means by which you might tie assessment data to instructional activities.
4. Organize environmental assessment teams to evaluate settings and practices within a program, school, or district.
5. Design and present training workshops for parents and families to highlight the critical features of good environments and the means by which you can support their development of these environments through your support and guidance.

Websites

California Childcare Health Program
www.ucsfchildcarehealth.org

Circle of Inclusion
http://www.circleofinclusion.org/

Council for Exceptional Children (CEC)
http://www.cec.sped.org

Creative Curriculum
http://www.creativecurriculum.net/

Division of Early Childhood (DEC)
http://www.dec-sped.org/

Embedded Instruction for Early Learning
http://www.embeddedinstruction.net/

Environmental Rating Scales
http://www.fpg.unc.edu/~ECERS/

Frank Porter Graham Center
http://www.fpg.unc.edu/main/about.cfm

High/Scope Curriculum
http://www.highscope.org

HOME Inventory
http://ualr.edu/case/index.php/home/home-inventory/

Inclusive Practices
http://www.truecoaching.com/pic/index.cfm

National Association for the Education of Young Children (NAEYC)
http://www.naeyc.org/

National Professional Development Center on Inclusion (NPDCI)
http://community.fpg.unc.edu/npdci

Positive Behavioral Intervention and Supports
http://www.pbis.org/

References

Abbot-Shinn, M., & Sibley, A. (1992). *Assessment profile for early childhood programs: Research version.* Atlanta, GA: Quality Assist, Inc.

Apter, S. J., & Conoley, J. C. (1984). *Childhood behavior disorders and emotional disturbance: An introduction to teaching troubled children.* Upper Saddle River, NJ: Prentice Hall.

Arnett, J. (1989). Caregivers in day-care centers: Does training matter? *Journal of Applied Developmental Psychology, 10,* 541–552.

Barnes, E. B., O'Flynn, J., & Saile, L. (2009). Autism spectrum disorders in your children. In G. Ensher, D. A. Clark, & N. S. Songer (Eds.), *Families, infants, & young children at risk: Pathways to best practice* (pp. 107–138). Baltimore: Brookes.

Blaustein, M. (2005, July). See, hear, touch: The basics of learning readiness. Beyond the Journal, Retrieved October 2, 2009, from www.journal.naeyc.org/btj/200507/01Blaustein.pdf

Bowman, B. T., Donovan, M. S., & Burns, M. S. (Eds.) (2001). National Research Council. *Eager to learn: Educating our preschoolers.* Committee on Early Childhood Pedagogy. Commission on Behavioral and Social Science Education. Washington, DC: National Academy Press.

Bradley, R. H., Corwyn, R. F., McAdoo, H. P., & Garcia Coll, C. T. (2001). The home environments of children in the United States Part 1: Variations by age, ethnicity, and poverty status. *Child Development, 7*(6), 1844–1867.

Bredekamp, S. (Ed.). (1987). *Developmentally appropriate practice in early childhood programs serving children from birth through age 8.* Washington, DC: National Association for the Education of Young Children.

Bredekamp, S., & Copple, C. (1997). *Developmentally appropriate practice in early childhood programs.* Washington, DC: National Association for the Education of Young Children.

Bricker, D., Pretti-Frontczak, K., & McComas, N. (1998). *An activity-based approach to early intervention* (2nd ed.). Baltimore: Brookes.

Caldwell, B., & Bradley, R. (1984). *Home observation for measurement of the environment (HOME)—revised edition.* Little Rock: University of Arkansas at Little Rock.

California Childcare Health Program. (2005). *CCHP health and safety checklist—revised.* Retrieved September, 12, 2009, from www.ucsfchildcarehealth.org

Commission on the No Child Left Behind Act. (2006). *Commission hears importance of properly supporting early childhood education.* Retrieved September 30, 2009, from http://www.aspeninstitute.org/policy-work/no-child-left-behind/newsroom/press-releases/release-nclb-commission-hears-importance-early-childhood-e

DEC/NAEYC. (2009). *Early childhood inclusion: A joint position statement of the Division for Early Childhood (DEC) and the National Association for the Education of Young Children (NAEYC).* Chapel Hill: University of North Carolina, FPG Child Development Institute.

Dodge, D., Colker, L., & Heroman, C. (2002). *The creative curriculum for preschool* (4th ed.). Eugene, OR: Teaching Strategies, Inc.

Dunst, C. J., Bruder, M. B., Trivette, C. M., & Hamby, D. W. (2005). Young children's natural learning environments contrasting approaches to early childhood intervention indicate differential learning opportunities. *Psychological Reports, 96,* 231–234.

Dunst, C. J., Bruder, M. B., Trivette, C. M., Hamby, D. W., Raab, M., & McLean, M. (2001). Characteristics and consequences of everyday natural learning opportunities. *Topics in Early Childhood Special Education, 21*(2), 68–92.

Fox, L., Dunlap, G., Hemmeter, M. L., Joseph, G. E., & Strain, P. S. (2003). The teaching pyramid: A model for supporting social competence and preventing challenging behavior in young children. *Young Children, 58,* 48–52.

Gomby, D. S., Larner, M. B., Carlosson, C. S., Lewit, E. M., & Behrman, R. (1995). Long-term outcomes of early childhood programs: Analysis and recommendations. *Future of Children, 5*(3), 6–24.

Hall, T. (2002). *Explicit instruction.* Retrieved September 13, 2009, from http://www.cast.org/publications/ncac/ncac_explicit.html

Harms, T., Clifford, R. M., & Cryer, D. (1998). *The Early Childhood Environment Rating Scale: Revised Edition.* New York: Teachers College Press.

Harms, T., Cryer, D., & Clifford, R. M. (2003). *Infant/Toddler Environment Rating Scale: Revised Edition.* New York: Teachers College Press.

Harms, T., Cryer, D., & Clifford, R. M. (2007). *Family Child Care Environment Rating Scale: Revised Edition.* New York: Teachers College Press.

High/Scope. (2003). *Preschool program quality assessment* (2nd ed.). Ypsilanti, MI: High/Scope Press.

Individuals with Disabilities Education Act Amendments of 1997. PL 105-17, 20 U.S.C. §§1400 et seq.

Individuals with Disabilities Education Improvement Act of 2004. 20 USC 1400.

Johnson, C., Ironsmith, M., Snow, C., & Poteat, G. (2000). Peer acceptance and social adjustment in preschool and kindergarten. *Early Childhood Education Journal, 27*(4), 207–212.

National Association for the Education of Young Children. (2009). *Position statement: Developmentally appropriate practice in early childhood programs serving children from birth through age 8.* Retrieved October 8, 2009, from http://www.naeyc.org/files/naeyc/file/positions/PSDAP.pdf

National Institute for Early Education Research. (2005). *Support for English language learners classroom assessment.* Rutgers, NJ: National Institute for Early Education Research.

Odom, S. L. (2000). Preschool inclusion: What we know and where we go from here. *Topics in Early Childhood Special Education, 20*(1), 20–27.

Odom, S. L., & Wolery, M. (2003). A unified theory of practice in early intervention/early childhood special education: Evidence-based practices. *Journal of Special Education, 37,* 124–133.

Piaget, J. (1955). *Sociological studies.* London: Routledge.

Regional Educational Laboratories' Early Childhood Collaboration Network. (1995). *Continuity in early childhood: A framework for home, school, and community linkages.* Greensboro, NC: SERVE Center.

Sandall, S., Hemmeter, M. L., Smith B. J., & McLean, M. E. (Eds.). (2005). *DEC recommended practices: A comprehensive guide for practical application in early intervention/early childhood special education.* Missoula, MT: Division for Early Childhood.

Schweinhart, L. J., & Weikart, D. P. (1997). The High/Scope preschool curriculum comparison study through age 23. *Early Childhood Research Quarterly, 12*(2), 117–143.

Sheridan, S. M., & Gutkin, T. B. (2000). The ecology of school psychology: Examining and changing our paradigm for the 21st century. *School Psychology Reviews, 29,* 485–502.

Shonkoff, J., & Phillips, D. A. (2000). *From neurons to neighborhoods: The science of early childhood development.* Washington, DC: National Academy Press.

Snow, E., & Hemel, S. B. (Eds.). (2008). *Early childhood assessment: Why, what, and how.* Washington, DC: National Academies Press.

Stipek, D. J., & Byler, P. (2004). The early childhood classroom observation measure. *Early Childhood Research Quarterly, 19,* 375–397.

Totsika, V., & Sylva, K. (2004). The home observation for measurement of the environment revisited. *Child & Adolescent Mental Health Journal, 9*(1), 25–35.

Vakil, S., Welton, E., O'Connor, B., & Kline, L. S. (2009). Inclusion means everyone! The role of the early childhood educator when including young children with autism in the classroom. *Early Childhood Education Journal, 36,* 321–326.

Vygotsky, L. S. (1978). *Mind in society: The development of higher psychological processes.* Cambridge, MA: Harvard University Press.

Winton, P., McCollum, J., & Catlett, C. (Eds.). (2008). *Practical approaches to early childhood professional development: Evidence, strategies, and resources.* Washington, DC: Zero to Three.

Observational Assessment

CHAPTER 8

CHAPTER OBJECTIVES

By the end of the chapter, you will be able to discuss the questions posed in Athena's case study. You will also be able to define observational assessment and be able to give examples of this type of assessment. You will also be able to give examples of checklists and rating scales commonly used by educators for early childhood settings. You will be able to identify informal assessment, authentic assessment, and the types and components of rubrics.

This chapter addresses Council for Exceptional Children (CEC) Standards 2 (Development and Characteristics of Learners), 5 (Learning Environments and Social Interactions), 8 (Assessment), and 10 (Collaboration). Information regarding human development and varying ability, active engagement and learning environments, informal assessment, and collaboration with families and professionals supply learning material involved with attaining goals.

Assessing Athena

Athena is a student in your preschool class. Your class consists of twelve children. You have two aides. In addition, a speech-language pathologist and a physical therapist work with the students and consult with you and the aides. Students in your class have been placed there because they have been considered high risk. Some students have been exposed to substances, such as drugs and/or alcohol. Other students have the diagnosis of developmental disorder. Athena is a 40-month-old student in your class. Through observation, you see that she uses mostly parallel play. That is, she will play next to other children using toys but typically will not interact directly with the other children. Some have characterized Athena as exceptionally shy. You also see that Athena uses about four single words consistently. She follows one-step directions (with cues) inconsistently. Athena is very quiet. She has the diagnosis of developmental delay.

Athena's mother is the sole provider and is very involved with Athena's medical and educational contexts. Athena's mother often reports on Athena's progress and seeks advice regarding how to best facilitate language and cognitive activities.

She is eager to try new techniques and strategies and participates in activities, such as visits to museums. Athena's mother states that formal tests often do not provide her with hands-on information and asks you about observational assessment to help her daughter and give her useful information.

What do you say to Athena's mother regarding formal and informal assessments? How would you approach observations to fit into the two types of assessments? What useful information can observations provide? How would the individualized family service plan (IFSP) interact with this performance-based assessment? What are some skills that you would assess first? How often would you evaluate? How would you describe the observational procedures?

As a teacher or educational professional in an associated field, you will deal with the day-to-day assessment processes linked to instructional practices. At times, this will be the loop associated with bridging informal assessment results, formal assessment results, the individualized family service plan (IFSP), the individualized education program (IEP) goals, and instructional practices. Data are used to determine progress toward goals. In addition, at a different level, this will be the spiral associated with continuous assessment of skills learned. For example, is the task too simple or too difficult for the child? This constant monitoring produces the enhancement of choosing appropriate skills and differentiated techniques for teaching skills.

Brown and Rolfe (2005) found that most early childhood practitioners and students reported use of informal assessment. Seventy percent of students and 10% of early childhood practitioners noted involvement or planned involvement in formal assessment. Appl (2000) reported that the evaluation process necessitates gathering information from multiple sources. Cook (2004) added that assessing young children with disabilities in natural environments is critical. Bagnato (2005) reported that standardized test may not capture authentic skills in everyday routines. Observations are an authentic fit with the natural setting.

Observations are possibly the most commonly used method of informal assessment (Taylor, 2009). According to Howel and Nolet (2000), observation data can consist of one to four categories. Overt behavior entails physical movements. Examples include kicking or spitting. Overt behaviors are witnessed by the educator. Covert behaviors are thoughts and feelings. The student may want a toy or food that makes him or her happy. State is a physical or psychological place. Examples include a location on a rug (overt) and being in a bad mood (covert). Critical effects are outcomes of situations. Reflecting on overt and covert behaviors allow the assessor to use ongoing assessment as a tool for instruction.

The student will often need to receive the information in different ways in order to understand and generalize the skill. Different intelligences (Gardner, 1993; Gardner, 2000) are tapped into by the educator to accomplish this goal (see Table 8.1). In addition, different senses (Birsh, 2005; Carbo, Dunn, & Dunn, 1986; Dede, Salzman, Loftin, & Sprague, 1999) are used in instructional and assessment materials and presentations (see Table 8.2). These assessment techniques are typically informal. That is, they are not norm-referenced, standardized tests. Informal assessments can include observations, interviews, **portfolios** (organized collection of work indicating learning), authentic assessments, and performance-based assessments. While participating in an instruction-to-assessment spiral, you will use these performance-based techniques with the aid of rubrics, checklists, and other teacher-made assessments.

In this chapter, we will focus on observation because the process is critical in the early childhood setting. Observation can be formal or informal. So, we will include both types of

TABLE 8.1	Gardner's Intelligences and Examples of Each
Linguistic: using language to understand and express oneself.	Writing a book report.
Logical-mathematical: manipulating numbers.	Organizing a calendar.
Spatial: representing spatial concepts.	Putting together letters to form words using letter blocks.
Bodily/kinesthetic: using the body to make something or perform.	Moving to a play performance.
Musical: hearing and using patterns.	Writing a rap song.
Interpersonal: understanding others.	Conducting cooperative groups.
Intrapersonal: understanding one's self.	Keeping a journal.

assessment in our discussion. In addition, we will discuss rubrics as they are commonly used for informal assessment in the early childhood setting.

DEFINITIONS

Rubrics

Rubrics allow us to measure skills examined in **authentic** (real-life application) and/or **performance-based** (student is constructing and demonstrating his or her knowledge) assessments. **Rubrics** include categories, scores, and descriptions that are used as a guide to evaluate projects or products. A well-conceived rubric involves a strong knowledge of the skills a teacher is expecting the student to master. In addition, the student and family members also know what is being measured. This information helps students understand, participate in, and improve on learning outcomes. We, as educators, must know what it is we are assessing and why we are assessing that skill. In developing measurements, those questions are at the forefront of the thought process. Those tasks and measures should relate to the curriculum used (Nitko, 2004).

Fischer and King (1995) reported a sequence of steps for developing a rubric. First, indicate the most significant elements of the learning activity. Second, determine the name (e.g., average) and number (e.g., 1–4) of criteria you will use for each scale. Third, write a description for each criterion level.

ANALYTIC RUBRIC. An **analytic rubric** is a type of rubric that may be used in a performance assessment task (Stiggins, 1997). Each skill is assessed separately with an analytic rubric. That is, there is a separate score for each criterion (Cohen & Spenciner, 2007). Descriptors are explanations of why a child's work falls into a specific evaluative category and may be included in an analytic

TABLE 8.2	Sensory Modalities and Examples
Visual	Pictures, video, color, graphic organizers.
Auditory	Music, rhymes, books on tape, assistive communication devices.
Kinesthetic	Jumping, dancing, clapping, skipping.
Tactile	Manipulatives, finger paints, play dough, water play.

TABLE 8.3   Analytic Rubric—Math

	Independent	Expanding	Emergent	Missing
Knowledge	Answer is complete and correct.	Shows almost complete understanding of the mathematic concept. Misses one or two pieces of the procedure.	Incorrect response.	Missing or inappropriate response.
Checks work	Student checks work and gets a correct answer.	Student checks work and gets an incorrect answer.	Student attempts to check answer but gets confused.	Missing or inappropriate response.
Explanation	Student accurately presents the process of solving the problem.	Student deletes some steps in his or her explanation or some steps are inaccurate.	Student's explanation is confusing.	Missing or inappropriate response.

rubric. The more detailed and clear the descriptor, the more useful the information is to the student. Analytic rubrics generally take a significant amount of time to develop. See Table 8.3.

HOLISTIC RUBRIC.   A **holistic rubric** is another type of rubric used in a performance assessment task (Stiggins, 1997). In this type of rubric, an overall evaluation of the product is given in terms of quality. The skills are evaluated as a whole; criteria are not assessed separately. Descriptors are also used in a holistic rubric. Rubrics can be used for assessment of understanding of young children. Pictures can be used to help the child visualize the assessment concept. Pieces of the picture can stand for components that are completed by the child. The child could see components of figures, such as a house or face. The full number of points would be awarded based on a complete picture. See Figures 8.1 and 8.2. A holistic rubric generally takes less time to develop than does an analytic rubric. See Table 8.4.

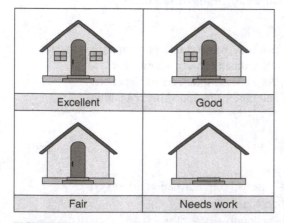

FIGURE 8.1   Basic House Rubric—Self-Assessment.

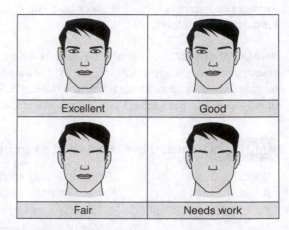

FIGURE 8.2   Basic Face Rubric—Self-Assessment.

TABLE 8.4	Holistic Rubric—Reading		
Exceptional	**Competent**	**Developing**	**Minimal**
Student reads target single words independently without assistance. Student uses various cues to achieve fluency and derive meaning.	Student reads target single words with assistance. Student knows most letters. Student uses some strategies to achieve fluency and derive meaning.	Student enjoys being read to. Student knows some letters. Student reads some of the target words. Student uses memorized language.	Student enjoys being read to. Student looks at pictures. Limited knowledge of print.

BREAKPOINT PRACTICE

1. Give an example of an analytic rubric for a 5-year-old child.
2. Give an example of a holistic rubric for a 5-year-old child.
3. Describe the pros and cons of analytic rubrics.
4. Describe the pros and cons of holistic rubrics.

Observations

Observations can be used in screening students, making educational decisions, collecting baseline data, and/or evaluating the effectiveness of an intervention program (Taylor, 2009). For example, Brown, Odom, Li, and Zercher (1999) found that children with disabilities differed from children without disabilities in two major ways when they looked at ecobehavioral assessment by using ecological context to look at behavior interactions (Greenwood, Carta, Kamps, & Arreaga-Mayer, 1990) in early childhood programs: Children without disabilities showed more child-to-child social behaviors; children with disabilities received more adult support.

Educators collect information regarding student performance through a combination of informal techniques in a number of different structured and unstructured contexts. One can collect information on a number of different areas through the observational technique. In the area of early childhood, researchers have identified some behaviors that educators can focus on in their data collection. For example, temperament could be an area of observational data collection.

Temperamental qualities include activity level (movement), rhythmicity (schedule), approach/withdrawal (attitude to a new situation), adaptability (adjustment), intensity of reaction, and mood (Berger, 1982; Bentzen, 2009). According to Bentzen (2009), observational foci can also include perceptual/sensory, sensorimotor/tool-using, conceptual/thinking, memory, representational/symbolic, communicative/linguistic, social/interactive, expressive/emotive, and self-regulatory/coping skills. In addition, Mindes (2007) reported that categories of observations can include motor (gross and fine), language (receptive and expressive), cognitive skills, relationships (adults, peers, self), play, group involvement, transitions and routines, and object manipulation. Piaget's (1936) stages are also often investigated in observational assessment (e.g., egocentrism, classification, one-to-one correspondence, conservation of number, causality, animism, artificialism).

Strengths and weaknesses of student learning are the most common purpose of teacher observation of students (Cook, Klein, & Tessier, 2004). The interviewer records information regarding the student, participants in the environment, and contextual factors within the observation. The observations are used for developing behavior intervention plans (BIPs). Several different types of recordings can be used. Direct observation can include the ABC (A = antecedent, B = behavior, C = consequences) procedure and observation recording system.

BREAKPOINT PRACTICE

1. List three characteristics of the child that might be observed.
2. Discuss validity aspects of observations.
3. Discuss timing issues of observations.

ABC PROCEDURE

In this particular method, the educator makes written entries about student behavior in a setting. The educator defines target behaviors and selects observational settings. In addition, the educator determines the time of day and the length of time the observation will occur (Beyda Lorie, 2010). *A* stands for the antecedent (i.e., shoe squeaking). *B* represents the behavior observed (antecedents) related to the target behavior. An example of an antecedent behavior is a task that is too difficult for the student (Chandler & Dahlquist, 2006). *C* signifies the consequences or events that follow the target behavior. Consequences reinforce the target behavior.

OBSERVATIONAL RECORDING SYSTEM

Another, more systemic direct observation method is the observational recording system. In this procedure, the observer defines a target behavior and identifies at least three observational settings (Yssledyke, 1998). In addition, like the ABC (A = antecedent, B = behavior, C = consequences) procedure, the educator determines the time of day and the length of time the observation will occur (Beyda Lorie, 2010).

Recording Techniques

Seven types of recording systems include anecdotal record, running record, event recording, interval recording, momentary time sampling, duration recording, and latency recording. See Table 8.5 for a list of types and definitions.

An **anecdotal recording** is a written account of an observation of a child after the event has taken place. In anecdotal recording (see Figure 8.3), the educator writes a narrative of the observation of the child after the observation has occurred. According to Overton (2009), a recorder writes down the behaviors that take place during a specific time period, such as a class period or lunch. Guddemi (2003) reports that it is important for these records to be as objective as possible. ABC recording is commonly used with this procedure. That is, the antecedent (event that precedes the target behavior) and the consequence (event that follows the target behavior) are used to decrease negative behaviors.

TABLE 8.5	Recording System Types and Definitions
Anecdotal record	An account, written after the event has taken place, of an observation of a child.
Running record	A written narrative documented during an observation of a child.
Event recording	Recording a frequency count of behavior.
Interval recording	Dividing an observation period into a number of short time spans and recording some target behavior.
Momentary time sampling	Dividing an observation period into equal time spans and observing the target behavior at the end of each time span.
Duration recording	Recording that focuses on the length of time some behavior lasts.
Latency recording	Recording how long it takes for an individual to initiate some target behavior.

A **running record** is a narrative of the observation of the child as the observation is taking place (see Figure 8.4). It is typically more detailed than the anecdotal record (Wortham, 2008). There are pros and cons to using anecdotal versus running records. A running record typically gives more detailed, objective information because it is recorded as the events take place. The anecdotal is written after the fact, so it is more prone to bias. On the other hand, a running record requires a teacher or other educator to take the notes during class, which generally necessitates having another person in the room to write the narrative.

School: Great Elementary School
Observer: Dr. University
Student: Junior
Location/Setting: Math Class

Events (What Happened)	Antecedent (Triggering Event)	Behavior (Student Action)	Consequences (Responses)

FIGURE 8.3 Anecdotal Recording Example.

Date: 12/13/10
Time: 9:15 to 9:55
Location: Reading Class
Student: Judy
Observer: Mr. Jones

At 9:15 class started. Mrs. Mann told the class to get out their folders. Judy looked at Irene and asked her for a pencil. Irene gave Judy a pencil. Judy then turned to Bruce and threw the pencil at him. Mrs. Mann asked Judy to go to the time-out table for 2 minutes. Judy refused to go to the time-out table. Mrs. Mann went over and asked Judy to go to the time-out table again. Judy walked over to the time-out table with Mrs. Mann. Judy stared at the ceiling for 2 minutes. Judy went back to her seat at the request of Mrs. Mann. The class continued with a reading exercise. At 9:28, Judy asked Oscar for a sheet of paper. Oscar told her that he did not have a sheet of paper for her. Judy started crying. Mrs. Mann went over to talk to Judy. Judy stopped crying and they continued with the lesson. At 9:47, Judy got up from her seat and she walked to the sharpener and the blackboard. Mrs. Mann asked Judy to sit down. Judy sat down and stared out the window for 2 minutes. Mrs. Mann verbally cued Judy to continue her assignment. She complied until the end of class.

FIGURE 8.4   Running Recording Example.

In **event recording**, a frequency count is used to provide evidence of the number of occurrences a target behavior takes place during a certain time period (see Figure 8.5). From that information, a rate of occurrence of the target behavior can be determined. The number of observed behaviors is divided by the number of minutes the student was observed. This recording method is typically used when a behavior occurs in a certain setting (Wortham, 2008). The teacher makes a tally mark each time a behavior occurs. Other measurement methods include a teacher putting a marble in a jar each time the behavior occurs. This technique is used most often when behaviors are distinct and short in time.

In **interval recording**, the observation period is divided into a number of short time spans and a target behavior is recorded. Interval recording is used by educators when behaviors are not discrete and occur often (i.e., speaking to a peer). See Figure 8.6. This technique can be documented in two different ways. The educator can use partial interval recording; here, more than one target behavior is measured. Examples include getting out of the seat and talking without

Date: February 14, 2011
Student: Vincent
Observer: Mrs. Smart

Observation Time	Subject	Target Behavior*
Monday: 11:00–11:30	Math	////
Wednesday: 10:20–10:50	Language Arts	///
Thursday: 1:15–1:45	Physical Education	////

FIGURE 8.5   Event Recording Example.
*The target behavior is speaking to peers during class time.

Date: May 4, 2010

Student: Gabriella

Observer: Mr. Cartledge

Target behavior: Gets out of seat

Time span/intervals: 30-second intervals over a 5-minute time span

1	2	3	4	5	6	7	8	9	10
−	+	−	+	+	−	−	+	−	−

FIGURE 8.6   Interval Recording Example.

raising a hand. Time periods are divided into smaller segments, usually measured in seconds. For example, a 2-minute time period in 15-second intervals could be used. A plus (+) or a minus (−) can be noted in each time interval to indicate the presence or absence, respectively, of the target behavior. A percentage of time can be calculated for on- and off-target behavior.

In **momentary time sampling**, an observation period is divided into equal time spans and the target behavior is observed at the end of each time span. Momentary time sampling is used to measure the frequency of the target behavior for a period of time (see Figure 8.7). The educator is interested in seeing what is occurring with one or more children (Mindes, 2007). The educator takes uniform time intervals and breaks those times up by minutes. An example would be 10 minutes.

Date: October 2, 2010

Student: Manny

Observer: Mrs. Trudeau

Target behavior: Works cooperatively with peers

Time span/intervals: 5-minute intervals over 50-minute time span

Time	Occurrence	Nonoccurrence
11:00	X	
11:05		X
11:10		X
11:15	X	
11:20	X	
11:25		X
11:30		X
11:35		X
11:40	X	
11:45	X	

Manny worked cooperatively with peers during a group activity 50% of the time (25/50 minutes).

FIGURE 8.7   Momentary Time Sampling Example.

Date: April 1, 2010

Student: Brandon

Observer: Mr. Wise

Target behavior: Tantrum

N	U	M	B	E	R	O	F	M	I	N	U	T	E	S
1	2	3	4	5	6	7	8	9	10	11	12	13	14	15

FIGURE 8.8 Duration Recording Example.

*Tantrum occurred between the sixth and eighth minute for 2 minutes.

A tally mark is made and/or comments are noted when the student uses the target behavior. A percentage can be computed based on the tallies over the observation time multiplied by 100. An advantage to this technique is that the sampling can be recorded at the end of the time periods.

Duration recording is used to document the length of time a target behavior lasts (see Figure 8.8). For example, continuous tasks or events, such as a temper tantrum, can be measured by seconds or minutes. This recording method needs much attention to the time (Taylor, 2009). **Latency recording** also measures time (see Figure 8.9). However, it is used to measure the initiation of a target behavior once a signal has been given by the teacher. For example, how long does it take the student to begin an assignment once cued to start the assignment? If the student walks around, sharpens his or her pencil, talks to his or her neighbor, doodles, and performs other extraneous tasks before beginning the assignment, those activity times would be included in the latency. The latency recording method also needs much attention to time (Taylor, 2009).

BREAKPOINT PRACTICE

1. Give an example of when you would use anecdotal recording in place of a running record.
2. Give an example of when you would use event recording.
3. Compare and contrast latency and duration recordings.

Student: Gina

Observer: Ms. Kean

Target behavior: Beginning classroom assignment

Date	Cue Time	Response Time	Latency Time
11/11/10	10:22:00	10:24:14	134 seconds
11/12/10	11:12:23	11:13:53	90 seconds
11/15/10	10:36:09	10:37:10	61 seconds
11/16/10	10:58:34	10:59:34	60 seconds

FIGURE 8.9 Latency Recording Example.

© zea_lenanet/Fotolia

The student is not asked to do anything specific regarding the observation within his or her natural environment (McLoughlin & Lewis, 2008). Examples of structured contexts include a classroom activity involving large-group discussion, greeting time, or closing time. Unstructured contexts include snack, lunch, and recess. When assessing young children, activities often center on play (Demchak & Downing, 2002). Play activities involve cognition (e.g., memory, symbolic), social, language, sensory, fine and gross motor, adaptive behavior, self-regulatory, and other important skills. Some examples include arts and crafts and blocks.

Observations and interviews can include the child, family, peers, educators, and other adults. Bernheimer and Keogh (1995) reported that family assessment is necessary for appropriate intervention planning. Therefore, it is critical to involve and look at family factors in the area of special education assessment, especially when evaluating young children (Bruder, 2000; Hanson & Bruder, 2001). Stress (Saloviita, Italinna, & Leinonen, 2003), mood (Hassiotis, 1997), and resilience (Patterson, 2002) have been examined in the area of providing intervention and assessment services to the families of young children with disabilities.

Margalit, Al-Yagon, and Kleitman (2006) investigated 80 mothers of infants with developmental disability whose children (ages 2 to 39 months) were receiving early intervention services. The researchers identified four family subtypes based on stress, mood, and coping: (1) cohesive families with high personal self-perception, (2) noncohesive families with medium maternal self-perception, (3) noncohesive families with low maternal self-perception, and (4) cohesive families with low maternal self-perception. These finding have implications in the early childhood setting. Educators should be aware of family subtypes and should adapt services in relation to family situations and needs. In fact, Reed-Victor (2004) noted that differentiated assessments based on individual differences could enhance children's adjustment and self-regulation. It was also noted in Reed-Victor's (2004) study, which involved 176 children with special needs (ages 3 to 9 years), that individualized support can offer the groundwork for later school achievement. Schuck and Bucy (1997) also noted that family assessment is a meaningful piece of evaluation for providing services to young children.

King, Zwaigenbaum, King, Baxter, Rosenbaum, and Bates (2006) studied belief systems on the families of children with autism or Down syndrome. They found that changes in family beliefs regarding disabilities and family/child contributions were achieved through changes in their views, values, and priorities. These findings can also provide useful information for educators providing support to families. Family beliefs are a critical contextual factor in an evaluation process. Families are particularly essential when assessing young children, and this includes the instruction-to-assessment spiral.

CHECKLISTS AND RATING SCALES

Checklists consist of criteria or descriptions where the observer indicates accuracy by checking yes or no to indicate the presence or absence of a characteristic or behavior (Cohen & Spenciner, 2007; McLoughlin & Lewis, 2008; Johnson, 2008). **Rating scales** include agreement to descriptions by choosing one out of three or more ratings. Examples of items on a checklist or rating scale are "sits appropriately" and "interacts appropriately with peers" (Spinelli, 2002).

According to Prestidge and Williams Glaser (2000), checklists and rating scales allow the assessor to compare students' behaviors with desired behaviors, facilitate progress on IEP goals, and focus families and teachers on student's goals. Difficulties with scales include unclear language, not enough choices, lack of descriptors, and using judgments based on perceptions (Layton & Lock, 2008). Hosp, Howell, and Hosp (2003) reported that often-used behavior rating scales were frequently composed of negative action questions and frequently did not indicate observable and measureable behaviors.

Checklists and rating scales can allow for multiple informants, such as parents, teachers, and students. These tools can be used as screening instruments or in a battery of tests for diagnostic purposes. Checklists and rating scales can also be used to assess the effectiveness of interventions. The most commonly used checklists and rating scales are discussed below. Sections are separated into instruments used for autism, attention deficit hyperactivity disorder (ADHD), atypical behavior, and environmental assessment.

Checklists and Rating Scales for Autism

The Autism Diagnostic Interview—Revised (ADI–R; Le Couteur, Lord, & Rutter, 2003) focuses on social interaction, communication, and repetitive behaviors. A clinician scores the responses of a caregiver based on a 4-point scale. Categorical result information is reported. Inter-rater reliability, test-retest reliability, and internal validity are reported.

The Autism Diagnostic Observation Schedule (ADOS; Lord, Rutter, DiLavore, & Risi, 1999) uses clinician observation to score behaviors. Four modules are based on the fluency of the child. Students who are nonverbal are not addressed by ADOS; social behavior, communication, and play are examined by this instrument. Researchers recommend establishing inter-rater reliability at the clinical setting of at least .8 before using this instrument. Norm data, inter-rater, and test-retest reliability and internal validity are addressed.

The Autism Screening Instrument for Educational Planning, 3rd edition (ASIEP–3; Krug, Arick, & Almond, 2008) includes five subtests: Autism Behavior Checklist, Sample of Vocal Behavior, Interaction Assessment, Educational Assessment, and Prognosis of Learning Rate. Current norm data, reliability, and validity are included.

The Checklist for Autism in Toddlers, Modified (M-CHAT; Robins, Fein, Barton, & Green, 2001) includes 23 items with yes or no responses. Items were modified from the original form to increase their sensitivity. Norms involving the New England states are available. Predictive validity data exist. Translations of the checklist in more than 20 languages are available.

The Childhood Autism Rating Scale (CARS; Schopler, Reichler, & Renner, 1988) uses 15 items on a 4-point scale. Researchers (Perry, Condillac, Freeman, Dunn-Geier, & Belair, 2005) note that norm data, reliability, and validity appear adequate. Test-retest data reveal a 12-month testing period between testing dates and inter-rater reliability results in the low .7 number frame. Predictive validity data are available.

The Gilliam Autism Rating Scale—Second Edition (GARS–2; Gilliam, 1995b) includes subtests in Stereotyped Behaviors, Communication, Social Interaction, and Developmental Disturbance. Items form three subscales: Stereotyped Behaviors, Communication, and Social Interaction. Norming was done on 48 states with over 1,000 participants. Test-retest and internal consistency reliability information are included. Content and concurrent validity data are also included.

The Gilliam Asperger's Disorder Scale (GADS; Gilliam, 2001) is scored on a 4-point scale. Four subtests include Social Interaction, Restricted Patterns of Behavior, Cognitive Patterns, and Pragmatic Skills. A norm sample of 371 participants was drawn from 27 states. Reliability and content validity are available. See Table 8.6.

TABLE 8.6	Checklists and Rating Scales for Autism			
Test Name	**Publisher**	**Content**	**Age or Grade Level**	**Time to Administer**
Autism Diagnostic Interview—Revised (ADI–R)	Western Psychological Services	A rating scale used to diagnose autism and differentiate autism from other developmental disabilities.	2 years and above	1½ to 2½ hours
Autism Diagnostic Observation Schedule (ADOS)	Western Psychological Services	A rating scale used to diagnose autism and pervasive developmental disorder.	Toddlers to adults	30 to 45 minutes
Autism Screening Instrument for Educational Planning—3 (ASIEP–3)	Western Psychological Services	A checklist used to diagnose autism and differentiate autism from other severe disabilities.	2 years through 13 years, 11 months	Varies
Checklist for Autism in Toddlers (Modified) (M-CHAT)	National Academies Press	A checklist used to identify toddlers with autism spectrum disorder.	16 through 30 months	5 to 10 minutes
Childhood Autism Rating Scale (CARS)	Western Psychological Services	A rating scale designed to identify children with autism.	2 years and above	5 minutes, unless a direct observation is needed
Gilliam Autism Rating Scale (GARS)	PRO-ED	A checklist to diagnose autism spectrum disorder and measure symptom severity.	3 through 22 years	5 to 10 minutes
Gilliam Asperger's Disorder Scale (GADS)	American Guidance Service	A checklist to diagnose Asperger's syndrome.	3 through 22 years	5 to 10 minutes

Checklists and Rating Scales for Attention Deficit Hyperactivity Disorder

The Attention Deficit Disorders Evaluation Scale—2 (ADDES–2; McCarney, 1995) consists of a school and home version on a 5-point scale. Subscales of Inattentive and Hyperactive-Impulsive are included in the scales. Norms appear adequate; however, age-gender norms are not evident. Reliability and validity data are reported.

The Attention Deficit/Hyperactivity Disorder Test (ADHDT; Gilliam, 1995a) is completed by educators and/or parents. Three subtests include Hyperactivity, Impulsivity, and Inattention. Psychometric information is included.

The ADHD Symptom Checklist (ADHD–SC4; Gadow & Sprafkin, 1997) is a 50-item scale completed by educators and/or parents. Norm data, reliability, and validity information is included.

The Connors Rating Scale—39 (CTRS–39; Connors, 1989, 1997) consists of parent, teacher, and student rating scales. Long and short (CPRS–27) forms are available. Norms appear to have an overrepresentation of Caucasian parents. Teacher scales appear racially proportional.

The Test of Variables of Attention (TOVA; Greenberg, 1993) is a computerized behavior test, which is scored by clinicians (clinical version) or educators (screening version). Visual and auditory responses are measured. See Table 8.7.

TABLE 8.7 Checklists and Rating Scales for Attention Deficit Hyperactivity Disorder

Test Name	Publisher	Content	Age or Grade Level	Time to Administer
Attention Deficit Disorders Evaluation Scale—2 (ADDES–2)	Hawthorne Educational Services	A rating scale used to identify students with attention deficit hyperactivity disorder.	4 through 18 years	Home version: 12 minutes. School version: 15 minutes.
Attention Deficit/Hyperactivity Disorder Test (ADHDT)	Psychological Assessment Resources, Inc.	A rating scale used to identify attention deficit hyperactivity disorder in children.	3 through 23 years	5 to 10 minutes
ADHD Symptom Checklist (ADHD–SC4)	Western Psychological Services	A checklist used to identify attention deficit hyperactivity disorder in children.	3 through 18 years	5 to 10 minutes
Connors Rating Scale—39 (CTRS–39)	Multi-Health Systems	A rating scale used to evaluate ADHD symptomatology.	3 to 17 years for both the teacher and the parent version	Long form = 15 to 20 minutes. Short form = 5 to 10 minutes.
Test of Variables of Attention (TOVA)	TOVA Company	A rating scale used to diagnose attention disorder.	4 to 80+ years	About 20 minutes

Checklists and Rating Scales for Atypical Behavior

The Early Childhood Behavior Scale (ECBS; McCarney, 1992) includes subscales in Academic Progress, Social Relationships, and Personal Adjustment. Norms were used from 17 states.

The Behavior Assessment System for Children (BASC-2; Reynolds & Kamphaus, 2004) was developed to measure adaptive and maladaptive behavior. The instrument consists of teacher-, parent-, and child-completed rating scales on a 4-point scale. Student Observation System and Structured Developmental History are included. Norm data appear adequate. Reliability and validity information also appears adequate.

The Social Skills Rating System (SSRS; Gresham & Elliot, 1990) consists of teacher, parent, and student scales. Items are scored on a 3-point scale. Normative data, reliability, and validity appear adequate.

The Temperament and Atypical Behavior Scale (TABS; Neisworth, Bagnato, Salvia, & Hunt, 1999) includes a screener (15 items) and an assessment tool (55 items). Four categories of rated behavior include Detached, Hypersensitive-active, Underreactive, and Dysregulated. Norm data, reliability, and validity information is included.

Vineland Social Emotional Early Childhood Scales (Vineland SEEC; Sparrow, Cicchetti, & Balla, 1998) includes information in Interpersonal Relationships, Play and Leisure Time, and Coping Skills. A Social-Emotional Composite is included in the instrument. Norm, reliability, and validity information is included. See Table 8.8.

Pevalin, Wade, and Brannigan (2003) stressed the importance of positive family environment as a buffer to developmental deficits during the first 47 months of life. Herring,

TABLE 8.8 Checklists and Rating Scales for Atypical Behavior

Test Name	Publisher	Content	Age or Grade Level	Time to Administer
Early Childhood Behavior Scale (ECBS)	Hawthorne Educational System	Rating scale used to determine emotional disturbance.	36 through 71 months	15 minutes
Behavior Assessment System for Children (BASC–2)	American Guidance Service	Teacher- and parent-completed rating scales used to assess problem behavior.	4 to 5, 6 to 11, and 12 to 18 years	15 to 20 minutes
Social Skills Rating System (SSRS)	Pearson	Rating scales used to evaluate student social skills.	3 through 18 years	10 to 25 minutes
Temperament and Atypical Behavior Scale (TABS)	Western Psychological Services	Rating scale used to assess problem behavior.	11 through 17 months	Screener: 5 minutes. Full scale: 15 minutes.
Vineland Social Emotional Early Childhood Scales (Vineland SEEC)	Pearson	Rating scale used to measure social emotional behavior.	Birth through 5 years 11 months	1 to 25 minutes

Gray, Taffe, Tonge, Sweeney, and Einfeld (2006) reported that child emotional and behavioral difficulties contributed to family stress and family functioning. Mahoney and Spiker (1996) also noted that parent–child interaction was important in early childhood services; however, they cautioned that perhaps assessment procedures were not developed enough in reliability and validity.

Checklists and Rating Scales for Environmental Assessments

Choosing Options and Accommodations for Children (COACH; Giangreco, Cloninger, & Iverson, 1998) helps families and educators identify strengths and needs in order to plan instruction. It is primarily an IEP planning tool.

The Early Childhood Environment Rating Scales—Revised (ECERS–R; Harms & Clifford, 2005) includes 43 items across 7 subscales. Subscales include Space and Furnishings, Personal Care Routines, Language-reasoning, Activities, Interactions, Program Structure, and Parents and Staff.

The Home Observation for Measurement of the Environment (HOME Scales; Caldwell & Bradley, 1984) measures the stimulation of the child's home environment. Forty-five items are grouped into 6 subscales: Parental Responsivity, Acceptance of Child, Organization of the Environment, Learning Materials, Parental Involvement, and Variety in Experience. Norm data, reliability, and validity appear adequate.

The Infant/Toddler Environment Rating Scales—Revised (ITERS–R; Harms, Cryer, & Clifford, 2006) includes 39 items across 7 subscales. Subscales include Space and Furnishings, Personal Care Routines, Listening and Talking, Activities, Interactions, Program Structure, and Parents and Staff. See Table 8.9. (For a more complete review of these measures, see Chapter 7.)

TABLE 8.9　Checklists and Rating Scales for Environmental Assessments

Test Name	Publisher	Content	Age or Grade Level	Time to Administer
Choosing Options and Accommodations for Children, 2nd ed. (COACH-2)	Brookes	A checklist used for planning education for children with disabilities.	3 through 21 years	1½ hours
Early Childhood Environment Rating Scales—Revised (ECERS–R)	Teachers College Press	Rating scales used to assess programs of students.	2½ through 5 years	Varies
Home Observation for Measurement of the Environment (HOME Scales)	Lorraine Coulson HOME INVENTORY LLC, Distribution Center	Rating scales used to assess environmental interaction factors.	Birth through 3 years	1 hour
Infant/Toddler Environment Rating Scales—Revised (ITERS–R)	Teachers College Press	Rating scales used to assess programs of students.	Birth through 2½ years	Varies

BREAKPOINT PRACTICE

1. Give three examples of information that can be gained from checklists and rating scales for autism.
2. Give three examples of information that can be gained from checklists and rating scales for attention deficit hyperactivity disorder.
3. Explain how information gained from checklists and rating scales for atypical behavior is similar to and/or different than checklists and rating scales for autism or attention deficit hyperactivity disorder.
4. Name two challenges that can arise with checklists and rating scales for environmental assessments.

Revisiting Athena

In the case of Athena, the educator can observe Athena in the classroom, in the playground, and at Athena's home and community. Not only would the educator look to include different places, but also different individuals within Athena's community, home, and school environments. Other contextual factors can include materials used, such as toys, but also classroom activities, such as routines (i.e., games, songs), learning centers, independent work, and large-group interaction (McAfee & Leong, 2007). The purpose and nature of the interaction are also significant contextual factors (Bentzen, 2009). Physical features such as lighting, temperature, and noise can also influence the environment of the observation.

You could ask questions regarding Athena's play at home with family, friends, and peers. How does she react to children in her age group whom she does not know? How does she interact with family members? How does she interact with friends? Does she play with the children or with a similar activity next to the children? Does she use eye contact? What language does she use? Does she use words? Sounds? Gestures? Does she smile when she plays with others?

After gathering the information and using the strategies noted in this chapter, you should be more comfortable discussing formal and informal assessments with Athena's mother. You can share Athena's strengths and needs with her mother. You can also note what has worked best with Athena in the classroom and encourage Athena's mother to use the same techniques at home. You can discuss how the IFSP goals feed into instruction and note whether Athena is assessed during each session. You can show Athena's mother how her daughter is assessed with rubrics, checklists, and other assessment methods. You can also mention that you are constantly tailoring the assessment process based on Athena's responses and performance. You can mention social and language (pragmatic) skills as a focus and stress the importance of self-assessment and self-determination coupled with choices.

Activities

1. Compare and contrast informal and formal assessment.

2. Give three examples of informal assessments.
3. Give two examples of formal assessments.

4. How would you measure performance-based assessment?
5. Which type of portfolio would you use in your classroom and why?
6. Give an example of a holistic rubric in the area of language arts.

7. Describe event recording.
8. Describe momentary time sampling.
9. Compare and contrast anecdotal and running recordings.
10. Compare and contrast checklists and rating scales for atypical behavior and environmental assessments.

Websites

American Academy of Pediatrics
http://www.aap.org

American Association of School Administrators
www.aasa.org

Chicago Public Schools
http://intranet.cps.k12.il.us/Assessments/
Ideas_and_Rubrics/Rubric_Bank/rubric_bank.html

Connect with Kids
http://www.connectwithkids.com

Early Childhood
www.earlychildhood.com

Kentucky Assistive Technology Service Network
Coordinating Center
www.katsnet.org

Reading Is Fundamental
www.rif.org

Rubistar
http://rubistar.4teachers.org/index.php

Teach-nology
http://www.teach-nology.com/web_tools/rubrics/

Zero to Three
http://www.zerotothree.org

References

Appl, D. J. (2000). Clarifying the preschool assessment process: Traditional practices and alternative approaches. *Early Childhood Education Journal, 27*(4), 219–225.

Bagnato, S. J. (2005). The authentic alternative for assessment in early intervention: An emerging evidence-based practice. *Journal of Early Intervention, 28*(1), 17–22.

Bentzen, W. R. (2009). *Seeing young children: A guide to observing and recording behavior* (6th ed.). Clifton Park, NY: Thomson.

Berger, M. (1982). Personality development and temperament. *Ciba Foundation Symposium*, 89, 176–190.

Bernheimer, L. P., & Keogh, B. K. (1995). Weaving interventions into the fabric of everyday life: An approach to family assessment. *Early Childhood Special Education, 15*(4), 415–433.

Beyda Lorie, S. (2010). Behavior assessment. In E. P. Kritikos (Ed.), *Special education assessment: Issues and strategies affecting today's classrooms*. Upper Saddle River, NJ: Merrill/Pearson Education.

Birsh, J. (2005). *Multisensory teaching of basic language skills* (2nd ed.). Baltimore: Brookes.

Brown, W. H., Odom, S. L., Li, S., & Zercher, C. (1999). Ecobehavioral assessment in early childhood programs: A portrait of preschool inclusion. *Journal of Special Education, 33*(3), 138–153.

Brown, J., & Rolfe, S. A. (2005). Use of child development assessment in early childhood education: Early childhood practitioner and student attitudes toward formal and informal testing. *Early Child Development and Care, 75*(3), 193–202.

Bruder, M. B. (2000). Family-centered early intervention: Clarifying our values for the new millennium. *Topics in Early Childhood Special Education, 20*(2), 105–115, 122.

Caldwell, B., & Bradley, R. (1984). *Home Observation for Measurement of the Environment (HOME Scales)*. Little Rock: University of Arkansas at Little Rock.

Carbo, M., Dunn, R., & Dunn, K. (1986). *Teaching students to read through their individual learning styles*. Upper Saddle River, NJ: Pearson Education.

Chandler, L. K., & Dahlquist, C. M. (2006). Functional assessment: Strategies to prevent and remediate challenging behavior in school settings (2nd ed.). Upper Saddle River, NJ: Merrill/Pearson Education.

Cohen, L. G., & Spenciner, L. J. (2007). *Assessment of children and youth with special needs* (3rd ed.). Upper Saddle River, NJ: Merrill/Pearson Education.

Connors, C. K. (1989). *Connors rating scales manual.* North Tonawanda, NY: Multi-Health Systems.

Connors, C. K. (1997). *Connors Rating Scales—Revised; technical manual.* North Tonawanda, NY: Multi-Health Systems.

Cook, R. E. (2004). Embedding assessment of young children into routines of inclusive settings: A systematic planning approach. *Young Exceptional Children, 7*(3), 2–11.

Cook, R. E., Klein, M. D., & Tessier, A. (2004). *Adapting early childhood curricula for children in inclusive settings* (6th ed.). Upper Saddle River, NJ: Merrill/Pearson Education.

Dede, C., Salzman, M. C., Loftin, R. B., & Sprague, D. (1999). In N. Roberts, W. Feurzeig, & B. Hunter (Eds.), *Computer modeling and simulation in science education.* New York: Springer-Verlag.

Demchak, M., & Downing, J. E. (2002). The preschool student. In J. E. Downing (Ed.), *Including students with severe and multiple disabilities in typical classrooms* (2nd ed.). Baltimore: Brookes.

Fischer, C., & King, R. (1995). *Authentic assessment: A guide to implementation.* Thousand Oaks, CA: Corwin Press.

Gadow, K. D., & Sprafkin, J. (1997). *ADHD symptom checklist.* Stonybrook, NY: Checkmate Plus.

Gardner, H. (1993). *Multiple intelligences: The theory in practice.* New York: Basic Books.

Gardner, H. (2000). *Intelligence reframed: Multiple intelligences for the 21st century.* New York: Basic Books.

Giangreco, M. F., Cloninger, C. J., & Iverson, V. S. (1998). *Choosing outcomes and accommodations for children: A guide to educational planning for children with disabilities* (2nd ed.). Baltimore, MD: Brookes.

Gilliam, J. (1995a). *Attention-deficit/hyperactivity disorder test.* Austin, TX: PRO-ED.

Gilliam, J. E. (1995b). *Gilliam autism rating scale.* Austin, TX: PRO-ED.

Gilliam, J. E. (2001). *Manual for the Gilliam asperger disorder scale.* Circle Pines, MN: American Guidance Service.

Greenberg, L. (1993). *Test of variables of attention.* Circle Pines, MN: American Guidance Service.

Greenwood, C. R., Carta, J. J., Kamps, D., & Arreaga-Mayer, C. (1990). Ecobehavioral analysis of classroom instruction. In S. Schroeder (Ed.), *Ecobehavioral analysis and developmental disabilities: The twenty-first century* (pp. 33–63). New York: Springer Verlag.

Gresham, F. M., & Elliot, S. N. (1990). *Social skills rating system manual.* Circle Pines, MN: American Guidance Service.

Guddemi, M. P. (2003). The important role of quality assessment for children ages 3 to 8 years. In J. Wall & G. Walz (Eds.), *Measuring up: Assessment issues for teachers, counselors, and administrators* (pp. 273–284). Greensboro, NC: ERIC Counseling and Student Services Clearinghouse.

Hanson, M. J., & Bruder, M. B. (2001). Early intervention: Promises to keep. *Infants and Young Children, 13*(3), 47–58.

Harms, T., & Clifford, B. M. (2005). *Early childhood environmental rating scale—revised (ECERS–R).* New York: Teachers College Press.

Harms, T., Cryer, D., & Clifford, R. M. (2006). *Infant/toddler environmental rating scale—revised (ITERS–R).* New York: Teachers College Press.

Hassiotis, A. (1997). Parents of young persons with learning disabilities: An application of the family adaptability and cohesion scales (FACES). *British Journal of Developmental Disabilities, 84,* 36–43.

Herring, S., Gray, K., Taffe, J., Tonge, B., Sweeney, D., & Einfeld, S. (2006). Behaviour and emotional problems in toddlers with pervasive developmental disorders and developmental delay: Associations with parental mental health and family functioning. *Journal of Intellectual Disability Research, 50*(12), 874–882.

Hosp, J. L., Howell, K. W., & Hosp, M. K. (2003). Characteristics of behavior rating scales: Implications for practice in assessment and behavioral support. *Journal of Positive Behavior Interventions, 5*(4), 201–208.

Howell, K. W., & Nolet, V. (2000). *Curriculum-based evaluation: Teaching and decision making* (3rd ed.). Belmont, CA: Wadsworth.

Johnson, J. (2008). *Early childhood special education.* New York: Thomson.

King, G. A., Zwaigenbaum, L., King, S., Baxter, D., Rosenbaum, P., & Bates, A. (2006). A qualitative investigation of changes in the belief systems of families of children with autism or Down syndrome. *Child: Care, Health & Development, 32,* 353–369.

Krug, D., Arick, J., & Almond, P. (2008). *Autism screening instrument for educational planning* (3rd ed.). (ASIEP–3). Austin, TX: PRO-ED.

Layton, C. A., & Lock, R. H. (2008). *Assessing students with special needs to produce quality outcomes.* Upper Saddle River, NJ: Pearson Education.

Le Couteur, A., Lord, C., & Rutter, M. (2003). *Autism diagnostic interview—revised.* Los Angeles, CA: Western Psychological Services.

Lord, C., Rutter, M., DiLavore, P. C., & Risi, S. (1999). *Autism diagnostic observation schedule*. Los Angeles, CA: Western Psychological Services.

Mahony, G., & Spiker, D. (1996). Clinical assessments of parent-child interaction: Are professionals ready to implement this practice? *Topics in early Childhood Special Education, 16*, 26–50.

Margalit, M., Al-Yagon, M., & Kleitman, T. (2006). Family subtyping and early intervention. *Journal of Policy and Practice in Intellectual Disabilities, 3*(1), 33–41.

McAfee, O., & Leong, D. B. (2007). *Assessing and guiding young children's development and learning* (4th ed.). Upper Saddle River, NJ: Pearson Education.

McCarney, S. B. (1992). *Early childhood behavior scale*. Columbia, MO: Hawthorne Educational Services.

McCarney, S. B. (1995). *The attention deficit disorders evaluation scale* (2nd ed.). Columbia, MO: Hawthorne Educational Services.

McLoughlin, J. A., & Lewis, R. B. (2008). *Assessing students with special needs* (7th ed.). Upper Saddle River, NJ: Merrill/Pearson Education.

Mindes, G. (2007). *Assessing young children* (3rd ed.). Upper Saddle River, NJ: Merrill/Pearson Education.

Neisworth, J., Bagnato, S., Salvia, J. A., & Hunt, F. (1999). *Temperament and atypical behavior scale*. Baltimore, MD: Paul H. Brookes.

Nitko, A. J. (2004). *Educational assessment of students* (4th ed.). Upper Saddle River, NJ: Merrill/Pearson Education.

Overton, T. (2009). *Assessing learners with special needs: An applied approach* (6th ed.). Upper Saddle River, NJ: Merrill/Pearson Education.

Patterson, G. M. (2002). Understanding family resilience. *Journal of Clinical Psychology, 58*, 233–246.

Perry, A., Condillac, R. A., Freeman, N. L., Dunn-Geier, J., & Belair, J. (2005). Multi-site study of the Childhood Autism Rating Scale (CARS) in five clinical groups of young children. *Journal of Autism and Developmental Disorders, 35*(5), 625–634.

Pevalin, D. J., Wade, T. J., & Branningan, A. (2003). Parental assessment of early childhood development: Biological and social covariates. *Infant and Child Development, 12*, 167–175.

Piaget, J. (1936, 1963). *The origins of intelligence in children*. New York: Norton.

Prestige, L. K., & Williams Glaser, C. H. (2000). Authentic assessment: Employing appropriate tools for evaluating students' work in 21st century classrooms. *Intervention and School and Clinic, 35*(3), 178–182.

Reed-Victor, E. (2004). Individual differences and early school adjustment: Teacher appraisals of young children with special needs. *Early Child Development and Care, 174*(1), 59–79.

Reynolds, C. R., & Kamphaus, R. W. (2004). *Behavior assessment system for children manual* (2nd ed.). Circle Pines, MN: American Guidance Service.

Robins, D., Fein, D., Barton, M., & Green, J. (2001). The modified checklist for autism in toddlers: An initial study investigating the early detection of autism and pervasive developmental disorders. *Journal of Autism and Developmental Disorders, 31*(2), 131–144.

Salovitta, T., Italinna, M., & Leinonen, E. (2003). Explaining the parental stress of fathers and mothers caring for a child with intellectual disability: A Double ABCX Model. *Journal of Intellectual Disability Research, 47*, 300–312.

Schopler, E., Reichler, R., & Renner, B. (1988). *Childhood autism rating scale*. Los Angeles: Western Psychological Services.

Schuck, L. A., & Bucy, J. E. (1997). Family rituals: Implications for early intervention. *Topics in Early Childhood Special Education, 17*(4), 477–484.

Sparrow, S. S., Cicchetti, D. V., & Balla, D. A. (1998). *Vineland social emotional early childhood scales*. Upper Saddle River, NJ: Pearson Education.

Spinelli, C. G. (2002). *Classroom assessment for students with special needs in inclusive settings*. Upper Saddle River, NJ: Merrill/Pearson Education.

Stiggins, R. J. (1997). *Student-centered classroom assessment* (2nd ed.). Upper Saddle River, NJ: Merrill/Pearson Education.

Taylor, R. L. (2009). *Assessment of exceptional students: Educational and psychological procedures* (8th ed.). Upper Saddle River, NJ: Merrill/Pearson Education.

Wortham, S. (2008). *Assessment in early childhood* (5th ed.). Upper Saddle River, NJ: Pearson Education.

Ysseldyke, S. (1998). *Assessment*. Boston, MA: Houghton Mifflin.

PART
Three

DEVELOPMENTAL DOMAINS

PART OUTLINE

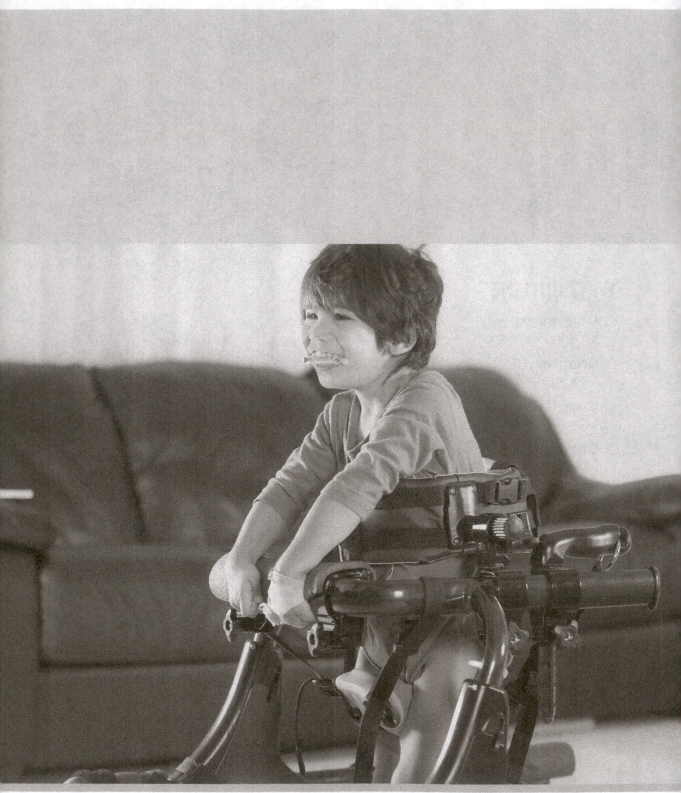

Sensory Assessment

CHAPTER 9

CHAPTER OBJECTIVES

After reading this chapter, you will understand the unique assessment needs of young children with sensory impairments, including visual, auditory, and sensory integration disabilities. This chapter addresses Council for Exceptional Children/Division for Early Childhood (CEC/DEC) Standards 4 (Instructional Strategies), 5 (Learning Environments and Social Interaction), 8 (Assessment), 9 (Professional and Ethical Practice), and 10 (Collaboration). It also addresses National Association for the Education of Young Children (NAEYC) Standard 3.

Assessing Louie

Louie is a 36-month-old who has just transitioned from a home-based program to your early childhood classroom. Louie was born with CHARGE syndrome (http://www.chargesyndrome.org/about-charge.asp). He has a bilateral mild conductive hearing loss and a retinal coloboma in his left eye. He also has generalized hypotonia. He has been receiving programming from an early interventionist and a speech pathologist and physical therapy since he was 12 months of age because of mild to moderate delay in all developmental areas. He presently receives speech and language services as well as physical therapy (PT). His speech and language goals include increasing the production of single words and clarity of initial phonemes. His PT goals include increase in **gross motor** strength (large muscle activity, for example, walking) and independent walking. His present mode of independent ambulation is crawling or using a gait trainer (adaptive in the classroom setting). Your main focus has been on skills that help Louie function independently.

Louie is able to communicate with a few words, but he is somewhat unintelligible because of the difficulty he has with initial phoneme productions. This often makes him appear vulnerable and less available to social situations typical for his age. He tends to participate mostly in similar activities that are repetitive in nature and resists changes in routines by protesting. Louie has recently transitioned to your program; as his classroom teacher, you are actively involved in the evaluation process and would like to concentrate on the assessment-to-instruction link within daily activities. You understand that Individuals with Disabilities Education Improvement Act (IDEIA) 2004 states that Louie's family members must be actively involved in the process and that, with young children, authentic assessment is best practice.

Which formal and informal assessment strategies would you use? Which specific vision, auditory, and sensory needs would you investigate?

How might you assess his self-regulation based on these sensory needs? Where would you go to receive information regarding the technologies that you would like to see Louie use? Which low- and high-level technologies would you explore? What other adaptations would you explore? How would you infuse the assessment information and outcomes within your classroom? What recommendations would you make to Louie's parents? How could you get more involved with the process?

You will be able to answer all these questions after reading this chapter. You will also be able to understand the aspects of your legal responsibility for using low- and high-technology devices in the classroom and give examples of the different types of technologies and adaptations that are applicable to children from birth to age 8.

VISION ASSESSMENT

According to the American Foundation for the Blind (AFB), approximately 93,600 children with visual impairment receive special education programming in the United States. **Visual impairment** involves central visual acuity of 20/70 or worse in the better eye with best correction, or a total field loss of 140 degrees. These statistics include degrees of vision loss, ranging from total blindness to having moderate residual vision. Considering the spectrum of visual abilities, it is understandable that assessment of a child with visual impairment would be comprehensive in nature, including input from medical, professional, and family resources.

Of those between birth and 21 years of age, approximately 57,000 are considered legally blind, meaning that their visual acuity is 20/200 or less in the better eye, after correction. **Visual acuity** is a clinical measure of the eye's ability to identify details of the smallest identifiable letter or symbol. It is a fraction measurement and is based on visible print size. Perfect vision is 20/20. If an individual sees 20/200, the smallest detail that a person sees at 20 feet can be seen by someone with perfect vision at 200 feet. Of these, 23% are considered prereaders, or in early childhood. Approximately 90% of these children use their residual vision as a mode of learning. Approximately 10% will eventually use Braille as a primary reading medium (2007 Annual Report: American Printing House for the Blind, Inc., www.aph.org/about/ar2007.html).

There continues to be discrepancies in the definition of low vision with no "universal definition" (Barraga, 2004, p. 581). American Printing House for the Blind (APH) uses a very specific definition in which **legal blindness** refers to a person with a central visual acuity of 20/200 or less in the better eye after correction (glasses) or a reduced peripheral field where the greatest diameter is 20 degrees or less. The Individuals with Disabilities Education Act (IDEA 2004), however, uses a less restrictive and more functional definition of visual impairment, defining the disability as vision that, even with correction, adversely affects a child's educational performance. The definition includes both partial sight and blindness.

Visual Process

To understand visual disability, you must first understand the visual process. Visual images are received in the form of light rays that enter the eye through the pupil and are projected on the fovea, the center of the macula that is the place on the retina that is the clearest point of central vision. These images are then transmitted to the optic nerve and eventually to the visual cortex (Jose, 1999). In perfect vision, the light rays enter the eyes and are focused exactly on the retina to provide a crisp, clear visual image.

The American Optometric Association (AOA) (2006) defines normal vision as the clarity of vision from a distance of 20 feet. A child who has 20/20 visual acuity can clearly see all information that is visible from a distance of 20 feet. What the child with 20/20 vision can see at 70 feet, the child with 20/70 acuity must be 20 feet from the same information in order to see with the same clarity.

When light does not focus perfectly on the retina, it is due to conditions known as **hyperopia** (farsightedness), **myopia** (nearsightedness), or astigmatism. Nearsightedness occurs when the eye is larger than normal, or its focal point is in front of the retina. Farsightedness occurs when the eye is smaller than normal, or the focal point is beyond the retina. **Astigmatism** is a variation in visual clarity due to irregularities in the shape of the cornea. Astigmatism results when there is a variation in refraction due to irregularities in the shape of the cornea (Jose, 1999). A refractive error can be corrected by a concave lens when a person is nearsighted, and with a convex lens if the person is farsighted. By wearing glasses with the prescribed lens, the person can see with normal vision.

Vision Disorders

Several disorders cause visual loss. However, the most common causes of visual impairment in children are retinopathy of prematurity (ROP), cortical visual impairment, albinism, cataracts, and optic nerve atrophy (Huebner, 2000).

Retinopathy of prematurity (ROP) is common in infants born at or less than 37 weeks gestation. Of the infants born at less than 3 pounds, approximately 66% will develop a degree of ROP; approximately 6% of these babies will require treatment (Palmer, 2003). The premature infant's eyes are typically underdeveloped, and exposure to oxygen causes a rapid growth of weak blood vessels that rupture easily. This results in retinal bleeding, which in turn results in the development of scar tissue. The scar tissue causes stress to the retina that results in retinal tearing or detachment. The outcome is mild to severe visual loss, with the possibility of blindness if left untreated (Howard, Williams, & Lepper, 2010).

Cortical visual impairment (CVI) is a condition in which the actual structure of the eye is intact. However, there is brain damage in the visual processing areas, visual pathways, or the visual cortex. CVI typically co-exists with another neurological impairment such as cerebral palsy. Many children with severe global disability show CVI. What is unique and also very confusing to the parent or educator is that the visual exam shows normal visual functioning. The indicators of CVI may be evident, however, on an abnormal magnetic resonance imaging (MRI) or computed axial tomography (CAT) scan (Roman-Lantzy, 2007).

Congenital cataract(s) is a cloudiness or opacity in one or both lenses of the eyes. This affects the internal structure needed for focusing. The lens is surgically removed, but visual blurriness can remain because of the inability to focus. With new surgical procedures, including the insertion of a lens into the eye and glasses, vision can return to a normal range. However, some continue to have difficulty with clarity, focus, and light sensitivity (Jose, 1999).

Optic atrophy is a visual disorder in which the optic nerve has deteriorated or shows atrophy. The optic nerve is instrumental in sending visual information to the visual cortex in the occipital lobe, and damage to it results in a loss in visual acuity and loss of all or parts of visual fields. Its effects on visual functioning range from mild visual loss to visual field cuts, to blindness. Secondary conditions usually include nystagmus, which affects the ability of the eyes to focus clearly (American Foundation for the Blind, 2006). **Nystagmus** involves involuntary rapid movement of the eyes; the eyes appear to flutter in a horizontal or vertical pattern.

Albinism is a sex-linked recessive disorder in which males exhibit the disorder and females typically are carriers, although some females may show traits of albinism. It is a disorder where the body lacks the ability to produce pigment; the results are fair complexion, platinum blonde or white hair and eyebrows, very lightly colored irises, and light sensitivity. Nystagmus may be present due to the underdeveloped macula, severe astigmatism is common, and the degree of visual impairment may vary (Jose, 1999).

Each of these visual disabilities carries unique visual characteristics that affect overall developmental progress. Research through the decades has revealed that children with visual impairment experience considerable as well as unique developmental delay in all areas of development (Brambring, 2007). Educators should understand the role that visual impairment plays in the child's presentation of developmental skills and should use appropriate and fair assessment procedures that show an accurate, unbiased account of the child's true potential and abilities.

BREAKPOINT PRACTICE

1. Coloboma isn't listed as one of the most common disorders causing visual impairment. How would you assist the family in understanding the implications of Louie's visual diagnosis?
2. As the early interventionist, what would you like to know about Louie's visual diagnosis and how would you find this information?
3. How familiar are you with the visual disabilities listed in this section? Discuss your familiarity with these disabilities as well as with visual impairment in general.

Visual Concerns

Visual acuity and clarity play a major role in the incentive to move and explore one's environment. This is observed as early as a few months of age when the development of head control appears to depend on visual motivation. The infant with intact vision moves, twists, and turns and uses head, neck, and trunk to accomplish the best position for visual reinforcement, but the child who does not have this visual incentive typically lies quietly and takes in auditory information rather than watch the environmental surroundings (Koenig & Holbrook, 2000).

Also, infants with intact vision eagerly lift their arms to swipe and bat at dangling toys, moving quickly and effortlessly through the hierarchal steps of fine and gross motor development, which in turn allows the infant to proceed smoothly through sensorimotor stages or cognitive stages of development. Infants with decreased vision are most interested in the auditory information provided by objects and toys and do not see the need to reach toward objects in order to receive more sensory information (Sigelman & Rider, 2009).

Because the infant lacks the incentive to move and use the muscles needed to develop the motor strength, muscles may appear flaccid, or hypotonic. Motor skills and cognitive development are delayed, not because of neurological impairment but because of the roadblock of visual impairment (Koenig & Holbrook, 2000). Without this understanding, the final diagnosis may be inaccurately defined and the potential of the child may be compromised.

As the child gets older, vision is the most enticing motivation to sit upright, crawl, and eventually walk. Although families and early interventionists look for ways to replace this motivation, looking for ways to motivate movement is a challenging and ongoing process.

Here are some signs of possible visual problems in an infant:

- Does not look at the speaker's face when someone is speaking to the infant.
- Does not look at/toward lights or windows.
- Eyes do not move together when looking around the room (older than 3 months).
- Eyes look different in a photograph than other children's eyes (other than eye color or red spot).
- Redness or puffiness, crustiness around the eye(s).
- Visible white, grayish-white, or yellow material in one or both pupils.
- Excessive tearing.
- Overly sensitive to light.
- Frequent rubbing of eyes.
- Appears to look at objects with one eye.
- Turns head to look at object or face.
- The eyes appear to vibrate.
- Does not follow the movement of a toy.

Toddlers with decreased vision may show decreased interest in fine motor tasks such as handling buttons and knobs on toys and puzzles, looking at picture books, or scribbling or coloring activities. **Fine motor** describes small muscle activity (i.e., writing). Many of the signs of possible visual problems in infancy are signs of visual concern for the toddler; however, the list also includes the following:

- Holds a toy close to eyes when looking at it.
- Holds a book close to eyes when looking at the pages.
- Tilts head to one side or the other when looking at toys or books.
- Avoids fine motor or visual-motor tasks (working with puzzles, stacking toys, coloring, and cutting).
- Doesn't appear to notice airplanes, birds, and other items of interest that are at a distance.
- Trips frequently over toys and objects; appears clumsy.
- Redness in eyes.
- Rubs eyes frequently or complains that eyes hurt.
- One eye crosses frequently or constantly.

Children in early childhood environments are commonly referred for evaluation by the classroom teacher because of a decrease in fine motor abilities including, decreased interest in classroom toys and manipulatives or difficulty with coloring, cutting, and pre-academic skills such as legibly writing letters. Many of the signs of possible visual problems for infants and toddlers are signs of visual concern for children in early childhood, but with a few additions, mostly concerning pre-academic development:

- Does not attend to a book in circle time or to other visual aids.
- Does not look at your face in circle time.

- Does not attend to movies or videos.
- Short attention span during table work or visual-motor activity.
- Difficult making letters and drawing and coloring.
- Difficulty writing on a line.
- Difficulty cutting on a line.

Once it has been established that there are warranted concerns about the child's vision, the next step for the early interventionist is to discuss the need for an examination by an optometrist or ophthalmologist. Typically, if there is no existing diagnosis, the optometrist is qualified to conduct an initial examination. If the findings from this exam suggest a more extensive workup, then a referral is made to an ophthalmologist. Depending on the outcomes of these visits, and if the visual issue cannot be corrected with lenses, the intervention team and family takes steps toward setting up the optimal learning environment with accommodations to adjust for the diagnosed visual needs of the child (Ricci & Kyle, 2009).

Functional Vision Assessment

If the infant or child has been diagnosed with a visual impairment, a person who is trained to work with children with visual impairment becomes part of the intervention team. This person conducts an initial functional vision assessment, which provides the information needed to make necessary adaptations and modifications in the home, daycare, or educational setting. **Adaptations** are changes to instruction or assessment. Medical reports provide the initial diagnostic information, such as severity and ongoing visual needs, but they typically do not include overall implications of the disorder (Chen, 1999).

Some visual disorders, such as ROP, have a wide range of developmental implications, depending on the stage or degree of loss. In some cases, the implication may be that the child has only light perception. In some cases, there may be vision in only the right or the left eye. However, it will be up to you to find resources that discuss the implications that will affect overall development. See Table 9.1 for more information about implications of visual disorders.

The functional vision assessment begins with observation of the environment and how the child is responding within this setting. Questions to consider during this step included the following:

- Does the infant/child appear to focus or visually attend to any information in the environment?
- What is the lighting like in the room?
- Does the room have direct lighting?
- If the toddler/child is mobile, how easy is his or her navigation in the room?
- How is the child playing with toys/objects (using vision?)

The person who conducts the functional vision assessment typically assesses the following skills:

- *Near distance*—where is the best visual clarity for books, toys, manipulatives.
- *Far distance*—maximum distance where objects are visible.
- *Visual fields*—seeing objects to the sides, and above or below eye level.
- *Localizing/scanning*—ease in locating visual information.
- *Tracking*—following movement.
- *Shifting gaze*—looking back and forth from one object to another.
- *Eye preference*—using one eye more than the other.
- *Eye-hand coordination*—reaching out to touch something or to pick up an object.
- *Color vision*—ability to perceive color out of the context of a functional task.

TABLE 9.1	Definitions and Implications of Visual Disorders	
Visual Disorder	**Definition**	**Visual Implications**
Albinism	Congenital hereditary disorder. It is due to the lack of or inability to produce pigment. It is characterized by a fair complexion; very blond to white body hair, eyebrows, and eyelashes; and very light-colored, often red-appearing irises.	Severe sensitivity to light, nystagmus, and decreased vision due to a poorly developed macula.
Aniridia	Underdevelopment of the iris of the eye, which controls the amount of light that enters the eye and focusing of the light rays on the retina.	Blurred vision and light sensitivity. Possible secondary visual conditions including nystagmus, cataracts, and glaucoma.
Congenital cataract(s)	Opacity in one or both lens of the eyes. This affects the internal structure needed for focusing. The lens is surgically removed, but visual blurriness can remain due to the inability to focus.	Light sensitivity, especially with glare. With new surgical procedures, including the insertion of a lens into the eye and glasses, vision can return to a normal range. However, some continue to have difficulty with clarity, focus, and light sensitivity.
Congenital glaucoma	Damage to eye tissue due to increased eye pressure. This condition is serious: If left untreated, the student may lose all vision.	Glaucoma causes a decrease in visual acuity and a loss of vision starting in the peripheral (outer) fields. Students experience light sensitivity and can develop cataracts.
Coloboma	Cleft or hole in various parts of the eye. Effects on vision depend on the severity of the coloboma and its location(s) in the eye.	The effects on visual performance include decrease acuity, nystagmus, and possible loss of certain visual fields or parts of fields. Possible secondary visual conditions include cataracts and microphthalmia (an abnormally small eye).
Cortical visual impairment	Damage to the visual cortex, the area of the brain that processes visual information. It is most often present with another disability such as cerebral palsy, or multiple disabilities. The eye sees, but the brain does not see.	These students appear as if they are looking at items and people. It is characterized by fluctuating visual performance, lack of attention to visual information and frequent light gazing.
Nystagmus	Secondary to many other visual disorders; however, it can be a condition by itself. Involuntary movement in one or both eyes. In some cases, it is hardly visible to the observer, but in other cases, it is very obvious, uncontrolled movement of the eyes.	Decrease in visual acuity. Many students with nystagmus locate a null point, or a positioning of the eyes that slows the eye movement, allowing for a clearer focus.
Optic atrophy	Optic nerve has deteriorated or shows atrophy. The optic nerve is instrumental in the transmission of visual information to the visual cortex in the occipital lobe.	Loss in visual acuity and loss of all or parts of visual fields. Its effects on visual functioning range from mild visual loss to visual field cuts, to blindness. Secondary conditions usually include nystagmus.

(continued)

TABLE 9.1	*(continued)*	
Visual Disorder	**Definition**	**Visual Implications**
Retinopathy of prematurity	Develops in premature infants, primarily those born at less than 32 weeks gestation. Because the retinas of the eyes of these infants are underdeveloped, exposure to the environment outside the uterus (including oxygen levels in the normal environment) causes a rapid growth of blood vessels that are fragile and rupture easily. This causes bleeding on the retina, in turn resulting in the development of scar tissue. The scar tissue causes stress to the retina, which results in tearing or detachment.	The outcome is mild to severe visual loss, with the possibility of blindness if left untreated.

Source: American Foundation for the Blind (2006).

- *Illumination*—how much or what kind of lighting does the child need to best use his or her vision, given the eye condition?
- *Color and contrast*—is there good visual contrast between the background and the object, person, or event?
- *Size*—what size object, picture, letters will allow the child to perform the task most easily?
- *Distance*—what is the best distance for learning? (Chen, 1999)

BREAKPOINT PRACTICE

1. What factors should be considered when assessing Louie's functional vision?
2. What questions would you ask Louie's parents regarding Louie's visual abilities?
3. What are the major differences between visual assessment of an infant and visual assessment of a young child?

Assessment of Visual-Motor Skills

Visual-motor skills refer to the ability to coordinate the visual system with body movements. Vision becomes a component of motor development starting as early as when the child looks toward an object and attempts to reach for it. The indicator that the child is ready for a visually directed grasp is when the child begins to look and examine his or her own hands and fingers (at approximately 3 months of age).

Delays in visual-motor development are most often identified in 4-, 5-, and 6-year-olds who are experiencing difficulty with prewriting skills or writing acquisition. Several assessments are designed to look specifically at visual-motor development and can be administered by the trained educator.

The Beery-Buktenica Developmental Test of Visual-Motor (BEERY™ VMI) (Beery, Buktenica, & Beery, 2010) is a standardized assessment that looks specifically for visual-motor deficits. It is commonly used for the assessment of preschoolers and kindergarteners who are having difficulty acquiring prewriting skills and early writing skills. It is designed to be used with children starting at age 2 and with adults. The only testing instruments are the writing booklet and a pencil. The overall assessment can be completed in less than 30 minutes, and it can be administered by an occupational therapist or an early childhood special education teacher.

The Wide Range Assessment of Visual Motor Ability (WRAVMA) (Adams & Sheslow, 1995) is an assessment that includes the comparison of visual-spatial, fine motor, and visual-motor integration and is standardized for children as young as 3 years of age. **Visual-motor integration** is coordination of motor skills from visual input. It includes drawing, visual-spatial matching, and pegboard tasks, with each subsection being administered in approximately 15 minutes.

The Bender Visual-Motor Gestalt Test (Brannigan & Decker, 2003) is an updated version of the work originally published in 1938 by Lauretta Bender. It is specifically designed to be administered by a psychologist and provides comprehensive information about visual-motor memory and the visual-motor skills of children starting at 3 years of age and those of adults. It is easy to administer; it asks the child or adult to reproduce simple line drawings.

BREAKPOINT PRACTICE

1. What may be some signs that a child is experiencing visual-motor difficulties?
2. Do you believe there is a separation between visual perception and visual-motor performance? If so, why?
3. What are some informal tasks that you can ask a child to complete to screen for visual-motor dysfunction?
4. What are some signs that vision may be the problem instead of visual-motor dysfunction?

Final Considerations

It is common for a visual impairment to coexist with other disabilities. It is critical that a comprehensive assessment take place so that the true problems can be identified and the child can receive the supports needed to have an optimal learning environment (Turnbull & Turnbull, 1998).

The National Agenda for the Education of Children and Youths with Visual Impairment, Including Those with Multiple Disabilities (2006) has recommended that a person with expertise in visual impairments be available to all children, including those in early intervention programs. It is your responsibility as a special educator to work with this person or persons so that you have the information needed to provide the environment setting that best meets the child's needs. Your input will be an integral part of the comprehensive assessment process and will be of utmost value in deciding on what is needed to make the home or setting accessible to all children, with or without a visual impairment.

HEARING ASSESSMENT

Hearing is also an essential component of any school assessment. Areas of communication, academic, behavior, and motor skills can be negatively affected if the hearing loss is not identified (Sattler, 2002). According to a report from the National Institute on Deafness and Other Communication Disorders (2006), each year about 12,000 children experience hearing loss. Approximately 28 million individuals in the United States have hearing difficulties. Identification of hearing loss as early as possible is critical, especially in the area of speech and language, because of the impact of hearing loss on speech and language development (Yoshinaga-Itano, Sedey, Cooulter, & Mehl, 1998). It is important to conduct a hearing screening and any possible follow-up assessments in order to rule out or pinpoint difficulties. In either case, identifying issues related to responding to expressive language can lead to providing appropriate services for the student (Moeller, 2000).

When students have frequent colds, allergies, upper respiratory infections, ear infections, and other health issues, hearing can often be negatively affected (National Institute on Deafness and Other Communication Disorders, 2002). Receptive language issues can also be misinterpreted as hearing problems if a hearing screening is not conducted. Hearing issues should be ruled out when assessing language (Wright, Sell, McConnell, Sutton, Thompson, Vaughn, & Bess, 1988). IDEA 2004 includes distinctions between a diagnosis of deafness and a hearing impairment. Deafness involves a hearing impairment that does not allow an individual to understand language through the hearing mode. Hearing impairment or hard of hearing involves difficulty hearing, but the individual can understand language through the hearing mode with or without hearing amplification (Individuals with Disabilities Education Improvement Act, 2004).

Physiology of Hearing

Hearing is associated with the auditory system, which is comprised of the peripheral and central auditory systems. The peripheral auditory system consists of the three segments of the ear: (1) outer ear (pinna and ear canal), (2) middle ear (tympanic membrane, malleus, incus, stapes, and Eustachian tube), and (3) inner ear (acoustic nerve and cochlea containing outer and inner hair cells). The outer ear serves as a resonator and conductor (funnels sound). The middle ear receives sound from the ossicles (malleus, incus, and stapes) beating against the tympanic membrane or eardrum. The inner ear receives sound through the hair cells via cochlear fluid (Paxinos & Mai, 2004). The central auditory system contains the brainstem and temporal lobe. Neural signals go from the brainstem to the temporal lobe for understanding (Bamiou, Musiek, & Luxon, 2001).

Hearing Testing

Types of hearing testing include pure tone screening, pure tone threshold (air conduction and bone conduction), tympanometry, speech recognition, and word recognition. See Figure 9.1 for more information regarding hearing tests.

Pure tone screening involves the use of an audiometer. This instrument (in air conduction) produces signals at distinct frequencies ranging in hertz (Hz) (high versus low pitch). The higher the number, the higher the pitch. Loudness is also included and is measured in decibels (dB). The higher the number of decibels, the louder the sound. For school-age students, the range of normal hearing is 1,000 to 4,000 Hz for pure tones (20 db) and adults (25 db). Each ear is tested separately

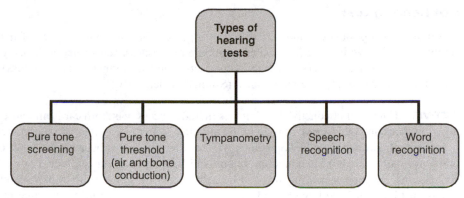

FIGURE 9.1   Types of Hearing Tests.

using headphones. The student raises his or her hand when the sound is heard. See http://www.asha.org/hearing/testing for more information).

During testing to establish pure tone threshold (the point at which an individual indicates awareness of the presence of sound), air conduction and bone conduction results are assessed. Bone conduction involves placing a vibrator at the back of the ear, on the mastoid bone. The vibrations bypass the ossicular chain of bones in the middle ear and use the mastoid bone to stimulate the cochlea. Therefore, the functioning of the inner ear can be assessed without engaging the ear canal. This allows the examiner to diagnose the presence or absence of conductive hearing loss (Niskar, Kieszak, Holmes, Esteban, Rubin, & Brody, 2001).

Tympanometry is used for the measurement of middle ear function. This handheld tool is inserted into the student's ear; it measures the movement of the middle ear and looks at the functioning of the eardrum in response to the vibration of the ossicles. A type A (normal peak), type B (flat, no peak), and type C (peak falls on negative part of graph) are possible outcomes of tympanometry (Onusko, 2004). A peak appears for a "normal" reading. Flat peak outcomes indicate possible middle-ear fluid, a stiff middle ear, tissue around the middle ear, or a tumor (Fowler & Shanks, 2002). A deep peak could indicate disarticulation of middle-ear bones (Onusko, 2004).

In speech audiometry, the evaluator investigates the student's ability to hear and understand speech at different loudness points. In language audiometry, the evaluator investigates the student's ability to hear and understand language at different loudness levels (Takayanagi, Dirks, & Moshfegh, 2002). Because there are very few tasks in real life that involve decoding only pure tones, routine screening of students should also include determination of speech reception thresholds (SRTs) (Hagerman & Kinnefors, 1995).

Sound field audiometry or visual reinforcement audiometry is used with young children who find it difficult to wear headphones or who are unable to show manual responses. The child looks toward the source of the sound. In conditioned play audiometry, the child performs an activity (i.e., placing a manipulative in a box) when he or she hears the sound (Roeser & Downs, 2004). Otoacoustic emissions (probe measuring vibration echoed to the middle ear) or auditory brainstem response (measurement of brain wave activity) can also be used to test infants for deafness (requires sedation). (See http://www.asha.org/hearing/testing for more information.) Many states such as Indiana require all infants born in medical facilities to undergo a hearing screening before being released (just like a phenylketonuria [PKU] heel stick is required).

Types of Hearing Loss

Results of these testing tools can indicate different types of hearing losses. Types of hearing losses include conductive hearing loss (outer or middle ear issues), sensorineural hearing loss (inner ear), mixed hearing loss (combination of conductive and sensorineural hearing loss), and central auditory hearing loss (processing issues) (Smith & Tyler, 2010).

CONDUCTIVE.   Causes of conductive hearing loss include excess wax, torn eardrum, otosclerosis (bony growth around the stapes), or fluid in the middle ear. In this case, air conduction results will not be normal, but bone conduction results will be normal. This is because the inner ear is functioning normally (i.e., bone conduction), but overall hearing function is affected by outer or middle ear issues. Surgery or hearing aids can be helpful and can reduce the impact. Common hearing aid problems include low or dead battery, technical issues with the instrument, and blocked earmold (see www.asha.org).

SENSORINEURAL.   In the case of sensorineural hearing loss, air conduction and bone conduction testing will reveal results that are not within normal limits. Etiology can include repeated exposure to high noise, head trauma, ototoxic drugs (drugs that cause damage in the ear—i.e., drugs that treat meningitis), viral diseases (e.g., mumps, cytomegalovirus), hereditary factors, Rh incompatibility, or head trauma. Hearing aids are generally not helpful with students affected by sensorineural hearing loss. More cochlear implants now occur at all ages.

MIXED HEARING LOSS.   Mixed hearing loss is revealed by air and bone conduction results that are out of range. Air conduction hearing is usually more out of range, and the causes were already listed. Hearing aids can be useful for students affected by mixed hearing loss. Auditory loops and transmitters are important tools in addressing the needs of a student in and out of the classroom. Auditory loops are used in rooms where there are many people. An auditory loop enhances the use of hearing aids. In the case of a transmitter, an individual receives amplified sound using an auditory device; in other words, the adult (parent or teacher) wears a microphone transmitter and the child wears a receiver. Background noise is not amplified, whereas the sound of the speaker is amplified.

Etiology

The etiology of about 33% of children with hearing loss is due to a genetic cause, 33% of hearing loss in children is due to a nongenetic cause, and 33% of hearing loss in children is due to an unknown cause (see http://babyhearing.org/HearingAmplification/Causes/index.asp and http://www.boystownhospital.org/parents/info/genetics/ten.asp). About 400 different genetic origins of hearing loss exist. These genetic origins could be part of a syndrome (i.e., Usher's syndrome, which involves progressive loss of hearing and vision). Most nongenetic hearing loss has an origin of illness or trauma that occurred before or during birth (see www.cdc.gov/ncbddd/ehdi/researchcompleted.htm).

Severity

The American Speech-Language-Hearing Association (ASHA) recognizes measurement of hearing loss levels in dB: normal range (−10 to 15 dB), slight hearing loss (16 to 25 dB), mild hearing loss (26 to 40 dB), moderate hearing loss (41 to 55 dB), moderate/severe hearing loss (56 to 70 dB), severe hearing loss (70 to 90 dB), and profound hearing loss (91+ dB) (see http://www.asha.org/public/hearing/disorders/types.htm). The American Academy of Otolarynology uses four levels of hearing loss defined in dB: mild (15 to 40 dB), moderate (40 to 60 dB), severe (60 to 90 dB) and profound (90+ dB) (see http://www.entnet.org/KidsENT/upload/KidsENT_HearingScreening.pdf). Research indicates that estimates of unilateral hearing loss involve 30 per 1,000 individuals (31.1% in the mild range, 31.8% in the moderate range, 15.3% in the severe range, and 12.0% in the profound range) and estimates of bilateral hearing loss involve 60 per 1,000 individuals (26.1% in the mild range, 28.3% in the moderate range, 16.0% in the severe range, and 18.0% in the profound range) (see http://www.cdc.gov/ncbddd/ehdi/FAQ/questionsgeneralHL.htm).

Modes of Communication

Different modes of communication exist for individuals who are hard of hearing or deaf. American Sign Language (ASL) is one language option. ASL has its own grammar and syntax and should not be viewed as a substandard version of standard English. Other sign systems include several versions of Signed English. This sign system utilizes the structure (grammar and syntax) of Standard American English. Cued Speech uses hand cues to supplement auditory and visual decoding of speech. Signs and speech reading is used in Standard American English language structure. Total Communication uses all communication modalities (speech reading, auditory training, signing, cues, and gestures). Assessment practices should take communication modality into consideration when these assessment practices are used to make educational decisions (http://www.asha.org/about/legistlation-advocacy/federal/idea/nat-env-child-facts.htm).

Professionals who are culturally competent, have the technological knowledge, are willing to collaborate with parents, are fluent in the student's communication modality, and can compare the student to peers who share the student's language modality are necessary in providing appropriate assessment services to students with hearing impairments (see http://www.asha.org/about/legislation-advocacy/federal/idea/nat-env-child-facts.htm). Note that professionals who provide services to students who are deaf or hard of hearing are in short supply (Bowen & Ferrell, 2003).

Educational Tests in the Area of Hearing Difficulties

If hearing difficulties are found in children, some educational test options are available specifically for this population. A test for phoneme decoding can include the Auditory Perception Test for the Hearing Impaired (Allen & Serwatka, 1994). The Carolina Picture Vocabulary Test for Deaf and Hearing Impaired examines receptive sign vocabulary (Layton & Holmes, 1985). The Test of Early Reading Ability—2: Deaf or Hard of Hearing (Reid, Jiresko, Hammill, & Wiltshire, 1991) addresses the ability to extract meaning from printed symbols. Note that, when assessing intelligence, a nonverbal intelligence test (see Chapter 6) is a more appropriate test compared to conventional intelligence testing for children with hearing loss.

BREAKPOINT PRACTICE

1. What types of results are connected with sensorineural hearing loss versus middle ear hearing loss?
2. What are some causes of hearing disorders?
3. What is the difference between deaf and hard of hearing?

Central Auditory Hearing Loss

In central auditory hearing loss, students usually pass air and bone conduction tests and tympanometry appears normal. However, the students have difficulty understanding speech and language in noisy environments. Students have difficulty with learning. Types of central auditory hearing loss include auditory comprehension and discrimination difficulties. Language and learning difficulties can also occur.

According to the American Speech-Language-Hearing Association (American Speech-Language-Hearing Association Working Group on Auditory Processing Disorders, 2005, p. 2), auditory processing means that "the perceptual processing of auditory information in the CNS and the neurobiological activity that underlies that processing . . . gives rise to electrophysiologic auditory potentials." That is, hearing uses electrical signals to carry information from the ear to the brain. **Auditory processing** is the retention of auditory information via neurological processing. According to ASHA, skills such as "sound localization and lateralization, auditory discrimination, auditory pattern recognition, temporal ordering and masking, auditory performance in competing acoustic signals, and auditory performance with degraded acoustic signals" make up auditory processing (American Speech-Language-Hearing Association Working Group on Auditory Processing Disorders, 2005). The American Speech-Language-Hearing Association Working Group on Auditory Processing Disorders (2005) lists seven types of central auditory processing disorder tests, including "auditory discrimination, auditory temporal processing and patterning, dichotic speech, monaural low-redundancy speech, binaural interaction, electroacoustic, and electrophysiologic assessments" (American Speech-Language-Hearing Association Working Group on Auditory Processing Disorders, 2005, p. 9). Schow, Seikel, Chermak, and Berent (2000) noted that auditory assessment measures should be simplified in an effort to connect classifications and test measures. They discussed four behavioral areas. which included "auditory pattern/temporal ordering, monaural separation/closure, binaural separation, and binaural integration" (p. 5).

Auditory processing issues can sometimes be misdiagnosed as attention deficit disorder, behavior disabilities, motivation problems, or other issues (Minnesota Department of Children Families & Learning, 2003; Schminky & Baran, 1999). Therefore, it is important that an audiologist participate in the testing and interpretation of auditory processing (Bellis, 2004). Auditory processing issues are associated with other disorders but are not due to other disorders, such as learning disabilities and language disorders (American Speech-Language-Hearing Association Working Group on Auditory Processing Disorders, 2005). Difficulties include following conversations; following directions; challenges with reading, spelling, and/or writing; and inability to hear in noisy environments (Learning Disabilities Association of America, 2006).

Subtypes of auditory processing disorders include difficulties with auditory decoding (e.g., analyzing sounds), auditory integration (i.e., word recognition), auditory associative issues (i.e., receptive language), and auditory output organization (i.e., directions) (see http://www.acenta.com/audiology.auditoryprocessing.asp). Researchers have identified intervention strategies in the area of auditory processing (Bellis, 2002, 2003; Chermak, 1998; Chermak & Musiek, 1997; Crandell & Smaldino, 2000; Musiek, 1999). Strategies have included, but are not limited to, perceptual (practicing limited stimuli, which is slowly changed), compensatory (increasing language, memory, and attention), cognitive training (could include phoneme manipulation), and modification of the environment (Keith, 1999).

Auditory processing includes auditory discrimination, which is commonly assessed. In auditory discrimination, the ability to differentiate phonemes is compromised. Some examples are high-frequency sounds that include /f/ and /s/, and /sh/ and /th/. Words are comprised of phonemes or sounds. Therefore, when the ability to differentiate or discriminate speech sounds is negatively affected, this affects one's ability to understand the speech of others. Issues with auditory discrimination can significantly affect classroom performance. In auditory discrimination tests, individuals are assessed on the ability to understand or use phonemes within spoken words. Some examples include identifying phonemes in the context of words, comparing phonemes, separating phonemes, and combining phonemes. For more information regarding auditory processing issues, see Chapter 9.

BREAKPOINT PRACTICE

1. How does an auditory processing disorder differ from a conductive hearing loss?
2. What types of difficulties would an individual with a central auditory disorder experience?
3. What are two examples of a central auditory disorder?

Auditory Processing Tests

Some common auditory processing tests include the areas of auditory discrimination, perception through the area of vision, and auditory processing. See Table 9.2 for examples of vision tests.

In the area of auditory discrimination, the Goldman-Fristoe-Woodcock Test of Auditory Discrimination (G-F-WTAD) and the Wepman Test of Auditory Discrimination, 2nd Edition (ADT–2), are commonly used. In investigating auditory perception, the Test of Auditory Processing, 3rd Edition (TAPS–3), is commonly used.

GOLDMAN-FRISTOE-WOODCOCK TEST OF AUDITORY DISCRIMINATION.   The Goldman-Fristoe-Woodcock Test of Auditory Discrimination (G-F-WTAD) (Goldman, Fristoe, & Woodcock, 1970) requires that students point to the specified pictures on plates (each plate consists of four drawings) by responding to directions that are presented via CD. No speaking or writing skills are required of the examinee for this test.

WEPMAN TEST OF AUDITORY DISCRIMINATION–2.   The Wepman Test of Auditory Discrimination, 2nd Edition (ADT–2) (Wepman & Reynolds, 1987) involves 40 pairs of words being read aloud to the student by the examiner. The student judges each pair presented as being the same or different.

TEST OF AUDITORY PERCEPTUAL SKILLS–3.   The Test of Auditory Perceptual Skills, 3rd Edition (TAPS–3), consists of the following subtests: Word Discrimination, Phonological Segmentation, Phonological Blending, Numbers Forward, Numbers Reversed, Word Memory, Sentence Memory, Auditory Comprehension, and Auditory Reasoning. Three cluster scores include Basic Auditory Skills, Auditory Memory, and Auditory Cohesion. Standard scores, scaled scores, stanines, percentile ranks, and age equivalents are available with this tool.

BREAKPOINT PRACTICE

1. Compare auditory processing tests and hearing tests.
2. Compare auditory processing tests and language tests.
3. Give an example of an item on an auditory processing test.
4. What could an auditory processing difficulty be mistaken for in the classroom?

TABLE 9.2	Vision Tests		
Test	**Author(s)**	**Description**	**Category**
Step by Step Charts, Sequence of Visual Development in Preschool	L. Harrell and N. Akeson	Checklist of normal visual development for children from birth to age 5 and ways to enhance that vision.	Vision development
First Look: Vision Evaluation and Assessment for Infants, Toddlers and Preschoolers, Birth Through Five Years of Age	B. Klingensmith, S. Smith, and J. Swanson (Eds.)	This kit includes parent interview, observation page, and definitions of skills watched for during the functional vision assessment of children from birth through age 5.	Functional vision evaluation
Individual Systematic Assessment of Visual Efficiency (ISAVE)	B. Langley	This functional vision assessment kit is used with all levels and ages of students with visual and multiple disabilities.	Functional vision evaluation, multiple impairments and visual impairments
Program to Develop Efficiency in Visual Functioning	N. C. Barraga and J. E. Morris	These materials help train students to use their vision more efficiently. The Diagnostic Assessment Procedure Kit identifies specific training needs. The Design for Instruction Kit contains lessons for vision training. For children age 3 and older.	Functional vision evaluation, vision efficiency training
What Can Baby See? Vision Tests and Intervention Strategies for Infants with Multiple Disabilities	D. Chen	This video provides and explains common techniques and instruments used for assessing vision in infants and toddlers.	Functional vision evaluation, multiple impairments and visual impairments
Oregon Project for Visually Impaired and Blind Preschool Children, Skills Inventory and Curriculum, 5th Edition	D. Brown, V. Simmons, J. Methvin, S. Anderson, S. Boigon, and K. Davis	This curriculum focuses on teaching preschoolers with visual and multiple impairments and parent–teacher partnerships.	Instructional strategies
The New York Lighthouse (LH) Symbols Test	L. HyvaÈrinen	A set of cards of varying sizes, each containing one of 4 symbols: circle, heart, apple, house, or square. Three cards can be used to assess near and distance acuity. The child identifies the symbol on the card by pointing, matching, or naming. The cards are used with high frequency for acuity testing.	Visual acuity

TABLE 9.2	(continued)		
Test	**Author(s)**	**Description**	**Category**
The Forced Preferential Looking (FPL) Tests	D. Teller	A set of cards with a variety of pattern lines based at different distances within a square. The child looks toward the square with the lines on it. The smallest pattern of lines that the child can see provides a measure of near visual acuity.	Visual development
STYCAR	M. Sheridan	A set of balls placed at varying distances from the child. Distance acuity is measured by determining the smallest ball that the child sees at the greatest distance.	Neurodevelopment
HOTV Charts	P. Good and O. Lippmann	A chart with lines composed of the letters H, O, T, and V in varying combinations and in different sizes. The smallest line of print that the child can read at 10 feet provides a measure of distance acuity. (*Note:* The local education agency [LEA] symbol acuity tests are used frequently for acuity testing.)	Visual acuity

ASSISITIVE TECHNOLOGIES

In assessment, instruction, and daily living, technology is a crucial tool. It is especially useful and necessary in the discussion of sensory assessment. It is important to keep in mind that technologies can be used as adaptations in many and in multiple areas. For example, language issues related to cognition or learning disabilities could necessitate technologies in order for the student to obtain optimal performance (i.e., adaptation of reading materials, communication devices). Therefore, many of the technologies that will be mentioned in the following sections could be used for a variety of students with various disabilities. See Chapters 10 and 11 for more discussion of cognition and adaptive skills, and communication, respectively.

Technologies are particularly significant in the area of sensory skills. **Assistive technology (AT)** is technology that permits individuals with disabilities to increase independence and quality of life. *Assistive technology (AT)* is a term used in IDEIA as an item used to "increase, maintain, or improve functional capabilities of a child with a disability" (20USC Sec. 602(1)), and these items are a focus in the Assistive Technology Act of 1998 (105-394, S.2432). Assistive technology devices can be used and/or developed for the student during an evaluation. When the evaluation supports the use of assistive technologies, and the information is included in the student's individualized education program (IEP), students can be provided training in and access (utilization or lease) to equipment for use in/or outside school. It is important for the team to train families, teachers, students, peers, and related service providers.

CEC Content Standard 8 specifically addresses the use of "appropriate technologies to support their [individuals with exceptional learning needs'] assessments" (see http://www.cec.sped.org/ps/perf_bases_stds/standards.html). These standards are endorsed by the National

Ian Shaw/Alamy

Council for Accreditation of Teacher Education (NCATE) (http://www.ncate.org). Teachers should have knowledge about, use, assess, and locate AT devices (Edyburn, 2003). However, special education educators report feeling unprepared to use AT with their students (Wahl, 2004). It is important for team members to request training when the team makes decisions to include technology in individualized family service plans (IFSPs), IEPs, individualized transition plans (ITPs), and statewide assessments.

Models of Assistive Technology

Researchers have investigated models for assistive technology approaches (Lenker & Paquet, 2003, 2004; Watts, O'Brian, & Wojcik, 2004). Two popular approaches include Students, Environment, Tasks, and Tools (SETT) (Zabala, 1995, 2005) and Matching Person & Technology (MPT) (Scherer & Craddock, 2002). SETT involves a dynamic process of collaboration among team members and revolves around the student's needs, type of AT needed, and strategies needed to optimize AT (Brady, Long, Richards, & Vallin, 2008). MPT is an approach that takes environment and individuality into consideration when the team chooses assistive technologies. Functionality of the technology is also addressed in this model.

Assistive Technology Areas

Assistive technology has many different applications in and outside the classroom. It can be used for mobility, communication (augmentative and alternative), hearing, orthotics, vision, and other daily living skills (Wehman & Kregel, 2004). **Low-level technologies** require little training, whereas **high-level technologies** generally require user training (Birnbaum, 1999). Examples of low-level technologies for the classroom include raised line paper, highlighters, correction pens, book holders, page turner aids, grips for writing tools, and calculators. Examples of high-level technologies include voice output devices, computer software, braille embossers, and wheelchairs.

VISION. The misconception has been that if a child has decreased visual acuity, then the modification would simply be to enlarge the visual images. However, many children with decreased vision actually read standard print more quickly and easily than large print (Wilkinson,

Trantham, & Koenig, 2001). Also, children who have residual vision may benefit from using optical or low-vision devices. A low-vision device is defined as any optical device made up of one or more lenses that are placed between the student's eyes and the information or object being viewed (Gardner & Corn, n.d.). Optical devices can be as simple as a tinted lens in a pair of glasses and as complex as a closed-circuit television system (Gardner & Corn, n.d.). When an individual is blind or visually impaired, output devices such as scanning/reading devices, books on tape, large-print display, braille display, braille embossers, screen-reading software, and screen magnification (low- and high-level technologies) are available options.

Braille.   The Perkins brailler continues to be used by children who are blind to create braille documents. It is best practice to introduce young braille readers to the brailler at a very young age so that the children can play with this writing tool, just as a sighted child would play with writing tools. The Perkins brailler has changed little since it was originally designed in 1951 (Perkins School for the Blind, n.d.). Many picture books and primary reading materials are in braille (American Foundation for the Blind, 2006). Braille technology has been one of the greatest advancements in making the sighted world more readily available to those who are blind. A braille display (placement of six raised dots in specific patterns) is a tactile device that provides braille navigation of computer systems such as Windows (American Printing House for the Blind, n.d.).

Other adaptations include books on tape, someone reading material for the student, appropriate lighting, and arranging furniture and room for more space (reduce obstacles). Depending on vision and other sensory and cognitive skills, the appropriate technologies can be chosen during an evaluation.

Exposure to and use of technological support is a priority for students with visual impairment. Hatlen (1996) stated that the ongoing development of technology has been instrumental in providing equal opportunities for those with visual impairment to the academic world, which is geared to those with sight. Assistive technology is the component that closes the technology gap and gives total access to students who are visually impaired. It includes any product that is used to improve the abilities of a student, including computer screen readers, screen magnification, scanners, adaptive keyboards, closed-circuit televisions, braille translation software, braille embossers, and braillers (American Foundation for the Blind, n.d.).

The availability of the continually expanding repertoire of assistive technology brings a wealth of information to students who can use it proficiently. The trained educator of students with visual impairment should conduct a comprehensive assessment of the unique needs of each student to find the appropriate match between technology and the student (American Foundation for the Blind, 2006).

MOTOR.   When an individual needs adaptations in the area of motor skills, a TouchWindow, alternate keyboards, joysticks, trackballs, switches, and alternative mice are possible input options (Wisconsin Assistive Technology Initiative, n.d.). During an evaluation and depending on the person's motor skills, one or more of these options will be examined. A TouchWindow is positioned over a monitor screen. The individual can then touch the screen to choose items. Alternate keyboards can have larger or smaller keyboards, and have a wider set of options, including keyboard labels, slant boards, and onscreen keyboards (Circle of Inclusion, 2006). The keys can be color-coded or arranged in ABC order.

Joysticks and trackballs are sold by a variety of companies. They come in many different sizes and shapes. Some joysticks have more angles of motion than others. A proper choice depends on the amount of control a student has. Trackballs allow the individual to maneuver a mouse more easily by using the tips of their fingers or their hand. An alternative mouse comes in a variety of sizes and colors that can be matched to the size of the student's hand and her or his motor skills.

Switches can be used when motor skills are more severely impaired. Switches can be operated by muscle movements (head, eye, mouth puffing, and sipping) and sound. During an evaluation, it is important to think about which part of the body the student would use, the amount of strength the student has, how much aim and range of motion the student has, and other sensory issues (Birnbaum, 1999). Switches can also control an individual's environment via appliances, televisions, alarms, and telephones. Low-level technologies around the environment can include mounts (to hold items in place), ramps, lifts, elevators, larger doorways, adapted furniture, adapted doorknobs, and specially designed kitchens and bathrooms (RehabTool, 2006).

Adaptations for students who have motor disabilities can also involve positioning. Proper positioning aids in the support of the body. Seating is one important aspect of positioning. According to Best, Heller, and Bigge (2005), pelvic position, foot support, and shoulder and trunk support are important elements of appropriate seating. They add that transferring students, and the location and mobility of students are other areas of importance.

Assistive walking devices, lifts, canes, crutches, and wheelchairs should all be part of the discussion about mobility (Lindsey, 2000). Depending on a person's motor skills in his or her arms, legs, and trunks, different options are appropriate. In the realm of assistive walking devices, walkers (reverse and nonfolding) and crutches (forearm and aluminum crutches) are options (Best, Heller, & Bigge, 2005).

An individual who has use of one or both arms can use a manual wheelchair. Electric or motorized wheelchairs assist individuals who have more severe motor involvement. Wheelchair options include conventional, power base, and scooters (Best, Heller, & Bigge, 2005). Adjustable wheelchairs that allow individuals to raise themselves vertically (to a standing position) exist. Some of the assistive technologies (i.e., joystick) aid individuals with this device. Adaptive eating utensils, drinking utensils, and specialized clocks are examples of technologies for use with daily living skills.

ASSISTIVE COMMUNICATION DEVICES.   When the motor domain is affected, labial (lip) and lingual (tongue) muscles are often affected. **Augmentative communication** devices represent an addition to natural spoken, written, or gestural speech. Alternative communication devices represent a substitute for natural spoken, written, or gestural communication (Lloyd & Blischak, 1992). **Alternative communication** includes devices that substitute for natural spoken, written, or gestural speech. So these assistive communication devices are assistive technologies. They can be low-level technologies, such as picture books, or high-level technologies, such as synthesized speech. **Synthesized speech** is electronically constructed speech.

Low-level communication devices can include communication boards made from cardboard or thick paper. Boards can incorporate photographs, pictures, markers, colored paper, and even real objects. Place one or more items on a backboard with a word label using Velcro or Dycem (sticky substance) to attach items. Picture Exchange Communication System (PECS) is an option included in this category. Medium-level technologies are sometimes referred to as talking devices that are not computer-based. Simple switches are used. The student presses on a switch and a recorded message of one or more words (i.e., "I need help" or "apple") is heard. In this case, a person records her or his speech on a device that has a microphone (digitized speech). **Digitized speech** is speech that is artificially compiled from recordings of human speech.

High-level technologies for assistive communication include electronically constructed speech, which is referred to as synthesized speech. It is important to match an individual's voice with a general age category and gender category. In other words, it is important to match the voice as much as possible to the person. For more information, see http://www.cini.org/glossary. html. Personalization is an important piece of the process. The student should be an active participant in choosing the voice that will "speak" for him or her. The individual can then access the constructed or recorded words by pressing a key or a button; pointing to a picture; using her or his voice; using a joystick or lever; using the eyes, head movements, and/or tongue movements; and sipping and/or puffing (Gragiani, 2006).

Synthesized speech products containing picture boards typically range from 4- to 32-key picture displays. Picture boards contain pictures, symbols, and/or letters. Based on the student's cognitive and language levels, key vocabulary can be programmed in to match what is often used by the student and/or what the student is learning. Expansion occurs by tapping on a picture and going into a new screen of symbols and/or pictures. For example, a student can access a collection of pictures for food, home, and vacation words (low-tech). Another option would be typing words into an assistive technology device for voice-synthesized output (text-to-speech) (high-tech). Word prediction software is also available for some of these devices.

HEARING.   Interpreters and note takers are adaptations who can help in assessment practices and in the classroom. Amplification systems, video relay services, sitting close to the teacher (but not closer than 2 to 3 feet), tape recorders, limited background noises, and visual aids are other adaptation tools (see http://www.deafweb.org/assist.htm and http://nclid.unco.edu). Other adaptations include alternate forms of standardized tests, modified scheduling, modified response mode, and extended time (Bowen & Ferrell, 2003). Braden (1992) reported that only nonverbal tests should be used in the assessment of a deaf student's intelligence (see Chapter 6).

Some other general adaptations include peer support, student groupings, sign language, repeating content, giving a study guide, highlighting important content, using manipulatives, allowing calculators, using raised or graph paper, using graphic organizers, reducing the number of items or the length of words, increasing the amount of breaks and/or break time, increasing prompts, using words of lower vocabulary level, inserting pictures, bolding material, and/or color-coding material.

Other assistive technology devices include speech recognition software, live captioning, telephone devices, environmental alert devices, cochlear implants, and listening devices (i.e., FM systems and hearing aids) (see http://www.nclid.unco.edu). In a study conducted by the Office of Vocational Rehabilitation Services in Oregon (www.oregon.gov), 73% of the participants who were deaf or hard of hearing noted that they used instant messenger programs (e.g., America Online Instant Messenger), 60% noted that they would use video remote interpreting, 61% noted that the use of web cameras was a good idea, and 80% supported video relay service. In terms of communication preferences, e-mail (92%), instant messenger (44%), and TTY calling (type text messages; 31%) were the top three preferences.

GENERAL ADAPTATIONS.   When conducting assessments, establishing the strengths and needs of the students is a vital part of the beginning of the assessment process to establish which supports a student needs (Downing, 2002). The supports allow the student to display his or her skills (Wehmeyer & Agran, 2005). Only 1% of all students at local school districts can be considered eligible to use alternate tests for the statewide assessments for students with the most severe disabilities (Committee on Education and the Workforce, 2006). So a widespread assessment mechanism for students who are low functioning focuses on standardized tests (Pratt & Stewart, 2006).

In this case, adaptations are used in the evaluation process. On an even wider scale, adaptations can include changes in the content and/or manner in which instructional methods, assignments, assessments, environment, and/or scheduling are delivered and/or responded to. This is meant to make tasks in instruction and assessment doable, meaningful, and fair to individuals. *Adaptations* is an umbrella term that can include providing additional or alternative ways for delivery or responses. Adaptations include modifications and accommodations. Modifications refer to significant changes in the instruction that changes the amount and/or level of material. Accommodations refer to providing materials to help level the playing field; they typically affect the form of the instruction or response mode. They could involve alternate goals and/or completing a portion of a program.

Wehmeyer (2002b) defines *curricular adaptations* as any changes in the curriculum, *curriculum augmentation* as any enhancing to the curriculum, and *curriculum alteration* as infusing aspects such as vocation or life skills into the curriculum. The Council for Exceptional Children lists examples of adaptations of lesson format and teaching style (Council for Exceptional Children, 1997). These would be important considerations when connecting instruction to assessment.

Rubrics, checklists, and other assessment tools can be adapted based on one or more of the general adaptations discussed previously. For more information regarding the literature on adaptations and accommodations and students with disabilities, see Williams (2001).

BREAKPOINT PRACTICE

1. In terms of responsibility for training in assistive technology, who do you think is the most critical? Why?
2. Describe how the Internet can be used specifically in the area of assessment of students with motor disabilities.
3. Which device would be most useful in the home environment for a person with a motor impairment (i.e., a person who is using a wheelchair with little use of her motor skills)? Why?
4. Which device would be most useful in the community environment for a person with a severe language impairment (i.e., to accomplish a grocery store task)? Why?
5. Which device would be most useful in the community for a person with a visual impairment (someone who has very little sight)? Why?

OTHER CONSIDERATIONS

An area of significant interest when discussing sensory disabilities is research on the deaf as related to special education assessment. Several recent studies have revealed results with significant implications for teachers and parents.

In a longitudinal study, Yoshinaga-Itano (2003) investigated language, speech, and social-emotional development of children who had hearing disabilities over the processes of screening, early identification, and intervention. This researcher found that language skills were positively related to the age at which the hearing impairment was identified. Speech and social-emotional development were highly linked to language development. Therefore, early identification was noted as a predictor to successful outcomes for students with hearing disabilities. These findings have significant applications to assessment practices.

Loots and Devise (2003) examined visual-tactile communication strategies of deaf and hearing parents of deaf toddlers who were between 18 and 24 months of age. Four groups of parents (deaf mothers, deaf fathers, hearing mothers, and hearing fathers) had significant differences. Deaf mothers and fathers adapted visual communication style to match the needs of the developmental period more than did the hearing parents. These findings have implications for increasing communication strategies with deaf children. Swisher (2000) noted similar results. Parents can become trainers for teachers and related service professionals.

Webster and Heineman-Gosschalk (2000) compared hearing teachers and deaf adults in supporting reading in deaf children. Results revealed that hearing teachers use discourse that is high in management (i.e., behavior), whereas deaf adults focus on responding to the child's intentions (i.e., communication and attention). Therefore, the students were receiving significantly different language input from adults. These findings are significant for application in the assessment/instruction settings. In a study by Calderon (2000), the researcher studied factors such as student's hearing loss, mother's educational level, mother's communication skills related to her child, and additional services used by the mother. Results revealed that poor communication skills in the mother were related to higher externalizing behavior issues (visible behaviors). Results reveal important information regarding the impact of a child's environment on his or her behavior.

BREAKPOINT PRACTICE

1. How can you use technology to better address linguistic variation in the assessment process?
2. How can you use technology to better address cultural factors in the assessment process?
3. How can you infuse technology into the assessment process in order to better involve family members?

SENSORY AND SELF-REGULATION ASSESSMENT

The early childhood years are significant for their focus on self-regulation, or the ability for children to engage in goal-directed behavior with greater independence and comfort. **Self-regulation** is the ability to manage one's actions and emotions within norms appropriate for a child's age. Children with dysfunctions in self-regulatory behaviors are prone to failures in both academic and social pursuits because their abilities to manage themselves and others may be compromised.

Parents will often describe their children with sensory regulation issues as having difficult **temperaments** (see Chapter 10), or a child's general orientation and reaction to his or her surroundings resulting in a failure to adapt successfully to his or her world with confidence and comfort. Quick to react, getting upset easily, having trouble adapting to change, and oversensitivity are hallmarks of children who find it difficult to self-regulate. The goal of the early education environment is to provide physical, social, and instructional supports to ameliorate these deficits and to build strong, prosocial patterns of behavior that assist children in increasing their executive functions associated with emotional and behavioral regulation.

Common goals in early childhood programs are "learning to get along with others," cooperative play, and following rules and routines, and children who are unable to access these schemes with ease tend to fall behind their same-age peers in most domains. It has been found that all aspects related to children's self-regulation are uniquely situated to support academic abilities, planning, problem solving, and goal-directed behavior (Blair & Razza, 2007).

The ability for children to self-regulate on entry to school is a significant factor for ensuring children's school functioning (Blair, 2002). In fact, Blair notes that "whether defined as the regulation of emotion in appropriate social responding or the regulation of attention and selective strategy use in the execution of cognitive tasks, self-regulatory skills underlie many of the behaviors and attributes that are associated with successful school adjustment" (p. 112). Shonkoff and Phillips (2000) note that "the growth of self-regulation is a cornerstone of early childhood development that cuts across all domains of behavior."

Early childhood environments are particularly predisposed to be a "central front" in supporting children (and their families) regarding goals and strategies associated with self-regulation. First, though, an accurate assessment to determine goals and strategies must be conducted. In addition, it is important to clearly identify and articulate those behaviors, or lack thereof, that are the basis for concern.

At present, there are no clear definitions of "self-regulation" or agreement on its "constituent elements" (Rimm-Kaufman et al., 2009, p. 959). Self-regulation is a concept that involves cognition, emotions, sensory integration, focus and attention, and behavioral inhibition. Each of these constructs is an assessment area unto itself. A good assessment of self-regulation often involves instruments and tools that measure the dynamic, or manifestation, of the whole of these constructs.

Sorting It Out

The definition of self-regulation is ambiguous, so it is important to consider a few factors that contribute to the inability of children to gain regulation commensurate with their chronological ages. One significant factor contributing to failure in self-regulation is in ability for children to process sensory information effectively. **Sensory integration disorder (SID)** might best be explained as a child's inability to process multiple sensory stimuli, which is typical of most environments. While most children assume the ability for sensory integration early in life, children with SID fall further and further behind when they are unable to do so.

SID involves the failure of children's abilities to process sensory input through visual, auditory, olfactory, taste, tactile, vestibular (e.g., balance and spatial orientation), and proprioceptive (e.g., body movement and position) means (Byrne, 2009). Many studies conclude that SID is highly correlated with a number of labels used for special education services: attention deficit hyperactivity disorder (ADHD), learning disabilities (LDs), autism spectrum disorders (ASDs), and nonverbal learning disabilities (NLDs) (Byrne, 2009). Failure in the sensory inputs of sight, sound, taste, and smell, and the inability for effective movement through time and space typify features associated with sensory processing and dysregulation. When sensory processing is compromised, children are prone to developmental failures in self-regulation that decrease their abilities for self-management and self-calming, and the acquisition of skills necessary for attaining age-appropriate autonomy: a major goal of early childhood programs.

Failures in sensory integration are directly related to compromised executive functioning. The term *executive function* refers to a set of cognitive abilities that are the basis of self-regulation across numerous developmental areas (see Chapter 10). Executive functions are necessary for goal-directed behavior and the ability to adapt to change. Skills such as planning actions, organizing resources, implementing an action plan, evaluating outcomes, and adapting plans and behaviors (including emotional regulation and behavioral inhibition) are traits associated with effective executive functioning. The failures in one or more of these areas lead to skews in development that can lead to developmental delays that in turn contribute to failures in academic and social skill acquisition. The ability to form conceptualizations and move toward abstract thinking is highly correlated with effective executive functioning. In fact, kindergarten teachers' ratings of children's "kindergarten readiness" point to the central role of self-regulation in their evaluations (see Blair, 2002).

BREAKPOINT PRACTICE

1. How do you think Louie's sensory deficits might affect his ability to process the environment around him?
2. What would you want to assess in Louie's social-emotional life to build a program of support for him?
3. How might you prioritize what is most important for Louie to increase his comfort with his environment, including building better social skills?

Failures in Self-Regulation

When sensory processing is compromised, children are prone to developmental failures in self-regulation that decrease their abilities for self-management, self-calming, and the acquisition of skills necessary for attaining age-appropriate autonomy: a major goal of early childhood programs. The failures in one or more of these areas lead to skews in development that can contribute to performance deficits in both academic and social settings (Chen & Boggett-Carsjens, 2005). The ability to form conceptualizations and move toward abstract thinking is highly correlated with effective executive functioning.

In the preschool setting, a variety of indicators point to compromised sensory integration and concomitant regulatory failures. Here are a few common signs as they relate to specific types of sensory dysregulation (Kranowitz, 2005; Smith & Gouze, 2004):

- Recoils when touched—even lightly.
- Overreacts to minor incidents, such as a scraped knee at recess.
- Bothered by clothing tags, rough clothing, and textures such as that of play dough.
- Engages in rough activities to seek additional sensory input.
- Underreacts to incidents such as bruising or being hit.
- Toe walking is a predominant pattern for mobility, especially at time of excitement.
- Difficulty performing fine motor tasks, such as buttoning or zipping, cutting with scissors, and drawing with crayons.
- Hypersensitive to movement: avoiding playground equipment and staying close to trusted adults.
- Hyposensitive to movement: a thrill seeker who is in constant motion.
- Low muscle tone—a limp body state, e.g., always slumping.
- Seeks out jumping and other active behaviors but may have difficulty judging space and movement.

- Distracted by sounds or appears not to hear others.
- Picky eater.
- Sensitive to bright lights.
- Difficulty getting along with peers; an ability to read peer social cues.
- Cannot accept changes in routines.
- Easily frustrated; difficulty delaying gratification needs.
- Avoidance of eye contact.
- Excessive irritability.

Many of these traits are associated with temperaments such as the "slow to warm child," the "difficult child," or "the overreactive child." Taken separately, many of these symptoms can be applied to most children at a given point in time. It is the clustering of symptoms and their extreme expression over longer durations that create dilemmas in the developmental trajectories of children.

Assessment

There are no clear avenues for assessing children with sensory regulation issues. Rather, one engages in a journey of discovery about the etiology, outcomes, and best practices to support better developmental trajectories of growth, learning, and maturation. Assessments for sensory and regulatory concerns range from informal checklists to formal, standardized assessments.

The Preschool Social Behavior Scale—Teacher Form (PSBS–T; Crick, Casas, & Mosher, 1997) assesses preschool children's social behavior, including aggression, depressed affect, and prosocial behavior. The assessment tool is comprised of 19 items clustered in the following subcategories: relational aggression (6 items), relational aggression (6 items), prosocial behavior (4 items), and depressed affect (3 items).

The Preschool Social Behavior Scale—Peer Form (PSBS–P; Crick, Casas, & Mosher, 1997) assesses relational and overt aggression and prosocial behavior. The measure includes 12 items clustered into the following subcategories: relational aggression (4 items), overt aggression (4 items), and prosocial behaviors (4 items). Children participate in two 15-minute interviews and are asked to point to pictures of peers who fit certain behavioral descriptors.

The Toddler Behavior Assessment Questionnaire (Goldsmith, 1987) assesses temperament traits including activity level, anger, fear, pleasure, and interest. This assessment includes 111 items that are rated using a Likert scale from 1 (never) to 7 (always).

The Young Children's Empathy Measure (Poresky, 1990) assesses empathy in children as measured by their ability to identify sadness, fear, anger, and happiness. Four vignettes are presented to the child to evoke a response. A rating scale from 1 (nonemotional response) to 4 (response matches the intended emotion of the vignette) is used to measure these responses.

The Child Behavior Checklist (CBCL) and the Caregiver-Teacher Report Form (C-TRF) (Achenbach & Rescorla, 2001) are used to assess areas of strengths and needs in term of behavior and language development. The tool can be used with teachers, parents, and other caregivers and is useful in identifying risk factors and support needs. The scale is comprised of 100 items with ranking from 0 (not true) to 2 (very true or often true).

The Infant/Toddler Symptom Checklist (ITSC; DeGangi, Poisson, Sickel, & Wiener, 1995) is a screening tool to assess sensory and regulatory concerns for infants and toddler ages 7 to 30 months. The instrument focuses on the following domains: (1) self-regulation, (2) attention, (3) sleep, (4) eating or feeding, (5) dressing, (6) bathing, (7) touch, (8) movement, (9) listening and language, (10) looking and sight, and (11) attachment/emotional functioning. This criterion-reference test is rated with 0 points (never or sometimes), 1 point (past), and 2 points (most times).

The ITSC checklist comes in six versions: a single short version for general screening purposes and five age-specific screens for both diagnostic and screening purposes (7 to 9 months, 10 to 12 months, 13 to 18 months, 19 to 24 months, and 25 to 30 months).

The Infant-Toddler and Family Instrument (ITFI; Apfel & Provence, 2001) assists early childhood service providers in the assessment of the well-being of children 6 months to 3 years of age and their families. The instrument is comprised of four sections: Caregiver Interview, Developmental Map, Checklist for Evaluating Concern, and the Plan for the Child and Family. The Caregiver Interview is conducted with parents or caregivers and is comprised of 35 items related to home and family life, child health and safety, and family issues and concerns. The Developmental Map involves an observation of infant-toddler behavior in the developmental areas of gross and fine motor, social and emotional, language, and coping and self-help. Observations include the child's behavior and interaction with others as well as the evaluator playing with the child using an established set of testing materials. The Checklist for Evaluating Concern is completed by the observer following the visit to assess the family in the areas of home and family environment; child health, development and safety; and stressors in the child's life. Ratings of 1 (low) to 10 (high) prioritize concerns. The Plan for the Child and Family determines the next steps in providing supports for the child and family.

BREAKPOINT PRACTICE

1. What assessments might you choose to evaluate Louie's development and why? What particular categories might be of interest to you in matching Louie's needs to an appropriate assessment measure?
2. What characteristics of sensory dysregulation (a discussion of which you can find in the previous section) do you think may be influencing Louie's development?
3. What do you want to know about Louie's self-management and self-soothing functions and how these help him? Can you think of ways that an accurate assessment of these needs can be channeled into more prosocial behavior (an increase in social-emotional skills)?

This representative sample of assessment tools encompasses a wide range of skill and developmental areas for which behavior can be assessed, goals and strategies can be determined, and evaluation of methods and procedures can be conducted. The chapter discussion conveys the breadth of assessment contexts, including the use of natural environments and key stakeholders, such as parents, teachers, and peers, and it includes numerous attributes associated with developmental failures in sensory integration and self-regulation Chapter 10 includes other assessment tools that measure self-regulation skills.

In addition to these formal assessments, many teachers use informal checklists for evaluating children's needs that are useful to their practice. For example, a Web-based service (see http://www.interventioncentral.com/index.php/behavorial-resources) offers a plethora of materials, checklists, and forms to support teachers in their evaluation, management, and recording of behaviors. The Classroom Report Card Resource Book (see http://www.jimwrightonline.com/pdfdocs/tbrc/tbrcmanual.pdf) provides examples of scales with behavioral indicators for general classroom behaviors, physical aggression behaviors, verbal behaviors, inattention/hyperactive behaviors, and socially withdrawn behaviors that can be adapted as needed for use in early childhood settings. Teachers can use existing scales as provided by the respective author(s), they can organize data for record keeping and evaluation of behaviors over longer periods of time, or they can create their own forms to assess identified behaviors of concern. The website includes a template that teachers can use for choosing relevant behaviors for evaluation, or they can fill in their identified behaviors to create daily report cards, weekly report cards, or report card monitoring charts. Jim Wright, author of this website, remarks that his design and distribution of quality response-to-intervention resources are based on his desire to make these tools available to teachers so that they are easy to access, easy to use, and available at no cost.

Many risk factors are associated with sensory and self-regulation failures in young children. Among these are constitutional factors (e.g., temperament), family or contextual issues (e.g., home environment), and developmental diagnoses (e.g., ADHD, ASD). Too often, difficult and challenging behaviors are attributed to the wrong sources and can include "shaming strategies" that accompany beliefs that children are misbehaving on purpose. The careful selection and use of instruments and checklists designed to determine etiology and developmental pathways more accurately aids educators in using best practices in their intervention approaches.

Children are resilient. Despite the numerous risk factors captured by these tools, children can and do thrive in spite of these developmental concerns. The manner in which children cope, develop, and mature depends on their mastery of essential skills associated with sensory and self-regulation. Early childhood professionals are in a unique and influential position to support this effort. It is the responsibility of those who support young children to make themselves aware of, and use, these tools for the betterment of program initiatives and children's outcomes.

Revisiting Louie

In reviewing Louie's case study, it is important to consider both formal and informal assessments that support his development and include his family in assessment and intervention processes that may enhance developmental outcomes. Examples of assessments you may have considered are the *Beery-Buktenica Developmental Test of Visual-Motor Integration*, 6th edition, for fine motor skills (Beery, Buktenica, & Beery, 2010), the Universal Nonverbal Intelligence Test (UNIT; Bracken & McCallun, 1998), the Woodcock Johnson II test of Achievement (Woodcock, McGrew, & Mather, 2001), and the Goldman-Fristoe Test of Articulation, 2nd edition (Goldman & Fristoe, 2000) for articulation skills. In addition, Louie has been diagnosed with a visual impairment that may influence the need for adaptations and modifications, including lighting, position of materials, and size and contrast of visual information, to traditional assessment methods.

Louie's developmental concerns include his ability to regulate his behavior, and based on his sensory deficits, you may have considered a number of instruments that would address these deficits and include his family in this process. For example, the Toddler Behavior Assessment Questionnaire (Goldsmith, 1987) assesses important temperament traits including activity level, anger, fear, pleasure, and interest that may provide information relevant to Louie's behaviors that are exhibited in the classroom setting. Or you may have considered use of the Infant-Toddler and Family Instrument (ITFI; Apfel & Provence, 2001) because of its distinct focus on family involvement to enhance the assessment process.

Adaptations to testing should also be incorporated as needed. Motor, speech/language, and other sensory needs affect the response mode (how the student responds) due to motor and speech/language difficulties, and use of assistive technologies would address these areas. In addition, augmentative communication devices (e.g., synthesized speech) as well as alternate keyboards may be a consideration.

In the informal assessment realm, observations and anecdotal behavioral data would be collected. Family interview and discussion should be incorporated. A technology specialist from the district could be contacted to assist in this effort with referrals, as needed, to other professionals who may be able to help. A thorough analysis of Louie's strengths would then be used to inform classroom practices. The teacher could then communicate with the technology specialist on an ongoing basis for support and revision of assessment and intervention strategies that will promote developmental outcomes through the use of these technologies. Any new high technology requires much training and support for all individuals involved with the student.

Finally, the teacher would collaborate with the speech-language pathologist, physical therapist, and other related personnel (e.g., occupational therapist, social worker) to monitor and tweak day-to-day assessment and instruction. It is imperative that the teacher devise strategies for effective communication with Louie's family to provide positive carryover activities in the home setting and to evaluate Louie's progress more accurately.

Activities

1. Name, explain, and give an example of four components of a comprehensive visual assessment.
2. How would the assessment of motor skills differ in a toddler and in a child who is school age?
3. Compare and contrast conductive, sensory-neural, mixed hearing loss, and central auditory processing.
4. List two adaptations for children in the following categories: motor, vision, language, hearing, and sensory regulation.
5. Generate a list of examples of how sensory impairments, such as Louie's, may manifest in the classroom setting.
6. Use your knowledge of assessment tools, approaches to sensory deficits, and the manifestations of sensory deficits in young children to discuss how you might make classroom modifications to meet children's needs.

Websites

Resources for materials and adaptations for children are blind or have visual impairments:

All About vision.com
http://www.allaboutvision.com/lowvision/reading.htm

American Foundation for the Blind
http://www.afb.org/

American Printing House for the Blind
http://www.aph.org/

Center for Disease Control and Prevention (CDC)
http://www.cdc.gov/ncbddd/dd/ddvi.htm

Enablemart: technology for everyone
http://enablemart.com/default.aspx?store=10&dept=12

Enabling Technologies
http://www.brailler.com/

Independent Living
http://www.independentliving.com/

The Low Vision Store.com
http://www.thelowvisionstore.com/catalog/

National Dissemination Center for Children with Disabilities (Vision Section)
http://www.nichcy.org/pubs/factshe/fs13txt.htm

Sight Connection
http://www.sightconnection.com/

Resources for materials and adaptations for the children with motor impairments:

Muscular Dystrophy Association
http://www.mda.org

Spina Bifida Association of America
http://www.sbaa.org

Spina Bifida Association of Illinois
http://www.sbail.org

United Cerebral Palsy
http://www.ucp.org

Web Accessibility in Mind
http://www.webaim.org/articles/motor/motordisabilities

Resources for materials and adaptations for the children who are deaf, have hearing impairments, auditory processing, or speech impairments:

American Association of the Deaf-Blind
http://www.aadb.org/

American Speech-Language Hearing Association
http://www.asha.org/public/hearing/disorders/

Hearing Disorders and Deafness: Medline Plus
http://www.nlm.nih.gov/medlineplus/hearingdisordersand-deafness.html

Learning Disabilities Online
http://www.ldonline.org/article/6390

Medicinenet.com
http://www.medicinenet.com/hearing/focus.htm
http://www.medicinenet.com/auditory_processing_disorder_in_children/article.htm

National Institute on Deafness and other Communication Disorders
http://www.nidcd.nih.gov/health/voice/auditory.asp

Resources for materials and adaptations for the children with sensory regulation impairments:

Intervention Central
http://www.interventioncentral.com

National Association for School Psychologists
http://www.nasponline.org/advocacy/pbs_resources.aspx

Teaching Tools for Young Children with Challenging Behavior
http://challengingbehavior.fmhi.usf.edu/tools.html

University of Kansas (Foundations of Positive Behavioral Support)
http://onlineacademy.org/modules/a201/lesson/a201c0_00100.html

References

Achenbach, T. M., & Rescorla, L. A. (2001). *Manual for ASEBA school-age forms and profiles.* Burlington: University of Vermont, Research Center for Children, Youth, & Families.

Adams, W., & Sheslow, D. (1995). *Wide range assessment of visual motor abilities.* Wilmington, DE: Wide Range.

Allen, S. G., & Serwatka, T. S. (1994). *Auditory perception test for the hearing impaired.* East Aurora, NY: Slosson Educational Publications.

American Foundation for the Blind (n.d.). Refreshabraille 18 user's guide. Retrieved February 14, 2011, from http://tech.aph.org/rbd_info.htm

American Foundation for the Blind. (2006.). *Specific assessments for students with low vision.* Retrieved October 25, 2006, from http://www.afb.org/

American Optometric Association. (2006). *Visual acuity: What is 20/20 vision?* Retrieved October 25, 2006, from http://www.aoa.org/

American Printing House for the Blind, New York (n.d.). Products catalog. Retrieved October 28, 2006, from http://www.aph.org/

American Speech-Language-Hearing Association. (2006a). *Guidelines for the roles and responsibilities of the school-based speech-language pathologist.* Retrieved October 10, 2006, from http://www.asha.org/about/legistlation-advocacy/federal/idea/nat-env-child-facts.htm

American Speech-Language-Hearing Association. (2006b). *Hearing screening.* Retrieved October 15, 2006, from http://www.asha.org/hearing/testing

American Speech-Language-Hearing Association. (2006c). *The prevalence and incidence of hearing loss in children.* Retrieved October 15, 2006, from http://www.asha.org/public/hearing/disorders/types.htm

American Speech-Language-Hearing Association Working Group on Auditory Processing Disorders. (2005). (Central) auditory processing disorders. *Technical Report,* 1–20.

Apfel, N., & Provence, S. (2001). *Manual for the infant-toddler and family instrument (ITFI).* Baltimore: Brookes.

Assistive Technology Act of 1998. Public Law 105-394, §2432.

Bamiou, D., Musiek, F., Luxon, L. (2001). Aetiology and clinical presentation of auditory processing disorders—a review, *Archives of Disease in Childhood, 85,* 361–365.

Barraga, N. C. (2004, October). A half century later. Where are we? Where do we need to go? *Journal of Visual Impairment & Blindness, 98*(10), 581–583.

Beery, K. E., Buktenica, N. A., & Beery, N. A. (2010). *Beery visual-motor integration,* (6th ed.). Upper Saddle River, NJ: Pearson Education.

Bellis, T. J. (2002). Developing deficit-specific intervention plans for individuals with auditory processing disorders. *Seminars in Hearing, 23*(4), 287–295.

Bellis, T. J. (2003). *Assessment and management of central auditory processing disorders in the educational setting: From science to practice* (2nd ed.). Clifton Park, NY: Delmar Learning.

Bellis, T. J. (2004, March). Redefining auditory processing disorder: An audiologist's perspective. *The ASHA Leader,* 22–23.

Best, S. J., Heller, K. W., & Bigge, J. L. (2005). *Teaching individuals with physical or multiple disabilities* (5th ed.). Upper Saddle River, NJ: Merrill/Pearson Education.

Birnbaum, B. (1999). *Connecting special education and technology for the 21st Century.* Lewiston, NY: Edwin Mellen Press.

Blair, C. (2002). School readiness: Integrating cognition and emotion in a neurobiological conceptualization of children's functioning at school entry. *American Psychologist, 57,* 111–127.

Blair, C., & Razza, R. (2007). Relating effortful control, executive function, and false belief understanding to emerging math and literacy ability in kindergarten. *Child Development, 78,* 647–663.

Bowen, S. K., & Ferrell, K. A. (2003). Assessment in low-incidence disabilities: The day-to-day realities. *Rural Special Education Quarterly, 22*(4), 10–19.

Bracken, B. A., & McCallem, R. S. (1998). *Universal test of nonverbal intelligence.* Itasca, IL: Riverside.

Braden, J. P. (1992). Intellectual assessment of deaf and hard-of-hearing people: A quantitative and qualitative research synthesis. *School Psychology Review, 21*(1), 82–94.

Brady, R. T., Long, T. M., Richards, J., & Vallin T. (2008). Assistive technology curriculum structure and content in professional preparation service provider training programs. *Journal of Allied Health, 36*(4), 183–192.

Brambring, M. (2007). Divergent development of gross motor skills in children who are blind or sighted. *Journal of Visual Impairment & Blindness, 212,* 225.

Brannigan, G. G., & Decker, S. C. (2003). *Bender visual-motor gestalt test—II.* Itasca, IL: Riverside.

Byrne, M. (2009). Sensory processing disorder: Any of a nurse practitioner's business? *Journal of the American Academy of Nurse Practitioners, 21*(6), 314–321.

Calderon, R. (2000). Parental involvement in deaf children's education programs as a predictor of child's language, early reading, and social-emotional development. *Journal of Deaf Studies and Deaf Education, 5*(2), 140–155.

Chen, D. (1999). *Essential elements in early intervention: Visual impairment and multiple disabilities.* New York: AFB Press, American Foundation for the Blind.

Chen, M., & Boggett-Carsjens, J. (2005). Consider sensory processing disorders in the explosive child: Case report and review. *Canadian Child and Adolescent Psychiatry Review, 14*(2), 44–48.

Chermak, G. D. (1998). Managing central auditory processing disorders: Metalinguistic and metacognitive approaches. *Seminars in Hearing, 19*(4), 379–392.

Chermak, G. D., & Musiek, F. E. (1997). *Central auditory processing disorders: New perspectives.* San Diego, CA: Singular.

Circle of Inclusion. (2006). Retrieved October 18, 2009, from http://www.circleofinclusion.org

Committee on Education and the Workforce. (2006). *Flexibility on testing students with disabilities.* Retrieved October, 18, 2009, from http://www.house.gov/ed_workforce

Council for Exceptional Children. (1997). Effective accommodations for students with exceptionalities. *1*(9), 1–15.

Crandell, C., & Smaldino, J. (2000). Room acoustics for listeners with normal-hearing and hearing impairment. In M. Valente, H. Hosford-Dunn, & R. Roeser (Eds.), *Audiology: Treatment* (pp. 601–623). New York: Thieme Medical.

Crick, N. R., Casas, J. F., & Mosher, M. (1997). Relational and overt aggression in preschool. *Developmental Psychology, 33*(4), 579–588.

DeGangi, G., Poisson, S., Sickel, R., & Wiener, A. S. (1995). *Infant/toddler symptom checklist: A screening tool for parents.* San Antonio, TX: Therapy Skill Builders, Psychological Corporation.

Downing, J. E. (2002). *Including students with severe and multiple disabilities in typical classrooms.* Baltimore: Brookes.

Edyburn, D. L. (2003). *What every teacher should know about assistive technology.* Boston: Allyn & Bacon.

Fowler, C. G., & Shanks, J. E. (2002). Tympanometry. In J. Katz., R. F. Burkard, & L. Medwetsky (Eds.), *Handbook of clinical audiology* (5th ed., pp. 175–204). Philadelphia: Lippincott Williams & Wilkins.

Gardner, L., & Corn, A. (n.d.). Low vision: Access to print. Retrieved February 14, 2011, from http://www.cecdvi.org/Postion%20Papers/low_vision_print.htm

Goldman, R., & Fristoe, M. (2000). *Goldman-Fristoe test of articulation* (2nd ed.). Circle Pines, MN: American Guidance Service.

Goldman, R., Fristoe, M., & Woodcock, R. (1970). *Goldman-Fristoe-Woodcock test of auditory discrimination.* Circle Pines, MN: American Guidance Service.

Goldsmith, H. H. (1987). *The toddler behavior assessment questionnaire: A preliminary manual.* Eugene: University of Oregon, Department of Psychology.

Gragiani, J. (2006). *Assistive communication devices by Dynavox.* Lecture for alternative curriculum course. Chicago: Dynavox.

Hagerman, B., & Kinnefors, C. (1995). Efficient adaptive methods for measuring speech perception thresholds in quiet and noise, *Scandinavian Audiology, 24*(1), 71–77.

Hatlen, P. (1996, Spring). The core curriculum for blind and visually impaired students, including those with additional disabilities. *Re:View, 28*(1), 25–32.

Howard, V., Williams, B., & Lepper, C. (2010). *Very young children with special needs: A foundation for educators, families, and service providers* (4th ed.). Upper Saddle River, NJ: Merrill/Pearson Education.

Huebner, K. (2000). Visual impairment. In M.C. Holbrook and A.J. Koenig (Eds.), *Foundations of education* (2nd ed.). *Volume 1. History and theory of teaching children and youth with visual impairments* (pp. 55–76). New York: AFB Press.

Individuals with Disabilities Education Improvement Act. (2004). Public Law 108-446 (20 U.S.C. 1400 et seq.).

Jose, R. (Ed). (1999). *Understanding low vision.* New York: American Foundation for the Blind.

Keith, R. W. (1999). Clinical issues in central auditory processing disorders. *Language, Speech, and Hearing Services in Schools, 30,* 339–344.

Koenig, A. J., & Holbrook, M. C. (2000). Ensuring high-quality instruction for students in braille literacy programs. *Journal of Visual Impairment & Blindness, 94,* 677–694.

Kranowitz, M. A. (2005). *The out-of-sync child: Recognizing and coping with sensory processing disorder.* New York: Penguin Books.

Layton, T. L., & Holmes, D. W. (1985). *Carolina picture vocabulary test for deaf and hearing impaired.* Austin, TX: PRO-ED.

Learning Disabilities Association of America. (2006). *Definition of learning disabilities.* Retrieved October 1, 2009, from http://www.ldaamerica.us/aboutld/parents/help/parents.asp

Lenker, J. A., & Paquet, V. L. (2003). A review of conceptual models for assistive technology outcomes research and practice. *Assistive Technology, 15*(1), 1–15.

Lenker, J. A., & Paquet, V. L. (2004). A new conceptual model for assistive technology outcomes research and practice. *Assistive Technology, 16*(1), 1–10.

Lindsey, J. D. (2000). *Technology & exceptional individuals.* Austin, TX: PRO-ED.

Lloyd, L. L., & Blischak, D. M. (1992). AAC terminology policy and issues update. *Augmentative and Alternative Communication, 8,* 104–109.

Loots, G., & Devise, I. (2003). The user of visual-tactile communication strategies by deaf and hearing fathers and mothers of deaf infants. *Journal of Deaf Studies and Deaf Education, 8*(1), 31–42.

Minnesota Department of Children Families & Learning. (2003). *Introduction to auditory processing disorders.* Retrieved October 1, 2009, from www.nesc.k12.mn.us

Moeller, M. P. (2000). Early intervention and language development in children who are deaf and hard of hearing. *PEDIATRICS, 106*(3), e43.

Musiek, F. E. (1999). Habilitation and management of auditory processing disorders: Overview of selected procedures. *Journal of the American Academy of Audiology, 10,* 329–342.

National Agenda for the Education of Children and Youths with Visual Impairment, Including Those with Multiple Disabilities. (2006). Retrieved October 25, 2006, from http://www.tsbvi.edu/agenda/index.htm

National Institute on Deafness and Other Communication Disorders. (2002). *Otitis media (ear infection).* (NIH Publication No. 974216). Bethesda, MD: Author.

National Institute on Deafness and Other Communication Disorders. (2006). Retrieved October 1, 2009 from http://www.nidcd.nih.gov/health/statistics/hearing.asp

Niskar, S., Kieszak, S., Holmes, A., Estegban, E., Rubin, C., & Brody, D. (2001). Estimated prevalence of noise-induced hearing threshold shifts among children 6 to 19 years of age: The third National Health and Nutrition Examination Survey, 1988–1994, United States, *PEDIATRICS, 108*(1), 40–43.

Onusko, E. (2004). Retrieved November 2, 2009, from http://www.aafp.org/afp/20041101/1713.html

Pacific Audiology. (n.d.). Example of audiogram. Retrieved August 17, 2007, from http://www.pacificaudiology.com/audiogram/uya.html

Palmer, E. (2003). Implications of the natural course of retinopathy prematurity. *Pediatrics, 111*(4), 885–886.

Paxinos, G., & Mai, K. (2004). *The human nervous system* (2nd ed.). Boston: Elsevier Academic Press.

Perkins School for the Blind. (n.d.). Retrieved February 14, 2011, from http://www.perkins.org

Poresky, R. H. (1990). The young children's empathy measure: Reliability, validity, and effects of companion animal bonding. *Psychological Reports, 66,* 931–936.

Pratt, C., & Stewart, R. (2006). *Teaching students who are low-functioning: Who are they and what should we teach?* Retrieved October 15, 2009, from http://www.iidc.indiana.edu/irca

RehabTool. (2006). Assistive technology resources and links. Retrieved November 3, 2009, from http://www.rehabtool.com

Reid, K. D., Jiresko, W. P., Hammill, D. D., & Wiltshire, S. (1991). *Test of early reading ability—2: Deaf or hard of hearing.* Austin, TX: PRO-ED.

Ricci, S. S., & Kyle, T. (2009). *Maternity and pediatric nursing* (1st ed.). Philadelphia: Lippincott, Williams, & Wilkins.

Rimm-Kaufman, S. E., Curby, T. W., Grimm, K., Nathanson, L., & Brock, L. L. (2009). The contribution of children's self-regulation and classroom quality to children's adaptive behaviors in the kindergarten classroom. *Developmental Psychology,* 45, 958–972.

Roeser, R., & Downs, M. (2004). *Auditory disorders in school children: The law identification and remediation* (4th ed.). New York: Thieme.

Roman-Lantzy, C. (2007). *Cortical visual impairment: An approach to assessment and intervention*. New York: AFB Pewaa.

Sattler, J. M. (2002). *Assessment of children: Behavioral and clinical applications* (4th ed.). San Diego: Sattler.

Scherer, M., & Craddock, G. (2002). Matching person & technology (MPT) assessment process. *Technology and Disability, 14*, 125–131.

Schminky, M. M., & Baran, J. A. (1999). Deaf-blind perspectives. Retrieved September 14, 2009, from http://www.tsbvi.edu

Schow, R. L., Seikel, J. A., Chermak, G. D., & Berent, M. (2000). Central auditory processes and test measures: ASHA 1996 revisited. *American Journal of Audiology, 9*, 1–6.

Shonkoff, J., & Phillips, D. (2000). *From neurons to neighborhoods: The science of early childhood development*. Washington, DC: National Academy Press.

Sigelman, C. K., & Rider, E. A. (2009). *Life-span human development* (6th ed.). Belmont, CA: Wadsworth Cengage Learning.

Smith, K. A., & Gouze, K. R. (2004). *The sensory-sensitive child*. New York: Harper-Collins.

Smith, D. D., & Tyler, N. C. (2010). *Introduction to special education*. Columbus, OH: Pearson.

Swisher, M. (2000). Learning to converse: How deaf mothers support the development of attention and conversation skills in their young deaf children. In P. Spencer, C. Erting, & M. Marschark (Eds.), *The deaf child in the family and at school: Essays in honor of Kathryn P. Meadow-Orlans* (pp. 21–39). Mahwah, NJ: Erlbaum.

Takayanagi, S., Dirks, D., & Moshfegh, A. (2002). Lexical and talker effects on word recognition among native and non-native listeners with normal and impaired hearing. *Journal of Speech, Language, and Hearing Research, 45*, 585–597.

Turnbull, H. R., III, & Turnbull, A. P. (1998). *Free appropriate public education* (5th ed.). Denver, CO: Love Publishing.

Wahl, L. (2004). Surveying special education staff on AT awareness, use and training. *Journal of Special Education Technology, 19*(2), 57–59.

Watts, E. H., O'Brian, M., & Wojcik, B. W. (2004). Four models of assistive technology consideration: How do they compare to recommended educational assessment practices? *Journal of Special Education Technology, 19*, 43–56.

Webster. A., & Heineman-Gosschalk, R. (2000). Deaf children's encounters with written texts: Contrasts between hearing teachers and deaf adults in supporting reading. *Deafness and Education International, 2*(1), 26–44.

Wehman, P., & Kregel, J. (2004). *Functional curriculum for elementary, middle, & secondary age students with special needs* (2nd ed.). Austin, TX: PRO-ED.

Wehmeyer, M. (2002a). *Promoting the self-determination of students with severe disabilities*. Eric EC Digest #E633.

Wehmeyer, M. (2002b). *Providing access to the general curriculum: Teaching students with mental retardation*. Baltimore: Brookes.

Wehmeyer, M. L., & Agran, M. (2005). *Mental retardation and intellectual disabilities*. Upper Saddle River, NJ: Merrill/Pearson Pearson.

Wepman, J. M., & Reynolds, W. M. (1987). *Wepman test of auditory discrimination—2nd edition (ADT–2)*. Los Angeles: Western Psychological Services.

Wilkinson, M. E., Trantham, C. S., & Koenig, A. J. (2001). Achieving functional literacy for children with visual impairments. *Visual Impairment Research, 3*(2), 85–95.

Williams, J. (2001). Adaptations & accommodations for students with disabilities. Retrieved October 13, 2009, from http://www.nichcy.org

Wisconsin Assistive Technology Initiative. (n.d.). Retrieved February 14, 2011, from http://www.wati.org/content/supports/free/pdf/form/Checklist-Form.pdf

Woodcock, R. W., McGrew, K. S., & Mather, N. (2001). *WJ-III tests of cognitive abilities and tests of achievement*. Itasca, IL: Riverside Publishing.

Wright, P. F., Sell, S. H., McConnell, K. B., Sutton, A. B., Thompson, J., Vaughn, W. K., & Bess, F. H. (1988). Impact of recurrent otitis media on middle-ear function, hearing, and language. *Journal of Pediatrics, 113*, 581–587.

Yoshinaga-Itano, C. (2003). From screening to early identification and intervention: Discovering predictors to successful outcomes for children with significant hearing loss. *Journal of Deaf Studies and Deaf Education, 8*(1), 11–30.

Yoshinaga-Itano, C., Sedey, A., Coulter, D., & Mehl, A. (1998). Language of early- and later-identified children with hearing loss, *PEDIATRICS, 102*(5), 1161–1171.

Zabala, J. (1995). *The SETT framework*. Closing the gap conference on the use of assistive technology in special education and rehabilitation. Minneapolis, MN.

Zabala, J. (2005). SETT and reSETT: Concepts for AT implementation. *Closing the Gap, 23*(5), 1–11.

Cognitive and Social-Emotional Assessment

CHAPTER 10

CHAPTER OBJECTIVES

Based on the case study of Joey, you will be able to categorize his developmental concerns within the constructs of a developmental framework and with knowledge of assessment strategies appropriate for assessing his strengths and needs in the cognitive and social emotional domains.

This chapter addresses the Council for Exceptional Children (CEC) Standards 2 (Development and Characteristics of Learners), 3 (Individual Learning Differences), and 8 (Assessment) and National Association for the Education of Young Children (NAEYC) Standard 3 (Understanding and Practicing Responsible Assessment to Promote Positive Outcomes for Each Child).

Assessing Joey

Joey is a 5-and-a-half-year-old boy in your preschool early childhood education classroom. His parents state that he has always been more sensitive, rambunctious, impulsive, and self-centered than his older sister. At first, his parents believed it was just a "boy versus girl thing." Now, they are more concerned because he is having trouble following directions, getting along with others, and managing his anger at school.

Joey appears to be a very bright, verbal young boy. He was adopted when he was 3 months old. His birth mother abused drugs and alcohol during the gestational period and lost custody of Joey. His parents describe him as having been a very difficult-to-soothe infant and say that they still struggle with getting him to "settle down." They say that Joey focuses on things that interest him for long periods of time, but if he is not immediately interested or there is too much going on around him, he cannot focus.

Joey's teachers have frequently discussed the concerns that they have about Joey with his parents: not getting along with others; easily frustrated; always wants to be first; reactive when he does not get his way immediately; inconsistent academic performance, particularly comprehension skills; and incoherent narratives, or getting lost in trying to engage with others through conversation.

Joey's teachers enjoy him very much. As one teacher said: "When Joey is sweet, he is really sweet, but when Joey is angry or upset, he will 'let you have it.'" Joey's teachers understand that this behavior is not about his intent but rather about developmental concerns that were present at birth. They support Joey by providing frequent, explicit direction and guidance to remind him of rules and expectations, give him breaks to allow him to relax, and help him work through his reactivity by supporting him in calming down and welcoming him back into the classroom environment as soon as he is able to do so. They are working to get Joey ready for kindergarten with the hope that he will be able to go as an independent student. They are worried, however, that his academic performance is inconsistent (e.g., reads without comprehension, loses main ideas in simple stories, has difficulty with numeration) and his social skills may hamper his success in the kindergarten setting.

Based on the case study of Joey, what do you think are the main elements of his development that might concern you? What steps might you take to understand his development so that you have a clearer understanding of his skills and abilities? What tools are available to support you in determining Joey's strengths, needs, and goals for intervention?

By the conclusion of this chapter, you will be able to respond to the questions posed in the case study about Joey. In addition, you will be able to understand developmental issues associated with cognition and social-emotional skill acquisition and assessment tools that may help you in understanding these domains in young children's lives. Throughout this chapter, you will be asked questions to help you apply concepts associated with the assessment of cognition and social-emotional skills in young children with special needs.

COGNITION AND SOCIAL-EMOTIONAL DEVELOPMENT

Cognitive and social-emotional skills are two distinct but highly interrelated domains that are critical to children's success in school and for which new paradigms are emerging. Although there has been a tendency to focus on these domains separately as predictors of school success, research indicates that the combination of these skill sets are critical to ensuring both academic and social achievement (Leerkes, Paradise, O'Brien, Calkins, & Lange, 2008), and they serve as a buffer to failure in a variety of contexts (Ewing Marion Kauffman Foundation, 2002).

The term *cognition* comes from Latin "to know" or "to recognize." In early childhood settings, **cognition** refers to a child's evolving mental and intellectual processes that guide children's actions toward more formal thinking patterns, or a complex set of mental processes by which one acquires, organizes, and applies knowledge. It is the construction of thought processes, including attention, memory, learning, language, thinking, and reasoning (decision making), that occurs across the life span. During infancy, this progression begins as sensorimotor actions, or infants' use of innate reflexes to engage and gain mastery of their environments. Assessment of cognitive skills in infancy tends to focus on object permanence, means to an end, and causality, among other early developmental milestones.

Gargiulo and Kilgo (2005) state that cognitive development is evident when "children attend to stimuli; integrate knew knowledge with existing knowledge and skills; perform preacademic skills such as counting, sorting and letter recognition; and perform increasingly complex problem-solving tasks" (p. 96). Included in their summary of early cognition is the role of short- and long-term memory and the ability to sequence activities, make distinctions between objects and events, and pursue avenues of planning. As children move into early childhood, cognition is typically measured through pre-academic skills (e.g., letter and number recognition, prewriting skills), with more formal academic skills assessed when children enter the primary grades.

Social-emotional development can be defined as emerging behaviors that are identified by children's use of secure attachments with their caregivers and peers and that manifest in positive relationships, increasing self-regulation, confidence, curiosity, motivation, communication, and social competence. These skills begin in infancy with the establishment of reciprocal interactions that emerge in the preschool years as turn taking, taking others' perspectives, and learning to communicate and manage emotions. In 1950, Erik Erikson described eight stages of development that encompassed the social-emotional tasks over the life span. The first four stages are relevant to social-emotional development in young children and the outcomes for which the children are striving. They can be summarized as learning to trust, learning to be autonomous, learning to take initiative, and learning to set and attain goal pursuits. The ability to negotiate these developmental stages successfully depends on both the constitutional characteristics of the child (e.g., temperament) and the role of caregivers in providing a "goodness of fit" with the child to promote these outcomes.

In early childhood settings, it is important to understand the interrelated nature of social-emotional development and its role in enhancing cognitive skill acquisition and mastery. For example, through infant observation, we know that learning processes are occurring from birth through infants' active engagement with their environment (sensorimotor). Through use of relationships (reciprocity), infants and young children learn to form meaning from the incorporation of new information and novel stimuli that develop and organize skills of perception and thinking. Through the interplay of a child's social and cognitive worlds, development is enhanced and skills emerge.

Over recent decades, there has been an increased focus on relationships and their central role in the assessment and evaluation of young children, especially children with special needs. The emerging literature suggests the importance of a more comprehensive approach for understanding the needs of and resources to support children with special needs in their development. The use of relationships to scaffold specific development outcomes within the context of children's everyday routines and interactions (Bruder, 2000) leads to greater comfort in skill acquisition (cognition), the use of others for support (social skill), and a great sense of self-worth (emotional skill).

MAJOR THEORIES

Among the significant contributors to our understanding of cognitive development and the use of the social contexts for learning are Jean Piaget (1932, 1969, 1970) and Lev Vygotsky (1978). Both men gave greater definition to the manner in which children develop cognitively through mental construction, or the way in which a child builds new **schemes** of thinking by fitting new information with what the child already knows. While Piaget and Vygotsky diverge in their conceptualizations of cognitive development, both view children's social context as highly relevant to learning and intellectual growth.

Piaget

Swiss biologist and psychologist Jean Piaget (1896–1980) was a pioneer in altering the view of children's thinking processes by examining the manner in which children's thinking evolved and developed. Piaget hypothesized that cognition is **epigenetic** in nature, or that it unfolds in a predictable sequence based on maturation and one's interaction with the environment. Schemes can be defined as the mind's representation of perceptions and ideas, and the actions that go along with them. As children interact with their world and gain more experience, schemes are modified to make sense of that experience and to categorize new experiences. Infants begin life with a limited repertoire of sensory and motor schemes (reflexes and sensorimotor skills) that increase and are modified by interactions with their environment. As children reach toddlerhood, these schemes increase in complexity and integrate with one another to form more complex mental representations that aid in perception, organization, thinking, and action to support adaptation to the environment.

Piaget defined a person's **adaptation** to the environment through two complementary processes that are used throughout the life span: assimilation and accommodation. In essence, assimilation and accommodation are the "bookends" of adaptation. **Assimilation** refers to the incorporation of new events into preexisting cognitive structures or mental representations that a child has already gained through past experience. **Accommodation** refers to the necessary changes that must take place in those existing structures and representations to incorporate new information. Here is an example:

A baby enjoys her "play keys," sucking on them and "batting them around" for pleasure. When the baby comes upon a piece of Mommy's heirloom jewelry, she repeats the same action, demonstrating that she has assimilated *the concept—much to her mother's dismay! However, when the infant attempts to replicate this action with her brother's football, she realizes that this scheme won't work—so the baby knocks the ball, watches it roll, and* accommodates *a new scheme of interaction with the objects around her.*

According to Piaget, when a child has a balance between what she or he knows and can do (e.g., playing with keys), the child has a sense of **equilibrium**. Alternatively, when a child is presented with information that is unfamiliar (e.g., a football), he or she experiences a sense of **disequilibrium** that sets in motion a child's need for developing new behaviors in order to master the environment.

Piaget asserted that cognitive development occurs in a series of four distinct stages that are universal and epigenetic in nature (see Figure 10.1). In other words, all development progresses through a successive set of stages, each building on the other, to form higher-level thinking abilities. Researchers have found that these processes unfold in the same manner for all children, regardless of their developmental status (Hooper & Umansky, 2009). Children with special needs, for example, may progress through stages of cognitive development more slowly, but they do so in the same sequence as their nondisabled peers. Piaget contributed many central notions to the understanding and assessment of children's cognitive development through his definition of specific concepts associated with cognitive development (see Figure 10.2).

BREAKPOINT PRACTICE

1. How would you describe Joey's stage of development and why?
2. What issues within what developmental stage would you want to assess for Joey?
3. What do you think you might want to know about Joey's adaptation to his environment?
4. Why might it be hard to understand equilibrium versus disequilibrium given Joey's developmental picture?

Stage	Age (in Years)	Characteristics of Stage
Sensorimotor	0–2	During this stage, children learn about themselves and their environment through motor activity and reflex actions. Children learn that they are separate from their parent(s), with the understanding that their parents are "still around" even when they are absent (object permanence). Knowledge is limited to sensations, movement, and experiences, primarily with parents. Limited symbolic language appears at the end of this stage.
Preoperational	2–7	During this stage, egocentric thinking is predominant, or children think people "think like they do." Thinking is irreversible and illogical, with limited flexibility. Although children in this stage are more capable of thinking about people and events that are not in the present, there is limited conceptualization of time. There is an increase in the use of symbols and language, and memory skills are developed. The use of imagination emerges, with vivid fantasies a hallmark of this stage.
Concrete operations	7–11	During this stage, children develop the capacity for abstract thinking and can make rational judgments about observable, concrete phenomena. Egocentrism diminishes. Operational thinking develops, with reversible, flexible thinking emerging. Thinking is demonstrated by use of logic and manipulation of symbols related to concrete objects.
Formal operations	12+	During this stage, thinking is demonstrated through the logical use of symbols and abstract concepts. Adolescence brings a brief return to egocentrism, but rational judgments are made using hypothetical and deductive reasoning.

FIGURE 10.1 Piaget's Stages of Child Development.

accommodation	The difference made to one's mind or concepts by the process of assimilation. Note that assimilation and accommodation go together: You can't have one without the other.
adaptation	Adapting to the world through assimilation and accommodation.
assimilation	The process by which a person takes in material from his or her environment, an event that may mean changing the evidence of his or her senses to make the information fit with preexisting knowledge.
classification	The ability to group objects together on the basis of common features.
class inclusion	The understanding that is more advanced than simple classification, that some classes or sets of objects are also subsets of a larger class. For example, there is a class of objects called dogs; there is also a class called animals. But all dogs are also animals, so the class of animals includes that of dogs.
conservation	The realization that objects or sets of objects stay the same even when they are changed about or made to look different.
decentration	The ability to move away from one system of classification to another, as appropriate.
egocentrism	The belief that you are the center of the universe and everything revolves around you; the corresponding inability to see the world as someone else does and adapt to it. Not moral selfishness, just an early stage of psychological development.
operation	The process of working something out in your head. Young children (in the sensorimotor and preoperational stages) have to act, and try things out in the real world, to work things out (like count on their fingers). Older children and adults can do more in their heads.
schema (or scheme)	The representation in the mind of a set of perceptions, ideas, and/or actions that go together.
stage	A period in a child's development in which he or she is capable of understanding some things but not others.

FIGURE 10.2 Piaget's Cognitive Processes.

Vygotsky

Lev Vygotsky (1896–1934) was a Russian psychologist who, like Piaget, believed that children's interactions with their environment are central to their cognitive development and acquisition of knowledge. Vygotksy hypothesized that children require psychological tools that mediate thoughts, feelings, and behaviors, with language being the most important of these tools.

Vygotsky divided thinking into lower and higher mental functions. **Lower mental functions** contain processes such as sensation, attention, and memory; skills with which we are born. **Higher mental functions** include focused attention, deliberate memory, and logical thinking (Sternberg & Williams, 1998). For example, when teachers sing the ABC song in their classrooms, children initially pattern this song and take great pleasure in singing it to themselves and others. Children who learn the song initially often do so in rote fashion (lower mental function), with no recognition of the letters as symbols that have meaning. In time, children learn that the letters have meaning and can apply this knowledge (higher mental function) to early literacy experiences, such as letter identification, phonetic awareness, and recognition of common or important words.

Vygotsky offers two constructs that are central to early childhood assessment: the zone of proximal development and scaffolding. Vygotsky (1978) defines the **zone of proximal development (ZPD)** as "the distance between the actual developmental level as determined by independent problem solving and the level of potential development as determined through problem solving under adult guidance or in collaboration with more capable peers" (p. 86). Through a process he termed **scaffolding**, or building sequential skills through the use of relationship-based guidance, Vygotsky asserted that independent functioning and the construction of new concepts depended on assistance provided by adults and more competent peers. (Scaffolding is also often called **mediated learning**.) Vygotsky held that relationships are essential to helping children scaffold new and emerging skills and that working within the ZPD was the optimal context for success. From a traditional perspective, assessment focuses on the measurement of skills and abilities on standardized measures where children "hit a ceiling" of performance. Conversely, Vygotsky focused on children's achievements within joint activity, or the abilities for children's potential learning when mediated by others (Lidz, 1995).

Vygotsky's theory of socially mediated learning is of paramount importance to early childhood settings serving children with special needs. Children with special needs are prone to manifest problems in their social interactions with others (Guralnick, 1990; Lowenthal, 1996) and, compared to their typically developing peers, use less effective social strategies, including lower rates of social initiation, maintenance, and response behaviors (Friend, 2007). Vygotsky (1978) asserts the critical importance of understanding children's use of social skills for cognitive development when he states that "every function in the child's cultural development appears twice: first, on the social level, and later, on the individual level; first, between people (interpsychological) and then inside the child (intrapsychological) … all the higher functions originate as actual relationships between individuals" (p. 57).

BREAKPOINT PRACTICE

1. Which characteristics in Joey's development would you consider a benefit to mediated learning alliances? Which of his characteristics would be a barrier?
2. How might assessment be altered by the characteristics that Joey presents?
3. How might the concept of ZPD be applied to Joey?

Intelligences	Descriptor
Linguistic	Words
Logical-mathematical	Numbers and logic
Spatial	Pictures
Musical	Music
Intrapersonal	Self-reflection
Body-kinesthetic	Physical experience
Interpersonal	Social experience
Naturalistic	Natural world experience

FIGURE 10.3 Multiple Intelligences.

Multiple Intelligences

Intelligence is an umbrella term to describe cognitive processes and acquired knowledge. While intelligence has been traditionally viewed as a finite set of innate traits and characteristics, other theorists have posited that intelligence is a multifaceted concept with many numerous caveats. Among these theorists is Harvard psychologist, Howard Gardner, who made a significant contribution to our understanding of intelligence by defining multiple intelligences in eight different categories (see Figure 10.3). Gardner's seminal work has been defined as a paradigm shift in thinking about intelligence and intelligence testing. Gardner refutes the notion that intelligence is a finite trait that can be measured simply by intelligence quotient (IQ) tests. Rather, he suggests that intelligence "is the ability to solve problems, or to create products, that are valued within one or more cultural settings" (Gardner, 1993, p. x). This fundamental change in the perception of intelligence is increasingly making its way into U.S. classrooms, informing both teaching and assessment practices.

Social-Emotional Intelligence

The term *emotional intelligence* was initially coined by Salovey and Mayer (1990) and has been defined as "the ability to perceive accurately, appraise, and express emotion; the ability to access and/or generate feelings when they facilitate thought; the ability to understand emotion and emotional knowledge; and the ability to effectively regulate emotions in ways that promote emotional and intellectual growth" (Mayer & Salovey, 1997, p. 10). In early childhood settings, **social-emotional skills** (emotional intelligence) are the behaviors and approaches necessary to self-regulate and participate successfully in school settings. Psychologist, Daniel Goleman (1995), has contributed significantly to our understanding of emotional intelligence in his delineation of skills necessary for optimal developmental outcomes (see Figure 10.4).

Steps	Descriptor
Knowing your emotions	Demonstrating self awareness
Managing your own emotions	Using a range of appropriate emotional responses
Motivating yourself	Using your emotions in pursuit of goals
Recognizing and understanding other people's emotions	Demonstrating empathy and social awareness
Managing the emotions of others	Recognizing and accommodating others' emotions in pursuit of goals

FIGURE 10.4 Goleman's Emotional Intelligence.

Function	Descriptor
Planning	The ability to make a mental picture of how we will reach our goals.
Organization	The ability to use a system to arrange resources and/or thoughts.
Time management	The ability to keep track of time, to allocate time limits for the completion of tasks, to stay within time constraints and meet deadlines.
Metacognition	The ability to step back and view oneself objectively and evaluate progress in solving problems.
Self-regulation of affect	The ability to manage emotions and to control behavior to achieve goals.
Inhibitory control	The ability to suppress certain thoughts or actions that impede goal attainment.
Working memory	The ability to keep information in mind while working on complex tasks.
Flexibility	The ability to adapt to new situations by revising plans when one encounters obstacles, setbacks, new information, or mistakes.
Goal-directed persistence	The ability to stay on task until a goal is attained without being diverted by distractions.
Theory of mind	The awareness and understanding of the mental states of others and their effects on our beliefs and behaviors.

FIGURE 10.5 Executive Functions.

One key indicator of social-emotional development is the use of **executive functions (EFs)**, or the cognitive processes that aid in behavioral planning and preparation. Horowitz (2007) describes these cognitive processes as behind-the-scenes activity that prepares one for planning, executing, and accomplishing tasks. Executive function is an overarching term that encompasses a broad range of skills necessary for regulation and goal-directed activity. Executive functions are most simply defined as one's abilities to solve problems. These abilities include the capacity for defining a problem, making a plan to solve it, implementing a plan of action to address the problem, assessing how that plan is working, and initiating corrective actions to rework plans that are ineffective. While definitions vary, there is general consensus regarding the processes that are at play in executive functioning (see Figure 10.5).

Evidence suggests that executive functions are fundamental to academic achievement. For example, in a recent study of self-regulation and academic performance, it was determined that children's self-regulation skills, specifically the abilities to shift and focus attention and to inhibit impulsive responding, were uniquely related to early academic success and account for a greater variation in early academic progress than measures of intelligence (Blair & Razza, 2007). The ability for children to regulate their attention with purposeful planning is an essential characteristic of academic achievement and is attained through synchronous relationships with others. Executive function failures in early childhood setting manifest in a variety of ways (see Figure 10.6).

A final characteristic of social-emotional development is the basic temperament traits that children bring into the world and that facilitate or hinder their success for effectively managing their environments. Thomas and Chess (1977) explain **temperament** as the characteristic way the child experiences and relates to the environment as defined in three broad categories: easy (laid back), difficult (more reactive), and slow-to-warm-up (inhibited). They define temperament traits along nine dimensions: mood, approach-withdrawal, intensity, threshold, rhythmicity, distractibility, attention span, persistence, and adaptability (see Figure 10.7). The ability to organize experience, which is largely enhanced or thwarted by temperament traits, is a necessary consideration in cognitive development and may warrant further assessment and investigation as a

Poor planning, organization, and execution of a project or play scheme, such as the need for getting a racetrack ready before a game of "cars" can be played.

Difficulty initiating tasks or generating ideas independently and becoming overreliant on others for directing play schemes and other interactions.

Lack of effective mental strategies, such as memorizing simple rhymes or recalling routine information (e.g., locating a familiar bathroom).

Trouble organizing information for task performance, such as independently remembering all of the items necessary for enjoying a snack (e.g., napkin, straw, etc.).

Lack of a coherent narrative or the fact that a child has trouble telling a story in an organized, sequential manner.

FIGURE 10.6   Examples of Poor Executive Function.

foundation for effective intellectual growth. When working with children from backgrounds other than your own, it is important to note that cultural referents inform the manner in which children's temperaments are understood. Different cultures place different values on the types of behaviors their children demonstrate. While some children are expected to be quiet and dutiful, others are welcome to explore their world and assert themselves in a spirited manner.

Many theoretical principles both support and underpin the effective assessment of cognitive and social-emotional domains and are beyond the scope of this chapter. The inclusion of the theoretical perspectives presented here provide a context for understanding the interplay of cognitive and social-emotional skill development and the importance of viewing the interaction of these skill sets as possible areas of focus for a more accurate assessment of children's development.

Temperament Dimension	Descriptor
Activity	The amount of physical motion that occurs during children's sleep, eating, play, dressing, bathing, or other typical daily tasks.
Rhythmicity	The ability of the child to develop a regular schedule associated with physiologic functions such as eating, sleep, and toileting.
Distractability	The child's efficacy in filtering out extraneous stimuli that interfere with continuous behavioral performance.
Approach/withdrawal	The manner in which children initially respond to new stimuli, including people, places, food, toys, situations, and changes in rules and routines.
Adaptability	The ease or difficulty in which children can modify their actions to work in a more effective manner.
Intensity	The level of energy children use to respond.
Mood	A range of behaviors from positive mood traits, such as happy go lucky, to more negative mood traits, such as frequent anger, depression, and disappointment.
Persistence and attention span	The ability to stay with a task and limit attention to the relevant details for task completion.
Sensory threshold	The degree of sensory stimulation necessary to evoke a response in a child. Children with a low sensory threshold may demonstrate greater sensitivity to extraneous details such as noise, temperatures, pain, textures, odors, and tastes.

FIGURE 10.7   Temperament Dimensions and Descriptors.

BREAKPOINT PRACTICE

1. What type or types of intelligence may represent strengths for Joey?
2. What difficulties might Joey have in acquiring emotional intelligence?
3. Why would it be important to understand Joey's skews in development as a means of knowing his abilities for emotional intelligence and for accurate assessment?
4. What might be difficult in using relationship-based approaches? How might this inform your assessment?
5. What elements of executive function (EF) do you believe might be a struggle for Joey to attain?
6. How might your answer to Breakpoint Practice 5 relate to assessment of Joey's cognition?
7. How might Joey's use of attention relate to the assessment process?

ASSESSMENT OF COGNITION

Standardized (Norm-Referenced) Assessments

The conceptualization of cognitive skills and their relationship to academic, social, and emotional development is complex (Kritikos, 2010). The use of standardized testing for young children, particularly those with special needs, has been debated for its usefulness, purposes, and application for planning appropriate programs for young children (Myers, McBride, & Peterson, 1996; Neisworth & Bagnato, 1992, 2000). Standardized testing of intelligence for young children with exceptionalities is especially precarious because of the skill-level variances unique within a categorical disability and across domains of exceptionality. In cases where a known syndrome or categorical disability exists, developmental milestone delays and difficulties in certain areas of assessment are expected to exist. For example, typical developmental milestones (e.g., walking) may be delayed and fail to meet norm-referenced standards, but they may fail to identify accurately the level of the child's cognitive development. Similarly, a child with a hearing impairment will perform quite differently on standardized tests than a child with a visual or motor impairment (LeDosquet, 2010). These considerations are essential in selecting and using standardized assessment measures and certainly indicate that caution should be used in interpreting data from these instruments.

The Bayley Scales of Infant and Toddler Development—Third Edition (Bayley–III) (Bayley, 2005) is a commonly used standardized assessment tool that was originally designed to assess infants and toddlers from birth to age 30 months. Revised editions have been expanded to assess infants and toddlers from 12 to 42 months.

The Bayley–III consists of three scales with child interaction (cognitive, language, and motor) and two scales with parent questionnaires (social-emotional and adaptive behavior). Examples of items in the cognitive domain are sensory/perceptual acuities, discrimination, and response; acquisition of object constancy; memory learning and problem solving; vocalization and beginning of verbal communication; basis of abstract thinking; habituation; mental mapping; complex language; and mathematical concept formation.

A benefit of the Bayley–III is the rich data that comes from combined observations of both professionals and those significant people who have daily interactions with the child (e.g., parents, caretakers). In addition to the full assessment tool, the Bayley–III Screening

Test is an easy-to-administer instrument that uses items from the full assessment. The Screening Test can be administered in 15 to 25 minutes and can more quickly determine if children are developing at an appropriate pace or if more in-depth assessment is indicated. An observation checklist is also available to assess children through incidental observations of their development; this checklist has items aligned with the full Bayley–III.

The Bayley–III was normed on 1,675 children using 2000 census data and includes populations within its sample that are representative of gender, race-ethnicity, region, and parental education. Validity studies have shown strong correlations between the Bayley–III and other standardized measures, such as the Wechsler Preschool and Primary Scale of Intelligence—3rd Edition (WPPSI–III). The technical manual reports high reliability (over .80) and specificity/sensitivity (.77–1.00) scores; the percentage of misdiagnosis is low, ranging from 2 to 8%.

The Battelle Developmental Inventory—2 (BDI–2) (Newborg, 2005) is a standardized tool that was developed in 1984 and revised in 2005 through the cooperative efforts of several disciplines. The inventory consists of 450 items (100 screening items) that assess skill development in five developmental domains: personal-social, adaptive, motor, communication, and cognition. The cognitive domain includes the following subscales: attention and memory, reasoning and academic skills, and perceptions and concepts.

The BDI–2 is unique in its design because it uses a 3-point (0–1–2) scoring system and allows for credit where skills are emerging. Data is collected through test administration, parent and teacher interviews, and teacher observations in the natural environment. It also allows for a variety of test administration modifications for children who have sensory or physical challenges. The BDI–2 also includes a screening tool that can be administered in 10 to 30 minutes, depending on the age of the child, instead of the comprehensive examination that takes 1 to 2 hours to administer. The screening test is an abbreviated instrument that includes 100 test items from the full BDI–2.

Test administration begins at the suspected developmental age of the child. If the screening instrument is used, it may determine the need for further assessment and can find the starting point for a full administration of the BDI–2. A basal score is established when a child receives a score of 2 on three consecutive items; a ceiling is reached when the child receives a score of 0 on three consecutive items. Normative data for the BDI–2 were gathered from over 2,500 children between birth and age 7 years 11 months. Reliability was determined with internal consistency, standard error of measurement, test-rest and inter-rater reliability. This instrument is available in English and Spanish.

The Wechsler Preschool and Primary Scale of Intelligence—Revised—Third Edition (WPPSI–III) (Wechsler, 2002) is one of the more common instruments used for assessing the cognitive ability of young children. The test is for preschoolers age 2.6 to 7.3 years, with the combination of subtest scoring designed to provide verbal intelligence quotients (VIQs), performance intelligence quotients (PIQs), and a full-scale intelligence quotient (FSIQ). The new version of the test features short, more gamelike activities designed to hold the attention of younger children. The purpose of the WPPSI-III is to measure more accurately the intellectual abilities in young children. The instrument contains four core subtests for ages 2.6 to 3.11 years: receptive vocabulary (VIQ), information, block design, and object assembly (PIQ), and 7 core subsets for ages 4.0 to 7.3 years: information, vocabulary, word reasoning (VIQ), block design, matrix reasoning, picture concepts (PIQ), and coding (FSIQ). The WPPSI–III was normed on a sample of 1,700 children in nine age groups and is representative of gender, race, ethnicity, parental education level, and geographic region. The reliability coefficient for the WPPSI–III subtests ranges from .83 to .95. Administration time for children ages 2.6 to 3.11 years is 30 to 45 minutes; for children ages 2.6 to 7.3 years, it is 60 minutes.

The Stanford-Binet—5 for Early Childhood (Early SB–5) (Roid, 2005) is designed to assess the intellectual functioning of children ages 2.0 to 7.3 years (2 to 5.11 years for the full battery, 6 to 7.3 years for the abbreviated battery). Norming is based on a representative sample of 1,800 children and is co-normed with the Bender Visual-Motor Gestalt Test and the Test Observation Form. Reliability data for the Early SB–5 are .97 to .98 for the FSIQ and .81 to .92 for the subtests. The Early SB–5 has 10 subtests. Two subsets, nonverbal fluid reasoning and verbal knowledge, cover ages 2.0 to 7.3 years. The remaining eight subtests offer scores in the pre-school range, from ages 2.0 to 5.11 years, and measure quantitative, visual-spatial, and working memory abilities. Administration time is 30 to 50 minutes for the full battery and 15 to 20 minutes for the abbreviated battery.

The Test Observation Checklist was newly developed for the revision of the Early SB–5 and identifies a range of behaviors that may indicate behavioral or cognitive difficulties. The checklist addresses 21 areas of behavior that help identify the need for further assessment and includes observation, interview, or contacts with parents or other caregivers. The Early SB–5 assesses cognitive and developmental delays; identifies developmental disabilities and exceptionalities; and aids in planning intervention, including individual education and family plans. The instrument includes child-friendly toys and manipulatives, nonverbal/low-verbal content, and low-end items for measurement of children functioning at a lower level of development, and reports its usefulness for evaluating children with limited English who are deaf and hard of hearing, and children with autism. A parent report is available to assist in facilitating communication with children's parents and caregivers.

Criterion- and Curriculum-Referenced Assessments

Educators are most often concerned about how assessment data can assist them in planning programs of support for the children they serve. Criterion-referenced and curriculum-referenced tests tend to offer information that is more readily useful to the classroom teacher because measurement is not based on a comparison of children to their same-age peers, as is the case with norm-referenced testing procedures. Rather, criterion-referenced tools are designed to

© Zurijeta/Shutterstock.com

assess specified criteria or master levels of performance in specific developmental domains (e.g., cognition, social-emotional). Curriculum-referenced assessment is a criterion-referenced approach and differs primarily by its design, which is intended to align specifically with the classroom curriculum.

The Brigance Inventory of Early Development—II (Brigance IED–II) (Brigance, 2004) is a skill-based, developmentally sequenced assessment tool with norm-referenced interpretation available; it is standardized and validated for children from birth to 7 years of age, with or without disabilities. Domains include pre-ambulatory motor skills, gross motor skills, fine motor skills, self-help skills, speech and language skills, and social-emotional development. Early academic skill sections include general knowledge and comprehension, readiness, basic reading skills, manuscript writing, and basic math. Of particular relevance to teachers is the sequence of behaviors in each domain, which helps in instructional assessment and planning for students. Time for administration varies (approximately 20 to 55 minutes), depending on the age of the child. Data may be collected in a typical test environment or via interviews with parents, teaching staff, caregivers, or a combination of these. Assessments may be administered in any order, with suggested entry points, basals, and ceilings provided. The IED–II reports having an internal consistency of .85 to .99, test-retest reliability of .89 to .95, and inter-rater reliability of .82 to .96. The instrument also ranks high for discriminant validity when given to children with and without disabilities and associated risk factors for developmental delays. These groups of children score significantly different on the instrument.

The Brigance Infant and Toddler Screen (Brigance & Glasgoe, 2002) provides a sampling of children's development and skills in the following key areas: fine motor, gross motor, expressive language, receptive language, self-help, and social-emotional skills. By combining scores on these subtests, an evaluator can obtain an indicator of cognitive development because development is emerging at this early phase. The Brigance Screens were initially standardized using a sample of 1,564 children. Additional standardization was conducted with infants and toddlers in 21 states to produce normative information for children from birth to 23 months (infant screen: birth to 11 months, toddler screen: 12 to 23 months).

The Hawaii Early Learning Profile (HELP) (Parks, 1997) is designed for assessing children from birth to age 3 and is a widely used curriculum-based, family-centered assessment. The HELP is not standardized, but it uses data for the identification of needs, tracking growth and development, and determining next steps for targeting appropriate objectives. Assessment domains include regulatory/sensory organization, cognition, language, gross motor, fine motor, social, and self-help. All of the skill sets are age-sequenced. The HELP is designed as a play-based assessment, with the environment being prearranged by the evaluator. Items on the HELP are scored as present, not present, emerging, atypical/dysfunctional, or not applicable. This information is used to measure outcomes and to track progress over a set period of time. An activity guide is provided for each skill area, which aids as a link to instruction.

The HELP for Preschoolers (Teaford, Wheat, & Baker, 2010) is designed to assess children ages 3 to 6 years and is also a curriculum-based assessment tool for documenting children's growth and progress both in home and school settings. Like the HELP, it is not standardized, but it aids in the identification of needs, growth tracking, and instructional planning. Assessment domains are the same as for the HELP. General assessment procedures are designed to elicit behaviors or examples of observation opportunities. Examples of adaptations for children with exceptional learning needs are also included. Many of the HELP instruments' documents are available in Spanish.

The Transdisciplinary Play-Based Assessment—Second Edition (TPBA–2) (Linder, 2008) was developed by Tony Linder in 1990 as a curriculum-referenced tool that assess four developmental domains: cognitive, language, social-emotional, and the sensorimotor development of children from infancy to age 6. This instrument is structured so that evaluators can obtain information regarding the growth and development children at five levels of play. The items for this assessment are arranged by the evaluator and are preselected to represent all domains of development. Successive stages of play are used, from imitation of activities to reciprocal interaction with peers and parents. The primary purpose of this instrument is to assist in developing a plan for specific interventions for young children. A play facilitator interacts primarily with the child during the evaluation, while a parent facilitator provides interpretations of observations. Video recording is used for scoring by team members (e.g., speech–language pathologist, occupational therapist).

The Early Learning Accomplishment Profile—Third Edition (Glover, Preminger, & Sanford, 2002) is a criterion-referenced assessment to assist educators, parents, and other service providers in assessing the individual skill development of children from birth to age 36 months across six domains of development: gross motor, fine motor, cognitive, language, self-help, and social emotional. Results of the E-LAP can be used for getting an overall picture of how children are developing. The test is useful for planning instruction, and it is appropriate for use with children who have exceptionalities. Administration of the E-LAP takes from 45 to 90 minutes. The E-LAP does not use age norms, although identified stages are based in research, with the manual suggesting that it is essential that ages for specific developmental gains be viewed as "approximate in nature."

The Carolina Curriculum for Infants and Toddlers with Special Needs—Third Edition (CCITSN–3) (Johnson-Martin, Attermeier, & Hacker, 2004) and its companion tool, the Carolina Curriculum for Preschoolers with Special Needs—Second Edition (CCPSN–2) (Johnson-Martin, Hacker, & Attermeier, 2004) are curriculum-referenced assessment tools that assesses children through observation in the following domains: personal-social, cognition, communication, fine motor, and gross motor. Both tools are described as a systematic curriculum that directly links assessment (observation) with activities that promote skills that children have not mastered. Administration time for the CCITSN–3 (children from birth to age 36 months) is 60 to 90 minutes; the administration time is 60 to 120 minutes for the CCPSN–2 (children ages 2 to 5). Assessment procedures can be divided into two sessions, if necessary. Instrument protocols are based on informal observations with directed assessment, and they include parents and other familiar adults in observation exercises. Assessment results are not normed, but they are based on approximately age-based levels of development in each domain. Assessment logs and developmental progress charts are available in Spanish. The preschool manual has been translated into Korean, and the manual for infants and toddlers is translated into Portuguese, Russian, Korean, Chinese, Spanish, and Italian.

The Ages and Stages Questionnaires—Third Edition (Squires & Bricker, 2009), is described as a tool to "screen infants and young children for developmental delays during the crucial first 5 years of life." Parents or caregivers complete questionnaires that take approximately 10 to 15 minutes to complete and 2 to 3 minutes to score. The tool is designed for children ages 1 to 66 months and screens children in the domains of communication, gross motor, fine motor, problem solving, and personal-social. Item responses are scored as yes, sometimes, and not yet, with scores compared to established screening cutoff points to indicate if more in-depth evaluation is necessary. The test manual reports strong validity and reliability and has versions available in English and Spanish (French and Korean are available in previous formats).

BREAKPOINT PRACTICE

1. What assessments (e.g., standardized, normed, criterion-referenced) might you use to assess Joey and for what purposes? How might a standardized test help or limit your understanding of Joey's needs?
2. Describe positive and negative indicators in using standardized versus criterion-referenced measures in assessing Joey.
3. What types of developmental information would you want to glean from the assessment process?
4. How might observation be a benefit for assessing Joey?
5. What might be appropriate contexts or settings for Joey's assessment and why?

ASSESSMENT OF SOCIAL-EMOTIONAL DEVELOPMENT

In early childhood special education settings, social-emotional skills are highly related to both cognitive skills and, in particular, executive functions. Although social-emotional skills are typically identified by relationships with others, use of play schemes as a means for interaction, and socially appropriate skills, such as turn taking, the case can be made that building solid executive functions are central to the aims of social-emotional skill development. For example, self-regulation (the ability to manage one's physical body and emotional reactions, and use focused attention) and the ability to perceive the needs of others (taking another's point of view, sharing with others, letting others be first) are typical social-emotional skills that are supported in special education settings (see Chapter 9). These same skills are synonymous with executive function skills, in particular, metacognition (knowledge of one's own thinking), self-regulation, inhibitory control, and theory of mind (understanding one's own mind and the minds of others). In choosing assessment tools, it is important to remember that, in addition to teaching curricular (content) skills, effective development of social-emotional skills is highly contingent on cognitive skills (executive functions) that support children's unfolding abilities for availability and receptivity for the acquisition of the instructional content.

An emerging pool of instruments is available for assessment of social-emotional skills and self-regulation (executive functions) (see the websites related to attention deficit disorder and learning disabilities that are listed at the end of this chapter). Other assessment tools are available that define a better understanding of children's temperament and the manner in which they approach and engage in the environments around them.

The ability to organize experience, which is largely enhanced or thwarted by temperament traits and the use of executive functions, is a necessary area of focus for understanding the innate characteristics that color the dispositions children exhibit in socialization and problem solving. Inclusion of assessment approaches for addressing these foundations of self-regulation and children's availability to their environments may be warranted.

Assessment Tools for Social-Emotional Development

The Vineland Social-Emotional Early Childhood Scales (SEEC) (Sparrow, Balla, & Cicchetti, 1998) is a standardized, norm-referenced evaluation for children from birth to age 6. Norms were developed from 1,200 children from birth to age 5 years 11 months, with consideration given to chronological age, gender, geographic region, parent education, race and ethnic group, and community size. The instrument helps to assess children's social-emotional functions through interviews with parents or caregivers most familiar with the child. Areas of assessment include the examination of the child's feelings, relationships, and interactions with others. Skills such as paying attention, reciprocal interactions, and self-regulating behaviors are significant features. Time for administration is 15 to 25 minutes. Parent communication reports are available in Spanish and English.

Social Competence and Behavior Evaluation Preschool Edition (SBCE) (LaFreniere & Dumas, 1995) is a standardized, norm referenced evaluation measure assessing social competence, affective expression, and adjustment in preschoolers ages 2.5 to 6 years. Its primary objective is not to diagnosis children, but to describe children's behavior for the purposes of socialization and education. The instrument is completed by teachers, contains 80 items, and can be completed in approximately 15 minutes. The basic scales include assessment of a range of behaviors, including depressive-joyful, anxious-secure, angry-tolerant, isolated-integrated, aggressive-calm, egotistical-prosocial, oppositional-cooperative, and dependent-autonomous. Summary scales include social competence, externalizing problems, internalizing problems, and general adaptation. A short-form assessment is available, as are translations in Spanish, English, and French.

The Social Skills Improvement System (SSIS) (Gresham & Elliott, 2008) is a norm-referenced tool that assesses individuals and small groups for the evaluation of social skills, problem behaviors, and academic performance. Teacher, parent, and student forms provide a comprehensive picture of skills across home, school, and community settings. The instrument is divided into three domains: social skills (communication, cooperation, assertion, responsibility, empathy, engagement, and self-control), competing problem behaviors (externalizing, bullying, hyperactivity/inattention, internalizing, and autism spectrum), and academic performance (reading achievement, math achievement, and motivation to learn). Frequency and importance ratings indicate behaviors that may require intervention. Administration time is 10 to 25 minutes and the age range for children is 3 to 18 years. A performance screening guide and classroom intervention guide are available. This assessment measure is available in English and Spanish. Also available is the SSIS Performance Screening Guide, a more time-efficient screening instrument that assesses the domains of prosocial behaviors, motivation to learn, reading skills, and math skills.

The Infant-Toddler and Emotional Assessment (ITSEA) (Carter & Briggs-Gowan, 2005) is a standardized, norm-referenced tool designed to detect social-emotional behavioral problems, and delays in the acquisition of competencies in children ages 12 to 48 months. Assessment occurs in natural environments and relies on parent and caregiver observations. The instrument can be administered as a questionnaire or structured interview. The measure includes four behavioral domains: externalizing problems (e.g., aggression), internalizing problems (e.g., depression/withdrawal), regulatory problems (e.g., sleeping, eating, unusual sensitivities), and competencies (e.g., compliance, empathy, emotional awareness). Items are rated on a 3-point scale: 0 (not true/rarely), 1 (somewhat true/sometimes), and 2 (true/often). There is a "no opportunity to observe" option, too. Administration time is 20 to 30 minutes to complete as a questionnaire, and 35 to 45 minutes to complete as an interview. There is also a short version, the Brief Infant-Toddler Social and Emotional Assessment, which can be used as an initial screen for the ITSEA. This tool is available in English and Spanish.

The Behavioral Assessment of Baby's Emotional and Social Style (BABES) (Finello & Poulsen, 1996) is a screening tool consisting of three scales: temperament, ability to self-soothe, and regulatory processes. The instrument is designed for children from birth to age 3 and for use in pediatric settings, including early intervention programs. The BABES is a 29-item scale that is completed by parents and takes approximately 10 minutes. Standardization is based on a limited sample of 128 parents, mostly mothers. It is available in both English and Spanish.

The Strengths and Difficulties Questionnaire (SDQ) (Goodman, 1997) is a brief questionnaire, with several versions, all designed around 25 attributes divided among five scales: emotional symptoms, conduct problems, hyperactivity/inattention, peer relationship problems, and prosocial behavior. This tool is designed for children ages 3 to 16 and takes 10 minutes to administer. The first four of the five domains can be summed to yield a "total difficulties" score. This tool is available in English, Spanish, and 45 other languages.

The Carey Temperament Scales (CTS) are comprised of questionnaires for five age groupings, four of which are appropriate to early childhood settings: the Early Infancy Temperament Questionnaire (EITQ) for infants ages 1 to 4 months, the Revised Infant Temperament Questionnaire (RITQ) for infants ages 4 to 11 months, the Toddler Temperament Scale (TTS) for children ages 1 to 3 years, and the Behavioral Style Questionnaire (BSQ) for children ages 3 to 7 years. The TTS is a set of items, using parental report of a child's temperament; it consists of 75 to 100 descriptions of behavior to assess nine New York Longitudinal Study (Thomas, Chess, & Birch, 1968) characteristics of temperament: activity level, rhythmicity, approach-withdrawal, adaptability, intensity, mood, attention span and persistence, distractibility, and sensory threshold. Each questionnaire contains up to 100 items that are rated on a 6-point scale of frequency ranging from almost never to almost always. Test items are tabulated to yield a category score for each of the nine target areas. The Caregiver Report includes the temperament profile and provides an interpretive report of scores written for the caregiver. Information gathered from interviews, observations, and related information collected by professionals is encouraged to enhance the use of this instrument.

The Temperament and Atypical Behavior Scale (TABS) (Bagnato et al., 1999) assesses atypical temperament and the self-regulatory behaviors of infants and young children, ages 11 to 71 months, for which they may be at risk for developmental delay. The instrument is comprised of two parts: (1) a screening tool, which is a one-page, 15-item checklist with yes or no responses that can be used to determine the need for further assessment, and (2) the full assessment tool, which is a 55-item checklist with yes, no, and "need help" responses used to obtain a total raw score called the Temperament and Regulatory Index (TRI). Raw scores are also provided for the four following subtests: detached, hypersensitive/active, underreactive, and dysregulated. The TABS can be used as a screening tool to identify serious developmental problems targeted for intervention, to provide assistance to parents in managing behaviors, and to evaluate the effects of intervention efforts.

BREAKPOINT PRACTICE

1. What indicators of Joey's temperament are relevant for understanding his behavior?
2. How might issues of self-regulation be a factor in understanding Joey's academic performance or his scores on assessments?
3. Which items (behavioral clusters) might you most be interested in so that you know more about Joey and his abilities?
4. Which tool(s) may provide you with the most information about Joey's relationships with other children?
5. In which of Joey's environments might you want to consider implementing assessments and why?

ASSESSMENT CONSIDERATIONS

Regardless of a child's age, the overall purpose of assessment, beyond determining eligibility for services, is to help teachers make instructional decisions that best meet the needs of the children they support. Because of the exponential changes in growth and development between birth and age 8, it is often difficult to pinpoint children's skills and abilities at a moment in time. Consequently, it is critical that consideration be given to assessment methods that support children's development along a continuum to garner reliable data useful for the specific needs of children across a variety of domains (Zaslow, Calkins, & Halle, 2000; Neisworth & Bagnato, 2004). The assessments already described in this chapter are representative of available instruments to meet this goal.

Several considerations should be reviewed when selecting appropriate instruments to meet the needs of children, families, and the educational setting. There has been significant research regarding the appropriate assessment of young children, including those with special needs. For example, the Division for Early Childhood (DEC) of the Council for Exceptional Children (CEC) (Sandall, McLean, & Smith, 2000) and the National Association for the Education of Young Children (NAEYC) (Bredekamp & Copple, 1997) have devised benchmarks that guide professionals in selecting appropriate tools for assessment endeavors. Bagnato (2007) highlights 10 of the 46 DEC standards for assessment worthy of consideration:

- *Utility*—the usefulness of the instrument for application to intervention.
- *Acceptability*—parent/teacher agreement regarding content and methods, including the culturally relevancy of the tool for the child and the family.
- *Authenticity*—use of natural settings and contexts that will more likely elicit actual skill performance than may be captured by standardized procedures.
- *Equity*—the acceptability of instruments for use with children having exceptionalities.
- *Sensitivity*—instruments have enough items to define more precisely age and skill levels that more accurately capture the developmental experience of the child.
- *Convergence*—the use of instruments that allow for input from multiple sources and thus enhance the developmental picture.
- *Collaboration*—the use of instruments that incorporate family–teacher teamwork.
- *Congruence*—ensuring that the instrument design was based on children similar to those you wish to assess.
- *Technology*—reduction of paper-and-pencil instruments and the incorporation of modern technologies.
- *Outcomes*—assessment are aligned with federal, state, and other required benchmarks.

As Bagnato has clearly outlined, the selection of appropriate assessments requires consideration of various dimensions relevant to the child, the family, educational goals, and targeted outcomes to be successful. Standardized testing is becoming more commonplace for older children, but younger children, particularly those with special needs, may require alternative assessment (see Figure 10.8). Because standardized instruments are often not validated with young children with disabilities, they are not prone to offer data relevant to the child's functioning or provide relevant information for intervention (Neisworth & Bagnato, 1992, 2004). Evidence suggests that, for many young children with disabilities, effective assessment occurs within the natural environments and their typical, daily routines (Keilty, LaRocco, & Casell, 2009). Informal interactions, "teachable moments," and real-life experiences of children's decision making, problem solving, use of language, and application of concepts are what offer a

Infancy	Early Childhood	Primary Grades
Assessment is primarily conducted by parent/caregiver and teacher through observation.	Assessment is conducted by parent/caregiver and teacher through observation, with the introduction of more formal measures.	Assessment is primarily conducted by teachers and related educational staff with the use of both formal and informal assessment measures.

FIGURE 10.8   Assessment Contexts for Infants and Young Children.

glimpse of the whole child within natural learning environments. With the careful selection of both formal and informal assessment measures, professionals can get the best picture of a child's developmental strengths, needs, pathways, and outcomes in order to align the most successful intervention.

Other instruments besides those described in this chapter are designed specifically for children with specific categories of exceptionality. Here are some examples: Meadow-Kendall Social-Emotional Assessment Inventories for Deaf and Hearing Impaired Students (Meadow-Orlans, 1983); INSITE Developmental Checklist: Assessment of Developmental Skills for Young Multidisabled Sensory Impaired Children (Morgan & Watkins, 1989); Reynell-Zinkin Developmental Scales for Young Visually Handicapped Children (RZS) (Reynell & Zinkin, 1981); and the Autism Screening Instrument for Educational Planning—3rd Edition (ASIEP–3) (Krug, Arick, & Almond, 2008). A summary of these and other instruments useful for assessment in the areas of cognition and social-emotional development can be found in the website section of this chapter.

BREAKPOINT PRACTICE

1. Describe the importance of authenticity and collaboration in meeting Joey's needs and those of his family.
2. What might be typical teachable moments throughout the school day that you can identify as situations for both assessment and intervention?
3. Describe the ways in which assessment changes from infancy through the primary grades.

Revisiting Joey

Early childhood represents a unique developmental period in the lives of children. Consequently, the use of both formal and informal test measures are used to gather data on the full range of children's abilities, characteristics, and thought processes. In offering guiding principles for assessment practices, Bagnato and Neisworth (Bagnato, 2007) suggest that assessment in early childhood special education "is not a test-based process primarily; early childhood assessment is a flexible, collaborative decision-making process in which teams of parents and professionals repeatedly revise their collective judgments and reach consensus about the changing developmental, education, medical, and mental health service needs of young children and their families" (p. 2).

Assessment is, to coin a phrase, a "fact-finding mission." As Neisworth and Bagnato (2004) suggest, it is a team responsibility that includes families and is focused on making clinical decisions in one of the following areas: screening and eligibility determination, individualized program planning, child progress monitoring, and program evaluation. Effective assessment criteria, tools, and strategies in the areas of cognition, and the related domains of social-emotional development and adaptive functioning are essential steps in finding facts, forming hypotheses, and testing strategies that may be applied to socially mediated learning alliances and that scaffold children's development toward maturity.

Joey and his family represent the many families who come to early childhood special education settings seeking an accurate definition of what the parents observe as unusual in their child's development. Several important developmental issues (of which you should now be aware) must be considered for the purposes of assessment:

- Joey's use of relationships
- Joey's socialization strengths and needs
- Joey's apparent intellectual capacity and his inconsistent academic performance
- Joey's lack of attention and focus
- Joey's emotional reactivity
- Joey's inability to delay gratification and tolerate frustration

As you now know from reading this chapter, these basic functions of cognition, or the unfolding of development to support higher-level mental functions, are at issue in assessing Joey. The consideration of these factors (and those that you may have added to the list) point to avenues for structuring your thinking about, planning for, and assessment of Joey. Based on the contents of this chapter, you will organize these issues within stages of intellectual development (Piaget), needs for promoting mediated learning alliances (Vygtosky), and various assessment strategies that address those issues for which you need information to determine his skill level and to plan for instruction. The goal of assessing any child is the discovery of her or his strengths and needs, finding pathways to establish relationships that promote comfort and development, and optimizing the child's abilities toward age-appropriate autonomy.

As stated previously, early childhood special educators are like investigators on a "fact-finding mission," "turning over as many stones" as necessary to increase understanding and draw conclusions. Or as Blackman (1995) suggests, through experimentation, a "menu of possibilities" can be adapted to various circumstances. After reading this chapter, you now have a better sense of assessment approaches, tools, and considerations that would inform your work with Joey and his family in determining his needs for educational services and tailoring supports to promote development. For example, you may now realize that standardized assessments (for IQ) provide certain data necessary for eligibility, but they may be limited in directing day-to-day instructional needs. Or you may see how the assessment process for a child like Joey needs to be fine-tuned in order to get the data you want to obtain. You may have also factored in Joey's environment, including the role of the family, and see this as a critical factor in accurately determining Joey's unique needs and promoting his development.

Assessing Joey and other children like him requires a focus on the what and how of assessment in order to gain the essential elements necessary for instruction and related supports. In the domains of cognition and self-regulation skills, this requires a focused inquiry, awareness of available tools, and a commitment to addressing interrelated components of development that, in sum, organize higher-level mental functions and regulatory behaviors that aid in the development of intelligence and the greater likelihood of school success.

Activities

1. Using a list of behavioral indicators for academic and social-emotional performance, design classroom activities for a student, such as Joey, that will aid in the achievement of next steps for development.
2. Devise activities and strategies that you might use in setting up situations to observe skills you wish to assess with a student such as Joey.
3. Design an inservice training for your peers and/or colleagues so that they may better understand assessment in the domains of cognition and social-emotional development.
4. Find an experienced practitioner who you can "shadow" to learn more about effective strategies, such as observation, that you may wish to use as an assessment tool.
5. Interview parents to learn what they want from assessment processes, how assessment information is best provided to them, and what assessment information is most useful for them.
6. In a small group of your peers, watch a video recording of a child at play or in another typical situation to experience the role of observation in effective assessment.
7. Use role playing with your peers and/or colleagues to assume the perspective of team members, parents, and others in the assessment process. Discuss your perspectives in order to better understand how each participant may experience the assessment process and how this perspective may affect his or her participation or the lens through he or she views the process.

Websites

OVERVIEW OF ASSESSMENT TOOLS

The Early Childhood Outcomes Center (ECOC) *Instrument Crosswalks*
http://www.fpg.unc.edu/~eco/pages/crosswalks.cfm

National Early Childhood Technical Assistance Center (NECTAC) *Developmental Screening and Assessment Instruments*
http://www.nectac.org/~pdfs/pubs/screening.pdf

Northern California Training Academy *Mental Health Screening and Assessment Tools for Children*
http://humanservices.ucdavis.edu/academy/pdf/final2mentalhealthlitreview.pdf

State of Washington—Office of Superintendent of Public Instruction *A Guide to Assessment in Early Childhood*
http://www.k12.wa.us/EarlyLearning/pubdocs/assessment_print.pdf

ASSOCIATIONS AND ORGANIZATIONS (INCLUDING INFORMATION ON EXECUTIVE FUNCTION)

Children and Adults with Attention Deficit, Hyperactivity Disorder (CHADD)
http://www.chadd.org

Collaborative for Academic, Social, and Emotional Learning (CASEL)
http://www.casel.org

Learning Disabilities Online (LD Online)
http://www.ldonline.org

Nonverbal Learning Disabilities Online (NLD Online)
http://www.nldonline.org

References

Bagnato, S. J. (2007). *Authentic assessment for early childhood intervention: Best practices.* New York: Guilford Press.

Bagnato, S. J., Neisworth, J. T., Salvia, J., & Hunt, F. S. (1999). *Temperament and Atypical Behavior Scales (TABS): Early childhood indicators of developmental dysfunction.* Baltimore, MD: Brookes.

Bayley, N. (2005). *Bayley scales of infant development* (3rd ed.). San Antonio, TX: The Psychological Corporation.

Blackman, J. A. (1995). *Innovations in practice in early intervention. Infants & young children series.* Gaithersburg, MD: Aspen.

Blair, C., & Razza, R. P. (2007). Relating effortful control, executive function, and false belief understanding to emerging math and literacy ability in kindergarten. *Child Development, 78*(2), 647–663.

Bredekamp, S., & Copple, C. (1997). *Developmentally appropriate practice in early childhood programs.* Washington, DC: NAEYC.

Brigance, A. H. (2004). *Brigance inventory of early development—II.* North Billerica, MA: Curriculum Associates.

Brigance, A. H., & Glascoe, F. P. (2002). *Brigance infant and toddler screen.* North Billerica, MA: Curriculum Associates.

Bruder, M. B. (2000). Family-centered early intervention: Clarifying our values for the new millennium. *Topics in Early Childhood Special Education, 20*(2), 105–115.

Carter, A. S., & Briggs-Gowan, M. (2005). *ITSEA BIT-SEA: The infant-toddler and brief infant toddler social emotional assessment.* San Antonio, TX: PsychCorp.

Ewing Marion Kauffman Foundation. (2002). Set for success: Building a strong foundation for school readiness based on the social-emotional development of young children. Kansas City, MO: Author.

Finello K. M., & Poulsen M. K. (1996). The Behavioral Assessment of Baby's Emotional and Social Style (BABES): A new screening tool for clinical use. *Infant Behavior and Development, 19*, p. 453–453.

Friend, M. (2007). *Special education: Contemporary perspectives for school professionals* (2nd ed.). Boston: Allyn & Bacon.

Gardner, H. (1993). *Multiple intelligences: The theory in practice.* New York: Basic Books.

Gargiulo, R., & Kilgo, J. L. (2005). *Young children with special needs* (2nd ed.). Clifton Park, New York: Delmar.

Glover, M. E., Preminger, J. L., & Sanford, A. R. (2002). *The early learning accomplishment profile for developmentally young children* (3rd ed.). Lewisville, NC: Kaplan Press.

Goleman, D. (1995). *Emotional intelligence.* New York: Bantam Books.

Goodman, R. (1997). The Strengths and Difficulties Questionnaire: A research note. *Journal of Child Psychology and Psychiatry, 38*, 581–586.

Gresham, M., & Elliott, S. N. (2008). *Rating scales manual. SSIS Social Skills Improvement System.* Minneapolis, MN: Pearson Education.

Guralnick, M. J. (1990). Social competence and early intervention. *Journal of Early Intervention, 14*, 3–14.

Hooper, S. R., & Umansky, W. (2009). *Young children with special needs* (5th ed.). Upper Saddle River, NJ: Merrill/Pearson Education.

Horowitz, S. H. (2007, March). Executive functioning: Regulating behavior for school success. *LD News.* Retrieved February 20, 2009, from http://www.ncld.org/content/view/1200/480

Johnson-Martin, N. M., Attermeier, S. M., & Hacker, B. J. (2004). *The Carolina Curriculum for infants and toddlers with special needs* (3rd ed.). Baltimore: Brookes.

Johnson-Martin, N., Hacker, B. J., & Attermeier, S. M. (2004). *The Carolina Curriculum for Preschoolers with Special Needs* (2nd ed.). Baltimore: Brookes.

Keilty, B., LaRocco, D. J., & Casell, F. B. (2009). Early interventionists' reports of authentic assessment methods through focus group research. *Topics in Early Childhood Special Education, 28*(4), 244–256.

Kritikos, E. P. (2010). *Special education assessment: Issues and strategies affecting today's classrooms.* Upper Saddle River, NJ: Pearson Education.

Krug, D. A., Arick, J., & Almond, P. (2008). *Autism screening instrument for educational planning* (3rd ed.). Austin, TX: PRO-ED.

LaFreniere, P. J., & Dumas, J. E. (1995). *Social competence and behavior evaluation* (preschool edition). Los Angeles: Western Psychological Services.

LeDosquet, P. (2010). Early childhood. In E. Kritikos (Ed.). *Special education assessment: Issues and strategies affecting today's classrooms* (pp. 207–229). Upper Saddle River, NJ: Pearson Education.

Leerkes, E. M., Paradise, M., O'Brien, M., Calkins, S., & Lange, G. (2008). Emotion and cognition processes in preschoolers. *Merrill Palmer Quarterly, 54*, 102–124.

Lidz, C. (1995). Dynamic assessment and the legacy of L. S. Vygotsky. *School Psychology International, 16*(2), 143–153.

Linder, T. (2008). *Administration guide for TPBA 2 and TPBI 2.* Baltimore: Paul H. Brookes.

Lowenthal, B. (1996). Teaching social skills to preschoolers with special needs. *Childhood Education, 72*(3), 137–140.

Mayer, J. D., & Salovey, P. (1997). What is emotional intelligence? In P. Salovey & D. Sluyter (Eds). *Emotional development and emotional intelligence: Implications for educators* (pp. 3–31). New York: Basic Books.

Meadow-Orlans, K. P. (1983). *Meadow-Kendall social-emotional assessment inventory for deaf and hearing impaired students.* Washington DC: Gallaudet University.

Morgan, E. C., & Watkins, S. (1989). *INSITE: Assessment of developmental skills for young multihandicapped sensory impaired children.* Logan, UT: Hope Publishing.

Myers, C. L., McBride, S. L., & Peterson, C. A. (1996). Transdisciplinary, play-based assessment in early childhood special education: An examination of social validity. *Topics in Early Childhood Special Education, 16*, 102–126.

Neisworth, J. T., & Bagnato, S. J. (1992). The case against intelligence testing in early intervention. *Topics in Early Childhood Special Education, 12*(1), 1–20.

Neisworth, J.T., & Banato, S.J. (2004). The mismeasure of young children: The authentic assessment alternative. *Infants and Young Children, 17*(3), 198-212.

Newborg, J. (2005). *Battelle developmental inventory,* (2nd ed.). Itasca, IL: Riverside.

Parks, S. (1997). *Inside HELP: Administration and reference manual.* Palo Alto, CA: VORT Corporation.

Piaget, J. (1932). *The moral judgement of the child.* New York: Harcourt, Brace Jovanovich.

Piaget, J. (1969). *The mechanisms of perception.* London: Rutledge & Kegan Paul.

Piaget, J. (1970). *The science of education and the psychology of the child.* New York: Grossman.

Reynell, J., & Zinkin, P. (1981). *The Reynell-Zinkin developmental scales for young visually handicapped children—part 1: Mental development.* Windsor, Canada: NFER-NELSON.

Roid, G. H. (2005). *Stanford-Binet intelligence scale for early childhood* (5th ed.). Itasca, IL: Riverside.

Salovey, P., & Mayer, J. D. (1990). Emotional intelligence. *Imagination, Cognition, and Personality, 9*, 185–211.

Sandall, S., McLean, M. E., & Smith, B. J. (2000). *DEC recommended practices in early intervention/early childhood special education.* Longmont, CO: Sopris West.

Sparrow, S. S., Balla, D. A., & Cicchetti, D. V. (1998). *Vineland social-emotional early childhood scales (SEEC).* Circle Pines, MN: American Guidance Service.

Squires, J., & Bricker, D. (2009). *Ages and stages questionnaires* (3rd ed.). Baltimore: Brookes.

Sternberg, R. J., & Williams, W. D. (Eds.) (1998). *Intelligence, instruction, and assessment: Theory into practice.* Mahwah, NJ: Erlbaum.

Teaford, P., Wheat, J., Baker, T. (2010). *Hawaii Early Learning Profile (HELP) for preschoolers* (2nd ed.). Palo Alto, CA: Vort Corporation.

Thomas, A., & Chess, S. (1977). *Temperament and development.* New York: Brunner/Mazel.

Thomas, A., Chess, S., & Birch, H. G. (1968). *Temperament and behavior disorders in children.* New York: New York University Press.

Vygotsky, L. (1978). *Mind in society: The development of higher mental functions.* Cambridge, MA: Harvard University Press.

Wechsler, D. (2002). *The Wechsler preschool and primary scale of intelligence* (3rd ed.). San Antonio, TX: Psychological Corporation.

Zaslow, M., Calkins, J., & Halle, T. (2000). *Background for community-level work on school readiness: A review of definitions, assessments and investment strategies.* Washington, DC: Child Trends.

Communication

CHAPTER 11

CHAPTER OBJECTIVES

By the end of the chapter, you will be able to describe the areas of receptive and expressive language (i.e., form-phonology, syntax and morphology, content-semantics, and use-pragmatics). You will be able to give examples of standardized and criterion-referenced language instruments for different age groups and in each area of language. You will also be able to give pros and cons for each of these tools. You will be able to identify factors related to individuals and families who are linguistically and/or culturally diverse.

This chapter addresses Council for Exceptional Children (CEC) Standards 2 (Development and Characteristics of Learners), 5 (Learning Environments and Social Interactions), 6 (Language), 8 (Assessment), and 10 (Collaboration), and National Association for the Education of Young Children (NAEYC) Standards 1 (Promoting Child Development and Learning) and 3 (Observing, Documenting, and Assessing to Support Young Children and Their Families). Chapter 11 includes information regarding human development and varying ability, active engagement and learning environments, communication skills, formal and informal assessment, and collaboration with families and professionals supplying learning material involved with attaining goals.

Assessing Anita

Anita is a 30-month-old toddler who was referred by a physician after the parents expressed some concerns. She is bilingual in Spanish and English. According to her parents, Anita was using two and three word phrases and over 400 words. However, within the past several months, Anita has been using fewer words, has become decreasingly interested in interacting with peers, and has decreased eye contact.

Your transdisciplinary team members (speech-language pathologist, occupational therapist, physical therapist, special education teacher, and social worker) schedule a home visit. Anita's parents introduce you to Anita's grandmother (who babysits Anita); Anita's brother, Joe (5 years old); and Anita's sister, Theresa (8 years old). Anita's parents report that Anita's birth and delivery were unremarkable. Developmental milestones occurred within normal limits. The neighborhood is a middle-class neighborhood, and both parents work. Many children's families in the family's neighborhood are at the same socio-economic level.

What information would you like team members to gather about Anita, her siblings, and her other family members? What formal and/or informal instruments would the team members use? How will you connect this information to instruction?

As an educator, you will work collaboratively with speech-language pathologists, occupational therapists, physical therapists, social workers, audiologists, and other team members involved in speech and language screenings, speech-language assessments, speech-language services, or language enrichment activities. It is very important, especially in the area of early childhood special education, that you collaborate closely with the student's family members. Areas involved in speech and language services may include **articulation** (using structures to form phonemes), swallowing, **fluency** (smoothness of speech), **voice** (appropriate pitch, tone, and resonance), **tongue thrust** (speaking with the tongue extending past the teeth), **receptive language** (understanding communication), and **expressive language** (using communication). This chapter will concentrate on the assessments of the areas of receptive and expressive language, which are the major components of language on which the communication assessment process focuses.

DEFINITIONS OF RECEPTIVE AND EXPRESSIVE LANGUAGE

Receptive and expressive language constitutes the full picture of communication when defined appropriately. Verbal and nonverbal components are considered in this process. Metalinguistic areas (i.e., thinking about language) are also included in the communication realm. Receptive language represents the understanding of language. Expressive language signifies the use of language (i.e., speaking, using sign language, using assistive/augmentative communication devices). In many cases, receptive and expressive language is the reason why most children have early childhood special education involved in assessment.

Hearing screenings are critical to the area of communication assessment. An audiologist or speech-language pathologist can conduct this screening to rule out hearing issues. During the screening, students hear tones bilaterally via headphones and respond by raising their hands or looking at the object making the sound to indicate that they hear the sound. With young children, conducting this screening can sometimes be difficult from a behavioral and cognitive perspective. It is important to note that speech reception thresholds can reveal much more useful information than pure tone testing alone. That is, identifying at what levels the individual understands speech instead of at what levels of pure sound thresholds he or she understands it is more reflective of understanding spoken language.

Form, Content, and Use

Components of both receptive and expressive language include form, content, and use. **Form** consists of *phonology, syntax*, and *morphology*. **Content** is comprised of semantics, and **use** contains pragmatics. For speech and language milestones, go to http://www.asha.org/public/speech/development/. See Figure 11.1 for more information on language components.

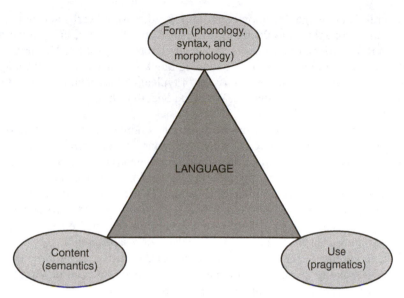

FIGURE 11.1 Language Components.

FORM. **Phonology**, one piece of form, incorporates how individuals understand (receptive language) and use sounds or phonemes and sound combinations (expressive language). English contains 44 phonemes, 25 consonantal and 19 vocalic sounds. Place (i.e., labio-dental), manner (i.e., stops), and voicing (i.e., voiceless) categorize consonants. Height (i.e., high) of the tongue and location of primary resonance (i.e., back of the mouth) are ways to categorize vowels (Rosner & Pickering, 1994). Timing, frequency, and duration of speech sound units are also included in the sphere of phonology. In young children, phonological processing and phonological awareness are important aspects to consider (Taylor, 2009).

Most individuals acquire phonemes in a developmental sequence. Building on phonemes, graphemes comprise the written symbols associated with these sounds. Sounds are assessed in isolation; in consonant clusters (i.e., /kl/); in syllables; by position in single words (i.e., /s/ beginning, /I/ middle, and /t/ final sound—"sit"); in phrases, sentences, and combination of sentences; in structured speech; and in spontaneous speech.

Syntax is the structure of sentences. The structure of sentences involves word sequences, sentence organization, word associations, word classes, and sentence components (Owens, 2005). As young children develop their language, they expand their use of noun phrases, verb phrases, passive sentences, rule exceptions, **embedding** (inserting grammar components), and **conjoining** (combining two or more grammar components) (Polloway, Miller, & Smith, 2004).

Morphology includes using and understanding **morphemes**, or meaningful grammatical units. Morphemes are the smallest units of language that have meaning. They include sounds, syllables, and words. Free morphemes, such as *bicycle* or *child* can stand alone, while bound morphemes depend on other functions (i.e., derivational morphemes, inflectional morphemes). Derivational morphemes can change class words. A verb such as *run* can therefore, be transformed to a noun like *runner*. Inflectional morphemes increase the accuracy of the morpheme. The *-est* in *fastest* indicates a more specific understanding of speed. For example, "Ellen is the fastest walker."

As the child's language development continues, the use of verbs serving as nouns, or gerunds (i.e., *running*); agents in relation to the main verb of a clause, or agentive forms (i.e., *runner*); and verb modifiers, or adverbs (i.e., *quickly*) improves (Hulit & Howard, 2006). So a child could say, "I love running" or "I love running quickly." Educators use language samples regularly in morphology analysis. For discussion of typical and atypical language development patterns in preschool children, see Shames, Wiig, and Secord (1998).

CONTENT. Content is comprised of **semantics**, which is defined as the meaning of a word or combinations of words. Young children develop vocabulary by advancing nouns. According to Polloway, Miller, and Smith (2004), nouns can include common (i.e., *car*), proper (i.e., *Alexander the Great*), concrete (i.e., *computer*), abstract (i.e., *strength*), collective (i.e., *university*), count (i.e., *door/s*), and mass or noncount (i.e., *air*). Adjectives (describe nouns), adverbs (describe verbs), pronouns (take the place of nouns), practical vocabulary (everyday vocabulary), and content (subject matter) vocabulary and verbs are also included in the expanding of nouns. Communicative purpose, such as rejection, nonexistence or disappearance, cessation or prohibition of action, recurrence, existence, action on objects, locative action (where), attribution (describing noun), naming possession, commenting, and social interaction, are also important when looking at word meanings (Bloom & Lahey, 1978).

Figurative language is also essential in the progression of semantics. This is an area of great interest for students with developmental difficulties, hearing disabilities, as well as individuals who are linguistically and/or culturally diverse. Examples include idioms, metaphors, similes, and proverbs. Idioms cannot be understood literally; an example is "Judy said that job was a piece of cake." Metaphors represent a thought in place of another to show that two seemingly dissimilar ideas are in fact similar. An example is "This classroom is a zoo." Similes also show that two dissimilar items are alike; however, the ideas are connected with the words *like* or *as*. An example of a simile using the word *like* is "Her face is red like a tomato". An example of a simile using the word *as* is "This bread is hard as a rock." Proverbs are culturally based. They are brief sayings regarding commonly held thoughts of a culture (i.e., "A stitch in time saves nine.") See Figure 11.2 for more information regarding idioms, metaphors, similes, and proverbs.

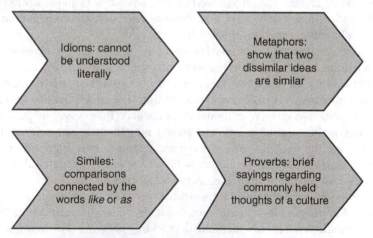

Idioms: cannot be understood literally

Metaphors: show that two dissimilar ideas are similar

Similes: comparisons connected by the words *like* or *as*

Proverbs: brief sayings regarding commonly held thoughts of a culture

FIGURE 11.2 Idioms, Metaphors, Similes, and Proverbs.

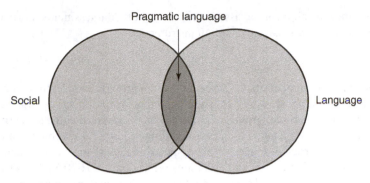

FIGURE 11.3   Pragmatic Language.

USE.   **Pragmatics** encompasses use and involves the intersection of language and social features. Communication is the focus of pragmatics. More specifically, the way individuals interact with speech acts, such as gestures and body language, is at the core of pragmatics. Loudness (volume), pitch (frequency of sound), intonation (rise and fall of voice), and stress (emphasis on syllables, words, or phrases) are also key in this process. See Figure 11.3 for an illustration of pragmatic language.

Intentions and presuppositions are commonly examined when assessing pragmatics in young children or early language development. Naming, commenting, requesting objects, requesting actions, requesting information, responding, protesting or rejecting, attention seeking, and greeting (Roth & Spekman, 1984) are types of intentions. Presuppositions describe the speaker's assumptions about what the person he or she is speaking with already knows. These assumptions may or may not be accurate in guiding communication. Inaccurate assumptions can impede the communication process.

It is important to note that pragmatic language depends heavily on contextual and cultural information. The assessor must be familiar with multiple contexts that the child participates in and the cultural communication meaning of those environments. Without culturally relevant communication information, the language assessment is not valid.

BREAKPOINT PRACTICE

1. What is the difference between receptive vocabulary and expressive vocabulary?
2. How would you assess morphology?
3. Give examples of an idiom, metaphor, simile, and proverb.
4. In your opinion, what is the most important aspect of language? Explain why you feel this way.

ASSESSING LANGUAGE

Language assessment can take a number of different forms. Formal assessment and informal assessment should both be used in a language assessment. Formal assessment involves using standardized tests, in which the test is given and scored the same way every time, and norm-referenced tests, in which the student's score is compared to the scores of other students of the same age and/or grade level. Informal assessments are all other assessments. Formal assessments can be screening or comprehensive evaluation instruments.

Screening

Screening is one method of assessment. Screenings often provide less depth than comprehensive evaluations in a content area. However, they are good tools for conducting large-scale programs (i.e., group testing). For example, groups of children can be assessed at the same time. One common use is a kindergarten screening on entry. According to Lerner, Lowenthal, and Egan (2003), screening is an efficient procedure in recognizing possible factors in developmental delays.

According to the Individuals with Disabilities Education Act (IDEA) (2004), all states must have a working plan for locating and screening infants, toddlers, and young children who may be at risk for a developmental delay. **Child find** is an important process of identifying and referring children for early intervention or special education services (IDEA Child Find Project, 2004). Child find actually extends from birth to age 21. According to information reported from the Dynamic Community Connections Project: A Process Model for Enhancing Child Find in Rural Areas, the University of Montana Rural Institute: Center for Excellence in Disability Education, Research, and Service (IDEA Child Find Project, 2004), a successful child find includes a target population that is defined and described, heightened public awareness, a robust referral and intake process, reliable and valid screening and identification of children who may be eligible for services, determination of eligibility, tracking for follow-up regarding individuals, and good interagency coordination. Key screening agencies include hospitals, social services, and public health agencies.

Screening Tools

Two common language screening instruments include the Bankson Language Screening Test–2S (Bankson, 1990) and the Boehm Test of Basic Concepts, Preschool—3rd Edition (Boehm, 2000). See Table 11.1 for more information about group language tests.

TABLE 11.1	Examples of Group Tests						
Name	**Author**	**Publication Date**	**Company**	**Technical Information**	**Content**	**Age Groups Tested**	**Time**
Bankson Language Screening Test—2nd Edition	Bankson	1990	PRO-ED	Internal consistency; content, concurrent, and construct validity	Semantic understanding, morphology and syntax rules, and pragmatics	3 years through 6 years 11 months	Varies
Boehm Test of Basic Concepts—3rd Edition	Boehm	2000	Psychological Corporation	Coefficient alpha and test-retest reliability	Understanding of verbal instructions (space, quantity, and time)	3 years through 5 years 11 months	About 30 minutes

The Bankson Language Screening Test–2S (Bankson, 1990) was normed on 1,200 children across 19 states. This test can be used with individuals from age 3 years through 6 years 11 months. It includes semantic knowledge information concerning body parts, nouns, verbs, categories, functions, prepositions, opposites, pronouns, verb usage/verb tense, verb usage, modal (i.e., *may*), copula (i.e., the weather is terrible), plurals, comparatives/superlatives, negation, and questions. Pragmatics information is also included. Ritualizing, informing, controlling, and imagining are included in this area. Internal consistency, content, concurrent, and construct validity are included in this tool. A short version is also included. It is important to note that researchers (Rhyner, Kelly, Brantley, & Krueger, 1999) revealed the possibility that this tool may overidentify individuals who are African American with low socioeconomic status. Test results from this population should be regarded with caution.

The Boehm Test of Basic Concepts, Preschool—3rd Edition appears to have an appropriate norm group. This test can be used with individuals from age 3 years through 5 years 11 months. Relational concepts, such as size, direction, position, time, quantity, classification, and general information, are assessed with this tool. Coefficient alpha and test-retest reliability were performed. Reliability and validity information is noted to be adequate. Suggestions for adaptations and a Spanish version are available with this test.

BREAKPOINT PRACTICE

1. If a 30-month-old toddler is not yet using words, where could the parents go to receive help or advice?
2. Lisa is 2 years old and does not look at toys or at faces. Her parents and extended family are concerned. How can they help Lisa?
3. Compare and contrast the Bankson Language Screening Test–2S and the Boehm Test of Basic Concepts, Preschool—3rd Edition.

COMPREHENSIVE ASSESSMENT

When a screening instrument reveals possible problems in language areas, a comprehensive multidisciplinary evaluation occurs. Each state has the opportunity to conduct assessment processes that are considered best for a child and her or his family, as long as a "timely, comprehensive, multidisciplinary evaluation" is family-directed, focused, and appropriate (IDEA, 2004, §635.3). In the case of language, we want multiple formal and informal valid assessment procedures, with input from the family.

Formal and informal assessment tools are used to determine whether a child is eligible for services. See Chapter 1 for more information regarding eligibility. Formal assessment involves norm-referenced, standardized testing. Some criticism has been presented in the literature regarding the use of standardized measures with young children. For example, Myers, McBride, and Peterson (1996) reported social validity concerns. Task familiarity (Pena & Quinn, 1997), prior experience (Campbell, Dollaghan, Needleman, & Janosky, 1997), type of task (Craig, Washington, & Thompson-Porter, 1998; Craig & Washington, 2000; Rodekohr & Haynes, 2001), validity of specific quantitative tests (Cole & Taylor, 1990; Saenz & Huer, 2003), and professionals' judgment (Bebout & Arthur, 1992; Roseberry-McKibbin & Eicholtz, 1994; Kayser,

1995; Kritikos, 2003) can all negatively affect the appropriate valid language assessment of children. Word meanings (Penegra, 2000), language loss (Schiff-Myers, 1992), and language patterns (Yavas & Goldstein, 1998) are also factors to consider in the language assessment process. Therefore, it is important to use tests for the purposes for which they were developed, the tests are administered by knowledgeable assessors, and instructions are strictly adhered to by the assessor (IDEA, 2004, Part B. §614.3.b.i.-i.i.i).

Comprehensive Standardized Assessment Tools

Comprehensive standardized assessment instruments are usually conducted individually. In the following sections regarding standardized assessment tools, diagnostic assessment will be discussed. Global testing, general language, receptive vocabulary, expressive vocabulary, auditory comprehension and discrimination, and language batteries will also be discussed.

Global Testing

The Bayley Scales of Infant Development—Second Edition (BISD–II) (Bayley, 1993) and the Battelle Developmental Inventory—2 (BDI–2) (Newborg, 2005) are commonly used assessments that tap into multiple development areas. See Table 11.2 for examples of standardized tests in multiple content areas.

TABLE 11.2 Examples of Standardized Tests on Multiple Content Areas

Name	Author	Publication Date	Company	Technical Information	Content	Age Group Tested	Time
Bayley Scales of Infant Development—2nd Edition	Bayley	1993	Pearson Education	Coefficient alpha, standard error of measurement, test-retest reliability, and inter-rater reliability	Cognitive	Birth to 42 months	45 to 60 minutes
Battelle Developmental Inventory—2	Newborg	2005	Riverside Publishing Company	Internal consistency; standard error of measurement; test-retest and inter-rater reliability; content, construct, and concurrent validity	Personal social, adaptive, motor, communication, and cognitive	Birth to 7 years 11 months	1 to 2 hours

The Bayley Scales of Infant Development—Second Edition (BISD–II) (Bayley, 1993) is a widely used standardized assessment instrument that was originally intended for use with children from birth to age 30 months. The second edition of this test can be used to assess children from birth to age 42 months. Three separate scales exist: (1) Mental Scale, (2) Motor Scale, and (3) Behavior Rating Scale. It is important to note that language skills are assessed in the Mental Scale. Language skills such as expressive phonology and pragmatic skills are targeted in this scale. The starting point depends on the child's chronological or supposed developmental age. The Mental Scale includes items 1 through 22. The norm group appears to be appropriate. Coefficient alpha, standard error of measurement, test-retest reliability, and inter-rater reliability were performed. Content, construct, predictive and discriminant validity were also performed. It is important to note that the author states that this tool was not designed to assess children with physical and/or sensory disabilities.

The Battelle Developmental Inventory—2 (BDI–2) (Newborg, 2005) is also a commonly used standardized tool. It has 450 items that tap into five domains: (1) personal social, (2) adaptive, (3) motor, (4) communication, and (5) cognitive. The communication domain addresses both receptive and expressive language. This test can be used with individuals from birth to age 7 years 11 months. Test administration begins at supposed age of development of the child. The instrument uses a scoring system from 0 to 2. Parent interview, teacher interview and observations, and test administration are used for collecting valuable test data.

The norm group utilized in the BDI–2 appears appropriate. Reliability includes internal consistency, standard error of measurement, test-retest reliability, and inter-rater reliability. Content, construct, and concurrent validity were performed. This test has a screening portion with 100 items. If further assessment is recommended, the full assessment instrument can be used. In addition, the test can be used for children with sensory or physical disabilities.

General Language Tests

The Preschool Language Scale—4 (PLS–4) (Zimmerman, Steiner, & Pond, 2002), the Receptive-Expressive Language Test—3rd Edition (REEL–3) (Bzoch & League, 2003), and the Test of Language Development-Primary—4th Edition (TOLD–P:4) (Newcomer & Hammill, 2008) are often used in the area of general language assessment. See Table 11.3 for examples of standardized tests of global language.

Preschool Language Scale—4 (PLS–4) (Zimmerman, Steiner, & Pond, 2002) is a test that evaluates the language of children from ages 2 weeks to 6 years 11 months. A new version, Preschool Language Scale—5 is due out in the spring of 2012. Two subscales (Auditory and Expressive Communication) and three additional measures (Articulation Screener, Language Sample Checklist, and Family Information and Suggestions form) complete the instrument. Conversational speech is included in the Language Sample Checklist.

The items can be scored with a check mark (correct), minus sign (incorrect), and the letters NR (no response). A graph protocol is included with this instrument. Test-retest and inter-rater reliability are reported. Concurrent and predictive validity are addressed. Guidelines for individuals with hearing disabilities, physical disabilities, and severe developmental delays are included. A worksheet for developing individualized family service plan (IFSP) goals and objectives is also a feature of this tool. The test has norm group information based on 1,500 children. Students with exceptionalities are included in the representative group from the 2000 census. Another interesting feature of the norm group is that 39.1% of the students in the sample are of an ethnic minority.

TABLE 11.3	Examples of Standardized Tests on Global Language Areas

Name	Author	Publication Date	Company	Technical Information	Content	Age Groups Tested	Time
Preschool Language Scale—4	Zimmerman, Steiner, & Pond	2000	Pearson Education	Test retest and inter-rater reliability, concurrent and predictive validity	Receptive and expressive language skills	2 weeks through 6 years	20 to 45 minutes
Receptive-Expressive Language Test	Bzoch & League	2003	PRO-ED	Test-retest reliability, concurrent validity	Prelinguistic skills	1 month through 36 months	20 minutes
Test of Language Development-Primary—4th Edition	Newcomer & Hammill	2008	PRO-ED	Content sampling; internal consistency; time sampling; inter-rater reliability; content construct, and criterion-related validity	Receptive and expressive vocabulary, grammar and phonology	4 years through 8 years 11 months	1 hour

Receptive-Expressive Language Test—3rd Edition (REEL–3) (Bzoch & League, 2003) is another commonly used standardized test. Educators use this tool to assess infants and toddlers from birth to age 3 in the areas of receptive and expressive language. Expressive Language Age, Receptive Language Age, and a Combined Age results score can be achieved using this instrument. The norm group for this test appears appropriate.

The Test of Language Development—4th Edition (TOLD–P:4) (Newcomer & Hammill, 2008) was renormed in 2005 on more than 1,000 children across 30 states. This test can be used with individuals from age 4 years to 8 years 11 months. The student responds through multiple-choice questions, open-ended questions, repetition of sentences, fill-in-the-blank questions, discrimination tasks, and picture naming. Subtests include (1) vocabulary, (2) relational vocabulary, (3) oral vocabulary, (4) syntactic understanding, (5) sentence imitation, (6) morphological completion, (7) word discrimination, (8) word analysis, and (9) word articulation. Three composites exist: (1) semantics and grammar; (2) listening, organizing, and speaking; and (3) overall language ability. Content sampling, internal consistency, time sampling, and inter-rater reliability results are presented. Content, construct, and criterion-related validity results are also included. Reliability and validity appear adequate.

Receptive Vocabulary

Receptive vocabulary can be investigated using tests that concentrate on this content area. The Peabody Picture Vocabulary Test—III (PPVT–IV) (Dunn & Dunn, 2007), the Test de Vocabulario en Imagenes Peabody (TVIP) (Dunn, Lugo, Padilla, & Dunn, 1986), and Receptive One-Word Picture Vocabulary Test (ROWPVT–2000) (Brownell, 2000b) are three commonly used tests of receptive vocabulary. See Table 11.4 for examples of standardized tests of receptive vocabulary.

The PPVT–IV requires no reading or writing by the examinee and contains full color pictures. This test can be used with individuals from age 2 years 6 months to 90+ years. The examiner shows

TABLE 11.4 Examples of Standardized Tests on Receptive Vocabulary

Name	Author	Publication Date	Company	Technical Information	Content	Age Groups Tested	Time
Peabody Picture Vocabulary Test—IV	Dunn & Dunn	2007	American Guidance Service	Internal consistency; alternate-form and test-retest reliability; content, construct, and criterion-related validity	Single-word receptive vocabulary	2 years 6 months through 90 and older	10 to 15 minutes
Test de Vocabulario en Imagenes Peabody	Dunn, Lugo, Padilla, & Dunn	1986	American Guidance	Internal consistency; alternate-form and test-retest reliability; content, construct, and criterion-related validity	Single-word receptive vocabulary (Spanish)	2 years 6 months through 17 years 11 months	10 to 15 minutes
Receptive One-Word Picture Vocabulary Test—2000 Edition	Brownell	2000	PRO-ED	Internal consistency; alternate-form and test-retest reliability; content, construct, and criterion-related validity	Single-word receptive vocabulary	2 years through 18 years 11 months	10 to 15 minutes

a page from the test booklet (IVA or IVB) with four items. The student then points to the picture in an attempt to match the examiner's spoken word. Norming appears adequate. Internal consistency, alternate-form, and test-retest reliability were performed. Content, construct, and criterion-related validity information were also included in the manual. Reliability and validity appear adequate.

The Test de Vocabulario en Imagenes Peabody (TVIP) (Dunn, Lugo, Padilla, & Dunn, 1986) is a Spanish version of the PPVT–III. This test can be used with individuals from age 2 years 6 months to 17 years 11 months. One hundred twenty-five items have been translated for this test. Norms were based on a population that consisted of individuals who are Mexican and/or Puerto Rican. Combined and separate standardization samples exist for these groups. The directions from the PPVT–III apply to the TVIP.

The Receptive One-Word Picture Vocabulary Test (ROWPVT–2000) (Brownell, 2000b) was designed to be compared to the Expressive One-Word Picture Vocabulary Test, 2000 Edition (Brownell, 2000a) in order to compare receptive and expressive vocabulary skills. This test can be used with individuals from age 2 years to 18 years 11 months. Like the procedure used with the previous receptive vocabulary measures, the child chooses from four possible choices (pictures) and attempts to match a picture to the assessor's spoken word.

Expressive Vocabulary

Another area of individual language assessment includes expressive vocabulary. Two commonly used measures are the Expressive One-Word Picture Vocabulary Test, 2000 (EOWPVT–2000) (Brownell, 2000a) and the Expressive Vocabulary Test—2 (EVT–2) (Williams, 2007). See Table 11.5 for examples of standardized tests of expressive vocabulary.

The Expressive One-Word Picture Vocabulary Test, 2000 Edition (EOWPVT–2000) (Brownell, 2000a) was normed with the Receptive One-Word Picture Vocabulary Test. This test

TABLE 11.5   Examples of Standardized Tests on Expressive Vocabulary

Name	Author	Publication Date	Company	Technical Information	Publication Date	Age Groups Tested	Time
Expressive One-Word Picture Vocabulary Test, 2000	Brownell	2000	PRO-ED	Split-half reliability and standard error of measurement, concurrent and content validity	Single-word expressive vocabulary	2 years through 18 years 11 months	10 to 15 minutes
Expressive Vocabulary Test—2	Williams	2007	American Guidance Service	Internal consistency; split-half, alternate-form; test-retest reliability; concurrent, construct, and content validity	Single-word expressive vocabulary	2 years 6 months to 90 years and older	10 to 20 minutes

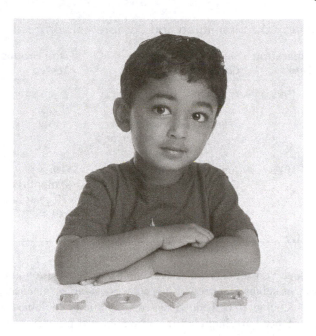

could be used with individuals, ages 2 years, 6 months through 90+ years. The child gives a one word oral response (English and Spanish versions exist) to match the target color drawing illustrations. The assessor could cue the child to focus on pertinent features of pictures. As with the receptive tests, no reading or writing is required to perform test. Split-half reliability and standard error of measurement are included in the manual. Concurrent and content validity information is also shared. It is important to note that the norm sample in this test is limited.

As mentioned previously, the Expressive Vocabulary Test—2 (EVT–2) (Williams, 2007) was normed on the same sample with the PPVT–IV. This test can be used with individuals from age 2 years to 18 years 11 months. The child is presented with a picture stimulus and uses one-word responses to label the target picture. The test has two forms, Form A and Form B, that consist of 190 items. Twenty content areas are included in these stimulus items. Norming appears adequate. Internal consistency, split-half, alternate-form, and test-retest reliabilities are provided in the manual. Concurrent, construct, and content validity are also included. Reliability and validity appear adequate.

Auditory Comprehension and Discrimination

Another important area of language includes auditory comprehension and discrimination. The Test of Auditory Comprehension of Language—3rd Edition (Carrow-Woolfolk, 1999) and the Goldman-Fristoe-Woodcock Test of Auditory Discrimination (Goldman, Fristoe, & Woodcock, 1970) can be used to investigate auditory comprehension and discrimination. See Table 11.6 for examples of auditory discrimination and comprehension tests.

The Test of Auditory Comprehension of Language—3rd Edition (Carrow-Woolfolk, 1999) includes three subtests: (1) vocabulary, (2) grammatical morphemes, and (3) elaborated phrases and sentences. This test can be used with individuals from age 3 years to 9 years 11 months. One hundred forty two multiple-item responses exist. Nouns, verbs, adjectives, adverbs, and basic concept words make up the vocabulary subtest. Prepositions, noun number, noun case, verb

TABLE 11.6	Examples of Auditory Discrimination and Comprehension Tests					
Name	Author	Publication Date	Company	Content	Age Groups Tested	Time
Test of Auditory Comprehension of Language—3rd Edition	Carrow-Woolfolk	1999	American Guidance Service	Receptive spoken vocabulary, grammar, and syntax	3 years through 9 years 11 months	10 to 20 minutes
Goldman-Fristoe-Woodcock Test of Auditory Discrimination	Goldman, Fristoe, & Woodcock	1970	American Guidance Service	Auditory discrimination	3 years, 8 months to 70 years and older	20 to 30 minutes

number, verb tense, noun-verb agreement, derivational suffixes, and pronouns are included in the grammatical morphemes subtest. Interrogative sentences, negative sentences, active and passive voice, direct and indirect objects, embedded sentences, partially conjoined sentences, and completely conjoined sentences are included in the elaborated phrases and sentences subtest. Reliability and validity information is needed.

The Goldman-Fristoe-Woodcock Test of Auditory Discrimination (Goldman, Fristoe, & Woodcock, 1970) does not require the child to write or speak. This test can be used with individuals who are 3 years 8 months and older. The child points to pictures that he or she listens to on tape. Quiet and noise backgrounds are used in the assessment of speech-sound discrimination.

Pragmatic Language

Pragmatic language tests include the Test of Pragmatic Language (Phelps-Terasaki & Phelps-Gunn, 1992), Let's Talk Inventory for Children (Bray & Wiig, 1987), and the Test of Pragmatic Skills—Revised (Shulman, 1986). It is important to note that more reliability and validity information is needed for these tests. See Table 11.7 for examples of pragmatic language tests.

TABLE 11.7	Examples of Pragmatic Language Tests					
Name	Author	Publication Date	Company	Content	Age Groups Tested	Time
Test of Pragmatic Language	Phelps-Terasaki & Phelps-Gunn	1992	Pearson Education	Pragmatic language	5 years through 13 years	30 to 45 minutes
Let's Talk Inventory for Children—Revised	Bray & Wiig	1987	Psychological Corporation	Pragmatic language	4 years through 8 years	20 to 30 minutes
Test of Pragmatic Skills—Revised	Shulman	1986	Out of print	Pragmatic language	3 years to 8 years 11 months	30 minutes

The Test of Pragmatic Language (Phelps-Terasaki & Phelps-Gunn, 1992) uses physical setting, audience, topic, purpose, visual-gestural cues, and abstraction. This test can be used with individuals from age 5 years to 14 years. The assessor shows the child a picture and asks questions related to the situation presented. Responses are examined in the areas of requesting, informing, regulating, expressing, ritualizing, and organizing.

The Let's Talk Inventory for Children (Bray & Wiig, 1987) also involves picture stimuli. This test can be used with individuals from age 4 years to 8 years. The assessor shows a picture about a communication situation with a short narrative examiner presentation. The child is assessed on ritualizing, informing, controlling, and feeling via oral response.

The Test of Pragmatic Skills (Shulman, 1986) involves play interactions presented in a script. These interactions are used to elicit responses from children age 3 years to 8 years. Puppets, pencil and paper, telephones and blocks are used. Requesting information, requesting action, rejection/denial, naming/labeling, answering/responding, informing, reasoning, summoning/calling, greeting, and closing conversation regarding communicative intents are examined.

BREAKPOINT PRACTICE

1. Which assessments would be appropriate for Anita? Why?
2. What overlap do you see in the various tests?
3. Compare and contrast the Preschool Language Scale—4 and the Receptive-Expressive Language Test.

CRITERION- AND CURRICULUM-REFERENCED ASSESSMENT

Criterion-referenced assessment investigates the strengths and needs of children. Curriculum-referenced assessment is a criterion-referenced tool *and* is designed in relation to the classroom curriculum. So in the case of criterion- and curriculum-referenced assessment, children are *not* compared to other children of the same age or grade level (norm-referenced assessment). Information regarding the child's skills is used to plan an instructional program for the child.

Many criterion- and curriculum-referenced assessments are commonly used with young children. Some of these assessments include the Brigance Inventory of Early Development II (Brigance IED–II) (Brigance, 1985), the Callier-Azusa Scale (Stillman & Battle, 1978–1985), the Early Learning Accomplishment Profile (E-LAP–3) (Hardin & Peisner-Feinberg, 2002), the Learning Accomplishment Profile—3 (LAP–3) (Hardin & Peisner-Feinberg, 2004), Carolina Curriculum for Infants and Toddlers with Special Needs—2nd Edition (Johnson-Martin, Jens, Attermeier, & Hacker, 2004), Carolina Curriculum for Preschoolers with Special Needs—2nd Edition (Johnson-Martin, Attermeier, & Hacker, 2004), Transdisciplinary Play-Based Assessment—2nd Edition (TPBA) (Linder, 2008), Hawaii Early Learning Profile (HELP) (Furuno, O'Reilly, Inatsuka, Hosaka, Allman, & Zeisloft-Falbey, 1987), the Play Assessment Scale—5th Revision (Fewell, 1986), Carrow Elicited Language Inventory (Carrow-Woolfolk, 1974), and Goldman-Fristoe Test of Articulation—Revised (GFTA–2) (Goldman & Fristoe, 2000). See Table 11.8 for examples of criterion-referenced and curriculum-referenced assessments.

The Brigance Inventory of Early Development—II (Brigance IED–II) (Brigance, 1985) also has a standardized portion with targeted skills. The instrument can be used with children

TABLE 11.8	Examples of Criterion-Referenced and Curriculum-Referenced Assessments					
Name	**Author**	**Publication Date**	**Company**	**Content**	**Age Groups Tested**	**Time**
Brigance Inventory of Early Development—II	Brigance	1985	Curriculum Associates Inc.	Pre-ambulatory motor, gross motor, fine motor, self-help, speech and language, general knowledge and comprehension, readiness, basic reading skills, manuscript writing, basic math, and social and emotional development	Birth through 7 years	20 to 55 minutes
Callier-Azusa Scale	Stillman & Battle	1978–1985	University of Texas at Dallas	Motor, perceptual, daily living, communication, cognitive, social	Birth through 6 years	30 to 40 minutes
Early Learning Accomplishment Profile	Hardin & Peisner-Feinberg	2002	Kaplan Early Learning Company	Gross motor, fine motor, cognitive, language, self-help, and social-emotional	Birth through 36 months	1½ hours
Learning Accomplishment Profile—3	Hardin & Peisner-Feinberg	2004	Kaplan Early Learning Company	Gross motor, fine motor, prewriting, cognitive, language, self-help, and personal-social	36 months through 72 months	1½ hours
Carolina Curriculum for Infants and Toddlers with Special Needs—2nd Edition	Johnson-Martin, Attermeier, & Hacker	2004	Brookes	Personal-social, cognition, communication, fine motor, and gross motor	Birth through 24 months	20 minutes
Carolina Curriculum for Preschoolers with Special Needs—2nd Edition	Johnson-Martin, Attermeier, & Hacker	2004	Brookes	Personal-social, cognition, communication, fine motor, and gross motor	24 through 60 months	20 minutes

TABLE 11.8 *(continued)*

Name	Author	Publication Date	Company	Content	Age Groups Tested	Time
Transdisciplinary Play-Based Assessment—2nd Edition	Linder	2008	Brookes	Cognitive, language, social-emotional, sensorimotor	Birth through 6 years	55 to 75 minutes
Hawaii Early Learning Profile	Furuno, O'Reilly, Inatsuka, Hosake, Allman, & Zeisloft-Falbey	1987	VORT Corporation	Cognitive, language, gross motor, fine motor, social-emotional, and self-help skills	Birth through 60 months	½ to 1½ hours
Play Assessment Scale—5th Revision	Fewell	1986	University of Washington	Perceptual and conceptual skills via play	2 months through 3 years	
Carrow Elicited Language Inventory	Carrow-Woolfolk	1974	PRO-ED	Expressive morphology and grammar	3 years through 7 years 11 months	20 to 30 minutes
Goldman-Fristoe Test of Articulation—Revised	Goldman & Fristoe	2000	American Guidance Service	Articulation	2 years through 21 years	15 minutes

from birth through 7 years. Child assessment, parent assessment, and parent observations are used with this instrument. Areas assessed include 11 domains: pre-ambulatory motor, gross motor, fine motor, self-help, speech and language, general knowledge and comprehension, readiness, basic reading skills, manuscript writing, basic math, and social and emotional development. Some examples of speech and language skills include prespeech gestures, prespeech vocalization, and picture vocabulary.

The Callier-Azusa Scale was developed for children who were deafblind and/or who had severe and profound disability. The instrument can be used with children from birth through 8 years of age. Five domain areas (motor, perceptual, daily living, communication, cognition, and social development) with 18 subscales are included. Observation is mainly used with this instrument, in addition to direct instruction with modifications (i.e., communication systems) input.

The Early Learning Accomplishment Profile—3 (E-LAP–3) (Hardin & Peisner-Feinberg, 2002) and the Learning Accomplishment Profile—3 (LAP–3) (Hardin & Peisner-Feinberg, 2004) both give a holistic picture of a child's development. The E-LAP–3 can be used to assess children from birth through 36 months, while the LAP–3 can be used to assess children from 36 months through 72 months of age. The E-LAP–3 assesses six areas: (1) gross motor, (2) fine motor, (3) cognitive, (4) language, (5) self-help, and (6) social-emotional. The LAP–3 investigates seven domains: (1) gross motor, (2) fine motor, (3) prewriting, (4) cognitive, (5) language,

(6) self-help, and (7) personal-social. Examples of language items include following directions and naming single-word picture vocabulary. Internal consistency, standard error of measurement, test-retest, and inter-rater reliability information is presented. Content, construct, and concurrent validity information is also presented.

The Carolina Curriculum for Infants and Toddlers with Special Needs—2nd Edition (CCITSN–2) (Johnson-Martin, Attermeier, & Hacker, 2004) and the Carolina Curriculum for Preschoolers with Special Needs—2nd Edition (CCPSN–2) (Johnson-Martin, Attermeier, & Hacker, 2004) assess children who have moderate to severe disabilities. The CCITSN–2 is used to assess children from birth to 36 months of age, while the CCPSN–2 is used to assess children from age 2 years through 5 years. Five areas assessed by both instruments include (1) personal-social, (2) cognition, (3) communication, (4) fine motor, and (5) gross motor. Some examples of items from the communication domain include conversational skills (i.e., smiles, gestures, or greets person speaking) and verbal comprehension (i.e., follows two-part commands). Reliability and validity information is not available.

The Transdisciplinary Play-Based Assessment—2nd Edition (TPBA) (Linder, 2008) taps into four developmental domains: (1) cognitive, (2) language, (3) social-emotional, and (4) sensorimotor development. This tool can be used with children from birth to 6 years of age. Assessors can investigate five levels of play through arranging toys and objects (preselected to represent all developmental domains). Stages include (1) child initiates play activities, (2) child initiates most play activities, (3) peer comes into the play environment, (4) play occurs between parents and child, and (5) a snack is served to the child and the peer.

The Hawaii Early Learning Profile (HELP) (Furuno, O'Reilly, Inatsuka, Hosaka, Allman, & Zeisloft-Falbey, 1987) includes six developmental domains: (1) cognitive, (2) language, (3) gross motor, (4) fine motor, (5) social-emotional, and 6) self-help skills. This tool can be used for children from birth to 6 years of age (strand 0–3 and strand 3–6). Examples in the language domain include receptive (i.e., understanding word meanings), expressive (i.e, following directions), sign language, and speech reading skills. Information is scored as present, not present, emerging, atypical/dysfunctional, or not applicable. Outcomes are then tracked over time via a chart. Activities link assessment to instruction.

The Play Assessment Scale—5th Revision (Fewell, 1986) investigates a child's play in the context of perceptual or conceptual skills. This tool can be used to assess children from age 2 months to 3 years. Condition I includes toys set on the floor, and the assessor makes introductory remarks and then scores the child's interaction with the toys. Condition II is implemented with the child who does not show more advanced behaviors. Here, the assessor uses more detailed instructions to facilitate behavior. The assessor chooses four of eight toy sets. The assessor also focuses on verbal cues and physical modeling. Two match the child's estimated age, one is below that age, and one is above that age.

The Carrow Elicited Language Inventory (Carrow-Woolfolk, 1974) investigates grammatical structures and syntax. This tool is appropriate for children from age 3 years to 7 years 11 months. Elicited imitation is used with this test. Test-retest and inter-rater reliability information is included. Content and concurrent validity information is provided. Reliability and validity are adequate.

The Goldman-Fristoe Test of Articulation—Revised (GFTA–2) (Goldman & Fristoe, 2000) uses imitation and spontaneous sound production. This tool is appropriate for individuals from age 2 years to 21 years. The child names pictures (in color), answers questions, and uses sounds in sentences. Three subtests include sounds in words (initial, medial, and final positions), sounds in sentences, and stimulability. Thirty nine consonant sounds and clusters are included in this test. Reliability data are adequate, but validity data is lacking.

BREAKPOINT PRACTICE

1. Which criterion-based/curriculum-based assessment could reveal useful information regarding Anita? Why?
2. Compare and contract the Brigance Inventory of Early Development and the Hawaii Early Learning Profile.
3. What is the difference between a standardized test and a criterion-referenced assessment?

INFORMAL MEASURES

Common informal measures in the area of early childhood special education and language include (1) interviews with caregivers, teachers, peers, and children; (2) observations of children in multiple contexts; and (3) classroom work and homework. Several types of informal measures should be collected in several authentic contexts ("natural environments") (Turnbull, Turnbull, Erwin, & Soodak, 2006; Dunst, Bruder, Trivette, Hamby, Raab, & McLean, 2001; Dunst, Hamby, Trivette, Raab, & Bruder, 2000). Natural environments are also important in order to examine the interactions between the young child and his or her caregivers (Bandura, 1969; Barnett, Ehrhardt, Stollar, & Bauer, 1994; McConnell, 2000). Families should have a significant role in supplying input into the assessment process (IDEA, 2004). The educator should be sensitive to the cultural and/or linguistic diversity of the family. It is important to create a relationship of respect. Some signs in the home, playground, or classroom that an evaluator should investigate include a child:

1. rarely initiating verbal interaction with peers or adults
2. not following requests
3. following requests incorrectly
4. not responding to peers or adults appropriately
5. using gestures in the place of words
6. repeating others' speech
7. having limited eye contact
8. having reduced speech intelligibility

A significant measure in the area of language is the language sample (Kayser, 1989; Mattes & Omark, 1991), which could be taken from observations of the child in her or his natural environment. Language samples should be spontaneous and from a natural setting. Language samples are then examined through the use of mean length of utterance (MLU) and developmental sequence analysis.

Language Samples

Usually 50 to 100 utterances are used to determine an MLU and developmental sequence analysis. In an MLU, the assessor elicits a response by asking open-ended questions. The responses are recorded and then transcribed. The analysis generally starts with the second page of transcription. Utterances can take the form of a sentence, phrase, or word. Morphemes are counted and divided by 100. MLU is based on Brown's (1973) stages. Spanish MLU procedures involving measurement was reported by Linares (1981). In developmental sentence analysis (Lee, 1974) grammatical types are extracted from the sample and points are assigned to words. Fifty complete sentences (subject-predicate) are required for this system. Children from age 2 years to 6 years 11 months can be assessed using this technique. Norms were gathered for this assessment; however, a low *number of participants* was used (i.e., 200 children). Therefore, this type of assessment can be considered an informal assessment (McLoughlin & Lewis, 2008).

Natural context is important in collecting language sample (Stockman, 1996). Washington, Craig, and Kushmaul (1998) examined the effect of language sampling context while evaluating African American English. Participants were from low socioeconomic status. The researchers compared free-play and picture-description responses. Results revealed that the picture-description context produced more use of African American English and took less time to gather a language sample than the free-play context.

Dynamic Assessment

Dynamic assessment is an important area to discuss in the context of the assessment-to-instruction loop. Intervention matched to the assessment is the key. This type of assessment focuses on how the student learns, how changeable the student is, and what types of instruction are most useful for the student (Lidz & Pena, 1996). A significant research base exists in the area of dynamic assessment and young children who are culturally and/or linguistically diverse (Fagundes, Haynes, Haak, & Moran, 1998; Laing & Kamhi, 2003). See Figure 11.4 for an illustration of the assessment-to-instruction loop.

Ukrainetz, Harpell, Walsh, and Coyle (2000) examined language learning ability in kindergarten children who were Native American (Arapahoe/Shosone). The researchers found that the participants' learning strategies were related to more effective language learning. Gutierrez-Clellen and Pena (2001) also looked at dynamic assessment with children who were culturally and/or linguistically diverse. The investigators examined three dynamic assessment methods: (1) testing the

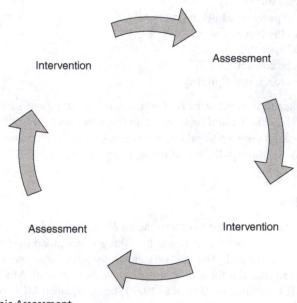

FIGURE 11.4 Dynamic Assessment.

limits, (2) graduated prompting, and (3) test-teach-retest. Results revealed that test-teach-retest methods were most effective with the participants. See Chapter 9 for information regarding assistive technologies.

Gutierrez-Clellen and Quinn (1993) also discussed dynamic assessment regarding children who were culturally and/or linguistically diverse in the area of oral narratives. The researchers investigated issues of narrative experience, exposure to narrative tasks, notions regarding audience involvement, paralinguistic strategies, and use of dynamic assessment as important in the assessment and instruction of language.

BREAKPOINT PRACTICE

1. What type of informal language assessments would be useful for assessing Anita? Why?
2. What aspects of a language sample would be tricky to accomplish?
3. In which contexts could you collect language samples?

Revisiting Anita

Because Anita's family has come to you with concerns, you would meet with the parents to get more qualitative examples of what has prompted their concerns. The parents would be able to compare Anita with their other two children in terms of development. Birth, medical, developmental, and family and language history would be collected. To evaluate Anita, informal and formal measures would need to be collected. Observations of Anita in multiple contexts would reveal language and social information important to the parents' concerns. Formal language measures can include receptive and expressive language testing in form, content, and use. Specific attention should be paid to the area of pragmatics because of Anita's reduced interest in toys and people. Results of this assessment process would indicate whether Anita needs services. If services are needed, an IFSP would be developed in collaboration with the family. A medical referral may be appropriate for autistic-like behaviors.

Activities

1. How could you find out more about child find efforts in your local area?
2. How would your assessment of a toddler who has vision impairments differ from your assessment of a toddler who is deaf?
3. Discuss the pros and cons of standardized testing.
4. Discuss the pros and cons of criterion-referenced assessment.
5. How does culture affect formal testing?
6. How does culture affect informal testing?
7. Give three examples of a standardized test.
8. Give three examples of informal assessment.

Websites

American Speech, Hearing, and Language Association
http://www.asha.org/public/speech/disorders

The Childhood Apraxia of Speech Association of North America
http://www.apraxia-kids.org

Illinois State Board of Education
http://www.isbe.state.il/us/earlychi

National Association for the Education of Young Children
http://www.naeyc.org

National Down Syndrome Society
http://www.ndss.org

The National Early Childhood Technical Assistance Center
http://www.nectac.org/ecprojects/ecproj.asp

National Institute for on Deafness and Other Communication Disorders
http://www.nidcd.nih.gov/health/voice/autism.asp

Nonverbal Learning Disabilities Association
http://www.nlda.org

Zero to Three: National Center for Infants, Toddlers, and Families
http://www.zerotothree.org

References

Bankson, N. W. (1990). *Bankson language screening test* (2nd ed.). Austin, TX: PRO-ED.

Barnett, D. W., Ehrhardt, K. E., Stollar, S. A., & Bauer, A. M. (1994). PASSKey: A model for naturalistic assessment and intervention design. *Topics in Early Childhood Special Education, 14,* 350–373.

Bayley, N. (1993). *Bayley scales of infant development* (2nd ed.). San Antonio, TX: Psychological Corporation.

Bebout, L., & Arthur, B. (1992). Cross-cultural attitudes toward speech disorders. *Journal of Speech and Hearing Research, 135,* 45–52.

Bloom, L., & Lahey, M. (1978). *Language development and language disorders.* New York: Wiley.

Boehm, A. E. (2000). *Boehm test of basic concepts* (3rd ed.). (BTBC–3). San Antonio, TX: Psychological Corporation.

Bray, C. M., & Wiig, E. H. (1987). *Let's talk inventory for children.* San Antonio, TX: Psychological Corporation.

Brigance, A. H. (1985). *Brigance diagnostic inventory of early development.* North Billerica, MA: Curriculum Associates.

Brown, R. (1973). *A first language: The early stages.* Cambridge, MA: Harvard University Press.

Brownell, R. (2000a). *Expressive one-word picture vocabulary test* (2000 ed.). Novato, CA: Academic Therapy.

Brownell, R. (2000b). *Receptive one-word picture vocabulary test* (2000 ed.). Novato, CA: Academic Therapy.

Bzock, K., & League, R. (2003). *Receptive-expressive emergent language test* (3rd ed.). Los Angeles: Western Psychological Services.

Campbell, T., Dollaghan, C., Needleman, H., & Janosky, J. (1997). Reducing bias in language assessment: Processing-dependent measures. *Journal of Speech, Language, and Hearing Research, 40,* 519–525.

Carrow-Woolfolk, E. (1974). *Carrow elicited language inventory.* Chicago: Riverside.

Carrow-Woolfolk, E. C. (1999). *Test of auditory comprehension of language—III* (TACL –3). Austin, TX: PRO-ED.

Cole, P. A., & Taylor, O. L. (1990). Performance on working class African-American children on three tests of articulation. *Language, Speech, and Hearing Services in Schools, 21,* 171–176.

Craig, H. K., & Washington, J. A. (2000). An assessment battery for identifying language impairments in African American children. *Journal of Speech, Language, and Hearing Research, 43*(2), 366–380.

Craig, H. K., Washington, J. A., & Thompson-Porter, C. (1998). Performances of young African American children on two comprehension tasks. *Journal of Speech, Language, and Hearing Research, 41,* 445–457.

Dunn, L. M., & Dunn, D. M. (2007). *Peabody picture vocabulary test—4* (PPVT–IV). Circle Pines, MN: American Guidance Service.

Dunn, L. M., Lugo, D. E., Padilla, E. R., & Dunn, L. E. (1986). *TVIP: Test de vocabulario en imagenes Peabody.* Circle Pines, MN: American Guidance Service.

Dunst, C. J., Hamby, D., Trivette, C. M., Raab, M., & Bruder, M. B. (2000). Everyday family and community life and children's naturally occurring learning opportunities. *Journal of Early Intervention, 23*(3), 151–164.

Dunst. C. J., Bruder, M. B., Trivette, C. M, Hamby, D., Raab, M., & McLean, M. (2001). Characteristics and consequences of everyday natural learning opportunities. *Topics in Early Childhood Special Education, 21*(2), 68–92.

Fagundes, D. D., Haynes, W. O., Haak, N. J., & Moran, M. J. (1998). Task variability effects on the language test performance of Southern lower socioeconomic class African American five-year-olds. *Language, Speech, and Hearing Services in Schools, 29*, 148–157.

Fewell, R. (1986). *Play assessment scale* (5th rev. ed.). Seattle: University of Washington.

Furuno, S., O'Reilly, K., Inatsuka, T., Hosaka, C., Allman, T., & Zeisloft-Falbey, B. (1987). *Hawaii early learning profile*, Palo Alto, CA: VORT Corp.

Goldman, R., & Fristoe, M. (2000). *Goldman-Fristoe test of articulation* (2nd ed.). Circle Pines, MN: American Guidance Service.

Goldman, R., Fristoe, M., & Woodcock, R. (1970). *Goldman-Fristoe-Woodcock test of auditory discrimination*. Circle Pines, MN: American Guidance Service.

Gutierrez-Clellen, V. F., & Peña, E. (2001). Dynamic assessment of diverse children: A tutorial. *Language, Speech, and Hearing Services in Schools, 32*, 212–224.

Gutiérrez-Clellen, V. F., & Quinn, R. (1993) Assessing narratives in diverse cultural/linguistic populations: Clinical implications. *Language, Speech, and Hearing Services in Schools, 24*(1), 2–9.

Hardin, B. J., & Peisner-Feinberg, E. S. (2004). *The learning accomplishment profile* (3rd ed.). Lewisville, NC: Kaplan Press.

Hulit, L. M., & Howard, M. R. (2006). *Born to talk: An introduction to speech and language development* (4th ed.). Boston: Allyn & Bacon.

Individuals with Disabilities Education Improvement Act. (2004). Public Law 108-446 (20 U.S.C. 1400 et seq.).

IDEA Child Find Project. (2004). Retrieved August 5, 2008, from http://www.childfindidea.org/

Johnson-Martin, N.M., Jens, K.G., Attermeier, S.M., & Hacker, B.J. (2004). *The Carolina curriculum for handicapped infants and infants at risk*. Baltimore: Brookes.

Kayser, H. (1989). Speech and language assessment of Spanish-English speaking children. *Language, Speech, and Hearing Services in Schools, 20*, 226–241.

Kayser, H. (1995). *Bilingual speech-language pathology: An Hispanic focus*. San Diego: Singular.

Kritikos, E. P. (2003). Speech-language pathologists' beliefs about language assessment of bilingual/bicultural individuals. *American Journal of Speech-Language Pathology, 12*, 73–91.

Laing, S. P., & Kamhi, A. (2003). Alternative assessment of language and literacy in culturally and linguistically diverse populations. *Language, Speech, and Hearing Services in Schools, 34*, 44–55.

Lee, L. L. (1974). *Developmental sentence analysis*. Evanston, IL: Northwestern University Press.

Lerner, J. W., Lowenthal, B., & Egan, R. (2003). *Preschool children with special needs: Children at risk and children with disabilities* (2nd ed.). Boston: Pearson Education.

Lidz, C., & Pena, E. D. (1996). Dynamic assessment: The model, its relevance as nonbiased approach, and its application to Latin American preschool children. *Language, Speech, and Hearing Services in Schools, 27*, 367–372.

Linares, T. (1981). Rules for calculating mean length of utterance in morphemes for Spanish. In J. Erickson & D. Omark (Eds.), *Communication assessment of the bilingual bicultural child* (pp. 291–295). Baltimore: University Park Press.

Linder, T. (2008). *Transdisciplinary play-based assessment* (2nd ed.). (TPBA). Baltimore: Brookes.

Mattes, L. J., & Omark, D. R. (1991). *Speech and language assessment for the bilingual handicapped* (2nd ed.). Oceanside, CA: Academic Communication Associates.

McConnel, S. R. (2000). Assessment in early intervention and early childhood special education: Building on the past to project into our future. *Topics in Early Childhood Special Education, 20*, 143–148.

McLoughlin, J. A., & Lewis, R. B. (2008). *Assessing students with special needs* (7th ed.). Upper Saddle River, NJ: Merrill/Pearson Education.

Myers, C. L., McBride, S. L., & Peterson, C. A. (1996). Transdisciplinary, play-based assessment in early childhood special education: An examination of social validity. *Topics in Early Childhood Special Education, 16*(1), 102–126.

Newborg, J. (2005). *Battelle developmental inventory—2*. Chicago, IL: Riverside.

Newcomer, P. L., & Hammill, D. D. (2008). *Test of language development—Primary:4* (TOLD–P:4). Austin, TX: PRO-ED.

Owens, R. E. (2005). *Language development: An introduction* (6th ed.). Boston: Allyn & Bacon.

Pena, E. D., & Quinn, R. (1997). Task familiarity: Effects on the test performance of Puerto Rican and African American children. *Language, Speech, and Hearing in Schools, 28*, 323–332.

Penegra, L. M. (2000). *Your values, my values: Multicultural services in developmental disabilities*. Baltimore: Brookes.

Phelps-Terasaki, D., & Phelps-Gunn, T. (1992). *Test of pragmatic language*. Austin, TX: PRO-ED.

Polloway, E. A., Miller, L., & Smith, T. E. C. (2004). *Language instructions for students with disabilities* (3rd ed.). Denver, CO: Love.

Rhyner, P. M., Kelly, D., Brantley, A. L., & Krueger, D. M. (1999). Screening low-income African American children using the BLT–2S and the SPELT–P. *American Journal of Speech-Language Pathology, 8,* 44–52.

Rodekohr, R., & Haynes, W. (2001). Differentiating dialect from disorder: A comparison of two processing tasks and a standardized language test. *Journal of Communication Disorders, 34,* 1–18.

Roseberry-McKibbin, C. A., & Eicholtz, G. (1994). Serving children with limited English proficiency in the schools: A national survey. *Language, Speech, and Hearing Services in Schools, 25,* 156–164.

Rosner, B. S., & Pickering, J. B. (1994). *Vowel perception and production.* Oxford, Eng.: Oxford University Press.

Roth, F., & Spekman, N. (1984). Assessing the pragmatic abilities of children. Part 1: Organizational framework and assessment parameters. *Journal of Speech and Hearing Disorders, 49,* 2–11.

Saenz, T. I., & Huer, M. B. (2003). Testing strategies involving least biased language assessment of bilingual children. *Communication Disorders Quarterly, 24,* 84–193.

Schiff-Myers, N. B. (1992). Considering arrested language development and language loss in the assessment of second language learners. *Language, Speech, and Hearing Services in Schools, 23,* 28–33.

Shames, G. H., Wiig, E. H., & Secord, W. A. (1998). *Human communication disorders: An introduction* (5th ed.). Boston, MA: Allyn & Bacon.

Shulman, L. (1986). Those who understand: Knowledge growth in teaching. *Educational Researcher, 15*(2), 4–14.

Stillman, R., & Battle, C. (1978–1985). *The Callier-Azuza scale.* Dallas: South Central Regional Center for Services to Deaf-Blind Children and Callier Center for Communication Disorders, University of Texas at Dallas.

Stockman, I. J. (1996). The promises and pitfalls of language sample analysis as an assessment tool for linguistic minority children. *Language, Speech, and Hearing Services in Schools, 27,* 355–366.

Taylor, R. L. (2009). *Assessment of exceptional students: Educational and psychological procedures* (8th ed.). Upper Saddle River, NJ: Merrill.

Turnbull, A., Turnbull, R., Erwin, W., & Soodak, L. (2006). *Families, professionals, and exceptionality positive outcomes through partnerships and trust* (5th ed.). Upper Saddle River, NJ: Merrill/Pearson Education.

Ukrainetz, T. A., Harpell, S., Walsh, C., & Coyle, C. (2000). A preliminary investigation of dynamic assessment with Native American kindergarteners. *Language, Speech, and Hearing Services in Schools, 31*(2), 142–154.

Washington, J. A., Craig, H. K., & Kushmaul, A. (1998). Variable use of African American English across two language sampling contexts. *Journal of Speech, Language, and Hearing Research, 41,* 1115–1124.

Williams, K. T. (2007). *Expressive Vocabulary Test—2.* Circle Pines, MN: American Guidance Service.

Yavas, M., & Goldstein, B. (1998). Phonological assessment and treatment of bilingual speakers. *American Journal of Speech-Language Pathology, 7,* 49–60.

Zimmerman, I., Steiner, V., & Pond, R. (2002). *Preschool Language Scale—4.* Upper Saddle River, NJ: Pearson Education.

Motor Development and Adaptive Skills

CHAPTER 12

CHAPTER OBJECTIVES

By the end of this chapter, you will be able to answer the questions at the end of the case study about Marcus. You will have a clear understanding of motor skills and the role they play in the ongoing growth and development of young children, including self-help skill development. You will realize the importance of understanding typical development in order to assess and provide programming for children who display atypical motor and self-help skills. You will be able to identify the assessments that evaluate motor and self-help skills most appropriately and make assessment decisions that lead to comprehensive program planning.

This chapter addresses Council for Exceptional Children/Division for Early Childhood (CEC/DEC) Standard 2 (Development and Characteristics of Learners) and Standard 8 (Assessment) and National Association for the Education of Young Children (NAEYC) Standard 1 (Promoting Child Development and Learning) and Standard 3 (Observing, Documenting, and Assessing to Support Young Children and Families).

Assessing Marcus

Marcus is a 9-month-old infant who has been receiving early intervention services since he was a newborn. Marcus was full term and weighed 8½ pounds at birth. Due to initial complications with breathing and eating following his birth, he was hospitalized for 10 days. During that time, he was diagnosed with a chromosome disorder. Generalized hypotonia (low muscle tone) and global developmental delay are common outcomes of this diagnosis. Marcus initially displayed overall low muscle tone, and it was most apparent in his oral motor control, causing initial feeding difficulties. His parents were provided with techniques for encouraging the development and strengthening of the muscles needed for independent feeding, as well as positioning techniques that would encourage better suck and swallow of liquids.

Marcus continues to show hypotonia in all extremities, with emerging head control. He can bring his hand to his mouth and loves to chew on his fingers. He bats at toys and grasps objects presented to him. He can bring toys to his mouth and chew on them. He prefers **supine position** (lying on his back) because this is most comfortable for him, and he appears to have the most motor control in this position. When he is in **prone position** (lying on his tummy), he has begun to push up on his forearms and lift his head 45 degrees for a few seconds. He has not been observed to roll independently; he sits with trunk support. He is presently receiving home visits weekly from an early interventionist, and biweekly from a physical therapist. He also receives consultation services from an occupational therapist and speech pathologist.

Marcus drinks formula from a bottle and he has begun to eat some puréed foods, including rice cereal and fruit. He chokes frequently when he is drinking and eating, and the parents have been looking for nipples that slow the flow of the milk.

Marcus has experienced frequent respiratory infections and has been hospitalized twice for pneumonia.

What other information would you like to know about Marcus and his family? What do you foresee as his needs in motor development and self-help skills? What are your concerns regarding feeding? What evidence suggests that this area needs to be monitored closely? What are his gross motor and fine motor development needs? How do you see Marcus's needs in this area being assessed most appropriately?

MOTOR DEVELOPMENT

The development of movement in the human body is a complex, comprehensive process. When children struggle with the acquisition of these skills, it affects their overall growth and learning. Your knowledge of the motor characteristics and needs of these children will influence the ways in which you provide intervention. It is imperative that you collaborate closely with the physical therapist and/or occupational therapist who provides intervention for children who experience gross motor and/or fine motor disabilities.

Motor or physical development is one of the five primary skills addressed in the early childhood special education curriculum and is listed as one of the descriptors of "developmental delay" in Part C of Individuals with Disabilities Education Improvement Act (IDEIA), 2004:

(B) CHILD AGES 3 THROUGH 9—The term "child with a disability" for a child aged 3 through 9 (or any subset of that age range, including ages 3 through 5), may, at the discretion of the State and the local educational agency, include a child—

(i) experiencing developmental delays, as defined by the State and as measured by appropriate diagnostic instruments and procedures, in one or more of the following areas: physical development; cognitive development; communication development; social or emotional development; or adaptive development; and

(ii) who, by reason thereof, needs special education and related services.

(Individuals with Disabilities Education Improvement Act (IDEIA), 2004)

GROSS MOTOR DEVELOPMENT

Gross motor skills are defined as the skills that require the coordination of the large muscle groups found in the arms, legs, trunk, and neck. This skill development is prerequisite for acquisition of independent movement. Newborn infants have no control over their body movements.

They are empowered only through **reflexes**, or involuntary processes. As the neurological system develops, involuntary movements are replaced by voluntary movement, and reflexes either integrate or disappear.

Reflex Assessment

There are many theories regarding how humans develop the ability to move independently. One of the oldest, the reflex theory, was developed by Sir Charles Sherrington in the late 1800s. He believed that the foundations for motor control were reflexes (involuntary movement) and that motor development was a process of maturation, moving toward voluntary control and movement. His approach continues to be respected today because most initial evaluations of motor skills include assessment of reflex development. Next, the hierarchical theory, developed by Hughlings Jackson at approximately the same time, states that motor development depends on various levels of neurological development. Jackson believed that lower skill levels are governed by higher levels; as higher levels develop, lower levels of development integrate or disappear (Foerster, 1977).

Both theories contribute to present therapeutic approaches to working with and understanding movement, and the absence of any reflex warrants concern for the infant's neurological development (Shumway-Cook & Woollacott, 2007). The earliest reflexes, primitive reflexes, have a specific purpose in initial human survival. The sucking reflex, for example, is instrumental in allowing the infant to take in nourishment. The rooting reflex (the infant turns in the direction of a touched cheek) assists the infant in locating the breast or bottle and the acquisition of food. As listed in Table 12.1, many of these primitive reflexes integrate or disappear a few months after birth. Jackson believed that they are replaced with higher level or voluntary motor abilities (Foerster, 1977). It is common for babies who experience problems at birth to have weak or no reflexes. Infants born prematurely frequently have difficulty with the sucking reflex. With time and with early intervention from a speech pathologist or occupational therapist, however, the reflex can be elicited, and further feeding adaptations may not be needed.

As the child learns to move independently, a new group of reflexes are observed called **postural reactions**, which include responses that protect the body from falling (**protective responses**) and righting responses. They are responses or reactions that the adult continues to use to protect and also keep the body in alignment with the environment. Early protection is observed in an infant if the infant is held in prone position by an adult and moved forward toward the ground. The infant will automatically extend the arms as a means of protecting the body from the potential fall. When the infant begins to sit, the infant extends the arms forward if the body bends forward. As the infant gains more independent balance, the arms extend to the left or right to protect from falling. Eventually, the equilibrium reactions (trunk control or rotation) work against gravity to keep the body from losing balance when in sitting position. **Righting reactions** develop as the child begins moving independently and are the reactions that automatically take place in an attempt to keep the body in an upright position. These responses can be elicited by tilting the infant toward the left or right side. The automatic response is for the infant to keep the head in midline, even though the body is tilted.

A variety of disabilities affect the development of postural reactions. Children with hypertonia or hypotonia may have delayed postural reactions, which inhibit natural motor developmental progression. Children who are visually impaired frequently have delayed responses because the visual system is instrumental in the motivation to keep the body in an upright position. Children with balance disorders or cognitive delay may also experience delays in postural reactions.

TABLE 12.1

Reflex	Onset	Stimulus	Inhibition
Sucking, rooting	24–28 weeks gestation	When the baby's cheek is touched, the baby turns in the direction of the touch.	3–4 months
Asymmetric tonic neck	Birth	In supine position, when head turns one way, limbs on that side extend out and the other side shows flexion.	6 months
Palmer	11 weeks gestations	A finger or object placed in infant's hand elicits the infant's grasp.	3 months
Placing or stepping	Birth	Infant is held upright. When dorsal (top) of foot touches a surface, hip and knee flex, causing the withdrawal of the foot, looking like a step onto the surface.	5 months
Grasp	Birth	When a stimulus is placed in the newborn's palm, the newborn's fingers wrap firmly around the finger or object.	5–6 months
Moro	9 weeks	Sudden movement, sound, and/or light causes extension of the neck, abduction and flexion of the arms, adduction and flexion of the extremities. Earliest form of survival response.	6 months
Traction	5 months	When pulled to sitting by its hands, infant anticipates the movement and resists by pulling against the pull and lifting head.	Ongoing
Landau	10 months	By eliciting flexion of the infant's head when she or he is in prone horizontal suspension, the infant displays leg and trunk flexion.	Before age 24 months
Parachute	10 months	When infant is moved headfirst in a downward direction, infant thrusts arms forward.	Ongoing
Head righting	4 months	Head stays in upright position, even though body is moved from one side to the other.	Ongoing
Trunk righting	8 months	When body is forced to either side while it is in a sitting position, the trunk resists and moves upright.	Ongoing
Equilibrium Responses	6–12 months	When the child is tilted or balance is offset, the child's trunk adjusts to bring the body to an upright position.	Ongoing

Reflexes are generally assessed by a medical professional, physical therapist, or occupational therapist. However, your understanding of reflexes and their presence or absence will assist you, as an educator, in realizing the underlying causes of specific motor barriers and will allow you to view and report realistically the child's developmental strengths and needs.

BREAKPOINT PRACTICE

1. To which of the two theories of the development of movement do you ascribe?
2. What steps would you take to ensure the optimal motor assessment of a child who has hypertonia and shows decreased postural reactions?
3. Describe how motor dysfunction affects the ways in which you assess a child's strengths and needs in other developmental domains.

Muscle Tone

A major indicator of typical motor development is evidenced by the child's overall muscle tone. **Muscle tone** refers to the tension of a muscle when it is at rest (Coleman, 2006). Normal muscle tone is not too tight or too flaccid, and it allows for smooth, precise movement of the body, including the head, neck, trunk, and limbs. When tone is increased or tight, it is described as spasticity, or **hypertonia**; when it is too flaccid, it is defined as **hypotonia** (Coleman, 2006).

Hypertonia is the most common characteristic of cerebral palsy and can range from mildly to severely increased tone in various muscle groups. Muscle tone involvement of various muscle groups is categorized as monoplegia (hypertonia in one extremity), diplegia (hypertonia in lower extremities), quadriplegia (hypertonia in all extremities), or hemiplegia (increased tone on one side of the body) (Hooper & Umansky, 2004).

Cerebral palsy is also grouped according to degrees and kinds of physical involvement. The terminology varies according to the author and the discipline, but usually there are four primary classifications. The most common classification is spastic cerebral palsy, also known as pyramidal cerebral palsy. It is characterized by a high degree of spasticity or hypertonia (Coleman, 2006). A second classification is labeled athetoid or athetosis. It is characterized by slow involuntary movements, often associated with writhing movements, particularity in fine motor control such as movements of the wrists, fingers, and feet. Commonly, there is intermittent fluctuating tone, which gives the appearance of severe clumsiness. Ataxia is the third grouping of cerebral palsy. It is identified by the lack of coordination. Children with this particular disorder may have difficulty with balance, and overall movement appears uncontrolled or jerky. Mixed type is also a classification and is characterized by ataxia, athetosis, and spasticity to varying degrees and in different parts of the body. Each classification of cerebral palsy has a unique affect on the child's ability to acquire gross and fine motor milestones at varying developmental periods.

Hypotonia is commonly observed in infants who are diagnosed with a chromosome disorder such as Down syndrome and in infants who are born prematurely. Low muscle tone also influences typical acquisition of gross and fine motor milestones. In some cases, hypotonia resolves with time. In Marcus's case, he presently shows delays in motor development due to his low muscle tone. However, information regarding his chromosome disorder is not provided; so the long-term affect is not provided. This is information that you would want to learn from researching his particular diagnosis.

Thorough assessment of muscle tone (again, typically assessed by a physical or occupational therapist) assists the educator in making allowances as needed for accurate overall evaluation and program planning. Common assessments used by therapists and physicians are listed in Table 12.2.

TABLE 12.2	Common Assessments of Motor Skills			
Assessment	**Areas Assessed**	**Age Range**	**Description**	**Who Administers**
Bayley Scales of Infant Development—III (Bayley, 2006)	Gross and fine motor developmental milestones.	0–42 months	Standardized	Trained evaluator
Milani Comparetti Motor Development for Infants and Young Children (Stuberg, 1992)	Postural control, active movement, primitive reflexes, righting reactions.	0–24 months	Standardized	Therapist
Newborn and Infant Neurological Assessment Tool (Amiel-Tisen, 2002)	Primitive reflexes and neurological capacity. Skills of newborns and also premature infants.	0–12 months	Not standardized	Physician, therapist
Test of Infant Motor Performance (TIMP) (Campbell, 2004)	For postural and selective control of functional movement	Preterm to 4 months adjusted age	Standardized	Physician, therapist
Developmental Assessment of Young Children (Voress & Maddox, 1998)	Physical skills and adaptive behavior	0–5 years	Standardized	Trained personnel
Peabody Developmental Motor Scales—II (PDMS–2) (Folio & Fewel, 2000)	Gross and fine motor skills	0–7 years	Not standardized	Therapists or educators
Mullen Scales of Early Learning (Mullen, 1995)	Gross and fine motor skills	0–5 years	Standardized	Trained personnel
Gross Motor Function Measures (GMFM) (Russell et al., 1993)	Gross motor skills	0–6 years	Not standardized; used with children with cerebral palsy	Trained personnel
Bruiniknks-Oseretsky Test of Motor Proficiency (Bruininks, 1978)	Gross and fine motor skills, running, balance, coordination, response speed, strength, visual motor skills, finger dexterity	4½–14½ years	Standardized	Trained personnel
Alberta Infant Motor Scale (AIMS) (Piper & Darrah, 1994)	Motor functions in supine, prone, sitting and standing	0–18 months	Standardized	Therapist

BREAKPOINT PRACTICE

1. When evaluating a young child who has developmental delay, what symptoms indicate that the child may have increased or tight muscle tone, or decreased or flaccid muscle tone?
2. In a classroom setting, what modifications are appropriate when assessing the strengths and needs of a child with hypertonia or hypotonia?
3. What information would you, as an educator, need to give a physical therapist to provide accurate information about gross motor development in the classroom environment?
4. What information would you like to receive from a physical therapist that may assist you in successful educational programming for Marcus?

Gross Motor Milestones

The acquisition of gross motor milestones is a sequential process in human development, starting with involuntary movements (reflexes) and going to simple voluntary movement, and eventually to refined actions that allow the child to function independently in all environmental settings. Development is cephalocaudal, meaning it moves in a head-to-foot progression. It is also proximo-distal, meaning that strength and coordination start in the center (the spine) and move out to the extremities. Large muscle movements develop before small muscle functions, and bilateral coordination precedes unilateral control (Lerner, Lowenthal, & Egan, 2003). Thus, in typical infant growth, head control develops first, followed by neck strength and control. The infant then displays strength and coordination in the trunk, which assists in the strengthening and control of muscles in and movements by the arms and legs (see Table 12.3).

Gross motor development is usually included in assessment tools as a separate domain. However, several assessments look specifically at gross and fine motor development. In most cases, these tools are standardized and are specifically designed to be administered by an occupational therapist or a physical therapist. Table 12.3 provides an outline of assessments that are commonly used to assess the motor skills of young children.

Bear in mind that children who have an existing diagnosis may have specific motor limitations. Consultation with physical and occupational therapists or other specialists who have unique expertise in the assessment of children with a specific diagnosis enhances the quality of your assessment results and assists you in making adjustments or adaptations to support the assessment and planning process.

FINE MOTOR DEVELOPMENT

Fine motor skills are defined as the skills that require the use of small muscle groups such as those found in the hands, fingers, and face. This skill development depends on the strength and refinement of basic gross motor skills. If gross motor skills are delayed, more than likely, delays will be observed in fine motor development. The major milestones of the fine motor domain include reach, grasp, release, and the manipulation of objects (Hooper & Umansky, 2004). Reaching consists of the ability to move the arm(s) forward toward a toy or object. This is

TABLE 12.3	Gross Motor Milestones
Age	**Milestone**
0–3 months	Holds head steady when held. Lifts head in prone position.
3–6 months	Holds trunk steady when held. Extends arms, legs, and trunk in prone position. Plays with feet in supine position. Bears weight on elbows, eventually on extended arms. Rolls from stomach to back and back to stomach. Reaches while supported on one elbow.
6–9 months	Moves to sitting from prone position. Moves to all fours from prone position. Sits without support. Pulls self forward in prone position.
9–12 months	Creeps on all fours. Pulls to standing. Stoops to pick up a toy with support. Stands alone momentarily. Begins to walk independently.
12–15 months	Moves from sitting to all fours, to standing. Creeps up stairs and backward down stairs. Squats to pick up object without support.
15–18 months	Walks sideways and backward. Walks up and down a few stairs. Attempts to kick a ball. Throws a ball. Enjoys swinging and sliding.
18–21 months	Maintains squatting position in play. Runs stiffly. Jumps. Walks up stairs with same-foot placement.
21–24 months	Jumps off stairs.
24–30 months	Walks on tiptoes. Begins running. Walks upstairs with alternating foot pattern.
30–36 months	Walking, running, and jumping become more coordinated. Can kick a ball 4–6 feet.
36–42 months	Walks 10 feet on tiptoes on a 1-inch line. Gallops at least 5 times. Hops in place. Jumps over 8-inch hurdle. Broad jumps at least 14–24 inches. Can throw and catch an 8-inch ball from 5 feet.

TABLE 12.3	*(continued)*
Age	**Milestone**
42–48 months	Skips. Hops on one foot. Jumps down from a 2-foot surface. Walks downstairs with alternating foot pattern. Peddles a tricycle several feet.
48–54 months	All motor skills (running, skipping, hopping, jumping) improve with balance and endurance. Pumps a swing.
54–60 months	Can change direction when running. Walks down several steps, alternating foot pattern without holding onto railing. Turns somersaults. Walks on a balance beam. Catches a 3-inch ball. Rides a two-wheel bicycle.

observed in supine, prone, and eventually sitting and standing positions. Independent grasp or hand use does not develop unless the trunk is strong enough to support reaching and free manipulation of toys. When the infant does begin manipulating objects, the process of **finger dexterity** (refined use of fingers for fine motor activity) improves (see Table 12.4).

The grasp reflex is initially observed as involuntary in the newborn. It is elicited when the palm is touched and is usually strong enough to hold the newborn suspended for a few moments. The grasp reflex eventually integrates and becomes voluntary movement at approximately 3 to 4 months of age. In contrast, the avoidant response is observed when the back of the hand is touched, eliciting opening of the fingers for release. Voluntary release of objects emerges at approximately

© mykeyruna/Fotolia

TABLE 12.4	Fine Motor Milestones
Age	**Milestone**
0–3 months	Actively moves arms when seeing or hearing an object. Looks to one side at hand or toy. Brings toy and hand into visual field and looks at them. Watches hands at midline. Raises both hands when object is presented. Looks at and manipulates a grasped toy.
3–6 months	Bats at dangling objects. Grasps object placed in hand. Reaches out and grasps a toy. Rakes and scoops small objects. Brings hands together at midline. Places both hands on toy at midline. Transfers objects between hands. Glances from one toy to another.
6–9 months	Imitates unfamiliar movements. Reaches for and picks up toys in visual field. Manipulates objects with fingers and hands. Voluntary release of object to pick up another object. Inferior pincer grasp is developing. Clasps hands.
9–12 months	Imitates gestures such as bye-bye. Uses index finger to poke. Uses neat pincer grasp. Removes objects from holders. Plays with toys at midline. Pulls string on a toy for cause and effect.
12–15 months	Imitation of gestures increases. Builds two-block tower. Grasps two small objects with one hand. Pulls apart pop beads. Hits drum with a stick. Marks paper with a writing tool.
15–18 months	Places pegs in holes. Builds three- to four-block tower. Uses stick to retrieve a toy. Scribbles on a paper.
18–21 months	Plays with play dough. Turns pages in a book. Unscrews small lids. Uses a hammer to pound in pegs.
21–24 months	Builds six- to eight-block tower. Puts pop beads together. Strings large beads. Imitates a vertical writing stroke. Moves from scribbles to marks.

TABLE 12.4	*(continued)*

Age	Milestone
24–30 months	Turns doorknobs.
	Puts small object in small opening.
	Imitates horizontal writing stroke.
	Pretends to write.
	Begins to show hand preference.
30–36 months	Unbuttons large buttons.
	Strings small beads.
	Screws on lids.
	Copies a circle.
	Snips with scissors and begins to make continuous cuts with scissors.
36–42 months	Makes simple forms with play dough.
	Turns a windup key.
	Laces lacing card.
	Copies a circle and a cross, and draws a simple person.
	Cuts on a line.
42–48 months	Holds writing tool with tripod grasp.
	Places several pellets in a small bottle.
	Ties single knot.
	Uses tongs.
	Draws person with at least four features.
	Cuts out a square.
48–54 months	Moves object from palm to pincer grasp easily.
	Does simple sewing.
	Holds deck of cards and sorts them.
	Copies a square.
	Draws simple pictures.
	Cuts out a circle.
54–60 months	Places paper clips on a paper.
	Folds paper in half.
	Consistently uses same hand for tasks.
	Traces outlines of a simple stencil.
	Draws person with many features.
	Cuts out a simple picture.

7 months of age, when the infant begins to transfer objects or toys from one hand to the other (Hooper & Umansky, 2004). Release of objects refines as the infant manipulates and explores toys. The asymmetric tonic neck reflex (ATNR), or arm and leg **extension** (straightening) toward the direction the head is turned, may provide the infant with an initial opportunity to link vision with grasp. Vision becomes an important part of fine motor development as the child learns to reach for an object within view. The visually guided use of hands and fingers (eye-hand coordination) becomes a critical component of the eventual development of writing, cutting, drawing, and typically any task that involves finger dexterity. See Table 12.5 for more information about typical fine motor development.

Fine motor skills can be affected by a variety of disorders, especially when the child is experiencing muscle tone dysfunction. When abnormal muscle tone is present, assessment

TABLE 12.5	Development of Grasp	
Age	**Type of Grasp**	**Illustration**
0–2 months	Reflex: ulnar side is dominant	
	Palmar: grasp is in the middle of the palm	
	Radial palmar: grasp includes the use of the thumb side of the hand	
	Radial digital: grasp includes thumb and fingers	
	Scissors: grasp is on the side of the index finger and the thumb	
	Fine pincer: grasp is from the tip of the index finger and the thumb	
	Transitional grasp: the initial grasp on a pencil usually is a palmer grasp	
	Tripod: Holds a writing tool with the thumb, index finger, and middle finger	

Source: Erhardt (1994).

considerations include positioning and posturing during reach and object manipulation. Poor positioning results in an inaccurate assessment of the child's true abilities in fine motor development. For a child who shows hypotonia, trunk support may make the difference in whether the child can display reaching, grasping, and object manipulation. This is true for Marcus because he is able to reach for objects when he is lying on his back. When a child is experiencing hypertonia, placing the child in positions where the spasticity does not overtake movement and hand usage is important (Johnson-Martin, Attermeier, & Hacker, 2004a). In both situations, it is best practice to include a physical therapist or occupational therapist in the assessment of fine motor milestones. The presence of this specialist ensures that the child is positioned so that optimal hand function can be elicited and observed.

Children with visual impairment commonly show delays in fine motor development. However, several adaptations can be made to provide optimal performance of ability (Johnson-Martin, Attermeier, & Hacker, 2004a). In this situation, it is best to include a teacher of the visually impaired in the assessment process. This person can give you key information regarding the adaptations needed to assist in the assessment of a child with a specific visual disorder.

Standardized assessments do not allow the evaluator the freedom to use environmental adaptations during the assessment process. This is a concern when assessing the skills of a child with exceptional learning needs. In many situations, best performance depends on the use of adaptations. Nonstandardized assessments allow you to make the adaptations needed to provide the child with the opportunity to display optimal performance. If you are uncertain about providing an adaptation for a given task, think in terms of what is being assessed: If you are not altering the intended outcome, then the adaptation is allowable. For example, when you are assessing the child's ability to draw a circle or make other prewriting strokes, the use of a pencil grip, a marker, or writing board will not alter the purpose of the task. If you are assessing the ability to secure an object from a surface in sitting position, placing Dycem™ under the object to keep it from sliding off the surface does not alter the intention of the task. Many nonstandardized assessments, such as the Carolina Curriculum (Johnson-Martin, Attermeier, & Hacker, 2004a) and the Hawaii Early Learning Profile (HELP) (Parks, 2006), provide considerations for children with specific diagnosed disabilities.

BREAKPOINT PRACTICE

1. What are the fine motor characteristics of a child who is diagnosed with hypotonia?
2. What assessment considerations are necessary for a child who is experiencing overall developmental delays?
3. Do you believe that the provisions of adaptations and/or modifications of assessment to accommodate the characteristics of various disabilities skew assessment results? How do they skew the results?

SELF-HELP AND ADAPTIVE DEVELOPMENT

The development of appropriate adaptive behavior is a critical issue in the assessment and programming of young children with exceptional learning needs. When young children have difficulties in the areas of adaptive behavior, they struggle to acquire the skills needed to meet their personal needs, show social responsibility, and respond appropriately in a variety of situations (Dunlap, 2009). Adaptive behaviors can be defined as those behaviors that allow the child to function appropriately according to her or his age level in all environments or settings, including social and community situations.

In young children, adaptive behaviors encompass, specifically, self-care skills or self-help skills (Bailey & Wolery, 1992). These are the specific adaptive behaviors that, at this age, allow the child to move toward independence in taking care of her or his needs and building feelings of independence and autonomy (Johnson-Martin, Attermeier, & Hacker, 2004b). Self-help skills are primarily categorized into four areas (eating, dressing, grooming, and toileting) and can depend to some degree on the development of gross and fine motor skills.

Feeding

Feeding is a social event and a time of connection and bonding starting from the early moments following birth. When an infant has difficulty feeding, the parent–child relationship can be strained, and the nutritional needs of the infant may be at risk. It is imperative that feeding problems be alleviated as soon as possible to create the environment needed for healthy physical and emotional growth (Hooper & Umansky, 2004). Basic knowledge of the skills needed to take in nutrition easily and adequately allows the early interventionist to assist families in creating the optimal feeding environment. This assistance can include support through consultation or contact with the appropriate experts in the field, such as feeding clinicians, which in many cases are trained speech-language pathologists or occupational therapists who have expertise and experience in assessing and supporting the feeding needs of infants and young children with disabilities or developmental delays.

Development of Feeding Skills

Typically developing infants have the ability to suck, swallow, and turn (root) toward the source of food with tactile input. Reflexive sucking and swallowing are strong during the first few months of age and diminish as they become voluntary (Conner, Williamson, & Siepp, 1978). During bottle feeding, the infant's sucking ability should be robust and rhythmic. If it appears to be weak, or if the infant appears to be unable to create an adequate seal around the nipple (causing excessive drooling during feeding), a referral to a feeding specialist is recommended. Marcus was observed to have difficulty with sucking and swallowing at a very young age, and intervention from the specialists assisted the parents in providing an optimal, comfortable feeding experience.

Initial assessment of feeding skills includes observation of the overall feeding environment to ensure that the infant and caretaker have created a comfortable and relaxed dyad. The infant's head should be slightly elevated, the trunk and limbs should be cradled, and the bottle should be held in proper alignment.

The following observations may be reasons to refer the child for further evaluation (Arvedson & Brodsky, 2001):

- Irritability during feeding
- Unable to finish the bottle in a timely fashion (30 to 40 minutes)
- Frequent gagging or choking while drinking
- Breathing disruptions while eating

By 4 to 6 months of age, the infant attempts to hold the bottle and begins to coordinate oral structure movements needed for eating solid food. At this age, the infant also begins drinking from a cup, which requires a lip closure quite different from that needed for sucking. When solid foods are introduced, the child moves from using a sucking motion to sophisticated tongue and jaw movements (Morris & Klein, 2000). By 9 months of age, finger feeding has begun, and the child begins to hold a cup independently. Independent feeding begins at approximately 15 months and refines over the next several months. By 2 years of age, most children can hold a cup and use a spoon independently. By age 3, the child can eat with a fork; by age 4, the child becomes an independent eater (Lerner, Lowenthal, & Egan, 2003).

Feeding problems are common for children with disabilities for various reasons and are frequently caused by oral motor difficulties. (*Oral motor* refers to the muscles in and around the mouth needed for adequate sucking, chewing, and swallowing.) Children with hypertonia may experience poor oral motor control due to involuntary tongue or jaw thrust or a strong biting reflex. This will result in decreased food intake as well as a lengthy, uncomfortable mealtime. Children with hypotonia may experience inadequate lip seal on a spoon or cup, resulting in drooling and food or liquid loss. Infants and children with decreased oral motor control are at risk for **aspiration** (entry of food or liquid into the respiratory tract), and early assessment and implementation of appropriate adaptations or modifications alleviate future health issues (Wagenfeld, 2005). In Marcus's case, he is experiencing signs of difficulty with swallowing liquids, which may be related to hypotonia. He has experienced upper respiratory issues frequently, which could be due to aspiration, especially because he has been hospitalized for pneumonia on two occasions. This would be reason to refer him for a formal suck-and-swallow test, which is administered by a trained clinician and usually in a clinical setting.

Other issues to consider are food hypersensitivity and tongue size. Some children, such as those with visual impairment or autism, may experience hypersensitivity to food textures. This hypersensitivity can result in defensive reactions, especially when the child is introduced to new foods. Children with Down syndrome commonly have oversized tongues, which can interfere with the development of refined oral motor control.

A knowledge base of the unique needs of each child results in realistic, comprehensive assessment procedures and outcomes. High-quality assessments incorporate a dynamic approach and a careful review of eating skills in the child's natural setting (Hooper & Umansky, 2004).

BREAKPOINT PRACTICE

1. After reading this section of Chapter 12, do you still have other concerns for a toddler who is experiencing feeding problems?
2. If a child is struggling with defensiveness to food texture, what can you do to assess oral motor skills and feeding skills without upsetting the child?
3. What do you think is meant by the term *dynamic assessment of feeding skills*?

Dressing

A child begins to cooperate in the dressing process as early as 9 months of age. The ability to dress and undress without assistance contributes to the child's feelings of autonomy and self-confidence (Johnson-Martin, Attermeier, & Hacker, 2004a). See Table 12.6.

TABLE 12.6	Sequence of Dressing Skills
Age	**Dressing Skill**
12 months	Begins to remove lose-fitting clothing. Unties shoes and can remove a hat.
18 months	Unfastens zippers. Puts a hat on.
24 months	Removes clothing such as a shirt, coat, or pair of pants.
36 months	Can dress without assistance. Can undo most fasteners.
36–42 months	Can put on a coat independently.
48 months	Can button most buttons independently.
60 months	Can dress and undress independently. Can zip clothing. Begins to tie a shoe.

Several factors can interfere with the development of independence in dressing. Lack of independence in gross and fine motor functioning can have varying affects. Children with increased or decreased muscle tone may have difficulty maneuvering their limbs as needed to put on a shirt, a pair of pants, or a jacket or for easy manipulation of fasteners.

Assessment of dressing skills includes the assessment of needed adaptations to make this process rewarding and as independent as possible. It may include placing rings on zippers to make grasping easier. Velcro fasteners may be considered until the child has the finger dexterity needed to secure snaps and buttons. Elastic waistbands create success in independence in pulling pants on and off. This is especially evident during toileting activities. Fashions in young children's clothing don't always include considerations for easy dressing or undressing. Therefore, family concerns and interests must be considered when altering the clothing items or suggesting easier fitting items to make dressing and undressing independent activities.

Grooming

Grooming independence in young children sets the stage for healthy habits throughout a lifetime. Grooming habits are necessary not only for health, but also for social acceptance, thus leading to a sense of pride and self-confidence (Johnson-Martin, Attermeier, & Hacker, 2004b). See Table 12.7.

Bathing, washing, brushing teeth, and combing hair are components of grooming. Children with disability, including motor, visual, and cognitive disability, have difficulties completing grooming tasks. Several adaptations are available to allow children to accomplish these tasks independently. Assessment must include the use of adaptations in order for children to learn and complete these tasks.

Toileting

Stages of acquisition of toileting independence are variable, with some children becoming independent by 2 years of age and others not until age 4. Boys may be more difficult to toilet-train, and nighttime training may be an issue for many children. Children with developmental

TABLE 12.7	Grooming Skills
Age	**Grooming Skill**
12–18 months	Cooperates in brushing of teeth.
18–24 months	Attempts to wash during bathing. Attempts to blow nose.
24–36 months	Brushes teeth with assistance. Can wipe nose independently. Attempts to comb own hair.
36–48 months	Wipes nose without a reminder. Washes hands and body independently.
48–60 months	Independence in most tasks, including brushing teeth, taking a bath, blowing nose.

disabilities frequently show delays in toileting. The stages of toileting are listed in Table 12.8. Sometimes bladder control may never be attained. For example, children with forms of spina bifida may have decreased bladder response and, as a result, toilet training may not be possible (Hooper & Umansky, 2004). Tone abnormalities also affect the ability to accomplish independent toileting. Children with cognitive impairment may be delayed in understanding the purpose or process of independent toileting.

BREAKPOINT PRACTICE

1. How would delayed acquisition affect the self-esteem of a child and affect a parent–child relationship?
2. What family issues should be considered when assessing the development of self-help skills?
3. What are some strategies that may assist in the assessment of toileting skills for a child such as Marcus, who is diagnosed with a chromosome disorder?

TABLE 12.8	Toileting Skills
Age	**Toileting Skills**
12–18 months	Indicates that diaper is wet. Has regular bowel movements.
24 months	Is dry for up to 3 hours. Urinates, has bowel movement when placed on toilet.
36 months	Urinates, has bowel movement when placed on toilet. Indicates need to use toilet.
36–48 months	Seldom has accidents.
48 months	Independence in toileting.
60 months	Shows day and night bladder control.

Self-Help Skill Assessments

Most assessment tools that evaluate developmental domains include a section on self-help skills. They offer detailed sequences of typical development in the areas of self-help skill acquisition. Nonstandardized assessments allow the evaluator to make adaptations as needed in order to achieve optimal performance in all areas of self-help development. Once again, the educator must look closely at what is being assessed, the intention of the activity, and the barriers that the child is experiencing in her or his attempt to accomplish this skill. It is important to remember that self-help skill acquisition is closely tied to gross and fine motor abilities. However, the intention of acquisition of these skills is autonomy, self-confidence, self-awareness, and eventual independent living. Therefore, assessment of modifications and adaptations that will allow successful completion of eating, grooming, dressing, and toileting is necessary.

Revisiting Marcus

Marcus has a diagnosis with unique characteristics. As you learned in the chapter, a characteristic of chromosome disorder is hypotonia with varying degrees of impact on motor development. It may be difficult to find information on this disorder because it is so rare. Therefore, a geneticist may be consulted to learn the most accurate implications of the specific diagnosis. Also, an Internet search of support groups, possibly rare chromosome disorder support groups, may provide you with some information about this disorder. Some adaptations will need to be incorporated into the assessment of Marcus's motor development and self-help skill development. Also, with low muscle tone and, more than likely, cognitive delays, Marcus may need to be given more time for completion of tasks. The implications of the neurological impairments should be considered during assessment. Hypotonia is present, so oral motor control should be assessed and a feeding clinician should be consulted. Marcus is having difficulty with feeding and has experienced frequent upper respiratory infections. You should seek medical assessment and consultation regarding the possibility of aspiration.

Activities

1. What kinds of assessments would you use with Marcus?
2. What would be the most appropriate assessment model to use during assessment?
3. Because of Marcus's specific needs, who would you consider as part of the assessment team?
4. What assessment adaptations should you consider?
5. What support systems would you provide for Marcus's family?

Websites

Adaptive equipment for young children
http://www.adaptivemall.com/

Children's Disabilities Information (Occupational Therapy plus simple adaptive equipment may help children who struggle with handwriting)
http://www.childrensdisabilities.info/cerebral_palsy/ handwriting-help.html

Choosing the right educational toys for children
http://www.brighttots.com/

Clinic 4kidz: Specializing in caring for children with pediatric feeding disorders, autism, and other special needs
http://clinic4kidz.com/

4MYCHILD Help and Hope for Life
http://www.cerebralpalsy.org/

Unique . . . but not alone Rare Chromosome Disorder
 Support Group
http://www.rarechromo.org/html/home.asp

References

Amiel-Tisen, C. (2002). Newborn and infant neurological assessment tool. *Pediatric Neurology, 27*(3), 196–212.

Arvedson, J. C., & Brodsky, L. (2001). *Pediatric swallowing and feeding assessment and management.* Clifton Park, NY: Thomson Delmar Learning.

Bailey, D., & Wolery, M. (1992). *Teaching infants and preschoolers with disabilities* (2nd ed.). Upper Saddle River, NJ: Merrill/Pearson Education.

Bayley, N. (2006). *Bayley scales of infant development* (3rd ed.). San Antonio, TX: The Psychological Corporation.

Bruininks, R. (1978). *Bruininks-Oserestsky test of motor proficiency.* Circle Pines, MN: American Guidance Service.

Campbell, S. K. (2004). *Test of infant motor performance.* Chicago, IL: LLC.

Coleman, J. G. (2006). *The early intervention dictionary: A multidisciplinary guide to terminology* (3rd ed.). Bethesda, MD: Woodbine House.

Conner, F., Williamson, G., & Siepp, J. (1978). *Program guide for infants and toddlers with neuromotor and other developmental disabilities.* New York: Teachers College Press.

Dunlap, L. (2009). *An introduction to early childhood special education: Birth to age five.* Upper Saddle River, NJ: Pearson Education.

Erhardt, R. P. (1994). *Developmental hand dysfunction: Theory, assessment, and treatment* (2nd ed.). San Antonio, TX: Therapy Skill Builders.

Foerster, O. (1977). The motor cortex in man in the light of Hughlings Jackson's doctrines. In O. D. Payton, S. Hirt, & R. Newman (Eds.), *Scientific basis for neurophysiologic approaches to therapeutic exercise.* Philadelphia, PA: Davis.

Folio, M. R., & Fewell, R. R. (2000). *Peabody developmental motor scales* (2nd ed.) *(PDMS–2).* Austin, TX: PRO-ED.

Hooper, S. R., & Umansky, W. (2004). *Young children with special needs* (4th ed.). Upper Saddle River, NJ: Merrill/Pearson.

Individuals with Disabilities Education Improvement Act of 2004. (2004).

Johnson-Martin, N. M., Attermeier, S. M., & Hacker, B. J. (2004a). *The Carolina curriculum for infants and toddlers with special needs* (3rd ed.). Baltimore, MD: Brookes.

Johnson-Martin, N. M., Attermeier, S. M., & Hacker, B. J. (2004b). *The Carolina curriculum for preschoolers with special needs* (3rd ed.). Baltimore, MD: Brookes.

Lerner, J. W., Lowenthal, B., & Egan, R. (2003). *Preschool children with special needs: Children at risk, children with disabilities* (2nd ed.). Boston: Allyn & Bacon.

Morris, S., & Klein, M. (2000). *Pre-feeding skills: A comprehensive resource for mealtime development.* San Antonio, TX: Therapy Skill Builders.

Mullen, E. M. (1995). *Mullen scales of early learning.* Circle Pines, MN: American Guidance Service.

Parks, S. (2006). *Inside HELP: Administration and reference guide.* Palo Alto, CA: VORT Corporation.

Piper, M., & Darrah, J. (1994). *Alberta infant motor scale.* St. Louis, MO: Health Sciences.

Russell, D., Rosenbaum, P., Gowland, G., Hardy, S., Lane, M., Plews, N., et al. (1993). *The gross motor function measure manual* (2nd ed.). Hamilton, CA: Psychological Corp.

Stuberg, W. (1992). *Milani Comparetti, motor development for infants and young children.* Omaha: University of Nebraska Medical Center.

Shumway-Cook, A., & Woollacott, M. H. (2007). *Motor control: Translating research into clinical practice* (3rd ed.). Philadelphia, PA: Lippencott, Williams, and Wilkins.

Voress, J. K., & Maddox, T. (1998). *Developmental assessment of young children (DAYC).* Upper Saddle River, NJ: Merrill/Pearson Education.

Wagenfeld, A. (2005). *Pediatric practice: For the occupational therapy assistant.* Thorofare, NJ: Slack Incorporated.

GLOSSARY

Accommodation: The necessary changes that place cognitive structures to accommodate new information.

Adaptation: Changes to instruction or assessment.

Alternate forms reliability: Consistency of item samples in different forms of the same test.

Alternative communication: Technological devices that substitute for natural spoken, written, or gestural speech.

Analytic rubric: Test in which each aspect of a task gets an individual rating.

Anecdotal recording: A written account of an observation of a child after the event has taken place.

Articulation: Using structures to form phonemes (place, manner, and voice).

Aspiration: Entry of food or liquid into the respiratory tract. Aspiration is a common concern for children with increased or decreased muscle tone.

Assimilation: Incorporation of new events into preexisting cognitive structures.

Assistive technology (AT): Technology that permits individuals with disabilities to increase independence and quality of life.

Astigmatism: Variation in visual clarity due to irregularities in the shape of the cornea.

Auditory processing: Retaining auditory information via neurological processing.

Augmentative communication: Addition to natural spoken, written, or gestural speech.

Authentic assessment: Assessment of a skill in a real-life application, situation, or setting.

Basal: Starting point of a test, as specified in the test manual.

Boundaries: The way that a family defines togetherness and separateness and their gate-keeping functions for outsiders.

Ceiling: Ending point of a test, as specified in the test manual.

Checklist: A list of questions or comments regarding the student that the teacher marks yes or no.

Child find: A service directed by each state that outlines plans and procedures for identifying children, from birth to age 6, who have disabilities and who are unserved.

Cognition: A child's evolving mental and intellectual processes.

Collaboration: Working together or working jointly in a cooperative interaction to attain a shared goal.

Communication: A means of exchanging information, including individual ideas, needs, and desires.

Concept of self: A continuum from self-reliance to consideration of one's group in decision making (i.e., individualistic versus collectivist).

Concept of time: One's orientation to time. Monochromic is a reliance on schedules and deadlines. Polychromic means that time is less quantified.

Concurrent validity: Comparison of two different measurements.

Conjoining: Combining two or more grammar components, for example, two sentences or two phrases.

Construct validity: Measurement of how well a psychological theory is covered.

Content: Semantics or meaning of words and/or word combinations.

Content validity: Measurement of an area of study or domain.

Criterion-related validity: Comparison of an instrument's scores to another measure.

Cross-cultural competence: Use of self-examination, values clarification, culture-specific knowledge, and systematic application of principles and practices.

Culture: The ways one perceives, believes, evaluates, and behaves.

Curriculum-based assessment: Assessment that is based on program or curriculum goals and objectives.

Developmental delay: A nonspecific diagnosis to indicate that a child is not achieving developmental milestones within expected timeframes; for purposes of eligibility, this category is limited for use with children from birth to age 9, or a subset of that age range, in states who have adopted this category.

Developmentally appropriate practices: Guiding principles to promote optimal learning and development based on research and evidence-based practices.

Deviation from the mean: How far away scores are from the mean of a distribution.

Digitized speech: Speech that is artificially compiled from recordings of human speech.

Disequilibrium: The state that exists between a child's ability to assimilate new information and then accommodate this new information, and thus attain equilibrium.

Duration recording: Recording that focuses on the length of time some behavior lasts.

Dynamic assessment: Assessment of a child's ability to learn while teaching is going on; learning is supported by scaffolding.

Early intervention services: Frequently used to define Part C of IDEA services for infants and toddlers with disabilities and their families.

Ecological principles: Consideration of the contexts and transactions between children and their environments and of their effect on development.

Education of All Handicapped Children Act: Passed in 1975 as the Education of All Handicapped Children Act and renamed the Individuals with Disabilities Education Act (IDEA), this law requires schools to provide a free and appropriate public education to all children with disabilities. Also known as *Public Law 94-142* or *P.L. 94-142*.

Embedded instruction: Opportunities for children to practice skills within naturally occurring activities.

Embedding: Inserting grammar components, for example, placing a phrase into a sentence.

Environmental analysis: A systematic examination of environments for elements that promote the development of young children with special needs.

Environmental ratings scales: Research-based instruments and tools designed to evaluate environments for young children.

Epigenetic: Naturally unfolding in development via a biological process.

Equilibrium: (1) A systems concept in which a family attempts to return to a steady state, especially during times of crisis, stress, transition, and change. (2) The balance between assimilation and accommodation. (3) The balance between what children know and can do.

Established conditions of risk: Developmental challenges that, left unattended, may result in developmental delays.

Event recording: Recording a frequency count of behavior.

Evidence-based practices: Interventions based on empirical research that promote quality outcomes for children.

Executive functions: Set of cognitive functions that control self-regulation and related cognitive processes, such as planning, organizing, and self-reflection.

Exosystem: The community level; extended relationships with other family members, neighbors, religious groups, and/or places of employment.

Expressive language: Using communication (form, content, use).

Extended school year services: Services provided to children in addition to services rendered during the school year.

Extension: The straightening of muscles in the body, such as the muscles in the trunk, neck, arms, and legs.

Family-centered: (1) An approach to assessment and intervention that recognizes the centrality of the family in supporting the needs of young children, including consideration of family concerns, priorities, and resources. (2) Individualized, flexible, and responsive; usually used to describe practices that treat families with dignity and respect.

Fine motor: Small muscle activity (i.e., writing).

Fine motor skills: Skills that require the use of small muscle groups such as those found in the hands and fingers.

Finger dexterity: Refined use of fingers for fine motor activity. The speed of finger use is a component of dexterity.

Fluency: Smoothness of speech.

Form: Phonology, syntax, and morphology.

Free appropriate public education (FAPE): The legal requirement that all children, regardless of disability status, receive appropriate services, at no cost to the parents, through the public school system.

Functional behavioral assessment: Problem-solving process for addressing problem behaviors of children and determining the causes or functions of the behaviors.

Gross motor: Large muscle activity, for example, walking.

Gross motor skills: Skills that require the use of the large muscle groups located in the arms, legs, and trunk. These large muscle groups are responsible for movements such as walking, running, and jumping.

Grouping: Arrangement of children in groups to promote instruction and social development.

Hierarchy: The order in which person(s) assume responsibility for decision making, control, and power in the family.

Higher mental functions: Mental functions that are developed through social interactions; they are socially or culturally mediated.

Holistic rubric: Measure in which all aspects are rated as one product.

Hyperopia: A condition in which a person can see items at a distance but not at close range. Also known as *farsightedness*.

Hypertonia: Increased muscle tone displayed through stiffness or rigidity of the muscles.

Hypotonia: Decreased muscle tone displayed by muscles appearing to be floppy or flaccid.

Inclusion: An educational approach in which special and regular education teachers collaborate to support children with disabilities so that the children may receive their education in a general education setting with same-age peers without disabilities.

Individualized education plan (IEP): A written education plan, for children ages 3 to 21 with disabilities, that is designed by a multidisciplinary team of professionals and parents to determine educational services based on assessment and evaluation of a child's individual strengths and needs; it is reviewed and updated yearly to describe a child's present performance, current learning needs, and services that will be required. Also known as an *individualized education program*.

Individualized family service plan (IFSP): A written education plan for children, from birth to age 3 with disabilities, that is designed by a multidisciplinary team of professionals and parents to determine both educational and family support services. The IFSP is reviewed and updated quarterly to determine a child's developmental outcomes; the concerns, priorities, and resources of the family; and services that will be required.

Individuals with Disabilities Education Act (IDEA): The federal law that was most recently amended in 2004 as the Individuals with Disabilities Improvement Act (IDEIA) and is an expansion of the original Education for All Handicapped Children Act of 1975 (PL 94-142).

Intelligence: An umbrella term used to describe cognitive processes and acquired knowledge.

Interdisciplinary approach: Team members perform their assessment independently but program development and recommendations are the result of sharing information, joint planning, and mutual decision making.

Internal consistency: Consistency of items within one test.

Inter-rater reliability: Consistency of rater scores.

Interval recording: Dividing an observation period into a number of short time spans and recording some target behavior.

Interval scale: Measurement scale used to name and rank; it has equidistant points.

Judgment-based assessment (JBA): Using information provided by a variety of individuals, including parents, teachers, daycare providers, nurses, and other team members, who know the child best.

Latency recording: Recording how long it takes for an individual to initiate some target behavior.

Least restrictive environment (LRE): An educational setting that provides optimal learning opportunities for students with disabilities while having maximum exposure to their nondisabled peers.

Legal blindness: Vision loss that refers to central visual acuity of 20/200 or less in the better eye after correction and/or a visual field of 20 degrees or less.

Locus of control: A means of attribution for causation; the locus of control is internal or external.

Lower mental functions: Mental functions that are genetically inherited; natural mental abilities.

Macroculture: The overarching values of the shared culture.

Macrosystems: Broader cultural ideas, values, policies, and customs that inform societal mores and practices.

Mean: Average score of a distribution.

Measures of central tendency: Scores clustering together about the mean.

Measures of dispersion: Scores spread about the mean.

Median: Middlemost score of a distribution.

Mediated learning: Use of relationship-based approaches to scaffold learning.

Mesosystem: The broader cultural ideas, values, policies, and customs that inform societal mores and practices.

Microculture: The unique institutions, values, and cultural elements that are shared primarily by members of specific cultural groups.

Microsystem: The immediate environments in which children frequently participate.

Mode: Most common score of a distribution.

Momentary time sampling: Dividing an observation period into equal time spans and observing the target behavior at the end of each time span.

Morphemes: Smallest meaningful grammatical units.

Morphology: The use and understanding of morphemes.

Multidisciplinary approach: (1) The collaboration of a group of professionals with parents to evaluate and intervene collectively on behalf of a child with disabilities. (2) Method used by professionals when they evaluate independently and complete other tasks, such writing reports and goals and objectives, independently.

Muscle tone: The amount of tension or resistance to movement in muscles. This tension should not be too tight (hypertonia) or too flaccid (hypotonia).

Myopia: A condition in which a person can see items near but not at a distance. Also known as *nearsightedness*.

Natural environments: (1) A mandate in Part C to consider the environment in which a child would ordinarily participate, regardless of disability status (i.e., home, daycare, community settings), where services should be provided. (2) Environments that are typical for children's participation and where they feel most comfortable, and the use of everyday learning opportunities to enhance these environments. They include home and community settings. Also known as *natural settings*.

No Child Left Behind (NCLB): Legislation designed to set high standards and measurable goals for improving children's educational outcomes.

Nominal scale: Weakest measurement scale; naming tool.

Nondiscriminatory assessment: Provision of the law requiring that assessments for determining eligibility, placement, and services be culturally sensitive, provided in the language of the child, and valid for the purposes of the evaluation.

Norm-referenced tests: Tests where students can be compared to other students of the same age or grade level based on data from a norm group.

Nystagmus: Involuntary rapid movement of the eyes. Eyes appear to flutter in a horizontal or vertical pattern.

Ordinal scale: Measurement scale where one can name and rank.

Paradigms: Thinking frameworks that influence the way in which people look at their social worlds.

Parental participation: The legislative mandates that require parental participation and decision making in educational programs for children with disabilities.

Part B of IDEIA: The subpart of the Individuals with Disabilities Education Act defining services for children ages 3 to 21 with disabilities.

Part C of IDEIA: The subpart of the Individuals with Disabilities Education Act defining services for children from birth to age 3 with disabilities.

Participatory practices: Structural aspects of relationships that allow for shared decision making, family involvement, and family choice.

Percentile rank: Percentage of scores that are equal to or lower than the scores of other students who have taken the same test.

Performance-based assessment: Assessment of skill acquisition through observation of the child's ability to complete a given task successfully. The child constructs and demonstrates his or her knowledge during the assessment.

Phonology: The use and understanding of phonemes or sounds (single and multiple combinations).

Play-based assessment: Assessment of a child's developmental abilities through interaction with familiar objects in familiar environments.

Portfolio: An organized collection of work indicating learning.

Portfolio assessment: An ongoing, comprehensive record of the child's skills supported by artifacts that show the child's ability and progress in any given developmental domain.

Positive behavior supports (PBS): Purposeful strategies designed to prevent and replace negative behaviors exhibited by children.

Postural reactions: The response of the body and limbs to the change in the body's center of gravity. These reactions develop when voluntary movements replace reflexive development. Righting reactions and protective responses are considered postural reactions.

Pragmatics: Social language, for example, turn taking, eye contact.

Procedural due process: Legal concept that guarantees and safeguards the rights of students with disabilities to receive a free and appropriate education.

Professional jargon: Terminology that is commonly used in a specific profession. These terms are frequently unfamiliar to those outside that particular profession.

Prone position: Lying on the front of the body, facing downward.

Protective responses: A response to sudden body movement that upsets balance. The arms and legs extend in an attempt to protect the body from a fall. The parachute reflex is an example: When the infant is lunged forward, head first, the infant reaches out with his or her arms to protect the body.

Public Law 94-142: Passed in 1975 as the Education of All Handicapped Children Act and renamed the Individuals with Disabilities Education Act (IDEA), the law requires schools to provide a free and appropriate public education to all children with disabilities.

Range: The highest score minus the lowest score of a distribution.

Rating scale: Observer chooses one out of three or more ratings.

Ratio scale: Measurement scale used to name and rank; it has equidistant points and has absolute zero.

Receptive language: Understanding communication (form, content, use).

Reflective practices: Systematic approaches to self-evaluation of clinical and professional practices.

Reflexes: Involuntary movements initially observed in newborn infants, with a variety of reflexes continuing through growth and development.

Relational practices: Relationship aspects of giving help, such as active listening, empathy, and a nonjudgmental stance.

Reliability: Consistency of test scores.

Righting reactions: Automatic movement responses that bring the head and body into an upright position. An example is holding the head upright, even though the body is tilted.

Roles: The prescribed and repetitive behaviors that family members routinely employ.

Rubrics: Measure that includes categories, scores, and descriptions that are used as a guide to evaluate projects or products.

Rules: Spoken or unspoken agreements that define family functioning and role performance.

Running record: A written narrative documented during an observation of a child.

Scaffolding: (1) Provision of needed supports such as modifications, assistance, or adaptations in order for skill mastery to take place. Once the child masters the skill, the supports are removed. (2) Building sequential skills through use of relationship-based guidance.

Schemes: The representation of perceptions, ideas, and/or actions that go together.

Semantics: The use and understanding of the meaning of words and word combinations.

Sensorimotor development: The first stage in Piaget's theory of human development, it occurs from birth through 2 years of age. During this stage, the child learns by interacting with the environment through auditory, visual, and kinesthetic sensory information.

Sensory integration disorder (SID): Failure to process sensory input effectively.

Social-emotional skills: The skills necessary to self-regulate and participate successfully in school settings.

Socially mediated learning: Problem solving under the guidance of an adult or peer who is more experienced than the learner.

Standard deviation: Square root of variance.

Standard error of measurement (SEM): Difference between the true score and observed score of a test.

Standardized tests: Tests that use the same materials and directions for administration and scoring guidelines.

Styles of communication: The means by which families communicate, including high-context (direct) and low-context (indirect).

Supine position: Lying on the back, facing upward.

Syntax: The use and understanding of the structure of sentences.

Synthesized speech: Electronically constructed speech.

Team: The group of professionals working toward a common goal.

Temperament: A set of inborn traits that are the characteristic manner in which children experience and relate to their environment.

Test-retest reliability: Consistency of scores over time.

Tongue thrust: Extending the tongue past the teeth, mostly evident in frontal sounds.

Transdisciplinary approach: Method by which professionals provide services yet relinquish their roles as service providers by teaching their skills to other team members, one of whom will serve as the primary interventionist.

Transition: Services mandated by the Individuals with Disabilities Education Act and, for purposes of early childhood education, used to support children and families as they transition from Part C to Part B services.

Use: Pragmatics or social language.

Validity: Quality of a test that indicates if the test measures what it says it measures.

Variance: How scores are dispersed.

Visual acuity: Clinical measure of the eye's ability to identify details of the smallest identifiable letter or symbol. It is a fraction measurement and based on visible print size. Perfect vision is 20/20. If an individual sees 20/200, the smallest detail that a person sees at 20 feet can be seen by someone with perfect vision at 200 feet.

Visual impairment: Central visual acuity of 20/70 or worse in the better eye with best correction, or a total field loss of 140 degrees.

Visual-motor integration: Coordinating motor skills from visual input.

Visual-motor skills: The ability to coordinate the visual system with body movements.

Voice: Appropriate pitch, tone, and resonance (free from pathology).

Zero reject: Principle that disallows exclusion of children with disabilities from the educational process.

Zone of proximal development: Part of Lev Vygotsky's learning theory that examines the supports needed in order for a child to complete a task successfully. The distance between a child's actual developmental level as determined by independent problem solving and that child's potential development through collaboration with others.

z-score: Standard deviation score's relation to the sample.

INDEX

Page numbers followed by *f* and *t* indicate figures and table respectively.